DIMENSIONS OF CHRISTIANITY

AN APPROACH TO GCSE IN RELIGIOUS STUDIES

▶ by Sister Anne Burke SND BA

 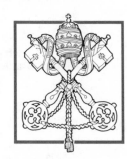 

SECOND EDITION

Kevin Mayhew Publishers

Author's Acknowledgements

I would like to thank the following people for their help and support during the production of the second edition of this book: Mrs Susan Paton for typing most of the text; Sister Gertrude Maria Caulfield and Sister Julie White for reading the proofs with me, and for assisting with the index; the Community at Notre Dame, Standish, who are always such a great support to me during 'busy' times; the numerous colleagues whose comments, ideas and suggestions have informed this second edition. I owe a debt of gratitude to Miss Judy Smith, the editor, for her help, patience and kindness.

Dedication

In memory of my parents and for my family.

Scripture quotations from the *Good News Bible*,
©American Bible Society, 1966, 1971, 1976,
published by The Bible Societies and Collins.
Used by permission.

First published 1986 in Great Britain by
KEVIN MAYHEW LTD.,
Rattlesden, Bury St Edmunds,
Suffolk IP30 0SZ.

2nd Edition 1988

ISBN 0 86209 093 8

Cover: detail from a painting in
St Alban's Cathedral; photograph by Carlos Reyes;
design by Geoffrey Philpott
Symbols for the three sections (Christianity (1) — Chi Rho;
Roman Catholic Church (2) — Keys of St Peter; Gospel of St Mark (3) —
the Lion of Mark) drawn by The Design People, Ipswich, Suffolk.
Illustrations on pages 13, 34, 37, 42, 45, 52, 69, 85, 96, 99, 100,
102, 130, 141, 143, 147 and 153 by John Ansell.
Illustrations on pages 10, 14, 17, 18, 19, 20, 25, 27, 48, 59, 73,
75, 79, 89, 109, 123, 133, 137 and 138 by The Design People.
Map on page 125 by The Design People.
Typesetting by Barry Sarling, Rayleigh, Essex.
Printed and bound in Great Britain at
The Bath Press, Avon

CONTENTS

Introduction to the second edition   **5**

Notes for the teacher   **5**

Notes for the pupil   **6**

SECTION 1   CHRISTIANITY

What is a Christian?   **8**

UNIT 1   Christian practice

1.1   Christian festivals   **9**

1.2   Places of worship   **16**

1.3   Public and private worship   **22**

1.4   Ceremonies for important events:
birth, marriage, death   **28**

1.5   The Eucharist — a sacred Christian meal   **34**

UNIT 2   Christian belief

2.1   The Apostles' Creed & the Lord's Prayer   **37**

2.2   Questions of interpretation & understanding   **41**

2.3   Christians and the Bible   **44**

UNIT 3   Christian values

3.1   The Ten Commandments and the teaching of the
New Testament   **47**

3.2   Christianity in action   **51**

SECTION 2   THE ROMAN CATHOLIC TRADITION

UNIT 4   The home and family

4.1   Baptism
A) The Roman Catholic ceremony   **57**
B) The Christian respect for human life   **60**

4.2   Marriage
A) The Sacrament of Marriage in the Roman
Catholic Church   **63**
B) Themes and problems relating to marriage   **64**

UNIT 5   Christian vocation

5.1   Discipleship: the Sacrament of Confirmation   **68**

5.2   Christian service   **71**
A) Lay ministries   **72**
B) Religious congregations   **74**

5.3   The Sacrament of Holy Orders   **77**

5.4   The ministry of the priesthood   **81**

UNIT 6   Eucharist and world-wide fellowship

6.1   The Mass   **83**

6.2   The Church/The Body of Christ   **87**

6.3   The poor   **90**

UNIT 7 Reconciliation — our way to God

7.1	*The Sacrament of Reconciliation (Penance)*	**94**
7.2	*Reconciliation in society*	**98**
	A) Crime and punishment	**98**
	B) Prejudice and discrimination	**101**
	C) War and peace	**104**
7.3	*Anointing of the Sick*	**108**
7.4	*Further themes*	
	A) Sickness and healing	**111**
	B) Death and eternity	**112**

SECTION 3   THE PERSON & MINISTRY OF JESUS — ST MARK'S GOSPEL

UNIT 8 The Gospel of Mark

8.1	*Social, political and religious background*	**117**
8.2	*The making of Mark's Gospel*	**120**
8.3	*The structure of Mark's Gospel*	**124**

UNIT 9 Christianity in Mark's Gospel

9.1	*'Who do people say I am?'*	**128**
9.2	*Disciples of Jesus*	**132**
9.3	*The Kingdom of God*	**136**
9.4	*Parable and allegory; miracle and sign*	**140**
9.5	*Opposition and conflict*	**146**
9.6	*The suffering, death & resurrection of Jesus*	**151**

Appendix A: Short tests on common scripture texts	**156**
Appendix B: 'What the Church says': Summaries of relevant conciliar and post-conciliar documents	**159**
Appendix C: Glossary of terms and religious vocabulary	**170**
Bibliography	**173**
Index	**174**

INTRODUCTION TO THE SECOND EDITION

The second edition of *Dimensions of Christianity* offers its readers the benefits of the experience I have gained through conducting courses in G.C.S.E. Religious Studies throughout Britain. I have listened to teachers' experience, and to accounts of good classroom practice. As a chief co-ordinator for the Northern Examining Association, I understand the need for course work suggestions. Many of the revised questions prepare pupils for this aspect of the examination. I have re-ordered the questions at the end of each chapter according to the skills required by the National Criteria for Religious Studies.

Teachers have used *Dimensions of Christianity* for the examinations of groups other than the Northern Examining Association. I have, therefore, abandoned the original intention to serve the requirements of the N.E.A., and have tried to cater more generally for any syllabus concerning Christianity as a world religion. In any case, it would not be practical to try to anticipate the changes of subject content of particular examination groups in the next few years.

The Christianity section has been expanded and adjusted to include the Orthodox Christian tradition. There is also a new chapter on rites of passage in the Christian religion. I have made some alterations to the Roman Catholic section in the light of comments and of my experience in the classroom. The wide use of this section for adult groups as well as G.C.S.E. candidates is most encouraging. One notable addition is the inclusion of the Church's teaching on *Respect for Human Life in its Origin and the Dignity of Procreation* (March 1987).

The section on the Gospel of Mark has been expanded into a fuller teaching course, with more insights into the themes of the Gospel, gained from my own research into the text, my experience of teaching the Gospel, and attendance at some excellent lectures at conferences and teachers' courses.

NOTES FOR THE TEACHER

This book sets out the subject content in Christianity, the Roman Catholic tradition, and the Gospel of Mark. Except where indicated, references to scripture are taken from the *Good News Bible*. The depth of treatment is suitable for candidates for G.C.S.E. Religious Studies. The questions at the end of each chapter distinguish the skills necessary in Religious Studies and follow the guidelines expressed in the National Criteria for G.C.S.E. The questions also take note of the recently published Grade Criteria, but for practical purposes I have grouped them under the broad objectives of **Investigation, Understanding** and **Evaluation**.

These objectives prepare for the course work element of the examination. The reading lists at the end of each chapter should help in the investigation of course work.

G.C.S.E. Religious Studies cannot be taught through a text book. There must be a wide range of approaches to the subject content of a syllabus, in order to achieve the aims of the subject. How can one encourage an enquiring, critical and sympathetic approach to the study of religion? The resources involved for such a teaching programme include:

▶ **written**
▶ **visual**
▶ **oral**
▶ **experiential**

Visits, speakers, audio-visuals and class projects are much more memorable than the written word! Many pupils do not naturally turn to a text book for information, so this book is a substitute for the class note book. It is a tool, a reference for preparation of course work, practice for the written examination, and revision for final papers. It would be disastrous to begin to use it as a traditional text book, the substance of the lesson. However, it would be useful if, for example, one wants to recall the main points of a baptism which the class has attended, or explore some of the symbols and their meaning.

The book is intended to stimulate imaginative and creative approaches to the teaching of Religious Studies in the fourth and fifth year, whilst providing a security of content for the final examination in the late fifth year.

G.C.S.E. is taken by a wide ability range of pupils. Teachers are most anxious about less able pupils who may be discouraged by the demands of the written examination, and the course work. For this reason, much of the text is summarised in the form of charts and illustrated diagrams. These may lead the less able pupil into reading appropriate paragraphs of the text.

As a tool, this book will be as effective as the teacher using it. The non-specialist teacher will find it useful as a guide to the appropriate subject content of many of the G.C.S.E. syllabuses based on the Christian tradition. It is essential that changes in syllabus subject content are noted each year, so a *current* syllabus for the examination is necessary.

Teachers are directed to the requirements of the separate examinations groups for the details of assessment of course work. Some examining groups have published useful information to support their regulations and all the groups have provided in-service training for this aspect of the examination.

The Appendices are a special feature of this book. There are basic questionnaires in Appendix A on some of the frequently recurring texts. They do not need to be answered in a written form, but they can be used as a basis for class-talk about the ministry of Jesus or the first Christians. Appendix B is especially useful for those who are studying the Roman Catholic tradition. It consists of short and simple summaries of important Church documents. The present edition contains a summary of *Respect for Human Life in its Origin and the Dignity of Procreation*.

Classroom relationships hold a 'touch of magic' from time to time. A teacher needs to be free to indulge in these moments. This book provides an outline of subject content in the dimensions of Christianity which make such moments possible.

NOTES FOR THE PUPIL

This book is a useful reference for basic information about the various traditions of the Christian religion, and for the study of a Gospel at G.C.S.E. level. You, the pupil, need to understand some important facts before you continue.

At the end of each chapter you will find questions. These will help you to prepare for:

▶ written examinations
▶ course work

Answering the questions will help you to find and develop the skills necessary for the study of religion.

Investigation involves:

▶ choosing appropriate factual information, reading and research;
▶ presentation of factual information — in various forms: as continuous writing, diagrams, statistics, or as illustrated information;
▶ organisation of factual information in a clear way, showing that you can use religious language and terms correctly.

Understanding involves:

▶ learning the meaning of religious language and terms;
▶ appreciating the importance, in religion, of special people (e.g. Jesus); of the writings of a religious tradition (e.g. the Bible); and of the special traditions of a religion (e.g. the spoken tradition of the early Church concerning the ministry of Jesus);
▶ realising that there is a link between what people believe and the way they live and behave towards others;
▶ looking at moral issues (e.g. prejudice, violence) and understanding how religious beliefs can be applied to these issues.

Evaluation involves:

▶ the expression of personal opinion and the opinions of others;
▶ the arguments involved in controversial issues (e.g. abortion);
▶ the ability to make a thoughtful, personal conclusion.

It is very important, therefore, not to limit yourself to text books and the written word, although you will find extra reading suggestions at the end of each chapter. It is important to join in class discussion, to listen to the news on T.V. and radio. Be interested in the world around you, read the newspapers. Interview other people about their religious views on various topics. Visit places of interest connected with religious groups or special people. Religious Studies is a challenging subject, and religion itself is a kaleidoscope of various traditions and practices.

Examinations

Remember that the G.C.S.E. examination will test the skills described above. You are *not* required to learn every word in your note books or files by heart! However, there *are* passages from scripture and quotations by famous people which are useful to know from memory. The examination will expect you to have a *working* knowledge of the subject content of the chosen syllabus. Make sure that you know what is on the syllabus you are following. If you are not sure, ask your teacher or tutor for details of the coursework and examination content.

A good guide to answering examination papers includes:

▶ reading the question carefully, and *selecting* the best information which answers that question;
▶ timing yourself carefully. Know beforehand what the examination paper will look like. Notice how many essays there will be, what will take up the most time, and what can be answered quickly. Look at the *number of marks* awarded for questions. Do not waste time on questions which carry only a few marks;
▶ presenting your work clearly. Remember that the examiner is a human being who appreciates a script which is easy to read!
▶ using the information contained in illustrations or passages which are meant to act as a stimulus;
▶ giving *examples* of what you mean;
▶ leaving enough time to *check* your answers at the end of the examination.

CHRISTIANITY

	What is a Christian?	8
UNIT 1	Christian practice	
1.1	*Christian festivals*	9
1.2	*Places of worship*	16
1.3	*Public and private worship*	22
1.4	*Ceremonies for important events: birth, marriage, death*	28
1.5	*The Eucharist — a sacred Christian meal*	34
UNIT 2	Christian belief	
2.1	*The Apostles' Creed & the Lord's Prayer*	37
2.2	*Questions of interpretation & understanding*	41
2.3	*Christians and the Bible*	44
UNIT 3	Christian values	
3.1	*The Ten Commandments and the teaching of the New Testament*	47
3.2	*Christianity in action*	51

A religious way of life

The first section of this book examines Christianity as one of the great religious traditions in the world. In one small area of a town or city in Britain today, people who have a religious faith may be Jewish, Hindu, Moslem, Sikh, Christian or Buddhist. These religions are the major religions of the world. In each of these major religions, there is a common core of belief, practice and values; and in each there is a variety of belief, practice and values. That seems contradictory, but it is difficult to find an exact model for the followers of any one of these religions. Christianity is no exception; so what is a Christian?

A follower of Jesus Christ

One of the definitions of 'Christian' in the Oxford English Dictionary is 'a person believing in, professing, or belonging to the religion of Christ'. Another is 'a person showing the character consistent with Christ's teaching'. These two descriptions reveal the fact that to ask the question, 'What is a Christian?', uncovers a search for another person. That person is Jesus Christ.

Some chapters of this book will describe the ways in which the life and death of Jesus Christ are celebrated by Christians in festivals of the Christian Church, such as Christmas and Easter, and the places and manner in which they are celebrated.

There will be an exploration of what Christians believe about God as Father, Son and Holy Spirit which follows from the teaching of Jesus about his Father in heaven, his own claim to be the Son of God, and his promise to send the Holy Spirit. The common sacraments of the Christian Church are baptism and the Eucharist, and there is some explanation of how these are celebrated.

A Christian Church

The word 'Christian' can also be used to describe a group of people, or a community claiming to follow the teaching of Jesus Christ. St Paul in his letters to the early Christians describes them as the 'Body of Christ', or 'God's field' or 'God's building'. These are images he used to describe how a group of individuals can at the same time be one community.

The idea of a Christian society is called 'Church'. Unfortunately, we have two distinct meanings in our own language for 'Church', and the most common answer to the question, 'What is the Church?' is that of the 'building used for public Christian worship'. 'Stones' and 'people' seem to be so different that it is difficult to think of the same word describing both in the Christian tradition.

A Christian is...

If one is going to write a conclusion to the sentence, then one is committed to an exploration of the kaleidoscope of Christian experience which the last two thousand years has produced. The following chapters will help to begin a journey through the maze of one of the world religions of our society — *Christianity.*

'Together for Christ.' An ecumenical gathering in Strawberry Hill.

1.1 CHRISTIAN FESTIVALS

Christians divide the year into seasons for the purpose of worship. These seasons are called the *liturgical year*. Each season has one or more major festivals which remind Christians of an important event in the life of Christ. Easter is the greatest of these festivals for all Christians, whether they are Orthodox, Roman Catholic, or Protestant. However, it seems puzzling when some Orthodox churches keep their great festivals on different dates from the rest of the Christian world. There is a simple explanation for this. Some Orthodox Churches still follow the calendar introduced by Julius Caesar (the Julian Calendar). The Church in the West follows the calendar introduced by Pope Gregory XIII. This means that some Orthodox Christians may be keeping Christmas or Easter about thirteen days later than other Christian groups. The Christian year (*liturgical calendar*) begins with Advent.

ADVENT

Advent is a period of four weeks when Christians prepare for the coming of Christ. During this time there are readings from the Bible about the Messiah and what the times of the Messiah would be like. The prophet Isaiah is frequently read. There are readings about the second coming of Christ, or the coming of the Lord at the end of time.

The story of the conception and birth of John the Baptist is important. This is read from the Gospel of Luke. John's father, Zechariah, says: '... *You, my child, will be called a prophet of the Most High God. You will go ahead of the Lord to prepare his road for him.*' (Luke 1:76)

Luke also records the incident of the annunciation of God's message to Mary by the angel Gabriel: '*You will become pregnant and give birth to a son, and you will name him Jesus... For this reason the holy child will be called the Son of God.*' (Luke 1:31, 35)

Matthew records the distress of Joseph when he discovered that Mary was going to have a baby: '*so he made plans to break the engagement privately.*' Joseph is given a message which explains and comforts: '*...it is by the Holy Spirit that she has conceived. She will have a son, and you will name him Jesus — because he will save his people from their sins.*' (Matthew 1:20-21)

The Advent readings demonstrate two important Christian beliefs:

1. That Jesus is the *Son of God* — his mother is Mary the Virgin who conceives by the power of the Holy Spirit.
2. That the baby born of Mary is the long awaited *Messiah* who will belong to the house of David. (For Joseph registered Mary his wife as a member of his own tribe.)

Advent Customs

The Advent Wreath: A wreath of evergreen is made, into which four candles are placed. Three of these candles are traditionally purple and one is pink. During the first week of Advent, one of the candles is lit for prayer; in the second week two candles, and so on until the fourth Sunday when they are all lit and Christmas Day is very near. The Advent wreath is a good example of the use of religious symbols:

▶ the circle of evergreen suggests the eternal life of God;
▶ the candle flame is a symbol of Christ — the light of the world;
▶ the candles and ribbons are purple, which is the liturgical colour for the seasons of preparation (Lent and Advent);
▶ one pink candle symbolises the joy of the third Sunday of Advent which is meant to remind people that their preparation may be hard, but it is for a feast of great joy.

The Advent Calendar: A twenty-four day calendar for December prepares for Christmas day. Children open one window of the calendar each day, and there is a picture and a text from the Bible, or a suggestion for Christian service to others. It is another way of preparing for the season of Christmas.

The Jesse Tree: People are always interested in their family tree, and the ancestry (genealogy) of Jesus Christ is often shown as a tree with all the famous ancestors of Jesus going back as far as Jesse, who was the father of King David. This family tree helps people to understand the basic Christian belief that Jesus was truly a man, born of Mary, with ancestors going far back into Jewish history.

CHRISTMAS

At Christmas, all Christians celebrate an important part of their faith: '*I believe...in Jesus Christ, his only Son, Our Lord, who was born of the Virgin Mary...*'

Christians believe that God became man in Jesus Christ. The mystery of this belief is called the *Incarnation*. Orthodox Christians are helped to understand this belief when they use *icons* of the Virgin and Child to help them pray. The word Incarnation literally means 'in flesh'. The Son of God was born of a woman, 'became flesh'. The Gospel accounts surrounding the birth of Jesus emphasise two truths:

JESUS IS THE SON OF GOD
and
JESUS IS THE SON OF MARY

Matthew begins his gospel account with the family tree of Jesus, or his *genealogy* (Matthew 1:11-17). He begins with Abraham, whom the Jews honour as the father of their race, and marks off three important periods in the history of the Jewish people, showing that Jesus was truly a Jew with a great ancestry.

The periods of history are:

1. *Abraham* to *David* (the greatest king of Israel);
2. *David* to the *exile* (a period when the great empire of Babylon conquered God's people);
3. The *exile* to the *birth of Jesus*. (During this period, the Empires of Babylon, Assyria, Persia, Greece and Rome conquered the chosen people and deported them or occupied their country.)

Matthew also emphasises that Jesus was the Son of God by giving the account of Joseph's struggle to decide to marry Mary. Matthew makes it quite clear that Jesus is not Joseph's son: *'For it is by the Holy Spirit that she (Mary) has conceived.'* Matthew quotes the prophet who speaks of the birth of **Immanuel** which means **God is with us**.

In Matthew's Gospel, Jesus is not just the saviour of the Jewish people. The Magi, who are foreigners, come to worship. There is death and danger from Herod who fears a rival in the birth of the child for whom the prophetic star appears.

Luke's Gospel begins with another miraculous conception and birth, that of **John the Baptist** whose mother was well past the age of child-bearing. The work which John would do as the announcer of the Messiah, is described in Zechariah's canticle (Luke 1:67-79).

The dialogue between the angel Gabriel and Mary makes it clear that Mary would be the mother of Jesus, but that he would be the Son of God by the power of the Holy Spirit.

The census of Caesar Augustus sets a date in history for the birth of Jesus. The tribe of David and the town of Bethlehem surround the birth of Jesus with an ancient Jewish heritage. Jesus is circumcised at eight days and made a member of the Jewish race. In Luke's Gospel, it is the poor and the faithful of the Jewish people who recognise the Messiah. These are the shepherds and Simeon, the old priest, together with Anna, the old and holy woman.

Date of Christmas

By tradition, the festival is kept on December 25th. The exact day on which Jesus was born is not known but the Christian Emperor Constantine fixed the day for the birth of Christ to coincide with an ancient festival of the sun. At one point in the winter the sun is farthest from the equator, and then it begins to return, giving longer days again. This point is called the **winter solstice**. The return of the sun and the coming of Jesus as the light of the nations are an appropriate coincidence for the Christian festival of Christmas.

CHRISTMAS CUSTOMS

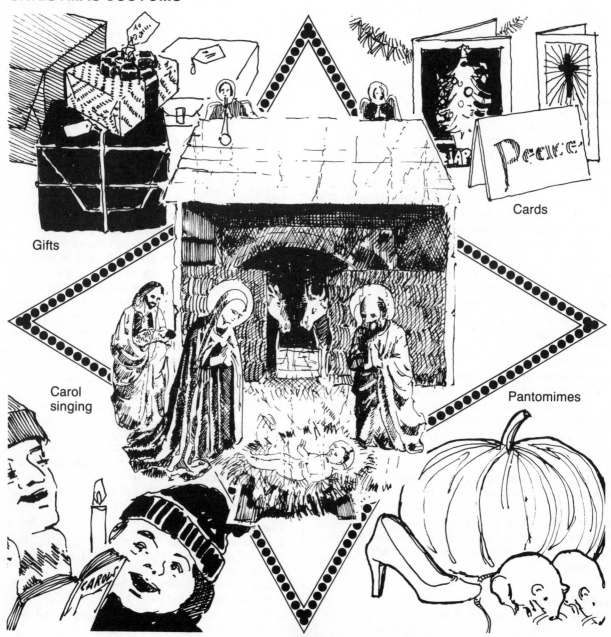

Gifts

Cards

Carol singing

Pantomimes

Customs of Christmas

Christmas customs often began from folk-lore. For example, an evergreen tree decorated with baubles and lights probably has its origins in old European customs of celebrating the life of the evergreen in the depths of winter. Sometimes, customs developed from the practice of Christian people who were inspired by the Gospel accounts of the life of Jesus. For example, the custom of decorating a tree with gifts reflects the gifts which the Magi brought to the child Jesus.

Cribs are often made in the Christmas season. St Francis is traditionally thought to have introduced the idea of a crib as a teaching-aid for simple people. The figures of the crib tell the story of the birth of Christ. There is a model stable or cave, and the animals which might have been found in a Palestinian stable are put into it. The manger is the centre-piece. Mary and Joseph are there. The Christ-child is placed in the manger on Christmas day. Other figures from the Gospel stories, the shepherds and the Magi, are also placed in the crib.

Gifts are an important feature of the Christian festival of Christmas. The exchange of gifts is a symbol of Christianity which teaches 'love your neighbour as yourself'. Gifts are given to children, and Father Christmas or Santa Claus (St Nicholas) is an important figure at this time. The feast of St Nicholas falls on December 6th, and it is the custom in some European countries for the exchange of gifts to take place on this day. *Boxing Day* is also associated with gift-giving and falls on December 26th which is the feast of St Stephen. Stephen was chosen by the apostles to distribute money and food for the poor in the early days of the Church.

Cards are a recent custom. Christmas cards are sent to friends and relations. Even non-Christian people send cards at Christmas because they are caught up in the commercial interests which surround the festival. Cards are meant to have a message or a picture which reminds people of the birth of Christ, but, because Christmas is now big business, many cards have no Christian message at all. Recently, groups of Christians began a poster campaign to *'Put Christ back into Christmas'*. They were trying to stop the use of 'Merry Xmas' which is not a Christian greeting at all.

Carols spread the Christian message most effectively. It is the custom for children particularly to go around the streets and sing carols in people's homes. Carols often tell the story of the birth of the Christ child, or they encourage the Christmas spirit of kindness and charity to others. Nowadays, carols are often sung to raise money for various charities, especially for the poor. Carols vary from country to country, but the basic Christian message is the same: *'Good tidings of comfort and joy'*.

Pantomimes are a most popular feature of Christmas celebrations. They are a family entertainment. The pantomime stories include stories about folk heroes like Dick Whittington, and fairy stories like Cinderella. There is always a great struggle between good and evil in the story. The hero of the pantomime always conquers the danger and evil in life. The theme of a Saviour is there, even if the story of Jesus is not being told!

EPIPHANY

Epiphany follows Christmastide in the Christian calendar. The word *Epiphany* is Greek, meaning *'to show forth'*. It is Jesus Christ who is shown in the Gospels as the Son of God, so the festival time of Epiphany concentrates on three 'showings' of Jesus:
- ▶ **the worship of the Magi** (Matthew 2:1-12)
- ▶ **the baptism of Jesus** (Matthew 3:13-17: Mark 1:9-12: Luke 3:21-23)
- ▶ **the transfiguration** (Matthew 17:1-10: Mark 9:2-13: Luke 9:28-36)

The Magi were non-Jews who recognised in Jesus the Saviour of the world. At the baptism of Jesus the voice said, *'This is my Son whom I love.'* The *transfiguration* of Jesus is an unusual account where Jesus speaks with famous characters of the Old Testament, Moses (the law-giver) and Elijah (representing the Jewish prophets). Again a voice says *'This is my Son, whom I love...listen to him.'*

THE EASTER SEASON

Lent

Easter is the greatest of the Christian festivals. For this reason there is a period of solemn preparation for the festival. This period is called Lent and is six weeks in length. It begins with **Ash Wednesday** when many Christians are signed with ashes. These ashes are made out of burning the previous year's palms. They are a sign that people are really sorry for their sins, and they are a promise of a return to living a good Christian life again.

'Remember man that you are dust and unto dust you will return.'

'Turn away from sin and be faithful to the Gospel.'

These are the thoughts which occupy the Christian who is seriously going to observe the solemn time of Lent.

Lent is a time of preparation for Easter. Easter celebrates the resurrection of Jesus from the dead. The preparation usually includes:

▶ **prayer**   ▶ **fasting**   ▶ **good works**

Extra time is given for reading the scriptures or attending special prayer services. Many Christians have their own programme of prayer during Lent. In some parts of the world Christians do extraordinary acts of penance which seem very harsh, but they are performed out of love and gratitude for the suffering of Jesus.

Fasting may take more than one form. It may literally involve giving up some meals or certain foods. However, it may mean trying to do something about having a bad temper or other faults of character. Giving up going to discos or football matches may also be a sign of the serious way in which Lent is being observed.

Lent is also a good time for helping various charities. Many people remember the 'giving up' aspects of Lent, but do not understand that much more time and effort should be given to this positive and creative way of preparing for Easter.

The length of Lent, about forty days, is important. After Jesus was baptized he went into the desert for forty days. He fasted there and prayed about the work he was going to do. It was a period of preparation by *prayer* and *fasting* before he began the many *good works* of his ministry. During Eastertide and Pentecost Christians remember the message which they must take to the world.

Lent resembles that period of preparation which Jesus himself made. The last week of Lent is called *Holy Week*. The days of this week have a special significance in the Christian calendar:

Palm Sunday (Passion Sunday)
Maundy Thursday
Good Friday
Holy Saturday
Easter Sunday

Palm Sunday

On this day, Christians recall the triumphal entry of Jesus into Jerusalem, riding on a donkey: *'See your king comes to you gentle and riding on a donkey, on a colt, the foal of a donkey.'*

It is difficult for us to see anything triumphant or kingly about riding on a donkey! However, the Jews of Jesus' time would consider the donkey to be an animal of peace. Horses were animals of war, but the donkey was a sign of commerce and progress in times of peace. Jesus was the King of peace. The prophets had written about him in these terms, and Isaiah described the Kingdom of the Messiah as a place where all conflict would be at an end, and even nature itself would be at peace: *'The lion will lie down with the lamb.'* The triumphant procession of Jesus was a signal that the *Messiah* had come.

The people put down their cloaks in his way and cut down branches from the trees in his honour. Christian services on Palm Sunday often take the form of processions. In some parts of the world these are great occasions, and the Gospel story is acted out. In Britain, some palm leaves are used in processions. These are sometimes made into crosses, as a reminder of the end of Holy Week when Jesus was crucified. Later in the year, they are burned to make ashes which are used on Ash Wednesday.

Maundy Thursday

On Thursday of Holy Week, Christians remember that Jesus celebrated the Passover with his disciples and, at the Last Supper, he performed two important acts. He washed his disciples' feet and then said to them:

> *'"Do you understand what I have just done to you?" he asked. "You call me Teacher and Lord, and it is right that you do so, because that is what I am. I, your Lord and Teacher, have just washed your feet... I have set an example for you, so that you will do just what I have done for you..."'*
> *John 13:12-15*

On Holy Thursday, Christians remember that it is important to be of service to others. This is the only way they can show that they follow the example and teaching of Jesus.

At the meal, Jesus took bread and wine and gave it to his disciples as his body and blood. Jesus was going to suffer and die, and his blood would be the new covenant between God and his people. Christians celebrate the Last Supper as Jesus told them to, because they remember the first Eucharist celebrated by Jesus on the night before he died.

In the Roman Catholic tradition, priests remember their solemn promise, made at their ordination ceremony, to consecrate bread and wine for the people. They celebrate the Eucharist on Maundy Thursday morning with the bishop of the diocese who consecrates the oils that will be used in the sacraments throughout the year.

Good Friday

Christians keep Good Friday in a most solemn way. They may join in processions which re-enact the last journey of Jesus to Calvary carrying his cross. The traditional hours, when the last moments of Jesus' life are remembered, are from 12 o'clock to 3 o'clock. The reading of the Passion of Jesus from one of the Gospels is a common feature of the Christian services, although the details vary from one denomination to another. Many Christians join in ecumenical (common) services on Good Friday to express the unity for which all Christians pray.

Good Friday is a very quiet day when people remember that Jesus, who was innocent of all sin, gave up his life willingly for all God's people who need forgiveness for their sins. Jesus also kept his promise that anyone who believed in his mission would be rewarded with eternal life.

Churches are usually stripped of all decoration on Good Friday. There are no flowers or other signs of devotion.

Holy Saturday

Holy Saturday is a time of anticipation. There are also signs of the excitement and joy of Easter as people prepare for the gorgeous displays of joy and celebration on the following day. Churches are cleaned and the best altar-linen and vessels are brought out ready for the Easter services. This is especially true for denominations in which formal liturgy is very important (e.g. Orthodox and Roman Catholic).

Easter Day

Many groups of Christians will begin their celebrations of the risen Christ at midnight on Holy Saturday.

Easter faith: Christians believe that Jesus rose from the dead on the third day after he was crucified. The Gospels give accounts of the women going to the tomb and finding it empty. In Mark's Gospel they are told by a young man in a white robe that Jesus has risen and that he will see the disciples in Galilee *'just as he told you'*. In Matthew's Gospel, an angel gives the message, and the women meet Jesus as they are on their way to tell the disciples.

In Luke's Gospel two men in clothes *'that gleamed like lightning'* give the message of the resurrection to the women. John's Gospel describes Mary Magdalen finding the empty tomb and alerting Peter and John who also come to the tomb. Jesus appears to Mary, who mistakes him for the gardener.

There are accounts of Jesus appearing to the disciples and to the women in all the Gospels, and these accounts make it clear that the disciples must witness to the fact that Jesus rose from the dead.

Easter services: The common features of Christian services at Easter are newness-of-life, new light, and joyful hymns with many 'Alleluias'. In some Christian traditions there are dawn services which are followed by an Easter breakfast. Most Christian Churches have a Communion service on Easter morning. The Orthodox begin Easter before midnight on Saturday. They walk in procession with lights, and then declare that *'Christ is*

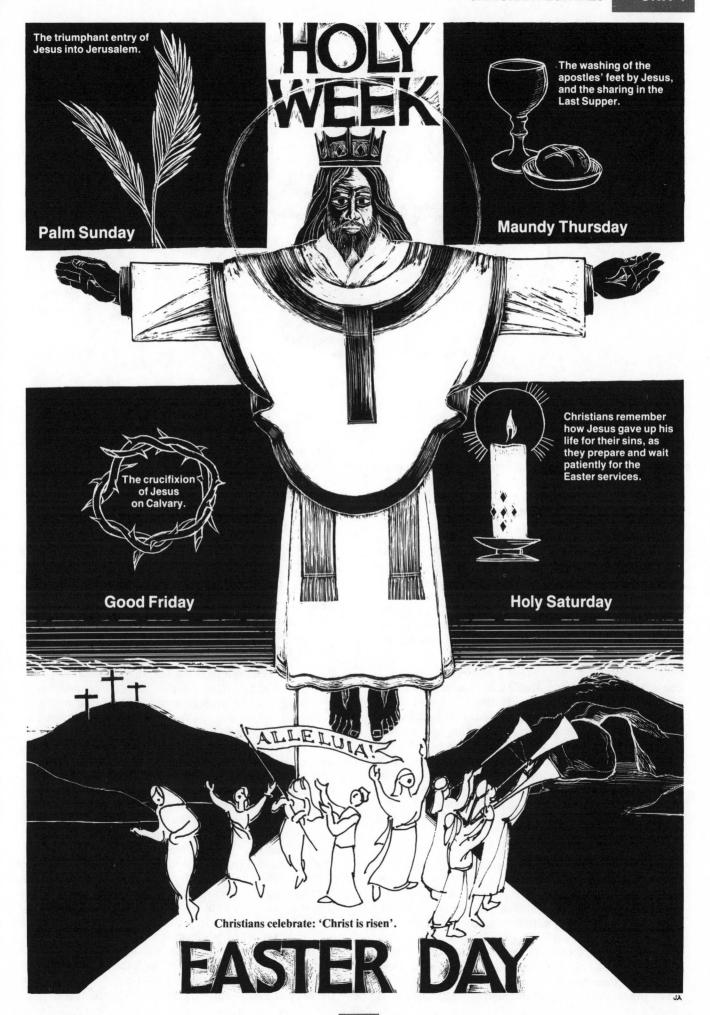

The triumphant entry of Jesus into Jerusalem.

Palm Sunday

HOLY WEEK

The washing of the apostles' feet by Jesus, and the sharing in the Last Supper.

Maundy Thursday

The crucifixion of Jesus on Calvary.

Good Friday

Christians remember how Jesus gave up his life for their sins, as they prepare and wait patiently for the Easter services.

Holy Saturday

ALLELUIA!

Christians celebrate: 'Christ is risen'.

EASTER DAY

JA

THE CHRISTIAN CALENDAR

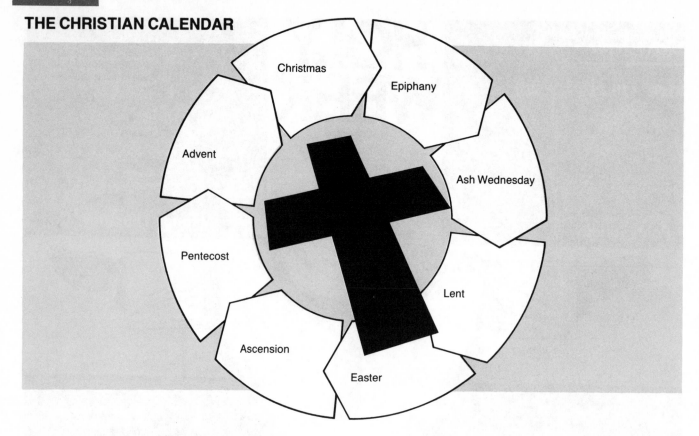

risen'. After a long service of about three hours, the people wish each other a joyful Easter and share special traditional Easter refreshments. The Roman Catholic main celebration of Easter is at midnight on Saturday. The service is called the *Easter Vigil*. The ceremony is in four parts: a service of light; a service of readings; a service of baptism; and an Easter Eucharist. (For local reasons, the Easter Vigil may be held earlier in the evening.) Most Christian denominations have a communion service on Easter morning. It is important to realise that some Christians do not think it necessary to have elaborate services for Easter. An example is the Religious Society of Friends, who consider that Easter can be renewed by their own simple style of worship. (See Unit 1.3)

The date of Easter: After March 21st, Easter falls on the Sunday after the full moon. If the full moon is on Sunday, Easter is the following Sunday. It is therefore possible to speak of Easter being 'early this year' or 'late this year'. What is meant is that the day is nearer to or farther from March 21st, depending upon the waxing or waning of the moon. From time to time there is a great debate about the advantages of fixing a set date for Easter, but the custom of dating Easter by the full moon between March 21st and April 25th is still the normal practice.

Easter customs: New life is celebrated in the custom of giving *eggs* at Easter. The way in which this is done varies from country to country, but in Britain chocolate eggs are given. The Orthodox Christians, however, paint real eggs in bright patterns and colours. The egg is a good symbol of new life. People also wear new clothes at Easter. Hats are specially decorated to make '*Easter Bonnets*', and Easter parades are held. The Easter *lamb* symbolises Jesus the 'lamb of God' who takes away the sin of the world. The lamb was slaughtered at Passover time in memory of the way in which God rescued the people of Israel from slavery in Egypt during the time of Moses. In the same way, Jesus was crucified to secure the safety of God's new people.

ASCENSION

Ascension day is forty days after Easter and marks the day when Jesus ceased to appear to his disciples and returned to his Heavenly Father. For ten days Christians remember how the apostles waited for the gift which Jesus had promised. This was the gift of the Holy Spirit, who would alter their lives completely.

PENTECOST

Pentecost is sometimes called the birthday of the Christian Church, because it is the day on which the apostles began to witness to the resurrection of Jesus before all the people. The fear they had of being handed over to the Jewish and Roman authorities was gone.

The word *Pentecost* means '*fifty*' and it falls fifty days after Easter. It coincides with the Jewish Feast of Weeks because of the relationship of the Christian Festival of Easter with the Jewish Passover.

Another name for Pentecost Sunday is *Whit Sunday* which means 'White' Sunday. Newly baptized Christians were given white clothes to wear which were a sign of their new faith. Often, people were baptized on Whit Sunday. Today, a link is made, by Christians joining 'Whit Walks', with the account of the apostles bursting out to preach to the crowds in Jerusalem. These walks are a public witness to Christian faith and teaching.

The festival of Whitsun is a celebration of the gift of the Holy Spirit given to the apostles and to all baptized Christians. The duty which the apostles had, to go out and *witness* to the resurrection of Jesus, is also the duty of every baptized person.

SUNDAYS

Sunday is the first day of the Christian week. Every Sunday, Christians celebrate the resurrection of Jesus. It is the most important belief in the Christian religion. In the New Testament it is known as *'the Lord's Day'*. Christians meet on this day to read the scriptures, to receive instruction, to sing hymns, and to celebrate the Eucharist.

The various Christian denominations have their own style of service, but the common factor is their faith in Jesus risen from the dead.

CONCLUSION

The Christian calendar is made up of regular Sunday services and in addition there are special days when events from the life of Christ or famous Christian saints are celebrated. In outline, the calendar is as follows:

► **Advent**
► **Christmastide**
► **Epiphany** — *(twelve days after Christmas)*
► **The Easter Season** — *(including Ash Wednesday and Lent)*
► **Ascension Day**
► **Whitsuntide**
► **Saints Days** *e.g. All Saints — November 1st; St Stephen — December 26th*
► **Special Sundays** *e.g. Trinity Sunday (Sunday after Whit Sunday)*

QUESTIONS

Investigation

1. Name the most important Christian festival.
2. What name is given to the *four* weeks of preparation for Christmas?
3. What was the main task of John the Baptist? (Look for Zechariah's prophecy.)
4. What did the angel Gabriel say about the identity of Jesus?
5. Investigate *one* Advent custom, and describe it in detail.
6. Describe the *three* traditional ways of observing Lent.
7. Outline the events of Holy Week in the life of Jesus up to Holy Saturday.
8. Name the *five* holy days of the last week of Lent.
9. What do Christians believe about Easter day?
10. Choose *one* account of Easter Sunday morning from one of the Gospels and describe what happened.
11. Read Luke 24:13-35. Summarise this appearance of Jesus in your own words.
12. Describe *two* Easter customs.
13. Investigate the way *one* Christian denomination celebrates Easter, and describe this briefly.
14. Name the festival which marks the return of Jesus to his Father in heaven.

Understanding

1. What does the term 'incarnation' mean?
2. What does the name 'Immanuel' mean?
3. What clues are there in the Gospels which emphasise that Jesus is Son of God and Son of Mary?
4. Explain why the winter solstice is a good time for the Christian festival of Christmas.
5. Explain the link between pantomimes and the meaning of Christmas.
6. Outline the meaning of some Christmas customs.
7. What is the meaning of the word 'Epiphany'?
8. Read the references for *one* of the 'showings' of Jesus, and explain how it reflects the Christian belief that Jesus is the Son of God.
9. Explain Ash Wednesday for a non-Christian.
10. Why is Lent part of the Easter season?
11. Explain how the date of Easter is fixed in the Christian calendar.
12. Explain the meaning and importance of *one* of the days in Holy Week (but not Easter Day itself).
13. What does the word 'Pentecost' mean?
14. Explain the origin of 'White Sunday'.
15. Why should Pentecost be called the birthday of the Christian Church?
16. Why is every Sunday of the year a Christian festival?

Evaluation

1. Discuss the importance of prayer, fasting and good works in the Christian tradition.
2. In what ways do you think that Advent customs help to explain the purpose of this season of preparation? Some Christians might not approve of such customs. Why?
3. By referring to some Christmas customs, show whether you think it matters that people should be aware of their religious meaning.
4. In what ways do Christians today keep Good Friday, and do you think these practices are good ways of showing the meaning of the event which is remembered on this day?
5. How would an Orthodox Christian and a Friend (Quaker) explain their Easter services to each other?

FURTHER READING

1. *The Christian Faith and its Symbols:* chapters 4-8; p.69-70; chapter 10.
2. *Christian Worship* (Chichester Project Book 1): chapter 5.
3. *Christmas and Easter* (Chichester Project Book 7).
4. *Christian Belief and Practice:* chapter 10.
5. *Christianity in Words and Pictures:* chapters 11, 12.
6. *Believers All:* pages 19-23.
7. *The Christian World:* pages 48-53; 59.

Note to teachers: The Westhill Project R.E. 5-16 is highly recommended, especially the Teacher's Manual, for the entire section on Christianity.

1.2 PLACES OF WORSHIP

The place where Christians gather for their acts of worship depends upon the people themselves and the times in which they live. Orthodox Christians worship in a building which is very different from that of a Meeting House for the Religious Society of Friends (Quakers). A great deal may be learned about Christianity as a world religion just by investigating the places where Christians meet.

THE EARLY CHURCH

Soon after Pentecost, many people became believers in 'the Way' and were baptized: *'Many of them believed his message and were baptized, and about three thousand were added to the group that day.'* (Acts 2:41)

This was the result of Peter's first sermon! These first Christians were mostly Jews who continued to go to the synagogue for worship. But they soon found that their new faith led them into special acts of worship:

> *'Day after day they met as a group in the Temple, and they had their meals together in their homes, eating with glad and humble hearts, praising God, and enjoying the good will of all the people. And every day the Lord added to their group those who were being saved.'*
>
> *Acts 2:46-47*

In this passage, the Temple courts are mentioned as a meeting place, and also the homes of the Christians. The needs of their worship together meant that they had to find a place suitable for that worship.

SHORT HISTORY OF PLACES OF CHRISTIAN WORSHIP

The first Christians were often referred to as the 'Church', so the Church is wherever the people gather. This is the origin of our use of the word 'Church' for a place of Christian worship. When the word 'Church' has a small 'c' it normally refers to the place of worship. When it has a capital 'C' it refers to the worshippers themselves.

In the early days, Christians met a great deal of opposition, first of all from the Jews who thought their teaching was blasphemous (an insult to God). Jesus could not be the Son of God, because the most important teaching of the Jewish faith was: *Hear O Israel, the Lord your God is one.'*

Then the Romans persecuted the Christians, particularly in the time of the Emperors Nero and Diocletian. However, one Roman Emperor, Constantine, was converted and Christianity became the religion of the State. From this time, public buildings were erected for Christian worship. The style of these buildings was determined by the needs of the services, and often public functions demanded space for processions, and accommodation for crowds of people.

The development of the monasteries also affected the style of churches, because the needs of a community of monks at worship meant that the church was built to meet these needs.

Each community of Christians had its own *bishop*, a successor of the apostles. The bishop had his chair or 'cathedra' in the main church of the area (known as a *'diocese'*) This church soon became known as the *'cathedral'*, and was usually much larger than the local churches. Its architecture was specially adapted to give an important place for the bishop's chair or throne.

At the Reformation in the sixteenth century, there was a reaction against the Mass, and against devotion to the Blessed Virgin Mary and the saints. There was a renewal of Bible-reading and Bible-study. Churches and meeting places for the reformers were much more simple. No statues or unnecessary devotions were permitted. Consequently, many churches were vandalised to make them plainer. As a group of Christians emerged from this period with their own practice of Christianity, different styles of churches, chapels and meeting houses developed.

It is important to realise that the Orthodox Christians never experienced the Reformation. Their services were always in the language of the people, and many of the basic reasons for the Reformation never touched the Orthodox Church.

THE TWENTIETH CENTURY

The following names are used for Christian places of worship today:

Cathedral: Only used for denominations which have bishops and priests e.g. Orthodox, Roman Catholic, Anglican.

Church: General word used for buildings specially designed for Christian worship.

Chapel: The name given to the meeting place of some Protestant groups; or the name given to a small area of a church which is dedicated to Mary or one of the saints.

Citadel: The name given to a place of worship for the Salvation Army. The word 'citadel' means a fortress, which is defended from the enemy. It is an appropriate name for the aims of the Army.

Meeting House: The name used for the place where the Society of Friends (Quakers) meet.

Note: Monasteries, Abbeys and Priories are sometimes used as names for a building of Christian worship. However, these words really refer to the whole complex of buildings which make up a monastery and abbey or a priory. The correct way to refer to such churches is: *monastery church, abbey church, priory church.*

Cathedrals

Christian traditions which have priests and bishops divide a country into regions (dioceses). Each region has its own bishop, but he is not able to care for all the Christians of that area alone so he is assisted by the priests of the diocese. The cathedral is the main church of the diocese.

The architectural style of the great cathedrals of the world developed from the work and worship which took place in them. Some of these influences were:

1. The fact that a cathedral was often part of some great monastery in the region e.g. Norwich Cathedral in England.

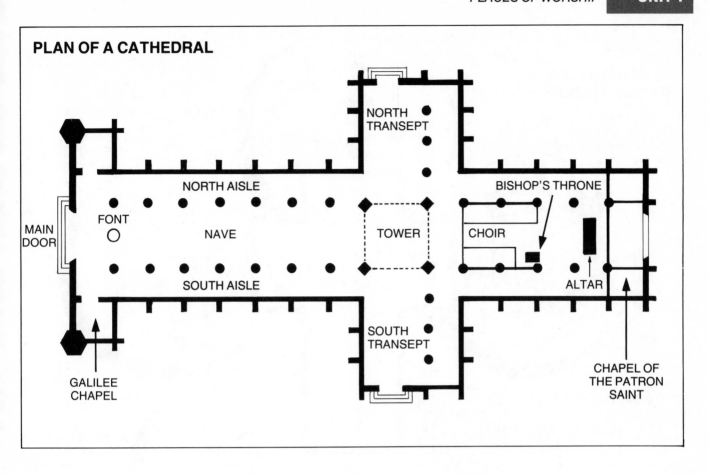

PLAN OF A CATHEDRAL

NORTH TRANSEPT

NORTH AISLE

BISHOP'S THRONE

MAIN DOOR

FONT

NAVE

TOWER

CHOIR

ALTAR

SOUTH AISLE

GALILEE CHAPEL

SOUTH TRANSEPT

CHAPEL OF THE PATRON SAINT

2. Local or national saints were often given honour by having their own special chapel in the cathedral e.g. St George; the Virgin Mary (sometimes called Our Lady) nearly always had her own 'Lady Chapel'.
3. Great celebrations and processions for the festivals of the Christian year meant that the cathedral had to have wide aisles and plenty of space. Great squares or piazzas allowed for crowds of people to gather e.g. St Mark's Square in Venice.
4. The cathedral church served the whole region or diocese, so that extra offices were often added for the administration that was necessary.

Churches

The form of worship which takes place in a church usually accounts for the style of the building. Just as a person will arrange their home to suit the family's needs, so the congregation of a local church will build somewhere suitable for the needs of their acts of worship. However, the needs of one generation of Christians are not the same as the next. So buildings get altered, and sometimes the original building is quite different from the needs of its present generation of worshippers.

Features of an Orthodox church

An eighth century patriarch of Contantinople, called Germanos said, *'The church is the earthly heaven in which the heavenly God dwells and moves.'* This saying explains a great deal about the main features of an Orthodox church, because many items in the church remind the worshippers of heaven. There are icons of Christ, of the Virgin Mary and of the saints in places of honour on the ceiling, walls and screens.

The most striking feature of an Orthodox church is the *iconostasis*. This is a screen which separates the people from the sanctuary where the priests celebrate 'the mysteries'. In the centre of this screen are the *royal doors*. These are double doors which are decorated with important *icons*. Icons are sacred paintings which are an important part of Orthodox worship. On the doors are icons which remind the people that God makes himself known to his people (e.g. the Gospel writers — evangelists, or angels who are God's messengers).

On the right side of these doors is the main icon of Christ. Next to this icon is one of the patron saint of the church, e.g. St Basil. On the other side of the royal doors is the icon of the Mother of God. Next to this is the icon of John the Baptist. On either side of these four icons, are two doors through which deacons emerge during the Orthodox service. On these doors are icons of the archangels. Depending on the size of the iconostasis, there may be other icons of incidents from the life of Christ, or more icons of the saints.

There are no seats in an Orthodox church because the people stand for prayer. There are stands which hold the many *candles* which are lit by the people and are a most important part of the liturgy. *Oil-lamps* often hang before icons. Frequently there will be a strong smell of incense because *incense* is regularly used in Orthodox worship.

The appearance of an Orthodox church from the outside varies as much as for other Christian churches, but a good example of the 'earthly heaven' Germanos spoke of may be seen in Red Square in Moscow — the Church of St Basil.

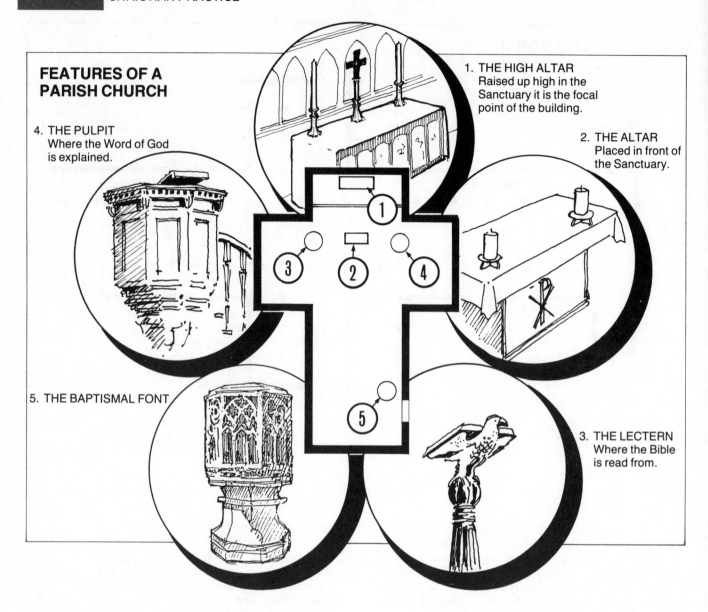

FEATURES OF A PARISH CHURCH

1. THE HIGH ALTAR
Raised up high in the Sanctuary it is the focal point of the building.

2. THE ALTAR
Placed in front of the Sanctuary.

4. THE PULPIT
Where the Word of God is explained.

3. THE LECTERN
Where the Bible is read from.

5. THE BAPTISMAL FONT

Features of a parish church
The oldest churches in Britain are usually Church of England, and their external appearance is of a building surrounded by a churchyard which contains a burial ground for the worshippers of that parish. The church itself will have a bell tower. This tower may have a *spire, square tower, round tower,* or *lantern tower*.

In days when people did not have clocks and watches the *church bells* were most important. They:
▶ **called to prayer**
▶ **announced a joyful occasion**
  (e.g. the end of war)
▶ **announced danger or sorrow**
  (e.g. after some local disaster)
▶ **rang the hour**
  (to remind people of the time of day)

Local parishes took great care to have fine bells cast in the *bell foundries*. Bells of different sizes and weights give different notes, and *bell ringers* form special groups in the parish to practise combinations of the bells for different purposes. Today, the art of bell ringing (campanology) is still kept on to preserve the Christian heritage of Britain.

A *spire* on a church can be seen for miles and is a reminder of the worship of the people whose prayers soar to heaven. Another feature of the parish church is the *nave*. This runs the length of the church, which allows enough space for the whole parish to gather. At the eastern end of the nave is the *altar* which is the focal point of the building. It may be very ornate and raised up in the *sanctuary* (or holy place). Sometimes the remains of a *rood screen* may be seen. This is used to screen off the sanctuary from the nave, and the priest from the people. It was thought that the priest was doing something so holy by consecrating the bread and wine, that people ought to adore from a distance.

There are *transepts* in a traditional parish church. These form a cross with the main body of the church. Originally these spaces might have surrounded the tomb of a martyr, and/or provided space for the tables where the people placed their gifts at the offertory of the Mass. Today transepts are often used for extra seating in the church.

Sometimes, old churches do not express the community aspect of worship, so another table is placed at the front of the sanctuary and is used instead of the High Altar at services. This allows the family of God to gather round his table for worship. In this way, the people are not cut off in either the transept or the nave from the main place of worship.

The service of the Word is also very important, so a *pulpit* has an important place, and also a *lectern*. From the lectern the Bible is read, and from the pulpit the word of God is explained to the people.

Quite near the entrance of the parish church, the *font* is placed. A font is the place where a person is baptized and made a member of the Christian community, and therefore of God's Family. It is near the entrance to act as a symbol of the 'entrance' of the new Christian into the parish community. Today the font is placed somewhere near the front of the church where the whole congregation can see and approve of the baptism.

These are the main features of the traditional parish church. A comparison of an old and a modern parish church shows how the role of the congregation in worship may alter the style and the contents of the building. It is interesting to note that the Orthodox church has never seen the necessity to change its style of worship, so the modern Orthodox church does not look so different from the traditional one.

Chapels

The word 'chapel' is used to mean two different things:

1. A little room opening off from the main part of the parish church, and dedicated to a particular saint e.g. Mary, Joseph or a saint important in the area e.g. Cuthbert, Edmund or Alban. In this chapel, people pray or give honour to the saint. Sometimes memorial chapels are built to remember or honour the dead soldiers of a particular war.

2. A 'chapel' may describe the entire building in which a particular denomination of Christians worship e.g. Baptist, Methodist or United Reformed. However, these Christians would still describe some of their places of worship as 'churches'. The features of chapel worship emphasise the importance of the Bible and scripture study, so a non-conformist chapel is simple with the *pulpit* and *lectern* having a central place. A table covered with a simple cloth is all that is used for the Communion service or the Lord's Supper.

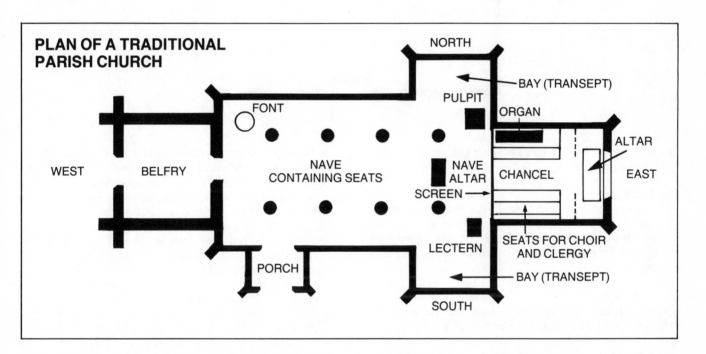

PLAN OF A TRADITIONAL PARISH CHURCH

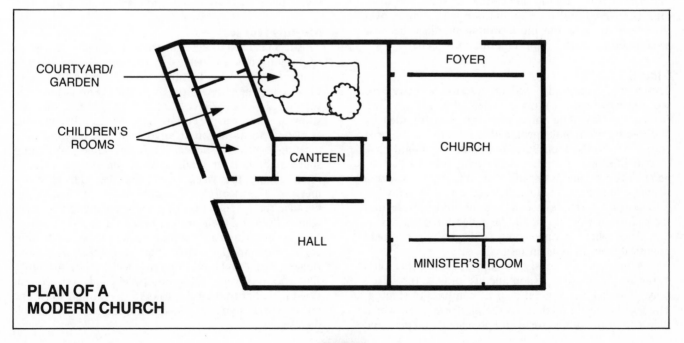

PLAN OF A MODERN CHURCH

PLAN OF AN ORTHODOX CHURCH

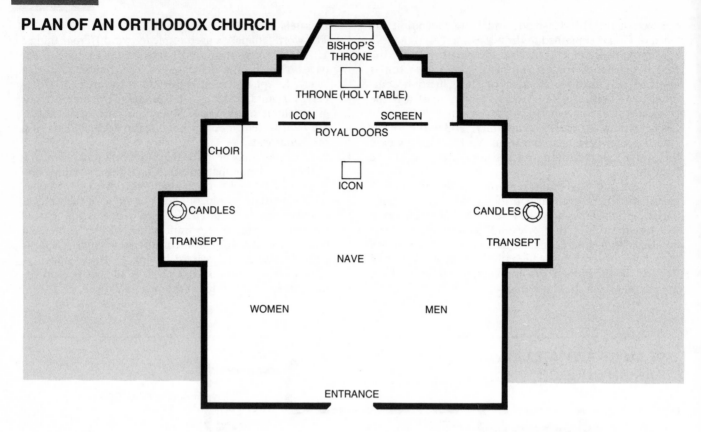

SOME SPECIAL FEATURES OF CHRISTIAN PLACES OF WORSHIP

Baptistry

This serves the same purpose as the font in a parish church, but is a more symbolic representation of the sacrament of baptism. Often there is a step down into the area of the baptistry and the font has a special place of honour there.

The step may represent the symbolic 'going down' into the waters of baptism where there is death to sin and new life in Christ when the person emerges again. In a Baptist church or chapel the baptistry is a tank sunk into the floor which may be filled with water for the baptism of adults by full immersion. At other times the tank is covered and the Communion table stands over the place. It is in the most prominent place because adult baptism is most important in Baptist belief.

Citadel

This word is normally used to describe a fortress of some kind where an army can defend a city or town from an enemy. The Salvation Army was founded by **William Booth** to make people have faith in Jesus Christ and accept him as their Saviour so that they might have eternal life. The enemy is Satan who tries to destroy people. The 'Army' is organised on military lines with a 'General' and officers of various degrees. The Army has 'cadets' and 'brigades' so it is quite appropriate that their place of worship should be called the citadel. It is the place where people come to find their personal salvation from all evils, in Jesus Christ.

Army worship consists of Bible reading, personal testimony, preaching, spontaneous prayer (no fixed prayer books) and a great deal of community singing. The focal point of a citadel is the platform from which the word of the Bible is read and preached, and personal testimony is given. 'Testimony' is when a person will tell others how the word of God and the example of others has changed their lives. The Salvation Army band has a place on the platform as well. Beneath the platform is the *'mercy seat'*. This is an important feature of a citadel, because people are invited to come to the mercy seat to show that they want to change their lives and turn away from sin. The mercy seat looks like a bench to sit on beneath the platform.

The flag bearing the motto *'Blood and Fire'* is given a prominent place in the citadel. The 'Blood' means the blood of Christ which saves all people, and 'Fire' is the symbol of the Holy Spirit used in the Acts of the Apostles, to show how the first Christians were given the courage to preach and teach about Jesus.

Meeting Houses

This term is used to describe the place where the Society of Friends meets. Just as in the citadel, the meeting house does not have features which reflect a formal act of worship like the Mass or Holy Communion. The Friends do not believe that sacrament and outward show are necessary. This is because they believe that God will speak through anyone at the meeting. The meeting is held in silence. However, some people may share a thought or reading which has meant a lot to them during the week or during the silence of the meeting. The meeting house does not resemble a church because the Friends do not draw a distinction between what is holy and their ordinary everyday lives.

The meeting room contains a simple circle of chairs or benches. In the centre there is a table with some flowers and a few books one of which will be the Bible. The room is very plain otherwise. This reflects the Friends' belief that God speaks to the human spirit and no external signs are necessary except the people themselves.

Another name which is given to the Society of Friends is *Quakers*. They got this name when the power of the Holy Spirit in their prayer meetings reminded people of the first Pentecost. Because they believe that everything in life is holy, the Friends have been famous for their work in society e.g. in prison reform and in other forms of social service.

OTHER FEATURES OF CHRISTIAN PLACES OF WORSHIP

Confessional. This is an important feature in a Roman Catholic church. It is a place in the church where a person can go to confess their sins to a priest. There are a variety of styles for these places, but there are two main types in a modern Roman Catholic church. One is a cubicle where the 'penitent' cannot be seen by the priest, and the other is a small 'room' where the penitent can talk face to face with a priest. (The explanation for this is given in Unit 7.1)

Cross. The cross is almost always found in a place of Christian worship. A crucifix has a figure on it and represents the suffering of Jesus by which all Christians believe they are saved. A plain cross emphasises the resurrection of Jesus which all Christians believe is a promise of eternal life for them. There is a type of crucifix which expresses the suffering *and* the resurrection of Jesus, and this shows Jesus on the cross but alive, dressed in the rich clothes of a king and wearing a crown.

Stained glass windows. These show Bible incidents which act as teaching aids for people. Sometimes they represent the lives of various saints. Sometimes they are memorial windows of famous people or events. It is worth visiting a church and finding out as much about the Christian religion as possible just by looking at the stained glass.

Statues. These represent saints or famous people. In Roman Catholic churches there will often be a rack for candles or votive lights in front of a statue. The Christian may light a candle to honour the saints or ask them to pray for the needs of their parish, their family and the world. Many Christians object to statues on the grounds that they are 'carved images' forbidden by the Commandments. However, Roman Catholics would say that the statues are not objects of worship but are reminders of the way they ought to follow Christ.

Stations of the cross. These are most often found in a Catholic church. They are fourteen crosses placed around the church. Near each cross there is a picture or a carving of an incident in the traditional account of the last journey of Jesus to Calvary. The Christian will walk (a symbolic 'journey') around the 'stations' and meditate on the suffering of Jesus at each stage. Usually the last station (or stage in the journey) shows Jesus being laid to rest in the tomb. Today a fifteenth station is often added to show the resurrection of Jesus.

Tabernacle. This is the place where the consecrated hosts for Communion of the sick are kept. It is usually a wooden or metal box fixed in a wall or standing on a plinth. Sometimes a curtain surrounds it or hangs in front. If this receptacle for the hosts hangs from the ceiling, it is called a *pyx*. This is a name which is also given to a much smaller metal box (usually silver) containing a few hosts when Communion is taken into the homes of the sick.

Sanctuary lamp. Somewhere near the tabernacle in a Roman Catholic church (and in some Anglican churches) a lamp is lit and kept burning as long as there are consecrated hosts in the tabernacle. Lamps are also an important feature in an Orthodox church.

Organ. Traditionally, the Christian church makes use of all types of musical instruments in its worship. However, the organ is a most popular instrument, because it is capable of reproducing all kinds of instrumental sounds. The Christian tradition also values the human voice in worship, and a great deal of church music is choral.

CONCLUSION

Buildings which are used for Christian worship suit the beliefs and practices of the people using them:
▶ Some Christians have highly organised services with bishops, priests, and other officers. Churches which belong to Orthodox, Roman Catholic, and some Protestant denominations (e.g. Anglicans) are examples.
▶ Some Christians have spontaneous services which depend upon the inspiration which is given by the Word and Spirit of God on that occasion. Their buildings provide for the needs of preaching, teaching, singing and praying, which is the main emphasis of their belief and practice of the Christian faith.

QUESTIONS

Investigation

1. Name *two* places where the first Christians worshipped.
2. What is the origin of the word 'cathedral'?
3. Name *five* types of buildings for Christian worship.
4. What is a diocese?
5. What is a citadel?
6. Describe *two* functions of church bells.
7. Describe a crucifix.
8. Outline the main features of a place of Christian worship which you have visited.
9. Describe a rood screen.
10. Describe a meeting house for the Society of Friends (Quakers).
11. What are the main features of an iconastasis in an Orthodox Church?

Understanding

1. Explain the function of the following: i) altar ii) nave iii) sanctuary iv) pulpit v) font.
2. Explain *two* of the Stations of the Cross.
3. Explain *three* features of an Orthodox church which remind the worshippers of heaven.

4. Give a simple explanation for the variety of church buildings in the twentieth century.
5. Choose *two* symbolic features of a baptistry and explain their meaning.
6. Why do Roman Catholic churches have statues in them?
7. Explain the purpose of the sanctuary lamp.
8. What is the purpose of a rood screen?
9. Explain the Christian teaching contained in an icon of your choice.
10. What is the 'mercy seat' used for?

Evaluation

1. Do you think stained-glass windows still have an important use today, or are they purely decorative?
2. Identify *two* of the items in an Orthodox church which a member of the Free Churches might find offensive to their own understanding of the Christian faith.
3. Do you like modern styles of church buildings or do you prefer traditional styles? Give reasons for your answer.
4. Do you think an organ is essential in a Christian place of worship? Give your reasons.
5. What are the arguments for a single building, for use by all Christians, in an area which is multi-denominational? Do you think a single building is a good idea? Give reasons for your opinion.

FURTHER READING

1. *The Christian Faith and its Symbols:* chapter 2.
2. *Christian Worship* (Chichester Project Book 1): pages 21, 22.
3. *Christian Belief and Practice:* chapters 8, 9.
4. *Christianity in Words and Pictures:* chapter 8; p.29.
   See also: Christian Denominations Series:
      1. *Roman Catholic Church:* chapter 3.
      2. *The Baptists:* chapter 5.
      3. *The Orthodox Church:* chapter 1.
   and: Meeting Religious Groups Series:
      1. *Visiting a Salvation Army Citadel:* chapter 2.
      2. *Visiting a Methodist Church:* chapter 1.
      3. *Visiting an Anglican Church:* chapter 3.
      4. *Visiting a Community Church:* of general interest.
5. *Believers All:* pages 7-10.
6. *The Christian World:* pages 32, 33.
7. *Religions of Man:* pages 157-168.

1.3 PUBLIC AND PRIVATE WORSHIP

PUBLIC WORSHIP

In the previous chapter, Christian places of worship and their furnishings revealed a great deal about the kind of prayer and praise which went on in them. It became obvious that there are different styles of worship in the Christian Church. The reasons for this are very complicated, but a simple explanation can be found by saying that the **Reformation** brought a move away from elaborate ceremonials to a different style of worship based on reading, preaching and teaching about the Bible.

Another explanation can be found in the fact that, from time to time, groups of Christian people want to return to the simplicity of worship which is described in the Acts of the Apostles (Acts 2:42-47). With these two reasons in mind, it is possible to look at the variety of Christian acts of worship in the following way:

LITURGICAL WORSHIP	NONCONFORMING WORSHIP (FREE CHURCH WORSHIP)
Eastern Orthodox	Presbyterian
Roman Catholic	Baptist
Church of England	Congregational
Church of Scotland	United Reformed
	Methodist
	Salvation Army

QUAKER WORSHIP	CHARISMATIC WORSHIP
Society of Friends	Pentecostal Churches

HOUSE CHURCH WORSHIP
House Church Movement

LITURGICAL WORSHIP

The word *'liturgy'* ('liturgical' is the adjective) comes from a Greek word which means an act of public service. In the Christian Church this is service to God. Worship is the best act of service to God and the word 'liturgy' is used to describe the different forms or patterns of the Eucharist in the Christian Church.

A comparison of an Orthodox service, a Roman Catholic service and an Anglican service reveals that there are features in common:
▶ **reading and explanation of scripture**
▶ **sermon**
▶ **prayers of intercession (Bidding Prayers)**
▶ **gifts of the people**
▶ **Jesus' words and actions at the Last Supper**
▶ **Communion service**

The special features of liturgical worship are:
1. A set form of service or ceremonial.
2. A service book. (Orthodox: Book of the Liturgy. Roman Catholic: Missal. Church of England: Book of Common Prayer, or Alternative Service Book. Church of Scotland: Book of Common Order.)
3. Vestments for the Ministers e.g. cassock, stole, alb, cope, chasuble, gown and hood, preaching band, mitre etc...
4. Use of symbolic actions and signs.

There is a pattern of standing, sitting, kneeling, for the people. The minister or priest also has set actions. Crosses and banners are carried in procession, or incense may be used. The sign of the cross is frequently used in Orthodox and Roman Catholic services. The 'pax' (sign of peace) may be used. Laying on of hands may be used.

FREE CHURCH WORSHIP
(Nonconformist worship)

After the Reformation and the introduction of the Bible in the English language, there was a move in the Re-formed Churches towards more reading and preaching and less ceremonial. People no longer listened to Latin or a language which they could not understand, so they took more part in the services themselves and eventually prayer books were issued for the people. It is important to realise that Orthodox services have always been conducted in the language of the people, and that the Orthodox Church never suffered the effects of the Reformation which took place in Western Christendom.

Instead of private prayers and devotions, the members of the congregation (after the Reformation) had an active part in the service. The public worship of the Free Churches has a strong bias towards community hymns, reading of the Bible, preaching and teaching. They do celebrate Holy Communion but less frequently than in the Roman Catholic Church, or the Church of England. Free Church services have the following in common:

Hymn singing. There is a great tradition of community hymn singing in the Free Churches. The worshippers are often greeted at the door of the church by an elder who will present them with a hymn book.

Prayer. In the Free Church tradition, prayers do not follow a set formula, and the minister will make them up according to the needs of the day. Prayers are of praise, thanksgiving, repentance and intercession.

Reading of the Bible. The Old Testament and New Testament readings are made, and in a Free Church there will be Bibles where one might expect prayer books in, for example, an Anglican Church.

Sermon. The sermon is long in the Free Church tradition and ministers, especially in the Methodist Church, receive very special training in preaching.

People's offerings. In the Acts of the Apostles 4:32-37 the generosity of the first Christians is emphasised: *'...there were no needy persons among them...they shared everything they had...'* Collections and gifts from the congregation are taken as part of the act of worship.

QUAKER WORSHIP

Liturgical worship emphasises the importance of the Eucharist and worship around the altar. Non-conformist worship emphasises the ministry of preaching and the importance of God's word in the Bible. The worship of the Society of Friends (Quakers), emphasises the importance of waiting for the action of God's Spirit in the hearts of the worshippers. The Friends have no set service, no priests and no sacraments. A Friends' meeting takes quite literally these words of Jesus: *'Where two or three are gathered together in my name, there am I in the midst.'*

The Friends believe that any person is likely to contribute to the prayer and insight of the meeting. They meet in silence, sit down in a circle, and wait for the Spirit of God to urge one or two of the Friends to speak. A Friend may say a prayer which comes to mind; share a particular worry about the amount of violence in society; ask the other Friends to be more concerned about the needs of the poor, or give an explanation of a part of the Bible they were reading during the week.

Quakers traditionally reject baptism and all sacraments. They believe that baptism in the Spirit is enough. They believe that there is no need for Holy Communion since Christ will dwell spiritually in the hearts of all who let him come into their lives.

PENTECOSTAL WORSHIP

The worship of the 'Pentecostal' Christians is also recognised by its emphasis on belief in the gifts of the Holy Spirit of God in the hearts of those who have faith in Jesus Christ as the Saviour of the world.

However, their worship contrasts strongly with that of the Quakers or Society of Friends. It has been noted that the worship of the Quakers was simple but that their commitment to the needs of the world was very strong. *'Love of God and love of neighbour'* is a good summary of their prayer and Christian action. Pente-costal Christians express the same belief of 'waiting on the Spirit' in their acts of worship, but their services are usually much more dramatic.

The word *'Pentecost'* shows that these Christians emphasise the same kind of gifts of the Holy Spirit which were given to the apostles on the first day of Pentecost, fifty days after the crucifixion and resurrec-tion of Jesus (Unit 5.1). The gifts of courage, prophecy, tongues, and preaching were most obvious on this day, and a Pentecostal service is recognised by the energetic conviction that Jesus is risen, he is Lord, and Saviour. In their service there is nearly always an element of calling people to change their lives, and be converted to God.

In a Pentecostal service the following are usually present:

▶ **hymns** (sometimes made up, or spontaneous)
▶ **prayer** (coming from any member of the congregation)
▶ **Bible readings**
▶ **preaching**
▶ **prophecy and tongues**

Pentecostal worship is different in the various parts of the world where there are Pentecostal Christians, because their worship is so individual and depends on the way the Spirit of God is expressed in the different gifts.

There are *'Pentecostal movements'* in the traditional Christian denominations like the Roman Catholic Church and the Church of England, but their services usually take the form of prayer groups outside the main liturgical services.

Pentecostal worship emphasises the fact that, during the service, prayer and praise may come from anyone in the congregation although there will be a minister or member of the Church who will lead the service. They are usually very long, perhaps taking up the whole evening. At the service some people will ask for 'laying on of hands' and they are prayed with individually by one or two members of the congregation after the main service.

HOUSE CHURCH MOVEMENT

This movement takes as its model the life and worship of the New Testament. People worship together in their homes, and everyone is important in the group's act of worship. A Sunday morning act of worship might follow this general pattern:

▶ **hymn** (hymns are specially composed by the movement although some suitable 'favourites' from other hymn books may appear)
▶ **prayer**
▶ **hymn**
▶ **speaking from the Bible** (a sharing of scripture)
▶ **thanksgiving for the bread** (the bread is passed round)
▶ **thanksgiving for the wine** (a cup of wine is passed round)
(The remaining bread and wine is covered and taken out)
▶ **hymn**

The group sits in a circle. On a table in the centre will be the bread and wine (an ordinary slice of bread and a cup of wine). Each group of perhaps 13 or 14 people will have its own bishop or elder, chosen according to the directions given in the New Testament. The Sunday evening service may consist of Bible readings from the New Testament, and there may be a mid-week service of readings from the Old Testament.

There will be two *ministers* in the area who will go from door to door inviting families to a meeting which would introduce them to the House Church movement. A hall is hired for the meeting. Each year there will be an annual convention for the members of the movement. The convention is organised by an overseer. A larger hall would be hired for a weekend for a convention.

Baptisms are performed by full immersion in the running water of the local river and are organised by the ministers of the area who will inform the local bishop or elder. *Marriages* are not a formal ceremony but the couple have a civil wedding in the registry office and then have a thanksgiving hymn for the marriage in the home. Sometimes the registrar may be invited to the home. *Funerals* take place in a hall or funeral parlour near to the cemetery. A prayer is said in the home before the coffin is taken away for burial.

It is important to realise that members of the House Church movement are *Bible Christians* who take their inspiration for worship in song and prayer from the worship of the early Church in the Acts of the Apostles and the other New Testament writings.

The lives of the members and the way they behave reflect Bible teaching. Therefore, any contributions or offerings which they give are private and generous according to the instructions of Jesus and the practice of the early Christians.

The movement is a world-wide one, and ministers who are serving overseas may speak about their mission at an annual convention.

PRIVATE WORSHIP

In the Sermon on the Mount, Jesus made two main points about personal prayer.

1. Prayer ought not to be a display that other people are meant to admire:

'When you pray, do not be like the hypocrites! They love to stand up and pray in the houses of worship and on the street corners, so that everyone will see them. I assure you, they have already been paid in full. But when you pray, go to your room, close the door, and pray to your Father, who is unseen. And your Father, who sees what you do in private, will reward you.'
Matthew 6:5-6

2. Prayer ought not to consist of long formulas as though God had to be persuaded by many words. This was a pagan idea which thought of gods being like human masters.

'When you pray, do not use a lot of meaningless words, as the pagans do, who think that their gods will hear them because their prayers are long.'
Matthew 6:7

This advice is followed by the Christian formula of the Lord's Prayer 'Our Father' (see Unit 2.1). Luke's Gospel records the teaching of Jesus in the parable of the friend at midnight (Luke 11:5-8), who kept on asking until he was given the bread he needed. The comparison being made was with the fact that people ought to be full of hope when they pray. *('You are not ashamed to keep on asking.')* In this teaching Jesus concluded: *'For everyone who asks will receive, and he who seeks will find, and the door will be opened to anyone who knocks.'* (Luke 11:10)

When Paul was writing to the Christians in Rome, he made the point that prayer was really the work of the Holy Spirit of God in a person, and that they were not to worry if they felt they didn't know how to pray: *'We do not know how we ought to pray; the Spirit himself pleads with God for us in groans that words cannot express.'* (Romans 8:26)

In the New Testament, therefore, the point is made that prayer is necessary but that God knows the needs of his people like a father knows the needs of his children (Luke 11:11-13).

Vocal and silent prayer

When Christians pray privately, they may use words or they may be quite silent. When they use words, it is called *vocal prayer*. There are four main kinds of vocal prayer:

1. The Lord's Prayer.
2. Liturgical prayers (e.g. 'Glory be to the Father, and to the Son and to the Holy Spirit, as it was in the

beginning, is now and ever shall be, world without end. Amen.').

3. Written prayers of other Christians (e.g. Anthologies of prayers for various occasions).

4. Spontaneous prayers (made up on the spot by the person).

Vocal prayers are often concerned with:

▶ **praise and adoration of God**
▶ **sorrow for personal sin**
▶ **thanksgiving for God's love in their lives**
▶ **intercession** (or blessings/favours) for oneself or for others.

Meditation

Meditation is a mixture of vocal and silent prayer. A common method of meditation is when a Christian reads a passage from the Bible, tries to picture the scene, and then speaks to God in prayer.

The *rosary* is a special method of meditation upon the most important events in the life of Jesus or of Mary. A rosary is a circle of beads. It has five sets of ten beads with one large bead between each set of ten. A crucifix on a short set of four beads is attached to the circle of beads. The person who is praying the rosary says the Lord's Prayer, ten 'Hail Mary's' and one 'Glory be to the Father', while thinking about an event in the life of Jesus or of Mary. Each event is called a 'mystery'. There are five joyful mysteries, five sorrowful mysteries and five glorious mysteries.

AIDS TO PRAYER

Joyful	Sorrowful	Glorious
1. Annunciation of the Angel to Mary	Agony of Jesus in the garden	Resurrection of Jesus
2. Visitation of Mary to Elizabeth	Scourging at the pillar	Ascension of Jesus
3. Nativity of Jesus	Crowning with thorns	Descent of Holy Spirit upon Mary and the apostles
4. Presentation of Jesus in the temple	Carrying of the cross	Assumption of Mary into heaven
5. Finding of Jesus in the temple	Crucifixion	Crowning of Mary as Queen of heaven and the glory of all the saints

Christians may also use other objects which help them to pray. Orthodox Christians use *icons* as a most important aid to prayer. An icon is a sacred picture, painted on wood, which has many symbolic features. These features include the style of the drawing; the colours of paint which are used, and special words and symbols which may be incorporated into the picture. These pictures seem strange to people who do not understand them, but they are regularly used in the home and in the churches of Orthodox Christians. Icons are often of Christ as teacher, of Mary and the child Jesus, and of the saints. Orthodox Christians will have an icon of the saint after whom they are named in their room with a lamp or candle before it. Other objects used for prayer may include:

▶ **stations of the cross** (small editions of the ones found in a Catholic church);
▶ **statues** (which remind Christians of Jesus, Mary, or of a saint they wish to pray for them);
▶ **pictures** (of Bible events, or nature, or holy people).

Contemplation

This is a silent form of prayer which relies on the promise that the Holy Spirit prays in the Christian without words being necessary. This kind of prayer is a loving conversation without words between God and the Christian. Contemplation is often compared with the image of two people who love each other so much that they do not need to put words to what they feel for each other. A story is told that when someone was questioned about what he did when he was praying, he said: *'Well you see, I just looks at him, and he looks at me!'*

Note: Many Christians pray in tongues. What this usually means is that these people allow many un-recognisable sounds to express their prayer. They feel that these sounds express what they cannot find 'real' words for. It does not always mean a gift of another language as on the day of Pentecost.

CONCLUSION

Public worship *(See illustration on p.27).*

In this chapter three main types of worship have been shown. They are:

1. *Liturgical worship* (services which have a set pattern and prayer book): This worship is centred around the altar and the celebration of the Eucharist and sacraments.
2. *Pulpit centred worship:* This worship emphasises the Bible and preaching. It is best expressed in the Non-conformist services (those of the Free Churches e.g. Methodist, Baptist etc.).
3. *'Waiting on the Spirit' worship:* The Quakers (or Society of Friends) and the Pentecostal Churches are examples of this type of worship, which is recognised by its emphasis on the gifts of the Spirit of God in the lives of ordinary people. There is an absence of priests and sacraments in this type of worship.

However, the various Christian denominations are beginning to adopt styles of worship different from their own without fear of losing their individual character. The ecumenical movement encourages any move towards Christian unity, and in this, worship is very important. It would be impossible for all Christians to have exactly the same style of worship, but today there is much less fear of adapting the styles of worship to the needs of the local congregation.

Private worship

Private prayer is very important in the Christian faith. The foundation of such prayer is in the teaching and example of Jesus who frequently went away by himself to pray alone. The two main kinds of private prayer are *vocal prayer* which may include meditation; and *silent prayer* or contemplation. Many Christians need nothing more than the Bible for their prayer. Others find many objects helpful to remind them of God. Usually the tradition in which the person has been brought up introduces him or her to a particular way of praying alone.

QUESTIONS

PUBLIC WORSHIP

Investigation

1. Give *two* examples, with names, of liturgical service books.
2. Describe *one* symbolic action used in liturgical worship.
3. Name *three* gifts of the Holy Spirit which are features of Pentecostal worship.
4. Describe baptism as it is given in the House Church Movement.
5. Identify *two* different types of 'Waiting on the Spirit' worship.
6. Describe the common features of liturgical worship.
7. Identify *three* items of the vestments of a Christian minister and draw or describe them.
8. Describe the main features of Free Church or Non-conformist worship.
9. Outline a typical meeting of the Society of Friends.
10. Describe a House Church meeting.
11. Describe *either:* a liturgical-style service, *or:* a Free Church style service which you have attended or watched on the television.
12. In public Christian worship, what activities are connected with: i) the pulpit, and ii) the altar?

Understanding

1. What does the term 'Reformation' mean for Christians?
2. Explain the origin and meaning of the word 'liturgy'.
3. Why is a meeting of the Society of Friends held in silence?
4. Why do 'the Friends' reject baptism and other sacraments?
5. Explain the importance of i) the gift of tongues, ii) the gift of prophecy.
6. Explain the purpose of the ecumenical movement.
7. Why did preaching and reading the Bible become emphasised in worship after the Reformation?
8. What is meant by the phrase 'Bible Christians', and what is involved in being this kind of Christian?

Evaluation

1. Do you think that public Christian worship is helpful for young Christians today?
2. When young Christians find Christian worship 'boring', how do you think they themselves could improve it?
3. Do you think that acts of Christian worship broadcast by the media (T.V., radio, video) are more effective than taking part in a live service? Give reasons for your answer.

PRIVATE WORSHIP

Investigation

1. Relate a parable which teaches about perseverance in prayer.
2. Name the *four* main kinds of vocal prayer.
3. Write out the Lord's Prayer from memory.
4. Describe a rosary.
5. Name *one* joyful, *one* sorrowful, and *one* glorious mystery of the rosary.
6. What advice did Jesus give about praying alone?
7. Describe some of the main points taught about prayer in the New Testament.
8. Choose an example of an icon and describe it in detail.

(Questions continued on page 28.)

THREE MAIN TYPES OF CHRISTIAN WORSHIP

LITURGICAL WORSHIP

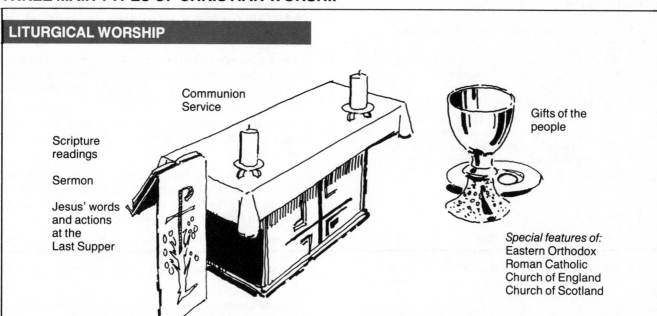

Communion
Service

Scripture
readings

Sermon

Jesus' words
and actions
at the
Last Supper

Gifts of the
people

Special features of:
Eastern Orthodox
Roman Catholic
Church of England
Church of Scotland

PULPIT CENTRED WORSHIP

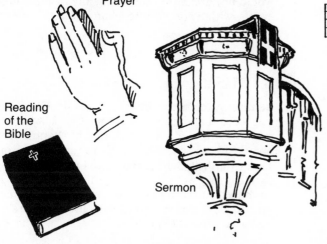

Prayer

Reading
of the
Bible

Sermon

Hymn singing

People's
offerings

Special features of:
Presbyterian   United Reformed
Baptist   Methodist
Congregational   Salvation Army

'WAITING ON THE SPIRIT' WORSHIP

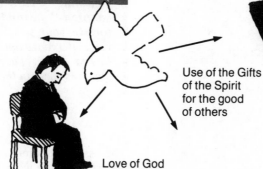

Action of the
Spirit in their
lives

Bible
reading

Use of the Gifts
of the Spirit
for the good
of others

Love of God
and neighbour

Prayer

Special features of:
The Quakers, or
   Society of Friends
Pentecostal Churches

Understanding

1. What did Jesus mean when he used the term 'hypocrite'?
2. What does the term 'vocal prayer' mean?
3. Explain the Christian concept of contemplation.
4. Write brief explanations for the following attitudes expressed in prayer: praise; sorrow; thanksgiving; intercession.
5. How do people pray when they meditate?
6. Explain the use made of an icon in prayer by Orthodox Christians.

Evaluation

1. What is your opinion about the usefulness or effectiveness of private prayer for Christians?
2. Some Christians are called 'contemplatives'. What do you think about the way they pray? Give reasons for your opinion.
3. Consider the main ways in which Christians pray on their own, and say what you think might be the value of such prayer.
4. A Roman Catholic attending a Quaker service might find the experience a strange one. Give some reasons for this.

FURTHER READING

1. *The Christian Faith and its Symbols:* chapter 3.
2. *Christian Worship* (Chichester Project Book 1): chapters 1, 3, 6.
3. *Christian Belief and Practice:* chapter 9.
4. *Christianity in Words and Pictures:* chapters 9, 10.
    See also: Christian Denominations Series:
        1. *The Society of Friends:* chapter 1.
        2. *The Salvation Army:* chapter 3.
        3. *The Pentecostal Churches:* chapter 1.
        4. *The Orthodox Church:* pages 39-41 (Icons), chapter 4.
    and: Meeting Religious Groups Series: *Visiting an Anglican Church:* chapters 4, 5.
5. *The Christian World:* pages 20-29: pages 34, 35 (Personal prayer).
6. *Religions of Man:* pages 126-131.

1.4 CEREMONIES FOR IMPORTANT EVENTS

Christians mark important events in the natural progress of a human life with ceremonies. These ceremonies answer the questions which people ask about the mystery of life itself:

▶ *baptism* or a Christian dedication service answers the questions 'Who am I?'; 'Why am I here?'; 'What am I here for?'

▶ *confirmation* ceremonies emphasise the purpose of life as a Christian which is to love and worship God and to serve the family of God by loving one's neighbour, with the help of the Holy Spirit.

▶ *marriage* ceremonies express important truths about the human family as a mirror of the love of God for his people, and the contract of love he has made with them.

▶ *funerals* express the firm belief of Christians in eternal life, and the communion of saints.

Sometimes these religious ceremonies for important 'milestones' in a person's life are called **Rites of Passage**. Many Christians who do not attend services regularly would not dream of celebrating any of these important events without a visit to church for the appropriate ceremony.

BAPTISM

Baptism is the rite of initiation into the Christian faith. The word 'baptize' comes from a Greek word 'baptizo' meaning 'to dip'. When John the Baptist began to preach, he asked all the people to turn away from their sins. (Matthew 3:1-6; Mark 1:2-8; Luke 3:3-18) As a sign that they were going to do this they came to John to be dipped in the water of the river Jordan. They were washed clean as a sign of the new life they were going to lead according to God's law.

> *'So John appeared in the desert, baptizing and preaching. "Turn away from your sins and be baptized," he told the people, "and God will forgive your sins." Many people from the province of Judaea and the city of Jerusalem went out to hear John. They confessed their sins, and he baptized them in the River Jordan.'*
>
> *Mark 1:4-6*

The essential points about baptism as it was done by John the Baptist were:

1. **Confession of sins**
2. **Washing in the River Jordan**
3. **Forgiveness of sins**
4. **Reform of life according to God's laws**

(See Luke 3:10-15. The people were told to share with each other; the tax-collectors were told to be honest; the soldiers were told to be content with their pay.)

The Baptism of Jesus
(Matthew 3:3-17; Mark 1:9-11; Luke 3:21-22)
Jesus presented himself to John for baptism. Matthew's Gospel points out that the conditions and necessity for baptism did not exist for Jesus:

> *'John tried to make him change his mind. ''I ought to be baptized by you,'' John said, ''and yet you have come to me.'' But Jesus answered him, ''Let it be so for now. For in this way we shall do all that God requires.'' So John agreed.'*

However, a new and important event occurred at the baptism of Jesus. The *Spirit of God* descended upon Jesus (in the form of a dove) and there was an announcement: *'This is my own dear Son, with whom I am pleased.'* (Matthew 3:17)

The baptism of Jesus was the opening act of his public life among the people as a wandering preacher, teacher and miracle worker. The event was a kind of ceremony of initiation into the life God wanted him to lead. The essential points about the baptism of Jesus were:

1. **He was one of the people who came to John**
2. **He was baptized like the others**
3. **The Spirit of God came in the form of a dove**
4. **A voice proclaimed him to be 'My own dear Son'**

Baptism in the New Testament Church
John the Baptist told the people that Jesus would baptize them 'with the Holy Spirit and fire.' After the first day of Pentecost, the apostles preached baptism just as John had done but they added the promise of the Holy Spirit. The gift of the Holy Spirit was very powerful among the early followers of Jesus: *'Many miracles and wonders were being done through the apostles, and everyone was filled with awe.'* (Acts 2:43) The essential points about baptism in the New Testament Church were:

1. **A confession and turning away from sin**
2. **Baptism in the name of Jesus Christ**
3. **Forgiveness of sins**
4. **The gift of the Holy Spirit**

Baptism in the New Testament was about adults recognising their sinfulness and changing their lives in a way God wanted. There was a promise to believe that God had raised Jesus from death and made him Lord and Messiah. People were baptized in great numbers and the ceremony admitted them to the company of the followers of 'the Way'.

Baptism today in the Christian Church
Christians understand the origins and purpose of baptism in different ways. There is a general understanding that the act of baptizing forgives all sin and is a sign of joining other Christians in their new life as followers of Jesus Christ. Baptism is a physical act which is a sign of a new birth. Water is the important symbol used, and the words of baptism express what is happening to the new member. However, methods of joining the Christian Church are different for various groups of Christians.

Infant Baptism
When a child is born into a family, there is great happiness and a celebration of the birth with a party or a family gathering. Christian parents also want the baby to be a member of the family of God. The idea is that the children of Christian parents belong to the membership of the Church and may, therefore, be baptized. Many groups of Christians practise the baptism of infants:

1. The Orthodox Church. There are special features for the baptism of a child. The most obvious is that the baby is completely dipped in the font. Traditionally, an orthodox baptism occurs on the eighth day after birth. The baby is held in the font facing the east (a symbol of resurrection). He or she is then dipped three times into the water in the name of the Trinity: *'The servant of God N. is baptized in the name of the Father, Amen; and of the Son, Amen; and of the Holy Spirit, Amen.'*

The Orthodox service has three parts: the order of holy baptism is the central ceremony of these three, and consists of:

1. Blessing the baptismal water with a prayer and breathing on the water in the form of the cross
2. A pre-baptism anointing with the 'oil of gladness'
3. The actual baptism as described above.

It is important to notice that **Chrismation** (the Orthodox equivalent of the sacrament of **confirmation** takes place immediately after the baptism in the Orthodox rite.

2. Roman Catholic and Anglican. In the Roman Catholic and other western Christian rites, the baby has water poured over the forehead with a formula of words: *'(Name) I baptize you in the name of the Father and of the Son and of the Holy Spirit.'*

Usually the parents bring the child for baptism and god-parents promise to watch carefully that the child will be brought up in the Christian faith. They promise to help the parents to do this. The essential parts of the ceremony are:

1. The child is presented for baptism by parents and god-parents.
2. Parents and god-parents profess their belief in the chief beliefs of the Christian Church.
3. There is a sharing of scripture which emphasises the importance of baptism.
4. The congregation welcomes the new member of the Church (the ceremony takes place at a public service).
5. The child is baptized with water poured and the words *'(Name) I baptize you in the name of the Father and of the Son of of the Holy Spirit. Amen.'*

Believers' Baptism
There are some groups of Christians who do not think it is appropriate to baptize babies. They think of the Church as a fellowship of people who believe that Jesus Christ is risen from the dead and is their Saviour and Lord. They confess their faith and are baptized in this faith. They take the example of the New Testament baptisms very seriously and only baptize those who wish to become Christians and ask for baptism.

Baptism takes place in a river or a place where the candidate can be fully immersed or dipped into the water. In a Baptist church there is often a tank sunk into the floor for baptisms. At other times it is covered and the communion table is placed over the tank.

When adult baptism is the custom, children usually go through a service of dedication. They are brought by parents to a public service where the minister will give thanks for the birth of the baby and bless the child. Both the parents and the congregation are asked to help in bringing up the child in the Christian faith.

The essential points in the baptism of believers are:

1. Candidates must be sorry for their sins and have faith in Jesus Christ. They often give a public testimony to the congregation about this.
2. Candidates present themselves in baptismal robes (a white garment or suitable clothes for the baptism).
3. Each candidate descends into the water and is completely immersed by the minister 'in the name of the Father and of the Son and of the Holy Spirit.'
4. The baptism is a symbol of forgiveness of sin and a new life of faith in Jesus Christ.
5. A certificate of the new baptism is given.

Note: Some Christians do not think it is necessary to have any external ceremony for the Christian commitment of baptism. Quakers, for example, think that baptism is an entirely spiritual event for a Christian.

BAPTISM AND CONFIRMATION

At first, in New Testament times, the baptism of Christians and the laying on of hands for the gift of the Holy Spirit (confirmation) was a simple affair and part of the conversion of adults. Over the centuries various traditions have grown up about the link between the two sacraments.

The Holy Spirit is given in baptism because people are baptized 'in the name of the Holy Spirit.' However, the laying on of hands for the gift of the Holy Spirit is still kept in either a sacramental or non-sacramental way. For example there is a frequent laying on of hands for the gift of the Holy Spirit in Pentecostal churches which is not a formal ceremony.

In the Orthodox tradition, anointing for the gift of the Holy Spirit follows the baptism of an infant. The newly baptized is anointed with chrism on the forehead, the eyes, the nostrils, the mouth, the ears, the breast, the hands and the feet. The words used are *'the seal of the gift of the Holy Spirit.'* This is called chrismation, but it is essentially the same anointing as for confirmation in the western Church.

The Roman Catholic tradition allows for confirmation at an early age i.e. before a first Communion, and also for confirmation at a later age of maturity. (See Unit 5.1)

The Anglican Church reserves the anointing for an age of maturity when a person can renew their baptismal vows, although some people argue for an earlier age.

The Methodist Church has a special service of 'Public Reception into Full Membership, or Confirmation'. This involves a promise of faithfulness to the Christian life, and a laying on of hands in blessing by the minister. The person is admitted to the fellowship of the Church.

There is a variety of practice in the Christian Church about chrismation/confirmation/reception into full membership, but it is clear that it is an important point in the milestones of the Christian life.

Baptism, confirmation and Eucharist are the three stages of membership of the Christian Church in the Orthodox and Catholic tradition. They are called *Sacraments of Initiation*. With some differences, this is the general pattern of initiation, but the degrees of formal ceremony among Christians vary according to the customs of the group or the country.

MARRIAGE

In the Gospel of Mark, there is an incident where Jesus is asked a question about divorce according to the law of Moses. The answer he gives contains an explanation about the meaning and purpose of marriage before the time of Moses: *'in the beginning, at the time of creation, "God made them male and female" as the scripture says.'* (Mark 10:6)

Jesus refers to the way God has made human beings: *'...And for this reason a man will leave his father and mother and unite with his wife, and the two will become one.'* (Mark 10:7,8)

The idea of leaving one family in order to establish another one is explained by Jesus as being according to God's plan. *'...So they are no longer two but one. Man must not separate, then, what God has joined together.'* (Mark 10:8,9) The holiness of marriage is explained in terms which describe God as the designer of marriage.

When Jesus was alone with his disciples, he gave them a further teaching:

'A man who divorces his wife and marries another woman commits adultery against his wife. In the same way, a woman who divorces her husband and marries another man commits adultery.'

Mark 10:11-12

It is almost certain that this incident contains the belief of the first Christian communities about the state of marriage, and the seriousness of divorce and second marriages. The Christian ideal which emerges from the incident is that marriage involves life-long companionship which is faithful and which excludes divorce and remarriage.

Christian forms of the marriage service

Christian forms of the marriage service emphasise a life-long commitment and faithfulness with the blessing of children.

Marriage in the Orthodox Church

The Orthodox Church has a very spiritual interpretation of marriage which is taken from scripture and particularly from the teaching of St Paul. Marriage is a sacrament in which two members of Christ's Body, the Church, become one. The ceremony emphasises the fact that it is Christ who unites the couple. The Orthodox priest, therefore, is the actual minister of the sacrament. There are many religious symbols used in the ceremony.

1. The Promises and the Rings. The marriage begins at the entrance of the church where the promises of marriage are made and the rings are exchanged. These are the usual worldly features of a marriage. Basic promises and exchange of rings may be seen at a registry office. The legal requirements of marriage are satisfied.

2. The Procession and Service of the Word. The spiritual meaning of the marriage is expressed when the couple process into the church. The marriage is going to be made as a reflection of the unity which Christ has with the Church. This is done through the mystery of the sacrament of marriage. The first stage is through readings from scripture which explain the meaning of marriage. These take place at a table or lectern in the centre of the church. The couple hold lighted candles which are a symbol of the light of Christ which comes through the word of God in scripture.

3. The Crowning. The priest places crowns or wreaths on the heads of the couple. The meaning of this action is that the man and woman are the king and queen of the family which is a little image of the Kingdom of God. They are told to *'increase and multiply, and see their children's children'*. The crowns are also symbols of the martyrs who are witnesses to Christ and his teaching, as the newly married couple will try to be. The Gospel reading is that of the marriage feast of Cana. The change of water into wine at this feast symbolises the change made for the couple from an ordinary contract of marriage (such as that made at the entrance of the church) to a holy and sacramental state of marriage.

4. The Cup of Wine. After the Gospel and prayers, a cup of wine is given. The couple drink from the same cup as yet another sign of the unity of their marriage in Christ. They share one life and they have one source of life which is Christ.

5. The Joining of Hands and Circling of the Centre Table. The bride and groom are led by the priest three times around the centre table. The circle is a symbol of the marriage which has begun with the sacrament but which will have no end.

CONCLUSION. The Orthodox service puts into practice an ideal of marriage which St Paul talked about to the Christians in Ephesus: *'There is a deep secret truth revealed in this Scripture, which I understand as applying to Christ and the Church.'* (Ephesians 5:32)

The Orthodox service is a good example of the form of Christian marriage which is sacramental. The Roman Catholic tradition also considers that marriage is a sacrament but that the couple give the sacrament to each other. The priest witnesses the marriage in the name of the Church and gives the nuptial blessing. (More details of this ceremony may be found in Unit 4.2.)

Protestant forms of marriage
All Christian Churches celebrate marriage as an important point in human life when a new family and a new generation of people will emerge. Marriage is therefore made in the sight of God. The Protestant Churches do not think of marriage as a sacrament in the same way as the Orthodox or Roman Catholic traditions, but it is still a very solemn occasion which is marked by a special service.

Baptist form of marriage
Baptists, for example, do not believe that marriage is a sacrament but they do recognise that God has instituted marriage and that believers should be married in the presence of God with prayers for his blessing on the marriage. There is no set marriage service, and there is great freedom about it, but the three main parts of the service would include:

1. The Introduction. A hymn. A talk about the meaning and purpose of marriage. A declaration by the couple that they do not know of any reasons why they should not be married (there are no 'impediments'). Prayer.

2. The Covenant. The promises of marriage are given and received. The couple join hands. Rings are given. The couple are declared married.

3. Service of the Word. Scripture is read. There is a sermon. There are prayers for God's blessing on the marriage. The service ends with a hymn and a blessing.

Church of England (Anglican) form of marriage
In the Church of England, banns are read on the three Sundays preceeding the wedding. Banns involve asking the congregation if they know of any reasons why the couple should not be married. A reason might be that one of them has been married before, or that the couple are too closely related.

The service begins with a procession of the bride to the altar where her father or another suitable person presents her to the groom. There is an explanation of the meaning and purpose of marriage. The couple make their promises to each other, and a ring is given to the bride as a sign of the marriage. The parish registers are signed, and the registrar is present to register the marriage legally if the priest or vicar is not himself a registrar. The couple process out of the church before the congregation, and often photographs are taken in the church grounds.

The Religious Society of Friends (Quakers)
In contrast to the elaborate symbolism of many marriage services, the marriage of 'Friends' is very simple. It takes place at a meeting called for the purpose of witnessing the promise made by the couple to each other: *'Friends, I take this my Friend (name) to be my wife/husband, promising through divine assistance, to be unto him/her a loving and faithful husband/wife, so long as we both on earth shall live.'*

There is no exchange of rings, but the couple do sign a certificate which is witnessed by the Friends present. The service continues like any other meeting, except that the Friends may speak about marriage, and about the couple who have just started their married life.

Legal requirements
It is important to realise that most Christian forms of marriage take into account the requirement of the law of the land about registering marriages. Some priests and ministers are also local registrars. Some Christians go to a registry office for the legal marriage and then return to the church or the home for a blessing by the minister.

In the case of divorced persons, there are some Christian groups who will allow a second marriage in church, but practice varies.

CHRISTIAN FUNERAL RITES

The Apostles' Creed says: *'I believe...in the Communion of Saints...the resurrection of the body and life everlasting.'*

All Christian funeral rites honour the body of the person who has died because he or she is still part of the Church. Faith in the resurrection also includes the belief that the body shares in the redemption won by Christ.

These rites usually express the natural sorrow which people feel when someone has died. Death is a great tragedy in itself. However, Christian burial rites remind people of the great victory over death which was won by Christ when he died but rose from death. Christians share in this victory over death because they have been baptized into Christ.

The Orthodox Service
This service is a good example of the kind of sorrowing and rejoicing which accompanies the funeral of a Christian.

1. The coffin is placed in the centre of the church facing the altar. It is open so that the body can be seen. Death is a tragedy and a sign of the separation of human beings from God which sin has brought. From this sad state springs the hope which all Christians have because of Christ.
2. The service takes the form of Mattins (morning prayer) which emphasises Christ's resurrection and his victory over death. The priest wears light coloured vestments.
3. There are symbols of life and light in the many candles burning and the incense with which the coffin is blessed.
4. All the readings are about the triumph of Christ and the hope which this brings for all who face death or who have died.

There are special rites for the burial of children.

Roman Catholic Church
Roman Catholics have special prayers and rites for the dying (See Unit 7.4).

The traditional funeral arrangements include:

1. Prayers in the home. This sometimes involves an all-night vigil or 'wake'. Sometimes the coffin is taken to the church the night before and people pray for the deceased there.
2. A service in the Church on the day of burial. This service may include the Eucharist.
3. Prayers at the graveside or at the crematorium.

There are two other rites which allow for:

1. A service at the cemetery chapel and at the graveside.
2. A service in the home. This may be necessary in some parts of the world.

Roman Catholics may be cremated if they wish.
Holy water, candles and incense are features of Orthodox and Catholic rites.

Church of England
The traditional parish church has its own graveyard. The custom was to bury the Christian within the church-yard walls. In modern times funeral rites have had to be adapted for use in cemetery chapels and at the crematorium.

Free Churches
Burial services held in Baptist, Congregational and other Free Churches have three features in common:

1. The opportunity for a service in the home with prayer, scripture and hymns.
2. A service in the church/chapel/meeting house, where a wider congregation may honour and pray for the deceased. This service may include a hymn, a short talk, scripture lessons and prayers. The prayers express faith in eternal life, comfort for the mourners and other suitable prayers for the occasion.
3. A service held at the graveside or in the crematorium.

The following prayer is taken from the Congregational service.

> *'For as much as it hath pleased Almighty God of His great mercy to take unto himself the soul of our dear brother/sister departed, we therefore commit his/her body to the ground: earth to earth, ashes to ashes, dust to dust; in sure and certain hope of resurrection to everlasting life through our Lord Jesus Christ...'*

Most Christian groups have special services for the burial of children, and some have a special service for suicides.

CONCLUSION

The Christian life is punctuated by special ceremonies which mark the important events in human life. These events are those of birth, growth, marriage and death. There are common beliefs held by Christians which underly these ceremonies, but there is also a rich variety of expression and practice among the various Christian groups.

QUESTIONS

BAPTISM

Investigation

1. Describe *two* features of John's baptism.
2. What did the voice say at the baptism of Jesus?
3. Describe *two* features of baptism in the New Testament Church.
4. Name the *two* kinds of baptism practised in the Christian Church today.
5. Outline the main points for the baptism of an infant in the Orthodox Church.
6. Describe a typical ceremony for 'believers' baptism'.
7. What are the words used at a Christian baptism?
8. Describe a ceremony of baptism from a denomination of your choice.

Understanding

1. Explain the purpose of Christian ceremonies which are 'Rites of Passage'.
2. What does the word 'baptize' mean?
3. What is 'repentance for sin'?
4. Explain the appearance of a dove at the baptism of Jesus.
5. Explain *one* difference between infant baptism in the Orthodox tradition and infant baptism in the R.C. or Anglican tradition.
6. What is meant by the term 'believers' baptism'?

7. Why do Quakers think that baptism is unnecessary?
8. Explain the effects of baptism for a person who has faith.
9. Explain the religious ideas behind infant baptism and believers' baptism.
10. Why is baptism important for a Christian?

Evaluation

1. What arguments would a Baptist bring against the baptism of infants?
2. Do you think that parents who are not practising Christians should have a course of instruction before their children are presented for baptism? Give reasons for your answer.
3. Do you think the ceremonies of baptism still mean something for people today?

CONFIRMATION

Investigation

1. Describe the ceremony of chrismation in the Orthodox Church.
2. Describe the essential features of a confirmation which involves anointing with oil.
3. Describe a ceremony for Reception into Full Membership (e.g. as practised in the Baptist Church).

Understanding

1. Explain the link between baptism and confirmation in New Testament times.
2. What is the purpose of initiation ceremonies in a religion?
3. Explain confirmation as part of the initiation ceremonies into the Christian religion.
4. Give reasons for the following symbolic acts linked with confirmation in the Christian Church: i) the laying on of hands; ii) anointing with oil.

Evaluation

1. By referring to the arguments used for confirmation at a later age, and the ceremony of chrismation by the Orthodox, what conclusions have you come to about the purpose of confirmation in the Christian Church?

MARRIAGE

Investigation

1. Outline the teaching of Jesus on the purpose of marriage from Mark 10:1-10.
2. Describe the ceremony of marriage in the Orthodox tradition.
3. Choose *one* other ceremony of marriage and describe how it is different from the Orthodox service.

Understanding

1. Choose *two* symbolic actions during an Orthodox wedding, and explain their meaning.
2. Explain why the marriage of Friends (Quakers) is very simple.
3. Explain these words of Jesus: 'Man must not separate, then, what God has joined together'.
4. Explain the term 'banns' as it applies to a Christian marriage ceremony.

Evaluation

1. Do you think that second marriages should be allowed in church? Explain the arguments which are put forward to support or reject the idea.

FUNERAL

Investigation

1. Which statement in the Apostles' Creed refers to what Christians believe about life after death?
2. What is a 'wake'?
3. Describe the main stages of the funeral rites for a Christian.

Understanding

1. Why do Christians honour the body of a dead person?
2. What does the term 'burial rite' mean?
3. Explain why the Orthodox leave the coffin open during a funeral service.
4. What is the meaning of the use of candles and incense at a funeral?
5. Explain the term 'mourner'.
6. What is meant by the term 'bereaved'?
7. What is the difference between a cemetery and a crematorium?

Evaluation

1. Find *three or four* prayers which are used at a Christian burial service and say whether you find the ideas expressed in them comforting for friends and relatives.
2. Discuss some of the views which are expressed about Christian belief in 'the resurrection of the body'.

FURTHER READING

1. *The Christian Faith and its Symbols:* pages 65-68.
2. *The Christian World:* pages 42, 43, 46, 47.
3. Christian Denominations Series:
    1. *The Orthodox Church:* pages 47-50.
    2. *The Baptists:* chapters 1, 6.
    3. *The Church of England:* chapter 3.
    4. *The United Reformed Church:* chapter 3.
4. *Christian Belief and Practice:* chapter 8.
5. *Believers All:* pages 4-7.
6. *Religions of Man:* pages 206-211.

1.5 THE EUCHARIST —
A SACRED CHRISTIAN MEAL

The ceremony which recalls the Last Supper of Jesus with his disciples is known by many names in the Christian tradition and is understood by Christians in different ways. The following is a simple outline of the important act of Christian worship as it is practised by the various Christian denominations.

NAMES FOR THE SACRED MEAL

EUCHARIST. The word means 'thanksgiving' and is a good name for the celebration of the sacred meal. Christians give thanks, as Jesus did, for the bread and wine which are the fruits of the harvest, and the work of mankind. Wheat and grapes are harvested and then made by people into bread and wine. There is also a deeper, spiritual thanksgiving for the gift which Jesus made of himself at the Last Supper and on the cross. This spiritual thanksgiving is brought out clearly in the Orthodox 'Liturgy'. 'The liturgy' comes from a Greek word which means 'an act of public service'. The Eucharistic service of the Orthodox is the most important form of public service — that of honouring God. It gives God thanks for what he has done for his people in rescuing them from sin. The Orthodox service emphasises worship and thanks to God through the Word of God, and through the great 'mystery' (another word for 'sacrament') of the Eucharist itself.

HOLY COMMUNION. The sharing of bread and wine emphasises the Christian fellowship of all those who believe in Jesus Christ as Saviour and Lord. The sharing or 'Communion' is a holy one because Christ brings his followers together in unity.

THE LORD'S SUPPER. This is a direct way of saying that Christians gather together to obey the command of Jesus at the Last Supper to: *'Do this in memory of me'.*

Some Christian groups always call this act of worship 'the Lord's Supper' because it is the title which is nearest to the New Testament event — the Last Supper of Jesus. Also the word 'Supper' emphasises the meal of Christian fellowship.

THE BREAKING OF BREAD. This title also describes the worship of Christians in the same way as that of the first believers. In the Good News Bible, Acts 2, verse 42 reads: *'They spent their time in learning from the apostles, taking part in the fellowship, and sharing in the fellowship meals and the prayers.'*

However, the original language of the New Testament, that is the Greek, is literally translated: *'...in the breaking of the loaf (or bread)'.* So the title 'the breaking of bread' is a good one for the Christians who like to worship with close reference to the Bible. Sometimes only one loaf is used in the service and it is broken into pieces for the congregation in imitation of the early Christian custom.

THE MASS. This title is one used by the Roman Catholic Church. It is taken from the Latin word 'missa' which means 'ended' or 'finished'. It was one of the last words of the service in Latin. It is thought that the 'missa' became used as 'Mass'. However, for most Christians, the word 'Mass' symbolises the special meaning given by the Roman Catholic Church to its central act of worship. At Mass, Roman Catholics remember the words and actions of Jesus at the Last Supper. They believe that the sacrifice of Jesus for the forgiveness of sins is represented in the sacrament. The Mass is also a sacred meal of thanksgiving which shows the love and unity of the Church through Communion with Jesus.

EUCHARIST
('Thanksgiving')
HOLY COMMUNION
('Christian Fellowship')
THE LORD'S SUPPER
BREAKING *of* BREAD
◇   THE MASS   ◇

FREQUENCY OF THIS ACT OF WORSHIP

Some Christians do not celebrate the Eucharist very often. Jehovah's Witnesses celebrate only once a year as a memorial of the Last Supper. Presbyterian Churches used to hold the service about four times a year, Congregational Churches about once or twice a month. After the Union of the Congregational Church in England and Wales and the Presbyterian Church of England into the one United Reformed Church, there had to be some adjustments about the frequency of the service.

The 'Sunday Service' of the Methodist Church allows for a service with or without the sacrament or sacred meal. A 'Communion Sunday' in a Baptist Church includes the Ministry or Service of the Word and the Ministry of the Table. At other times the service may be just a service of the Word, or a Bible service of prayer and praise, without the sacred meal.

The Church of England celebrates Holy Communion frequently, at least once a week. The Roman Catholic Church and the Orthodox Churches celebrate daily.

WAYS OF CELEBRATING THE EUCHARIST

The various ways in which Christians celebrate the Eucharist depend on the way they understand the sacred meal. The various names given to the service usually point out the particular emphasis which is being given i.e. Sign of Fellowship, Holy Meal, Thanksgiving, Sacrifice, Communion, Last Supper, and Memorial Act of Worship.

Churches which have *altar-centred worship* have a priest or minister to conduct the service. In the Churches where there is an ordained priesthood, only priests have the authority to consecrate the bread and wine. In such Churches, there is usually a three-part service:

1. **Worship of the Word**
2. **Worship of the Eucharist**
3. **Communion Service**

At the Communion Service in an *Anglican Church* (Church of England) the people come before the altar or Communion table and receive, first the bread, and then the wine from a single chalice (or cup). In the Roman Catholic Church the outward appearance of the people going to Communion is much the same as in an Anglican Church, only the chalice is not given at all Masses.

The *Orthodox Church* gives Communion on a spoon where the consecrated bread has been dipped into the consecrated wine.

Churches which have a *pulpit- or Bible-centred worship* tend to have a slightly different way of giving Communion. The actual service of Communion may be the last part of the morning or evening act of worship, and may not be the main point of the service as in Churches which have an altar-centred liturgy. For example, in a Baptist Church the minister or one of the appointed lay persons will bring Communion to the people in the benches, chairs or pews.

Today, the bread is often in the form of small unleavened wafers or small pieces of bread, and there are generally individual cups for the wine in a Baptist church. Some groups of Christians do not necessarily use wine but prefer a non-alcoholic juice of some kind. The bread is eaten by the minister and congregation at the same time. This contrasts with other Churches where the priests or ministers will receive Communion first and then take it to the people.

In the *Baptist Church* the people decide on the order of their service, but there is a familiar pattern of worship in their churches. It is important to realise that the Free Churches have a more improvised pattern of worship and do not have set prayer-books like the Orthodox, Roman Catholic and Anglican Churches. It is also customary among some Christian groups to break one large loaf for Communion.

'Waiting on the Spirit' Christians also have a Communion service, with the exception of the Society of Friends (Quakers) and the Salvation Army. Pentecostal Churches have a Eucharistic Service once a week or once a month according to custom. They are free about following a written service, or making up the prayers and praises as the Holy Spirit moves them.

WHO MAY RECEIVE COMMUNION?

In most Christian denominations, only Church members are allowed to receive Communion. In some Churches it was the custom for people to leave the service before the Communion service began. In the *Congregational Church*, older children who were being instructed for full membership would be allowed to receive Communion as part of that preparation.

In a *Baptist Church* there may be a practice of Communion for full members, but most Baptist Churches will give a general invitation to anyone who believes in Christ and are *'in love and fellowship with the Brethren'*. The tradition in the Free Churches varies according to the local custom. The local congregation is considered to be the real authority on all matters of worship.

In the *Orthodox tradition*, the Eucharist is given at the time of baptism. Baptism, chrismation and the Eucharist are the 'mysteries' of initiation. Orthodox Christians do not receive Communion at every Eucharist. They prepare very carefully for such a solemn occasion.

In the *Roman Catholic tradition*, it is the custom for children to be specially prepared for their first Holy Communion, usually while they are attending primary school. Confirmation follows some time after this.

The *Church of England* usually confirms a person first, and then as full members of the Church (i.e. they have been baptized and confirmed) they may receive Communion. The best explanation of the situation in these two Churches is that baptism, confirmation and Eucharist are looked upon as sacraments by which a person becomes a full member of the Christian Church. They are sometimes called the *Sacraments of Initiation*. This is an important point to remember as a criterion for receiving Communion.

It is also important to note that where the main service of a Christian denomination is the Eucharist, people may not always go to Communion but will attend the service anyway. It may be that they receive Communion only on great festivals or on special days like birthdays or anniversaries. They may decide not to go to Communion because they feel unworthy or too sinful.

THE MINISTER. In the Orthodox, Catholic and Anglican traditions, only an ordained priest or minister may consecrate the bread and wine at the Liturgy (the Mass or the Eucharist). This is very important, and there is a great debate as to whether women should or can be ordained. In the various Free Churches there is a great emphasis upon all the people having a spiritual authority. The minister may conduct the service of Communion, or one of the elders of the Church or another person chosen by the congregation may be allowed to do so.

THE COMMON HERITAGE. Despite the different ways of celebrating the Eucharist, the different names given to it, and the different people who conduct the service, there is a common foundation for this most important act of Christian worship. This foundation is the Christian understanding of the Jewish festival of Passover and the New Testament account of the Last Supper of Jesus.

PASSOVER. The Jewish people still celebrate a sacred meal which recalls the way in which God freed the children of Israel from the slavery of the Egyptian Pharoah in the time of Moses. The Old Testament gives an account of this meal in *Exodus 12:21-28*:

'Moses called for all the leaders of Israel and said to them, "Each of you is to choose a lamb, or a young goat, and kill it, so that your families can celebrate Passover. Take a sprig of hyssop, dip it in a bowl containing the animal's blood, and wipe the blood on the doorpost and the beam above the door of your house. Not one of you is to leave the house until morning. When the Lord goes through Egypt to kill the Egyptians he will see the blood on the beams and the doorposts and will not let the Angel of Death enter your houses and kill you.

You and your children must obey these rules forever. When you enter the land that the Lord has promised to give you, you must perform this ritual. When your children ask you, "What does this ritual mean?", you will answer, "It is the sacrifice of the Passover to honour the Lord because he passed over the houses of the Israelites in Egypt. He killed the Egyptians but spared us."

The Israelites knelt down and worshipped. Then they went and did what the Lord had commanded Moses and Aaron.'

THE LAST SUPPER. Jesus celebrated the Passover with his disciples, and was doing so on the night he was arrested. However, during this meal, he performed two actions which altered the meaning of the Passover for the disciples and for all Christians in the years to come. Paul gives an account of the institution of the Eucharist by Jesus at the Last Supper when he is writing to the Christian community at Corinth.

'For I received from the Lord the teaching that I passed on to you: that the Lord Jesus, on the night he was betrayed, took a piece of bread, gave thanks to God, broke it, and said, "This is my body, which is for you, do this in memory of me." In the same way, after the supper he took the cup and said, "This cup is God's new covenant, sealed with my blood. Whenever you drink it, do so in memory of me."

This means that every time you eat this bread and drink from this cup you proclaim the Lord's death until he comes.'

1 Corinthians 11:23-26

QUESTIONS

Investigation

1. Name the various titles given to the Christians' sacred meal.
2. What event in the life of Jesus is the foundation for the sacred meal of Christians?
3. Relate the words and actions of Jesus at the Last Supper, as they were recorded by Paul in his letter to the Corinthians.
4. Describe the conditions for being admitted to Holy Communion in the various Christian traditions.
5. Describe the way in which Holy Communion is given in the Orthodox Church.
6. Which Jewish festival helps Christians to understand the Eucharist?

Understanding

1. What does the word 'Eucharist' mean?
2. Explain the different ideas which are expressed by the titles for the Christians' sacred meal.
3. Why is the 'breaking of bread' a good way of speaking about Christian fellowship?
4. Explain the various beliefs which Christians have about the Eucharist.
5. Why do some Christians attend a service of the Eucharist, but do not receive Holy Communion on every occasion?

Evaluation

1. Can you think of reasons why some Christian denominations celebrate Holy Communion more frequently than others?
2. Discuss the different methods by which Holy Communion is given to the people in the Christian Church.

FURTHER READING

1. *The Christian World:* pages 44, 45.
2. Christian Denominations series:
   The Orthodox Church: pages 12-16.
3. *The Eucharist* (Chichester Project Book 9).

CHRISTIAN BELIEF

2.1 THE APOSTLES' CREED AND THE LORD'S PRAYER

The Apostles' Creed and the Lord's Prayer are two prayers used by all Christians to express their beliefs. The essential beliefs of the Christian faith are found in these prayers, but just as with baptism and the Eucharist, time and practice have led to differences of understanding about these beliefs among Christians themselves.

THE APOSTLES' CREED

1. *I believe in God, the Father Almighty maker of heaven and earth*
2. *and in Jesus Christ his only Son Our Lord who was conceived by the Holy Ghost born of the Virgin Mary,*
3. *suffered under Pontius Pilate was crucified, died and was buried he descended into hell; the third day he rose again from the dead, he ascended into heaven*
4. *and sitteth on the right hand of God the Father Almighty; from thence he shall come to judge the living (the 'quick') and the dead.*
5. *I believe in the Holy Spirit;*
6. *the Holy Catholic Church;*
7. *the Communion of Saints;*
8. *the forgiveness of sins the resurrection of the body and the life everlasting. Amen.*

The Apostles' Creed has been printed above in eight statements of belief. They are the central statements of the Christian faith.

(1) God
Christians believe that God is One and that he has created all things. They also believe that God may be known as three persons. He is Father of all, and father of Jesus. Jesus talked to God in a most familiar way, as his *abba* which is the common Aramaic name for 'daddy'. Christians believe that God became a human being in Jesus, so he is revealed to the world as God the Son. God also dwells and acts in the hearts of Christians by the Holy Spirit. The way in which Christians understand God as three persons and yet one God is a great mystery. Although Christians are certain that this way of knowing God is true, they do not understand how this way may be true. This mystery is called the *holy (or blessed) Trinity*.

SUMMARY:

God is Three and God is One
*God the Father
*God the Son
*God the Holy Spirit

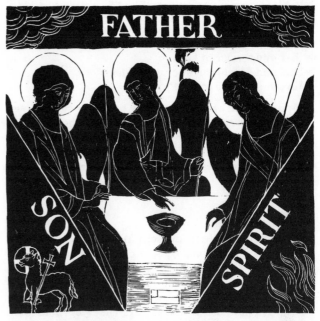

A Christian prayer of praise which is often used is: *'Glory be to God the Father, and to the Son and to the Holy Spirit, as it was in the beginning, is now, and ever shall be, world without end. Amen.'*

(2) Jesus Christ — the Incarnation of God
Christians believe that Jesus Christ is truly human and truly divine. They say that he is the Son of Mary by the power of the Holy Spirit. The teaching that Jesus was born of a virgin mother is important to the claim that he is the Son of God. However, there is much discussion as to how this teaching should be understood (see Unit 2.2). The word 'incarnation' comes from a Latin word meaning 'in flesh'. It means that the Son of God became a human being at a definite time in the history of the world.

(3) The Crucifixion, Resurrection and Ascension of Jesus
The Gospel accounts of the arrest, trial and crucifixion of Jesus are very detailed and the fact that Jesus really died on the cross on Calvary (or Golgotha) is of great importance to the Christian faith. The resurrection of Jesus on the third day after his burial is the heart of the Christian faith.

By rising from the dead, Christ defeated the power of death over the human race and he gave the promise of eternal life to all. The death of Christ who was without sin also obtained forgiveness for the sins of the world. The ascension of Jesus means that he returned to be with God the Father, and only after his personal return to heaven did he fulfil his promise of sending the Holy Spirit of God.

(4) The Judgement

In parables like 'the sheep and the goats' (Matthew 25:31-46) Jesus spoke about people being judged at the end of their lives or at the end of the world. The parables make it clear that all people will have to account for the way in which they have managed their own lives. The three areas of their lives which would be judged are:

▶ **love and service of God**
▶ **love and development of their talents**
▶ **love and service of God's people**

The judgement would decide whether a person was worthy of eternal life or whether they had chosen to live apart from God for ever. Christians believe that if they live according to the life and example of Jesus Christ himself, their judgement will be a joyful occasion.

(5) The Holy Spirit

In the absence of Jesus himself, after his ascension into heaven, the Holy Spirit of God came on Pentecost day into the hearts and minds of the apostles. The apostles were strengthened in their faith that Jesus had risen from the dead, and they were able to preach to the people in a new and powerful way. They were able to do what Jesus himself had done because the Holy Spirit of God made them holy and full of God's power. Christians believe that they also receive the gift of the Holy Spirit which makes them strong and powerful in faith.

(6) The Holy Catholic Church

Most Christians will say the Apostles' Creed which contains this phrase, but they will not all give the same meaning to the words. The word 'Church' here does not refer to a building called a church, but it does mean what it meant in the New Testament times — all the people who believe in Jesus Christ and follow his way. The Church is the people of God. The word 'catholic' means 'world-wide'. People in the reformed Christian traditions mean *'I believe in the holy world-wide company of those who follow Christ'*. The Roman Catholic tradition, on the other hand, has a different interpretation. Catholics will agree that the Church means all the people of God who are led by Jesus Christ. They will also say that Jesus appointed a visible leader of his Church on earth, St Peter, and all those who followed in this position of authority. These people are the popes of the Roman Catholic Church.

(7) The Communion of Saints

In the New Testament, it is clear that the word 'saints' refers to those who follow Jesus Christ. In the *Revised Standard Version* and the *Jerusalem Bible*, Paul addressed his letters to *'The Saints who are also faithful in Jesus Christ'*. (Ephesians 1:1) By 'the Saints', Paul meant the groups of Christians to whom he was writing. (The *Good News* translation replaces the word 'Saints' with 'God's people' which makes the meaning clearer for modern readers.) Christians generally mean by the phrase 'communion of saints' a fellowship of all those, living or dead, who have believed in Jesus Christ and followed his way of life.

(8) The forgiveness of sins
The resurrection of the body
Life everlasting

These three promises of the Christian faith are fundamental for anyone who says that they are a Christian. Forgiveness of sins in the Christian religion involves also the forgiveness of others, but it is clear that all sin will be forgiven by God for people who believe that Christ died for their sins. There are various interpretations of what is meant by 'the resurrection of the body' but Christians believe in the bodily resurrection of Jesus based on the New Testament accounts of his appearances to his disciples when he ate and drank with them and showed them his wounds.

Christians believe in their own personal resurrection after death because of the promises made by Jesus himself. Everlasting life and what this means is also something which Christians find difficult to explain but which they firmly believe is true. They mean that they believe they will in some way be with God for ever if they have lived according to the way shown to them by Jesus Christ, God's own Son.

THE LORD'S PRAYER

The Lord's Prayer is mentioned in the Gospels of Matthew (Matthew 6:7-16) and Luke (Luke 11:2-5). The phrases of the Prayer concentrate a great deal of Jesus' teaching and example into a few words. The Prayer also sums up some of the main points of the Christian faith.

Our Father who art in Heaven

Jesus surprised many of his followers by talking about God as a loving Father, and by referring to God as his Father in a most familiar way. He often used the term 'your heavenly Father' or 'my Father'. In the parable of the lost (prodigal) son, the character of the boy's father was meant to describe God's attitude towards anyone who is a sinner. Christians find it comparatively easy to understand what they mean by describing God as a Father to whose family they belong, but they find it much more difficult to say what they mean by 'heaven'. Explanations vary from a simple view of heaven as a place where God dwells, to a 'being with God' which is outside any human experience. A Christian must decide what they understand by their belief in heaven, or accept the opinion of a Church authority which can be trusted.

hallowed be thy name

'Hallow' is a word which is not used very often by ordinary people. In a prayer, it means 'to honour as holy'. Christians praise and honour God's holy name. They do this because praise is an important act of worship. They also honour God's name because it is an aspect of their religion which has come down from the Jewish religion. One of the Commandments is 'Do not use my name for evil purposes.' In ancient religions the name of God was a powerful word in worship. As a result of this Commandment, the Jews never spoke the name of God. Jesus took away the fear of the Commandment by praising the name of God. Christians generally disapprove of people who use the names 'God', 'Jesus Christ' etc. in a casual way, or as a way of expressing surprise or anger. They consider that such people are swearing.

thy Kingdom come,
thy will be done,
on earth as it is in heaven
Christians believe that God takes care of all that he has created. They use the title of 'King' to describe his status over all mankind. The 'Kingdom of heaven' was described by Jesus in parables like the mustard seed, the hidden treasure, or the fine pearl. He told his disciples that the parables gave them 'the secret of the Kingdom of God' (Mark 4:11). The Old Testament spoke about the Messiah bringing the Kingdom of God, and Jesus demonstrated by his life what it would mean for God to reign in the hearts of all people. That is why Christians work very hard to improve the injustice, poverty and violence which prevent the world from being what God intended when he created it. Christians are convinced that this can only happen when people live according to the teaching and example of Jesus who came to show people what God is like. Christians are helped by their belief in the goodness of God to accept suffering and disaster and to say 'thy will be done'.

give us this day our daily bread
Jesus uses bread, which is a basic food, and a good symbol of what supports human life, as a sign of the teaching about God. He multiplied bread for the crowds who followed him. He said, *'I am the bread of life'; 'the one who eats this bread will live for ever'* (John 6:35, 51). In the Lord's Prayer 'daily bread' represents all the needs of God's people, and is an example of the prayer of petition, or request, which is one of the main types of Christian prayer.

forgive us our trespasses as we forgive
those who trespass against us
A trespass is an offence against a person, a law, a principle or a right. Christians speak about 'sins', and they believe that Jesus was the Lamb of God whose life and death made up for the sin of the whole world. Asking for forgiveness, or sorrow for sin, is another important feature of Christian prayer. The parable of the unforgiving servant was told by Jesus in answer to Peter's question: *'Lord, if my brother keeps on sinning against me, how many times do I have to forgive him?'* (Matthew 18:21)

Forgiveness of others is an important condition for personal forgiveness in Christian prayer and practical life situations.

and lead us not into temptation,
but deliver us from evil
Christians believe in a powerful force of evil. Sometimes this force is given a personal name, as in the Bible. The Devil, Satan and Beelzebul are names for the evil one used in scripture. Fundamentalist Christians accept these descriptions as literally true, and others understand them as names for the evil which exists in people and in the world. Christians also believe in the power of God over evil. They believe that sin and the power of evil (death) were overcome by the life and death of Jesus. In this phrase of the Lord's Prayer, Christians claim the victory of Christ over sin and death.

The Lord's Prayer in Scripture
The Lord's Prayer occurs in Matthew 6:9-14 and in Luke 11:2-5.

Matthew 6:9-14	**Luke 11:2-5**
Our Father in heaven:	*Father*
May your holy name be honoured;	*May your holy name be honoured;*
May your Kingdom come;	*May your Kingdom come.*
May your will be done on earth as it is in heaven.	
Give us today the food we need.	*Give us day by day the food we need.*
Forgive us the wrongs we have done, as we forgive the wrongs that others have done to us.	*Forgive us our sins, for we forgive everyone who does us wrong.*
Do not bring us to hard testing, but keep us from the Evil One.	*And do not bring us to hard testing.*

(Good News Bible)

Modern translations of the Lord's Prayer help with the meaning of the older translation from which the Christian Prayer has been taken.

The Doxology
'Doxology' means prayer of praise. Christians add a prayer of praise to the Lord's Prayer:
for thine is the Kingdom, the power and the glory, for
ever and ever. Amen.

CONCLUSION

Several aspects of Christian belief are contained in the Lord's Prayer (sometimes called the 'Our Father'). They can be summarised as follows:
▶ **God is a father to his people**
▶ **God is the ruler of his people**
▶ **God is to be trusted**
▶ **People can work with God for his Kingdom**
▶ **God will provide**
▶ **Forgiveness from God depends upon forgiveness of others**
▶ **God will strengthen his people in a time of temptation**

The Lord's Prayer also contains, and is a summary of, all Christian prayer of praise, sorrow, thanksgiving and petition.

QUESTIONS

Investigation

1. What are the *three* titles for God which are given in the teaching on the Holy Trinity?
2. Describe crucifixion as the Romans practised it.
3. Where did Jesus die?
4. When did Jesus keep his promise to send the Holy Spirit?
5. On what day did the Holy Spirit come to the apostles?
6. Outline the effect of the Holy Spirit on the apostles.
7. Find *one* account of the resurrection of Jesus in the New Testament, and write it in your own words.
8. What do Christians state about their belief in what happens after death?
9. Choose *one* main idea contained in the Lord's Prayer, and describe this idea in greater detail.
10. Write out the doxology to the Lord's Prayer which is used by Christians.
11. Select examples of the prayer of Christian praise, sorrow, thanksgiving and petition from the Lord's Prayer.

Understanding

1. Explain the term 'creed' as it applies to the Christian religion.
2. Why did Jesus call God his 'abba'?
3. What does the word 'Church' mean when it does *not* refer to a building?
4. What do Christians mean by the term 'Communion of Saints'?
5. What does the word 'hallow' mean?
6. Explain the title 'Son of God' briefly.
7. What does the term 'doxology' mean?
8. Explain why the resurrection of Jesus is the most important belief in the Christian faith.
9. Read the parable of the sheep and the goats (Matthew 25:31-46) and explain in your own words the teaching of this parable.
10. Give *three* examples of Christian care and concern which illustrate the teaching of the parable of the sheep and the goats.
11. Explain the Christian belief in the 'Holy Catholic Church'.
12. What do Christians mean when they call God 'Father'?
13. Explain the meaning of the term 'Kingdom of God'.
14. Explain the following phrase of the Creed: 'he sits on the right hand of God, the Father Almighty, from thence he shall come to judge the living and the dead.'

Evaluation

1. Think about the following Christian beliefs, and then say what a Christian and then a non-Christian would say about them: i) forgiveness of sin; ii) the resurrection of the body; iii) life everlasting.
2. Say what your opinions are about the beliefs in the previous question. Give reasons for what you think.
3. Some people say the traditional words of the Lord's Prayer without really understanding its meaning. Do you think that modern translations help people to understand the Lord's Prayer better, or do you prefer the familiar traditional formula? Give reasons for your opinion.

FURTHER READING

1. *Christian Belief and Practice:* chapter 3.
2. *Christian Experience* (Chichester Project Book 3).
3. *Christianity in Words and Pictures:* chapter 5.
4. Christian Denominations Series:
    1. *The Salvation Army:* chapter 4.
    2. *The Pentecostal Churches:* chapter 5.

2.2 QUESTIONS OF INTERPRETATION AND UNDERSTANDING

What is an Orthodox Christian?

There are two senses in which the word *Orthodox* is used in the Christian religion. In the first sense, there is a whole Christian tradition which is called the Eastern Orthodox Church and all its members are called Orthodox Christians. In the second sense, an Orthodox Christian is a person who understands and interprets the Apostles' Creed (or the Nicene Creed), the Lord's Prayer, and the Bible in the accepted way of the Christians of their time. The word 'Orthodox' will be used in this sense for this chapter.

Someone who understands a basic Christian teaching like, 'Jesus is the Son of God', in an independent way which does not agree with the majority or accepted Christian view is said to be 'unorthodox' or sometimes even a 'heretic'. The history of Christianity is littered with controversial characters whose arguments illustrate what a true Christian should or should not believe about Christ. Christian Churches with a strong sense of authority can usually state quite clearly what they understand by the Creed etc. However, there is always the attitude that the Christian religion is a journey of faith, a pilgrimage, and that mankind will grow in understanding of the mysteries of Christianity as progress is made.

There are three questions which cause much argument in Christianity today. There is a variety of opinion as to the understanding and interpretation of these questions. They are:

▶ **Do Christians believe in the Virgin birth?**
▶ **Did the body of Jesus rise from the dead?**
▶ **How do Christians understand life after death?**

Each of these questions is answered differently by the following people:

Fundamentalist Christians
Orthodox Christians
Unorthodox Christians

THE VIRGIN BIRTH

The Gospels of Matthew and Luke emphasise that Jesus was born of a virgin:

> 'Now all this happened in order to make what the Lord had said through the prophet come true, "A virgin will become pregnant and have a son, and he will be called Immanuel" (which means, "God is with us").'
>
> *Matthew 1:22-24*

Matthew is quoting from the prophet Isaiah 7:14. The Jews who were reading the passage would find a most important point which Matthew was making. Luke puts words onto Mary's own lips: *'Mary said to the angel, "I am a virgin. How, then, can this be"?'* (Luke 1:34)

Fundamentalist Christians believe in the literal truth of the Bible. Their understanding of the Virgin birth would be that Mary was a virgin, and as a virgin conceived Jesus by the power of God the Holy Spirit. They might not necessarily agree that Mary remained a virgin afterwards or that she and Joseph did not have any children after the birth of Jesus.

The Orthodox Christians take as their interpretation the following phrase from the Apostles' Creed: *'I believe... in Jesus Christ, his only Son our Lord, who was conceived by the power of the Holy Spirit and born of the Virgin Mary.'*

The accepted understanding of this phrase for the Orthodox Christian is that Mary was still a virgin when Jesus was conceived and that as God's Son, Jesus had no human father.

There are unorthodox ideas about this phrase from the Apostles' Creed and the Gospel story. These ideas suggest that the accounts of the Virgin birth in Matthew and Luke were stories put on to the front of the Gospels to make it quite clear that Jesus was the Son of God in a very special way. However, it would not be necessary for Mary to have been a virgin. The suggestion is made that Jesus was born normally of human parents, Mary and Joseph, but that by the special power of the Holy Spirit, Jesus was Son of God.

Roman Catholic tradition states that not only was Mary a virgin when Jesus was conceived, but that she remained a virgin and never had other children.

THE RESURRECTION

The New Testament has many references to the resurrection of Jesus. The Gospels describe how those who came to the tomb on the third day after the crucifixion of Jesus found it empty and the body of Jesus gone. There are various accounts of appearances of Jesus: to Mary Magdalen, to the apostles, and to Thomas. Paul emphasises the importance of the fact that there were witnesses to the risen Jesus:

> '...he was raised to life three days later, as written in the Scriptures; that he appeared to Peter and then to all twelve apostles. Then he appeared to more than five hundred of his followers at once, most of whom are still alive, although some have died. Then he appeared to James, and afterwards to all the apostles. Last of all he appeared also to me...'
>
> *1 Corinthians 15:4-8*

Some of the accounts of Jesus' appearances emphasise the physical nature of his risen body. He invites Thomas to touch the wounds. He eats and drinks with the apostles by the lakeside in Galilee. And yet he is different. The two disciples on the way to Emmaus do not recognise him. Mary Magdalen recognises him only after Jesus calls her by name. The New Testament presents a picture of the same Jesus who is also different. Time and space do not seem to be any problem, and neither does a locked door!

The statement in the Apostles' Creed, 'The third day he rose again from the dead', is basic to Christianity. Christians will often quote the words of Paul to the Corinthians: *'If Christ has not been raised, then your faith is a delusion and you are still lost in your sins.'* (1 Corinthians 15:17)

The way in which Christians understand the resurrection of Jesus, however, does vary a good deal.

Fundamentalist Christians accept exactly what the New Testament says. They continue the great tradition, begun by the apostles, of witnessing to the resurrection of Jesus. They understand the nature of his resurrection to be not just a spiritual one, but a resurrection of his body.

Orthodox Christians also believe that the body of Jesus rose from death just as the New Testament reports. The Articles of Faith of the Church of England explain the phrase from the Apostles' Creed like this: *'Christ did truly rise again from death and took again his body with flesh, bones and all things pertaining to the perfection of man's nature.'* In other words, the Church of England says that whatever is needed before one could describe a person as a human being, belonged to Jesus after his resurrection.

The Roman Catholic Church says that he now lives a new, immortal, human bodily life, and that in this life he appeared several times to his followers.

Unorthodox views doubt the *bodily* resurrection of Jesus and say that it is not necessary to believe that the body of Jesus rose from death. They explain the stories and the empty tomb by saying that these are added to the Gospel after the event to explain the preaching of the early Christians.

However, the unorthodox views also emphasise the essential Christian truth that Jesus is alive. The argument is that the Christian faith is open to different interpretations from time to time because mankind gets a little nearer in each generation to an understanding of the mysteries involved in being a Christian.

Obviously, different interpretations of the Gospels and the Creeds lead to great arguments, but the fact of the resurrection is absolutely essential to the Christian religion.

LIFE AFTER DEATH

One event is certain in every person's life and that is their death. Christians believe in a life after death because Jesus rose from the dead for all those who believe in the promises he made on earth. *'I am telling you the truth: he who believes has eternal life.'* (John 6:47)

Fundamentalist Christians understand life after death according to the evidence of the New Testament. They believe that Jesus came back from death to tell them that this life was certain. They believe that Jesus will come at the end of time to judge all mankind. The second coming of Jesus was an important part of the preaching of the early Church.

The end of time was often referred to by Jesus himself in the parables of judgement e.g. the ten virgins ('the ten girls' in the *Good News Bible*). These parables speak of everlasting happiness or everlasting punishment, but either way they teach the fact of life after death. The early Christians were constantly looking for

CHRISTIAN DEBATE

the second coming of Christ, and one of the earliest prayers was *'Maranatha'* which meant 'Come Lord Jesus'. Heaven, paradise, eternal life, all describe the reward of the good; hell, gehenna, a place of weeping and gnashing of teeth, all describe the punishment of evil people. Heaven and hell are described in visual ways in the New Testament. The 'Kingdom of God' is also referred to in ways which create images or pictures of a place. However, even fundamentalist Christians will admit that it is difficult to be certain about the details, after death, of heaven and hell. When Paul tried to talk about life after death to the Corinthians he just said: *'What no one ever saw or heard, what no one even thought could happen, is the very thing God prepared for those who love him.'* (1 Corinthians 2:9)

Orthodox Christians express their belief in life after death in the following phrase of the Apostles' Creed: *'I believe in the Resurrection of the body and the life everlasting.'*

Orthodox Christians, therefore, believe that the resurrection of Jesus is a guarantee for their own survival in a fully human form after death. But the Christian belief is not just in immortality but in the transforming power of God. The traditional pattern of Christian belief is:

▶ sin results in death for mankind:

▶ the sacrifice of Jesus takes away the power of sin and death:

▶ the resurrection of Jesus is the proof that sin and death are defeated:

▶ every person baptized into the death and resurrection of Jesus is saved from sin and death:

▶ a Christian's death is followed by a meeting with Christ by the power (Holy Spirit) of God:

▶ there will also be a judgement at the end of time.

Unorthodox views challenge the traditional understanding of the Apostles' Creed. A person might say that they believe what the Creed says, but only as they understand it. If that person holds unorthodox views about the resurrection of Jesus as an historical fact, then it will have an effect on what they mean when they say that they believe that after death they will see God and be happy with him for ever. Heaven cannot really be described in detail, because it is a fact which is believed but is beyond human understanding.

However, a person who attempts a different and perhaps disturbing explanation of the resurrection and life after death will soon be labelled 'unorthodox'.

CONCLUSION

Christians are clear about what they believe but they cannot always explain the divine mysteries in which they believe. Explanations of the Christian faith are generally of three kinds: *fundamentalist* (taking the words of the Bible as the literal truth); *orthodox* (traditional understanding of Christianity on the acceptance of authority in the Christian Church); and *unorthodox* views which accept the Christian message but interpret that message in different and disturbing ways.

There is always room for growth in understanding the Christian message. Human beings are capable of progress, and a Christian is on a journey of faith, but basic Christian teaching (or doctrine) is said to have been revealed by God in the person of Jesus Christ. Christians, therefore, accept the truth of the teaching of Christ and then make great efforts to understand and interpret that teaching.

QUESTIONS

Investigation

1. Write out the phrase from the Apostles' Creed which mentions the Virgin birth.
2. What do Roman Catholics say about the Virgin birth?
3. Make a list of the people to whom Jesus appeared after his resurrection (cf. what Paul told the Christians in Corinth).
4. Write *two* New Testament phrases for hell.
5. Describe a point of view which might be labelled 'unorthodox'.
6. Relate the parable of the ten girls (virgins) in your own words.
7. Find the phrase 'traditional pattern of Christian belief' in this chapter, and then write out what follows about life after death in your own words.

Understanding

1. Write *three* statements to show that you understand what is meant by: i) a fundamentalist Christian; ii) an orthodox Christian (remember! *not* the Orthodox Church!); iii) an unorthodox Christian.
2. What does 'Maranatha' mean?
3. What is meant when Christians refer to the second coming of Jesus?
4. What do Christians mean when they say that something is 'revealed by God'?
5. What do people mean when they say that the Christian religion is 'a journey of faith'?
6. Explain why some Christians accept the authority of others concerning the mysteries of the Christian religion.

Evaluation

1. Why is it difficult to describe heaven or hell?
2. Summarise some of the ways in which Christians explain the Virgin birth of Jesus, and say which one you most agree with and why.
3. Summarise the arguments concerning the resurrection of Jesus and give your own views.
4. Why do Christians accept certain beliefs without being able to explain them fully? What do you think about the fact that Christian belief involves this kind of mystery of faith?
5. Outline a topic concerning Christian belief which is debated frequently (e.g. the problem of evil) and say what you think about the topic.

FURTHER READING

1. *Christian Belief and Practice:* chapter 10, pages 45-47.
2. *The Christian Faith and its Symbols:* pages 41-45.
3. *Christian Experience* (Chichester Project Book 3): chapters 3, 6.
4. *Jesus* (Chichester Project Book 4): chapter 8.

2.3 CHRISTIANS AND THE BIBLE

SACRED WRITINGS

All the world religions (Buddhism, Hinduism, Sikhism, Judaism, Islam etc.) have writings which they consider very holy. The writings usually form the basis of their:
- **belief (faith) and**
- **behaviour (ethics)**

The holy book of Islam is the ***Koran***. Jews are guided by the Old Testament which they call the ***Law (Torah)***, the ***Prophets***, and the ***Writings***. The sacred book of Christians is the ***Bible***. The word Bible comes from the Greek word 'biblos' meaning 'a book'.

THE CHARACTER OF THE BIBLE

Structure: The Bible is usually thought of in two main sections:
- **the Old Testament**
- **the New Testament**

The word 'testament' means covenant, and the covenant of the Bible is the agreement or relationship between God and his people. In the Old Testament, the people of God are the Jews (sometimes called 'children of Israel', 'Hebrews', or just 'Israel').

In the New Testament, Jesus makes it clear that all nations are God's people if they live in his way. It is the birth of Jesus which makes the beginning of the New Testament or covenant between God and his people.

The Old Testament is not one continuous account of God and his people. It is a collection of writings which broadly cover what we would recognise as the writings of:
- **law**
- **history**
- **prophecy**
- **poetry**
- **stories**

There are thirty-nine books in the Old Testament, but the Roman Catholic Church includes fifteen other writings taken from Greek manuscripts written in the period after the Hebrew writings and before New Testament times. The agreed Hebrew list of writings is called the ***canon*** of the Old Testament. The other agreed writings are called the ***deutero-canonical books***. (The first part of the word means 'second', so one could say that they are the second 'canon'.) Another name used for deutero-canonical is ***Apocrypha***.

The word 'Apocrypha' means 'hidden away': it suggests that these writings were not considered by some Christians to be sacred and inspired by God.

The New Testament is a collection of twenty-seven books or writings. We would recognise the following kinds of writing:
- **gospels**
- **history**
- **letters**
- **personal visions**

The Gospels are four accounts, sometimes very similar in content and sometimes quite different, of the person of Jesus Christ and his teaching.

The historical part of the New Testament is contained in the Acts of the Apostles which describes the growth of the early Church after Pentecost day. Peter and Paul play a very important part in the Acts. There are thirteen letters written by Paul to groups of Christians which give them encouragement and discuss their various difficulties. There are eight letters written by other Christians. The Book of Revelations (sometimes called the ***Apocalypse***) is an account of visions which describe how God and his people would be victorious over evil.

The Bible writings were composed over a period of about one thousand years from 900 BC onwards, and from a human point of view they have experienced the same kind of hazards and difficulties faced by any writings which have survived for centuries. Before the invention of printing these difficulties could be quite critical, and Christians have often puzzled over the correct meaning or message of a passage.

STUDY OF THE BIBLE

In order to ensure that the text of the Bible is as accurate as possible some scholars specialise in archaeology, ancient languages, preservation of manuscripts etc. Translations into many languages have been made with particular care being given to the culture of the people reading the translations.

There are many translations in the English/American languages, and these take into account words which come into the language and those which fall into disuse and become old-fashioned or difficult to recognise. The Bible, therefore, is studied and cared for in the same way as any other great writings or literature of the world. But, as the Bible is the ***sacred book of Christians***, there are other aspects to consider. These are the:
- **authority**
- **inspiration** and
- **interpretation** of the Bible.

Authority
Christians have been very careful in saying which writings may be included in the Bible. There are many other writings about the Old and New Testament times which are not included in the Bible. The books of the Bible are sacred to Christians, and some groups of Christians accept only what is in the Bible as the basis for their Christian belief and practice. The authority of scripture was emphasised at the time of the Reformation, when the existing human authority of the Christian Church was challenged.

Throughout the history of the Christian religion, three kinds of authority have been accepted by the people as a guide for their beliefs and actions:

1. **Leaders** (apostles, witnesses of the resurrection, popes, bishops and ministers).
2. **Tradition** (these grow up among people from customs over many years).
3. **The Bible**.

Also, the combined voice of Christian people has been accepted as the authority for declaring, for example, that a particular person is worthy of the formal title 'saint'.

OLD TESTAMENT

תורה נביאים וכתובים

Law, History, Prophecy, Poetry, Stories

NEW TESTAMENT

Η ΚΑΙΝΗ ΔΙΑΘΗΚΗ

Gospels, History, Letters, Personal visions

BOOKS OF THE OLD & NEW TESTAMENTS

On the whole, there are, and always have been, different opinions about the authority of the Bible for Christian belief and practice. Obviously the Bible was written in very different times from the twentieth century and does not deal with all the practical problems which Christians meet today, for example, drug addiction, or nuclear warfare. However, some Christians only accept the authority of the Bible because they think that God has revealed himself and commanded worship, justice, and brotherly love in terms which are broad enough to be applied to any age.

Inspiration

The revelation of God through the writings of a human person is called *inspiration*. It is thought that the writer has been influenced by God and has written the genuine intentions of God himself. At times in the history of Christianity, people say that the books of the Bible can only be read according to the original intention of the writer and are not influenced by God at all. But phrases like 'God's Word', and the 'Liturgy (Worship) of the Word', give away the fact that Christian belief and worship and practice relies heavily on the truth that the scriptures are inspired. In general, Christians behave as though the Bible is the word of God in the words of man. Because this is so, Christians make a study of the writings themselves in order to understand what God is saying to them. This requires some interpretation.

Interpretation

The Bible can be quoted to justify almost any course of action, and is frequently misused in this way. When, for example, a saying is taken out of its place or context, it often takes on a different meaning. This is as bad as repeating only part of a conversation in order to get someone into trouble! It is like telling a half-truth. The interpretation of scripture is, therefore, a very delicate task.

The interpretation of scripture is often thought of as a special gift of the Holy Spirit of God, and Bible services are held to ask for that gift.

CONCLUSION

The Bible is a guide to Christian *worship, beliefs, practice and values*. It is the holy book of the Christian religion. In using it as a guide to the Christian religion, one needs to be very careful to note the variety of responses to its *authority, inspiration and interpretation*.

QUESTIONS

Investigation

1. Name the sacred book of Christians.
2. Name the *two* main parts of the Bible.
3. What kind of writing may be found in the Old Testament?
4. What is the agreed list of books in the Old Testament called?
5. What kind of writing may be found in the New Testament?
6. What do we call the kind of studies which help to make the text of the Bible as accurate as possible?
7. Name *three* kinds of authority which are accepted by Christians as a guide for their beliefs and actions.
8. Select and describe *three* examples of the different kinds of writing to be found in the Bible, and say which books illustrate the kinds of writing you have chosen.

Understanding

1. Explain the term 'Apocrypha'.
2. What does the term 'inspiration' mean when it is applied to the scriptures?
3. What phrases do Christians use to show that they think the Bible is inspired by God?
4. What is meant by the *interpretation* of scripture?

5. Explain the relationship between the Old Testament and the New Testament in the Bible.
6. Why is the interpretation of scripture a very difficult task for a Christian?
7. Why is it important to Christians that the Bible should be inspired by God?

Evaluation

1. How far do you think that the Bible is a good guide to belief and behaviour for Christians to follow in the twentieth century? Give your reasons.
2. Explain the reasons why some people say that the Bible 'is not true' and say whether you agree with their point of view.

FURTHER READING

1. *Christian Belief and Practice:* chapter 2.
2. *The Christian's Book* (Chichester Project Book 6).
3. *Christianity in Words and Pictures:* pages 4, 5 and chapter 2.
4. *Religions of Man:* pages 83-85.
5. *Believers All:* pages 14-16.
6. *The Christian World:* page 16.

CHRISTIAN VALUES

3.1 THE TEN COMMANDMENTS AND THE TEACHING OF THE NEW TESTAMENT

People who have religious faith act according to the teachings of that faith. The behaviour of Christians depends a great deal on the vocation to which they think God is calling them. The rules of behaviour which the Jews held as sacred were the *Ten Commandments*.

Jesus was a Jew, so he and his followers kept the Ten Commandments, but Jesus showed them that God expected something more than the basic standards which the Commandments required. Christians base their behaviour towards God and their neighbour on *the teaching of Jesus*.

THE TEN COMMANDMENTS

These were given to Moses by God in the Old Testament. They can be found in Exodus 20:1-17. They are not numbered one to ten in the Bible: the numbering of the Commandments is for convenience. The following two lists are the common ways of numbering the Commandments.

1. Worship no God but me.

2. Do not make for yourselves images of anything in heaven or on earth, or in the water under the earth. Do not bow down to any idol or worship it.

3. Do not use my name for evil purposes, for I, the Lord your God will punish anyone who misuses my name.

4. Observe the Sabbath and keep it holy. You have six days in which to work but the seventh day is a day of rest dedicated to me.

5. Respect your father and your mother.

6. Do not commit murder.

7. Do not commit adultery.

8. Do not steal.

9. Do not accuse anyone falsely.

10. Do not desire another man's house; do not desire his wife, his slaves, his cattle, his donkeys, or anything else that he owns.

1. Worship no God but me.
Do not make for yourselves images of anything in heaven or on earth. Do not bow down to any idol or worship it.

2. Do not use my name for evil purposes, for I, the Lord your God will punish anyone who misuses my name.

3. Observe the Sabbath and keep it holy. You have six days in which to work but the seventh day is a day of rest dedicated to me.

4. Respect your father and your mother.

5. Do not commit murder.

6. Do not commit adultery.

7. Do not steal.

8. Do not accuse anyone falsely.

9. Do not desire another man's wife.

10. Do not desire another man's house; do not desire his slaves, his cattle, his donkeys, or anything else that he owns.

The difference between these two numberings is that in the left-hand list, there are *four* Commandments which refer to a man's relationship with God, and *six* Commandments which refer to the way he treats his neighbour. In the right-hand list, commonly used by the Roman Catholic Church, there are *three* Commandments which refer to the relationship with God and *seven* which refer to one's neighbour. The difference in the numbering occurs by separating verses 3 to 6 into two Commandments or counting them as all one Commandment. Next, by making a distinction between envying a man's wife and his possessions in verse 17, one or two Commandments are formed. In the end, in both methods of numbering there are Ten Commandments, but there is a slight difference in the organisation of the numbers — perhaps the best way of looking at the demands of the Commandments is in the following summary:

- ▶ **worship no God but me**
- ▶ **do not worship idols**
- ▶ **do not use my name for evil purposes**
- ▶ **observe the Sabbath and keep it holy**
- ▶ **respect your father and your mother**
- ▶ **do not commit murder**
- ▶ **do not commit adultery**
- ▶ **do not steal**
- ▶ **do not accuse anyone falsely**
- ▶ **do not desire a man's wife**
- ▶ **do not desire any of his possessions**

The Commandments can be recognised as the basic rules for peaceful living in any society. However, they are so basic that they are not particularly helpful for leading a positively good life. Most of the Commandments tell people what to avoid, like committing murder or stealing. Jesus taught a more refined and positive way of loving God and other people.

THE TEACHING OF THE NEW TESTAMENT

First of all Jesus taught the people that **God is Love**.

If one wanted to summarise the teaching of Jesus into a single word it would be **love**. Jesus taught his followers to be loving people because in that way they would be like God himself, and he wanted them to know what God was like. It was for that reason Jesus became the Son of Mary.

Mark 12:28-31

Jesus was asked the following question by a teacher of the law, who admired the kind of answers Jesus was giving to those who tried to test him: *'Which Com-* mandment is the most important of all?'* Jesus replied:

'The most important one is this, Listen Israel!
The Lord our God is the only Lord.
Love the Lord your God
with all your heart
with all your soul
with all your mind, and
with all your strength.
The second most important Commandment is this:
Love your neighbour as you
love yourself.
There is no other Commandment more important
than these two.'
(Mark 12:28-31)

It is quite easy to see that Jesus put the Ten Commandments of the Old Jewish law into two very positive statements about loving God and each other. The teacher of the law was very pleased with the answer Jesus gave, and Jesus was pleased that he could see the Commandments so positively, so he said to him: *'You are not far from the Kingdom of God.'* (verse 34)

THE GREATEST COMMANDMENT OF ALL

'Love the Lord your God
with all your heart
with all your soul
with all your mind,
and with all your strength.'

Give food

Comfort

Make peace

Pray

'Love your neighbour as yourself.'

Shelter

Bear wrongs

Matthew 5:1-12

Jesus illustrated what he meant by loving God and one another by a variety of comments and parables. He said, for example, that the poor widow who put all she had into the temple treasury really knew what it meant to worship God with love. He told the parable of the Good Samaritan to illustrate that anyone in need of help is a neighbour, not just friends, relatives and fellow countrymen.

In the Sermon on the Mount, however, Jesus explained in greater detail what he thought God-like behaviour consisted of. The teachings he gave are sometimes called *the Beatitudes*.

The word *Beatitude* comes from a translation of the original language of the New Testament in which the first word of each of Jesus' sentences meant 'Blessed are' or 'How happy are those who'.

Each of the eight Beatitudes can be seen as a trade-mark of Christian behaviour in the twentieth century. The next chapter will develop this point but some illustrations will be given here.

'Happy are those who know they are spiritually poor, the Kingdom of Heaven belongs to them.'

In Jesus' day, many Pharisees thought that if they kept all the rituals and laws of the Jewish religion, they could count themselves quite definitely as holy men. They tried to control God by their observance of religious ceremony. Jesus made it quite clear that all people owe their whole lives to God and that it is this goodness which governs their lives. In the Christian Church, it is the people who rely entirely upon God who often give a better example of God's goodness to their neighbour than people who observe a lot of religious customs.

'Happy are those who mourn, God will comfort them.'

People who mourn are generally sorrowful because they have lost people and things which are important to them. There are great sorrows today for people who are the victims of hatred, war or natural disasters. The goodness of God comes to these people when Christians organise themselves to bring relief.

'Happy are those who are humble, they will receive what God has promised.'

It is a pity that the word 'humble' often means 'weak' in a sense which people despise. This is not what Jesus meant by humility. Jesus told a parable about what God expects of people who have been given various talents. Humble people are those who accept their responsibilities according to the gifts they have. In a Christian home, a mother, father or child who really pulls their weight, is behaving in a humble way.

'Happy are those whose greatest desire is to do what God requires; God will satisfy them thoroughly.

Jesus makes great promises with confidence in his knowledge of what God is like. Jesus' own life was an example of someone who listened carefully to what God wanted of him even to death on the cross, when he said: *'not what I want, but what you want.'* (Mark 14:36)

'Happy are those who are merciful to others, God will be merciful to them.'

This teaching of Jesus about Christian behaviour is also repeated often in the Lord's Prayer in the phrase: *'forgive us our trespasses as we forgive those who trespass against us.'*

Forgiveness and mercy are the special trade-marks of Christian behaviour. That is why it is so difficult to see Christianity in the behaviour of people towards one another in Northern Ireland. Christians give rise to most scandal and set bad examples in situations where there is no forgiveness. The Jews had a law 'Lex talionis' which allowed them to return as much hurt as they had received, for example 'an eye for an eye'. Jesus, however, taught, 'do not take revenge on someone who wrongs you' (Matthew 5:39).

'Happy are the pure in heart, they will see God!'

In the Old Testament it was taught that God was so holy that if a man were to see God he would die. Jesus taught that close friendship with God was possible, but people would have to sort out for themselves what was acceptable to God in human life. These people would be the 'pure in heart'.

'Happy are those who work for peace, God will call them his children!'

The great Peace Movements in the twentieth century can be assured that they follow the example set by Jesus who, as the Messiah, would also be the Prince of Peace.

'Happy are those who are persecuted because they do what God requires; the Kingdom of Heaven belongs to them! Happy are you when people insult you and persecute you and tell all kinds of evil lies against you because you are my followers. Be happy and glad, for a great reward is kept for you in Heaven.'

It is not easy, says Jesus, to live in God's way. It is likely that Christian behaviour will upset the plans of many people. In the Old Testament, God spoke through his prophets against the dishonesty and injustice of the world. He said that it was wrong to ignore or take advantage of people who were naturally poor and weak such as orphans and widows. He said that it was wrong to use power so as to cheat the poor etc.

God spoke through Jesus in the New Testament, and his teaching invited people to live dangerously in this world, and to speak for the values he gave them. Great characters of the twentieth century like Martin Luther King, Maximilian Kolbe, and Dr Shelia Cassidy discovered that they had to suffer for the values which they believed to be true.

'Prisoners of conscience' are people who speak out against the political views of the State and are imprisoned and tortured for doing so. Not all of them are Christians, but many are, and they suffer for the values which Jesus gave them.

1 Corinthians 13

The writers of the New Testament letters usually encourage the early Christians with their own understanding of the teaching of Jesus. Paul underlines the values which Jesus taught in a particular way when he writes about love to the Corinthians in Corinth:

> *1 Corinthians 13*
>
> 'I may be able to speak the languages of men and even of angels, but if I have no love, my speech is no more than a noisy gong or a clanging bell. I may have the gift of inspired preaching; I may have all the knowledge and understand all secrets; I may have all the faith needed to move mountains — but if I have no love, I am nothing. I may give away everything I have, and even give up my body to be burnt — but if I have no love, this does me no good.
>
> Love is patient and kind; it is not jealous or conceited or proud; love is not ill-mannered or selfish or irritable; love does not keep a record of wrongs; love is not happy with evil, but is happy with the truth. Love never gives up; and its faith, hope, and patience never fail.
>
> Love is eternal. There are inspired messages, but they are temporary; there are gifts of speaking in strange tongues, but they will cease. For our gifts of knowledge and of inspired messages are only partial; but when what is perfect comes, then what is partial will disappear.
>
> When I was a child, my speech, feelings, and thinking were all those of a child; now that I am a man, I have no more use for childish ways. What we see now is like a dim image in a mirror; then we shall see face to face. What I know now is only partial; then it will be complete — as complete as God's knowledge of me.
>
> Meanwhile these three remain: faith, hope, and love; and the greatest of these is love.'

Several phrases from this chapter in Corinthians illustrate and emphasise the teaching of Jesus in the Gospels: *'If I have no love I am nothing.'*

People like Mother Teresa base their whole lives on words like these. She has spent her life with the destitute and dying in the belief that everyone should enter and leave human life knowing that they are loved.

Love is patient
— kind
— not jealous
— not conceited
— not proud
— not ill-mannered
— not selfish
— not irritable
Love does not keep a record of wrongs
Love never gives up

Each one of these phrases echoes the teaching of Jesus in the Beatitudes. Wherever Christian service has these trade-marks, it is truly a Christian work. Otherwise, as Paul says to the Corinthians: *'If I have no love, this does me no good'.*

Sometimes Christians' actions are very puzzling to people who do not believe in the promise made by Jesus. When Maximilian Kolbe offered to die in the hunger cells in the place of a man with a wife and children, his action was not particularly appreciated by his prison guards. Also, a Christian person may have a great struggle to forgive real wickedness, but Paul explains: *'What we see now is like a dim image in a mirror...what I know now is only partial — then it will be complete.'*

What Paul is saying here is that God will make things clear when *'we shall see face to face'*. In other words, the rewards promised by Jesus are very important motives for the actions of a Christian. These rewards will be:

▶ **the Kingdom of Heaven**
▶ **God's comfort**
▶ **God's promises**
▶ **to be satisfied by God**
▶ **God's mercy**
▶ **to see God**
▶ **to be a child of God**

(Read the Beatitudes again!)

QUESTIONS

Investigation

1. The Jews based their behaviour (moral code) on the Ten Commandments. What do Christians base their behaviour on?
2. Write out the answer which Jesus gave to the teacher of the law.
3. What parable did Jesus tell to illustrate the question 'who is my neighbour?'.
4. What kind of people did God use in the Old Testament to point out dishonesty and injustice in society?
5. Describe a 'prisoner of conscience' and give an example of one.
6. Name a society which helps 'prisoners of conscience' (See Unit 3.2).
7. Write a list of the qualities of love outlined by Paul to the Christians of Corinth.
8. Write an account of *one* Christian in modern times who has suffered for acting according to the teaching of Jesus.
9. Write out the rewards promised to Christians and contained in the Beatitudes.
10. Describe the life and work of one Christian who has put love first in his or her life.
11. Describe the work of *one* Christian who has been a 'peacemaker'.

Understanding

1. What does the word 'beatitude' mean?
2. Explain the connection between the Ten Commandments and the Christian religion.
3. Using the summary of the Ten Commandments in the chapter, explain why they are basic rules for any civilised society.

4. Outline any parable told by Jesus which teaches about *either* love of God *or* love of neighbour.
5. Choose *one* beatitude and explain its meaning, giving an example of its application to modern life.

Evaluation

1. Do you agree that Christian behaviour could upset many people's plans?
2. Where do you think injustice is practised in the world, and do you think it can be overcome by the life and work of Christians?
3. Why do you think some people reject the rewards of a Christian life?

FURTHER READING

1. *Christian Belief and Practice:* chapter 5.
2. *Christian Ethics* (Chichester Project Book 8).
3. *Revise Religious Studies:* pages 28-33.
4. *Religions of Man:* pages 122-125.

3.2 CHRISTIANITY IN ACTION

This chapter will develop the theme of what it means to put the teaching of Jesus into action in the world today. The present generation of people live in quite different circumstances from the wandering teacher, preacher and wonder-worker of two thousand years ago! However, Christians believe quite firmly that the values given to the first followers by Jesus, must be practised by Christians in every age.

CHRISTIAN MISSION AND SERVICE

The writers of the Gospels record the great compassion of Jesus for the poor, the sick, the 'possessed' and the outcasts of his day. It is not difficult to identify the weak in our modern society:

▶ **children**
▶ **the elderly**
▶ **the mentally handicapped**
▶ **the physically handicapped**
▶ **one-parent families**
▶ **drug addicts**
▶ **alcoholics**
▶ **prisoners**

(See illustration on page 52.)

Christians care for the weak in society for religious reasons. They recognise others as members of God's family, brothers and sisters of Christ. Worship of God, and care for their neighbour are part of the way they understand the meaning of their lives.

Some Churches have a *Social Responsibility Sunday* when their members think especially about neighbours who might be needing care or help of some kind. Many schemes for the poor and the weak are run by voluntary Christian organisations.

The Society of Friends believe that religion affects every aspect of life, and they are active in many areas of social life. In 1961 they founded Amnesty International for all prisoners of conscience throughout the world. Quakers (Friends) have often been imprisoned for being conscientious objectors during a war, and refusing to use weapons.

The Salvation Army is famous throughout the world for its concern for the outcasts of society. Some of their activities include: industrial training homes and occupational centres; homes and centres for alcoholics; remand and probation homes; training farms and settlements; homes for the elderly; children's homes and day nurseries; holiday homes and camps; play centres; students' residences; centres for the blind, the deaf and the crippled; canteens and hostels for service men and women; assistance for people in court cases; family welfare work and emergency relief. The list is very impressive! Wherever there is any kind of need, the Salvation Army responds with a true Christian charity. The Church Army is the Church of England's equivalent of the Salvation Army. Every Christian denomination has its own special heroes and heroines of Christian charity.

Religious Orders in the Roman Catholic Church have traditionally cared for children, the elderly, the handicapped, and needy families. The Missionaries of Charity are the Sisters of Mother Teresa's religious congregation. Mother Teresa deeply believes in what she thinks and what she does. She tells her Sisters to do

The weak in society

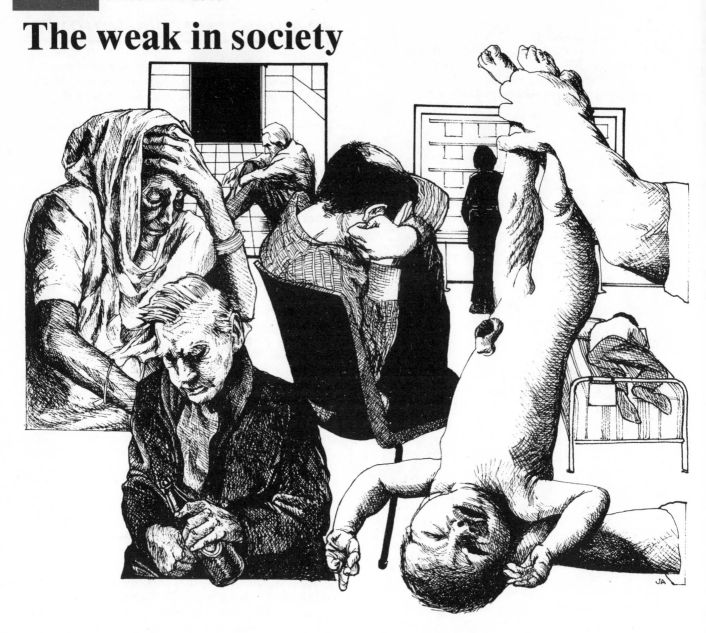

small things with great love. She tells them that it is not how much they do that counts but how much love there is in what they do. She believes that people who are dying in the most terrible circumstances must know that somebody cares. This care of the dying does not take any notice of colour or nationality, wealth or poverty. Mother Teresa believes that by dying one awakens to eternal life, so it is a privilege to be with someone, and loving them, at the moment of their death.

There are international Christian organisations like the *Tear Fund* and *Christian Aid* which care for the needs of the developing nations (the Third World). These organisations co-ordinate the many kinds of aid which helps to overcome the injustice of people who suffer poverty and disease unnecessarily. Mother Teresa has said: 'Poverty is not created by God. It is created by you and me.' The work of Christian international relief organisations often includes projects which provide:

▶ clean water   ▶ community development
▶ technical skills   ▶ food production
▶ health care   ▶ education

(see also Unit 6.3 — The Poor)

ISSUES CONCERNING CHRISTIAN MISSION AND SERVICE

There are some areas of Christian mission and service which are not always open to women. Some Christian Churches which have an ordained priesthood will not allow women to become priests. (See Unit 1.5)

Christian decision-making
It is sometimes difficult to decide how Christian values ought to be applied. Jesus met lepers, epileptics, the blind, the deaf and dumb, the lame and the paralysed. He cured them all. But he did not have to make decisions concerning organ transplants from one person to another, or about *in vitro* fertilisation (test-tube babies) and artificial insemination. These advances in medical science had not taken place.

Transplant surgery
Sometimes a person needs a transfusion of blood for their life to be saved. Some operations can only be performed when blood is available to replace the amount of blood lost by the operation and to keep the patient alive.

Most Christians see no obstacle to being a blood donor, or to receiving blood in a transfusion. However, there are some Fundamentalist Christians who believe that blood transfusions are forbidden by the Bible. Jehovah's Witnesses will not allow transfusions. Sometimes the objection to such an idea rests on the understanding of the resurrection of the body. It seems wrong to these Christians to donate blood or organs when the body will rise again at the last day. When people understand such things quite literally, normal medical procedures present great difficulties. Some Christians are selective about transplant surgery, and say that it would be right to transplant some organs but not others. There can be great problems for Christian doctors who have to decide between one patient and another for a transplant operation.

In vitro fertilisation

The natural method of transmitting human life is by conception and birth. Some women are unable to conceive normally. Some men are unable to fertilise a woman's ovum. Some women are unable to go through a normal pregnancy and to give birth, even with all the modern methods of childbirth. In the twentieth century it has been discovered that a human embryo can be artificially nurtured from a human ovum and sperm. It may be possible one day to nurse the embryo to complete growth outside the womb. This medical progress has given hope to childless couples. It has also presented great problems. Here are three cases where there may be conflict between medical progress and Christian teaching.

1. A woman is unable to conceive. It is possible that a woman cannot conceive because her ovum cannot travel into the womb. In this case, it is now possible to take the ovum and let the fusion with the male sperm occur under artificial conditions (hence the phrase 'test-tube' baby). The fertilised ovum can then be transplanted into the womb of the mother and a normal pregnancy can follow. Difficulties may arise if it is discovered that the foetus is abnormal in some way. Can it just be discarded and the experiment begun again? At what stage of the development of the foetus would one say that human life was present?

The whole area of experimentation at the early stage presents great problems, even to non-Christians who see that human beings may be entering into a dangerous stage in the history of the human race. For Christians, who believe that life is a gift from God, there are great difficulties about tampering with the sacred nature of human life itself.

2. Deep frozen sperm and conception at a future date. A man's sperm can be frozen and used for conception by *in vitro* methods at a later date. Actual examples have occurred where the father of a child was already dead at the moment of conception. Of course, this could be a great consolation to the man's wife who otherwise might have been very sorry that she had not had children earlier in the marriage. On a practical level, this has already led to law-suits about whether a child can inherit the estate of his father who may have died some years before the child's birth. From a Christian point of view, the possibility of a normal family group of mother, father and baby does not exist. Also, the same problems of experimentation in the early stages of the foetus are present.

3. Surrogate motherhood. *In vitro* fertilisation also makes it possible for a childless couple to have their own baby with the help of a second woman who will take the pregnancy through and give birth to the child. This might happen, for instance, when a woman is unable to sustain pregnancy and childbirth, but still wants to have children. The father's sperm would fertilise the surrogate mother's ovum, and the child would be given to the infertile woman at birth or soon after.

Again, there are many practical and legal problems which can occur. From a Christian point of view the sanctity of human life is at risk. The surrogate mother may feel one way before the pregnancy, but may not want to give the baby up after childbirth. The whole ideal of Christian family life may be held in question, because the surrogate mother is not the father's wife.

Artificial Insemination by Donor (A.I.D.)

In the case of a husband being infertile, his wife can now be fertilised by an anonymous donor. The semen is donated and kept in a sperm bank until it is required. From a practical point of view, a childless couple can have a family. However, there can be problems about inheriting illnesses through the genes of the father. There can be quite severe genetic problems. The Christian is faced with a situation where the father of the child is unknown, and the values of Christian family life are again compromised.

In the cases of *in vitro* fertilisation and artificial insemination by donor, severe emotional and psychological problems can arise from the artificial methods being used. On the other hand, a Christian would always recognise that medical progress itself is a way of giving thanks to God for the gifts of intelligence and creativity which are being used in experimentation.

In March 1987 the Roman Catholic Church issued an instruction called *Respect for Human Life in its Origin and the Dignity of Procreation*. This instruction gives guidance on the serious moral problems involved in medical progress. The point is made that what becomes technically possible in science is not necessarily morally acceptable. The human embryo must be respected, and artificial techniques for creating the embryo are generally rejected as unacceptable in the instruction. (See Appendix B.)

Note: Use of animals in medical experiments.
Animals are used extensively in medical science and many groups oppose such experiments. The animal rights movement may well have members who are Christians. These people would say that it was against the teaching of Christ to cause unnecessary suffering to God's creatures. Other Christians would say that God gave human beings authority over all creation, and that animals may be used for experiments if the lives of human beings can be saved as a result.

QUESTIONS

Investigation

1. Make a list of all the kinds of people cured by Jesus.
2. Who are the weak and powerless people in modern society?
3. Make a special study of *two* types of social work undertaken by the Salvation Army today and describe the work.
4. Describe the difficulties of *one* group of people who need help in modern society.
5. Find out some more details about the life and work of Mother Teresa of Calcutta.
6. Describe the work of Amnesty International.
7. Find out more about the Tear Fund *or* Christian Aid and describe some of the work this organisation does.
8. What is a transplant?
9. What is a transfusion?
10. What is the medical term used for experiments on the human foetus outside the womb?
11. Give examples of some case studies which have already occurred concerning surrogate motherhood. (Try to find examples in newspapers, magazines etc...)

Understanding

1. Explain the *religious* reasons why Christians care for the weak and the powerless in society.
2. Why does Mother Teresa consider that it is a privilege to love someone when they are dying?
3. Explain some of the moral problems which a Christian doctor might face today.
4. Explain the position of the Roman Catholic Church with regard to *in vitro* fertilisation and surrogate motherhood. (See Appendix B)
5. Why does the Roman Catholic Church speak with authority on moral issues for Roman Catholics?
6. What is meant by the phrase 'test-tube baby'?
7. Why do Christians believe that human life is sacred?

Evaluation

1. Evaluate some of the reasons why Mother Teresa has captured the heart and imagination of the whole world! What evidence is there that she is greatly loved and admired as a saintly person and a great Christian missionary?
2. Give some arguments for and against medical progress, and then say how a Christian might comment on these arguments.

3. Do you think that there can be *general* answers for the problems presented by medical science today, or do you think that answers depend on each individual case?
4. What conclusions have you come to about the relationship of Christian values to medical progress?
5. Are there any human organs which you think ought *not* to be used in transplant operations. Give reasons for your opinions.
6. What are the main arguments made by Christians for and against the use of animals in experiments? What is your opinion?
7. Do you think that Christian family life could be threatened by surrogate motherhood?

FURTHER READING

1. *Christian Belief and Practice:* chapters 4, 6, 11.
2. *Christian Experience* (Chichester Project Book 3): pages 20-24.
3. *Christianity in Words and Pictures:* chapters 6, 7.
4. *Revise Religious Studies:* pages 133-135.
5. *Framework* (Christianity and Life): chapter 19.

*T*HE ROMAN CATHOLIC TRADITION

UNIT 4 The home and family

4.1 *Baptism*
    A) The Roman Catholic ceremony   **57**
    B) The Christian respect for human life   **60**
4.2 *Marriage*
    A) The Sacrament of Marriage in the Roman
    Catholic Church   **63**
    B) Themes and problems relating to marriage   **64**

UNIT 5 Christian vocation

5.1 *Discipleship: the Sacrament of Confirmation*   **68**
5.2 *Christian service*   **71**
    A) Lay ministries   **72**
    B) Religious congregations   **74**
5.3 *The Sacrament of Holy Orders*   **77**
5.4 *The ministry of the priesthood*   **81**

Units 6 and 7 overleaf

THE ROMAN CATHOLIC TRADITION continued

UNIT 6 Eucharist and world-wide fellowship

6.1	*The Mass*	**83**
6.2	*The Church/The Body of Christ*	**87**
6.3	*The poor*	**90**

UNIT 7 Reconciliation — our way to God

7.1	*The Sacrament of Reconciliation (Penance)*	**94**
7.2	*Reconciliation in society*	**98**
	A) Crime and punishment	**98**
	B) Prejudice and discrimination	**101**
	C) War and peace	**104**
7.3	*Anointing of the Sick*	**108**
7.4	*Further themes*	
	A) Sickness and healing	**111**
	B) Death and eternity	**112**

4.1 BAPTISM

(A) THE ROMAN CATHOLIC CEREMONY

Baptism is one of the seven sacraments of the Catholic Church. It is the first of three *sacraments of initiation* which make a person a full member of the Church. These sacraments are *baptism*, *confirmation*, and *Eucharist*. There is a special ceremony or rite for the Christian initiation of adults into the Church, but the following account is for the baptism of infants.

A baby is not able to make the promises of faith, but he or she belongs to a family who have faith, and the parents and god-parents promise to make the faith known to the child as it grows up.

> *'Whoever believes and is baptized*
> *will be saved:*
> *whoever does not believe*
> *will be condemned.'*
> (Mark 16:16)

The reception or welcome into the Christian community

This takes place at the entrance to the church. The priest welcomes the child and its parents, and invites them to come to the baptismal font.

> *'You have asked to have your child baptized. In doing so, you are accepting the responsibility of training him to the practice of the faith. It will be your duty to bring him up to keep God's Commandments as Christ taught us, by loving God and our neighbour...'*

The priest asks the god-parents if they are prepared to help the parents to do this. The child is welcomed into the Christian family:

> *'(Name), the Christian Community welcomes you with great joy. In its name I claim you for Christ our Saviour by the Sign of his Cross. I now trace the Sign of the Cross on your forehead, and invite your parents and god-parents to do the same.'*

The sign of the cross is a symbol that the child now belongs to God.

A celebration of the Word of God

An important part of the celebration of every sacrament is a reading of the Bible, the Word of God. The scripture reading for the sacrament of baptism may describe the baptism of Jesus, or it may be Jesus' conversation with Nicodemus in John chapter 3, about being born again to eternal life. Paul, in his letter to the Romans, explains the importance of baptism in the Christian life. The priest will give a short homily or sermon to explain the reading to the congregation.

The *'Prayers of the Faithful'* or the *'Bidding Prayers'* follow. These prayers will be for the child, the parents and god-parents. There should be a prayer for the new life given in baptism, and for the serious responsibilities which are being taken on by the parents and god-parents. There may be a prayer asking the saints to pray for the child, especially the saint whose name is being taken as the child's name. A name may be chosen which is not the name of a saint in the Church, but great care must be taken that the name would not take away the respect due to, and the holiness of, the occasion.

The exorcism and anointing

Jesus told his apostles to 'cast out devils in my name'. At this point in the ceremony, the priest will hold up his hand and say:

> *'O God, you sent your Son to cast out the power of Satan, set this child free from Original Sin.'*

At an exorcism, the power and control that evil has over mankind is driven out. In baptism, the child will be freed from the control of all evil forces. However, he or she will still have free will, and can deliberately choose sin when the time comes for understanding right from wrong. An example of Jesus casting out devils may be found in Mark 5:1-20.

The priest anoints the child on the chest with the *oil of catechumens* (a catechumen is someone who is preparing to be baptized). Oil is a sign of strength and healing.

> *'We anoint you with the oil of salvation in the name of Christ our Saviour: may he strengthen you with his power...'*

Baptismal promises — a declaration of faith

The celebration of the baptism begins. The child is brought to the font. The font may be near the entrance of the church if the baptism is not taking place during Mass. Otherwise, the font is brought into the sanctuary or to a place where the whole congregation can witness and approve the ceremony. The water is blessed. Then the priest asks the parents and god-parents to renew their faith:

> *'Dear parents and God-parents. You have come here to present this child for baptism. By water and the Holy Spirit he is to receive the gift of new life from God, who is love. On your part, you must make it your constant care to bring him up in the practice of the faith. See that the divine life which God gives him is kept safe from the poison of sin, to grow always stronger in his heart.'*

The baptismal promises are basic questions and answers which make up the promises made by someone who intends to live a Christian life. The priest asks the following questions: (Responses are given in bold letters.)

> *'Do you reject Satan and all his works and all his empty promises?'*
> **'I do'**
> *'Do you believe in God the Father Almighty, creator of heaven and earth?'*
> **'I do'**
> *'Do you believe in Jesus Christ, his only son, our Lord who was born of the Virgin Mary, was crucified, died, and was buried, rose from the dead, and is now seated at the right hand of the Father?'*
> **'I do'**

'Do you believe in the Holy Spirit, the Holy Catholic Church, the communion of Saints, the forgiveness of sins, the Resurrection of the body and life everlasting?'
'I do'
'This is our faith. This is the faith of the Church. We are proud to profess it in Christ Jesus our Lord.'

The baptismal promises include a rejection of all sin and an open statement or declaration of all the basic Christian teachings, which are found in the Apostles' Creed.

The baptism
Jesus drew near and said to them:

> *'I have been given all authority in heaven and on earth. Go, then, to all peoples everywhere and make them my disciples: baptize them in the name of the Father, the Son, and the Holy Spirit, and teach them to obey everything I have commanded you. And I will be with you always, to the end of the age.'*
> *Matthew 28:18-20*

The child is baptized in the following way: water is poured three times over the forehead while the following words are said: *'(Name) I baptize you in the name of the Father and of the Son and of the Holy Spirit.'*

This is the sacrament of baptism. The actual baptism is surrounded before and after by ceremony which acts as a setting for the sacrament itself, just as a jewel is placed into a beautiful and valuable setting.

The anointing with chrism
Baptism is followed by a second anointing. A different oil is used this time. It is called **chrism**. This oil is used again at confirmation, and also in the ordination of a priest. It is a symbol of being chosen for a special task in life (in this case, the child is being called to take up the challenge of living according to the values which Christ gave his followers). Oil is used at the coronation of a King or Queen. In the Old Testament, prophets were anointed. Jesus was God's priest, his prophet and a King (the Messiah). The anointing with chrism after baptism is a reminder that the new Christian shares in the life of Jesus who was **priest, prophet** and **King**. Christians have a great dignity in the sight of God.

> *'Learn, O Christian, how great you are...do not return to your former base condition by behaviour unworthy of your dignity...'*
> *Pope St Leo the Great*

The rest of the ceremony of baptism emphasises the new faith, new life, and new dignity of the Christian.

Clothing with the white garment
In the early days of the Church, new Christians were given a white garment to wear as a sign of their new life in which they rejected all sin. White is a colour associated with innocence and purity, so it is a good sign.

The priest puts the garment (usually a white shawl) around the child:

'See in this white garment an outward sign of Christian dignity...bring that dignity unstained into everlasting life in heaven.'

(See the parable of the wedding garment in Matthew 22.)

The baptismal candle
A candle is given to one of the parents who lights it from the great paschal candle which represents the resurrection of Jesus. The paschal candle is blessed and lit for the first time at the Easter Vigil on the evening of Holy Saturday. The ideal time for baptism is at the Easter Vigil which celebrates the rising of Jesus from death to new and everlasting life. Christians believe that his resurrection is the guarantee of their own change from death to life with God. A candle at an individual baptism represents this belief.

'Receive the light of Christ...to be kept burning brightly...this child of yours...is to walk always as a child of the light. May he keep the flame of faith alive in his heart.'

(See the parable of the ten bridesmaids/virgins/girls in Matthew 25:1-13.)

Conclusion at the altar
If the baptism is performed at a time other than a Mass, the 'Our Father' is said at the altar. The child now belongs to the family of God and can call God his Father. Three blessings follow:

One is for the mother:

'May God bless this mother who gives thanks for the gift of her child...'

One is for the father:

'God bless this father. He and his wife will be the first teachers of the child in the ways of faith...'

A third is for all who attend the baptism

'May God continue to pour out his blessings over all present here. May he make them faithful...'

SUMMARY
▶ **reception — the welcome**
▶ **the Word of God — homily**
▶ **prayers of the faithful**
▶ **exorcism and anointing**
▶ **declaration of faith (baptismal promises)**
▶ **baptism**
▶ **anointing with chrism**
▶ **clothing with white garment**
▶ **baptismal candle**
▶ **Lord's Prayer and blessing**

SIGNS AND SYMBOLS OF BAPTISM
Water is a powerful, natural symbol of life and death. Water gives life in a desert, or in a time of drought and famine. Water can also be very cruel, and rough seas have caused many deaths by drowning. In the sacrament of baptism, water is a symbol of death and life. There is a death to sin and a rising to new life in the family of God. An unborn child floats in water in its mother's womb, and birth takes place out of this water. Out of the water of baptism, a child of God is born and a new Christian is welcomed into the Church. Jesus spoke about a new birth to Nicodemus. Baptism by dipping or full immersion is recommended by the Church because the full symbolism of the sacrament can be seen more clearly.

SIGNS AND SYMBOLS OF BAPTISM

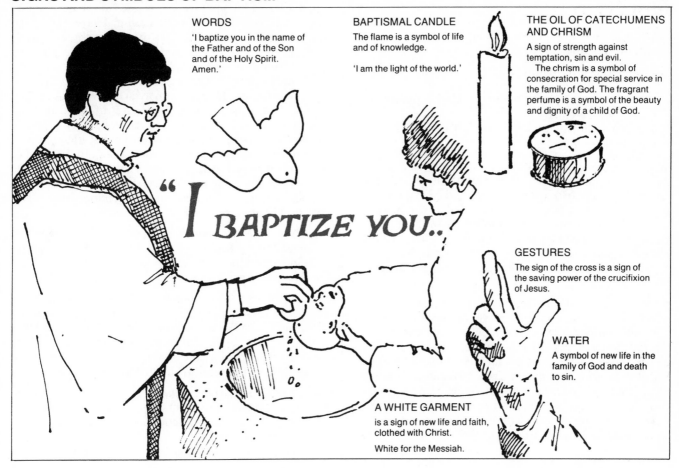

WORDS
'I baptize you in the name of the Father and of the Son and of the Holy Spirit. Amen.'

BAPTISMAL CANDLE
The flame is a symbol of life and of knowledge.

'I am the light of the world.'

THE OIL OF CATECHUMENS AND CHRISM
A sign of strength against temptation, sin and evil.
The chrism is a symbol of consecration for special service in the family of God. The fragrant perfume is a symbol of the beauty and dignity of a child of God.

"I BAPTIZE YOU..."

GESTURES
The sign of the cross is a sign of the saving power of the crucifixion of Jesus.

WATER
A symbol of new life in the family of God and death to sin.

A WHITE GARMENT
is a sign of new life and faith, clothed with Christ.
White for the Messiah.

Oil: Two kinds of oil are used at baptism: the oil of catechumens and the oil of chrism. One is used before the baptism and is a sign of strengthening for the life-long struggle with the power of temptation, sin and evil. In the early days of the Church, a person preparing for baptism would be stripped and anointed all over with oil. The use of oil is not so commonly understood by modern society, so this part of the ceremony is sometimes misunderstood, or not understood at all! The second anointing is after baptism and the oil of chrism is used. Chrism is a mixture of balsam, which is a fragrant perfume, and olive oil. The symbolism is two-fold: there is a consecration for special service in the family of God, and the fragrant perfume symbolises the beauty and dignity of a child of God.

White garment: In the early Church, a candidate (or catechumen) for baptism was clothed in a white robe as a sign of the fact that he was clothed with Christ when he was baptized. It was a sign of his new life of faith in Jesus Christ. The symbol is still used in baptism as a sign of new life and faith. The garment is usually provided by the mother. It is white because, in the Bible, the colour for the clothing of the Messiah was white.
(See the account of the Transfiguration of Jesus in Mark 9:2-9.)

Candle: Light is very important in the Christian faith because Jesus said, *'I am the light of the world'*. This was another way of saying that he was the Messiah sent by God. The flame of a candle is alive and is a sign of life. Sometimes, when a person dies, their relatives say that the 'light' of that person has gone out. Death is always thought of in symbols of darkness. Ignorance is thought of as darkness in the mind. So, light in the Christian faith is a symbol of life and knowledge. All the candles lit for use in the sacraments have a special relationship to the great paschal candle which represents the resurrection of Jesus.

Words and gestures: The important words of the sacrament of baptism are: *'I baptize you in the name of the Father and of the Son and of the Holy Spirit. Amen.'*
    In this formula, the Christian belief in the Holy Trinity is expressed. In baptism, the new Christian is a child of God the Father; he shares in the new life of Christ who is God the Son; and he belongs to the family of the Church which is a family of love in the Holy Spirit of God.
    The most important gesture in the ceremony of baptism is the ***sign of the cross***. The cross represents the saving power of the crucifixion of Jesus. It is special to the Christian religion and is the most commonly used sign of blessing, protection and faith.

(B) CHRISTIAN RESPECT FOR HUMAN LIFE

When a baby is brought to church for baptism, three celebrations occur:

1. The parents give thanks for the gift of a new human life.
2. Parents ask for membership of God's family on behalf of their baby.
3. The local Christian community welcomes the baby into the Church.

The ceremony underlines the fact that human life is a gift from God, and that all human life is sacred as a result. There are two issues concerning the beginning of human life which put the sanctity of that life at risk. They are *contraception* and *abortion*. Both these issues cause great problems to Catholics, and the teaching of the Church about them is challenged by other Christian denominations and sometimes by Catholics themselves.

Contraception is the use of contraceptives, i.e. methods which enable a couple to have sexual intercourse without risking the chance of a child being conceived. One method involves using the natural time of infertility called 'the safe period' for sexual intercourse. There is a length of time in every month when a woman is naturally most unlikely to conceive because the right physical conditions for conception are not present. This is the only form of planning the length of time between births which is advised by the Roman Catholic Church. Other methods interfere with conception in an artificial way (e.g. by the use of medication, 'the pill', a condom or a cap.) Some methods cause abortion after conception has taken place. The coil does this, and so does a 'pill' which is taken the morning after intercourse.

Contraception and the Roman Catholic Church
(a) The teaching authority of the Church
Roman Catholics believe that the Holy Spirit of God guides the hearts and minds of *all* who believe in what God has promised through the life, death, and resurrection of Jesus his Son. Throughout the history of the Church, however, when there have been serious questions about the meaning of the Christian faith or guidance about Christian behaviour (morality), Catholics have relied upon the combined authority of the pope and the bishops for a teaching on the matter. The great *councils* of the Church, and the letters of the popes to the people, are very important documents for Catholics. This *teaching ministry* of the church is called *the Magisterium* (the word comes from the Latin word 'magister' meaning teacher).

In general, when people talk about 'what the Church says' they are thinking about this special ministry of the pope and the bishops. This is an important fact to remember before any points about contraception can be discussed. It can never be forgotten that the Holy Spirit of God is present in all his people and that the definition of 'the Church' in the twentieth century is *the people of God*. This matters when the teaching authority of the Church is misunderstood as some kind of threatening control over people, instead of a ministry of love and care after the example of Jesus who called himself the Good Shepherd. Authority in the Catholic Church is the loving service and guidance of God's people.

(b) Marriage and the responsibilities of parents
In marriage, human love is expressed at the deepest and most intimate level. In a *Christian* marriage, the life of two people reflects the love of Jesus for all God's people. In the New Testament, God's people (the Church) are called the *Bride of Christ*. Jesus gave his life for his people, just as a husband would give his life for his wife and family. In marriage, love means much more than sexual activity. Love gives life, and this can be understood in two ways. In the first, when a person experiences sympathy and understanding, they grow in confidence, and we say they 'come alive'. In the second, the act of love which we call sexual intercourse, is the way in which human life is carried on or transmitted. When a discussion about contraception arises, two points about marriage need to be remembered:

1. *The loving relationship* of the married couple which needs to be kept alive as a sign and expression of God's love for people.
2. The sexual act as *the source of a new human life*.

Responsible couples think about the number of children they can reasonably care for and support. Sometimes, therefore, they want to express their love for each other without the possibility of conceiving another child. This is when they consider the best way of making sure that a new life does not result from their love-making.

(c) The guidance of the Church
There are several documents which contain the teaching of the Catholic Church about contraception. The most important ones are:
— *The Church in the Modern World* (Second Vatican Council).
— *Letter on the Regulation of Births* (Pope Paul VI).
— *The Christian Family in the Modern World* (Pope John Paul II).
— *Respect for Human Life in its Origin and the Dignity of Procreation.*
(See Appendix B)

There is another document which guides priests who are advising married couples.

The basic teaching about contraception is in the letter on the regulation of births which says: *'Any use whatsoever of marriage must retain its natural potential to procreate human life.'* (Paragraph 11)

This sentence means that all sexual intercourse in marriage should be natural and open to the possibility of a new human life. The only form of family-planning would therefore be the natural method of using the infertile period of the woman. All artificial chemical and physical methods of contraception are rejected by the teaching authority of the Church.

(d) Christian concern for the protection of human life
In his letter on family life, Pope John Paul II repeats the teaching that human life is sacred and must be protected from the threats which can arise from problems about population control:

'The Church is certainly aware of the many complex problems which couples in many countries face today in their task of transmitting life in a responsible way. She also recognises the serious problem of population growth in the form it has taken in many parts of the world...'

The Pope is concerned about the fact that some governments might force contraception upon people by law:

> '...any violence applied by such authorities in favour of contraception or, still worse, of sterilisation and procured abortion, must be altogether condemned and forcefully rejected.'

Sometimes countries might be offered money and resources but only on the condition that they are willing to take part in programmes of population control. The Pope also condemns this kind of mass bribery.

SUMMARY
▶ **The teaching authority of the Catholic Church is a loving service and guidance of God's people.**
▶ **Marriage involves love for each other and the transmission of human life.**
▶ **Responsible parenthood is important in marriage.**
▶ **Natural methods of spacing births are permitted.**
▶ **Chemical and physical methods of contraception are condemned in Catholic teaching.**
▶ **Chemical and physical methods which cause abortion after conception are also condemned.**
▶ **There is a world-wide threat to human life in the contraceptive programmes of some governments.**

Other views about contraception
General discussion about contraception includes an approval of chemical and physical methods of contraception, a fear of the medical dangers of these methods, and the effects on the attitude of people to sex as a result. The advantages of contraception for married couples are seen as helping them to space their families and limit them to a certain number. There is no fear of an unwanted pregnancy, and there is a feeling of security during the act of sex. The problems involved in contraception for the married couple include selfishness, which might prevent one partner from having the children he or she wants, and a knowledge that the act of love-making is closed to the possibility of a new life.

Outside marriage, people are often pleased that the possibility of illegitimate children is avoided, and unmarried mothers do not have to seek an abortion. The fact that it is possible for people to have sexual relationships freely leads to a great deal of human unhappiness and jealousy, and the real value of humam love is often lost in the process. Some people would say that there is more temptation to commit adultery when they feel they have the 'security' of practising contraception. There is no general agreement about contraception even among those who disagree with the Roman Catholic teaching. There is real concern about the medical effects of some methods of contraception and their link with the causes of cancer, and about their effect on the natural functions of the body.

Abortion
'Human life is sacred — all men must recognise that fact.' (The Regulation of Births — Pope Paul VI) Abortion, or the loss of a baby before birth, sometimes occurs naturally. There are many medical reasons for this. However, when people discuss abortion they do not mean a natural miscarriage of birth. They mean **procured abortion** or a miscarriage which is induced artificially. Abortion may also involve an operation to remove the foetus.

The teaching of the Catholic Church is expressed in the *Declaration on Procured Abortion (1974)*. In this document, the Church points out that respect for human life is not just a Christian duty. Respect for life is deeply embedded in the mind and heart of the human race. In the twentieth century, people have been specially aware of **human rights**.

▶ **the first right of the human being is his life**

The *Declaration* says:

> 'From the time that the ovum is fertilised, a life is begun which is neither that of the father nor of the mother. It is rather the life of a new human being with its own growth. It would never be made human if it were not human already.'
>
> *Paragraph 12*

Methods of contraception which cause abortion after conception defy the teaching contained in this *Declaration*.

Reasons why abortion is thought necessary by some people.
1. A question of health: the mother is thought to be in great danger by starting a pregnancy.
2. Another child in the family would be a great burden.
3. The child is likely to be abnormal or retarded e.g. Down's Syndrome baby.
4. The mother is unmarried, and the family may be disgraced among their relatives and friends.
5. The mother may be the victim of rape.

The Church teaches:

> '...never, under any pretext, may abortion be resorted to, either by a family or by the political authority, as a legitimate means of regulating births.'
>
> *Vatican Council II*

Abortion is considered to be the murder of an unborn child. However, the reasons why people ask for an abortion are sometimes very serious and involve great suffering.

> '...this does not mean that one can remain indifferent to these sorrows and miseries. Every man and woman with feeling, and certainly every Christian, must be ready to do what he can to remedy them.'
>
> *Declaration of Procured Abortion Para. 26*

There are situations when an operation for another disease (e.g. cancer) might also result in an abortion, and this is permitted, but an operation to take away the life of an unborn child is wrong.

Other opinions concerning abortion
Even people who do not agree with the teaching of the Catholic Church find it difficult to draw the line between one good reason for an abortion and another. Once one reason is accepted, it becomes difficult to refuse another reason and so on. Some Christian denominations will accept abortion for the following reasons:

1. Danger to the physical or mental health of the woman.
2. Rape.
3. The risk of a defective child being born.

There is some concern, among those who approve of abortion for certain reasons, that the availability of abortion may encourage people to become more promiscuous. They fear that human life may be counted too cheap if an 'unwanted' pregnancy can be ended. There is a similar debate when euthanasia is seriously considered as a solution to suffering, old age, and mental/physical handicap. Some people worry that life may be ended too easily under the pretext of being merciful. (See Unit 7.4, page 112)

CONCLUSION

The sacrament of baptism brings out the great respect which is due to human life. Christians may agree about the sanctity of human life when they are present at a joyful occasion like a baptism. However, once they have accepted that human life is a holy thing, they have to face great practical problems about preventing new life by contraception or abortion. The *Society for the Protection of the Unborn Child*, and the *LIFE* movement uphold the teaching of the Catholic Church on these issues.

QUESTIONS

Investigation

1. Name the *three* sacraments of initiation into the Catholic Church.
2. Outline the promises made by parents at the baptism of the child.
3. Select and describe a suitable reading from the Bible for a baptism.
4. What is the name of the first oil which is used in the ceremony of baptism?
5. Name the second oil used in baptism.
6. Describe the *basic* teaching of the Catholic Church about contraception (one sentence only).
7. Describe the *basic* teaching of the Catholic Church about abortion (one sentence only).
8. Search this chapter for information about contraception and explain in your own words the concern for human life which is contained in it.
9. Name *two* societies concerned with opposing abortion.
10. Give an account of *either* the baptism of Jesus *or* the conversation between Jesus and Nicodemus.
11. Select and describe an incident when Jesus cast out devils.
12. Write out clearly the way in which a child is baptized and the words used.
13. Outline the *main* parts of the ceremony of baptism.
14. Describe the work of *one* society which opposes abortion.

Understanding

1. What does the sign of the cross symbolise in baptism?
2. What does the word 'exorcism' mean?

3. Explain what the baptism promises are about.
4. What is the purpose of a white garment in the ceremony?
5. What does the paschal candle represent?
6. Why are God's people in the New Testament sometimes called the Bride of Christ?
7. Explain what is meant by a 'procured abortion'?
8. Explain in your own words what is meant by the words 'set this child free from original sin'.
9. What is the purpose of having god-parents at baptism?
10. What is the purpose of the second anointing with oil at a baptism?
11. Make a pictorial summary of the use of water, oil, a white garment, and a candle in the sacrament of baptism, to show that you understand *why* they are used.
12. Explain how the ceremony of baptism emphasises a new birth and eternal life.

Evaluation

1. Explain the purpose of the teaching authority of the Catholic Church and give the reasons why this purpose is sometimes misunderstood. Do you think these reasons are justified?
2. What are the most frequent objections which are made about the teaching of the Catholic Church on contraception. (Use Appendix B, No. 8). What conclusions have you come to about this teaching?
3. Outline some popular arguments in favour of abortion, and then answer them using information from SPUC or LIFE.
4. Some people think that children should not be baptized if their parents do not intend to bring them up in the practice of the Catholic faith. What is your opinion on this?

FURTHER READING

THE ROMAN CATHOLIC CEREMONY

1. *You Gather a People:* pages 22-28.
2. *A Child for You* (Bavidge).
3. *The Illustrated Catechism:* question 35: supplement page ix.
4. *Focus on Baptism* (Wilkinson).

CHRISTIAN RESPECT FOR HUMAN LIFE

1. *Framework* (Christianity and Life): chapters 9, 10.
2. *Facing the Issues:* chapter 5.
3. *Christian Way:* Book 3, chapter 8.
4. *Revise Religious Studies:* pages 124-134 (Family Planning): pages 149-150 (Abortion).
5. *Real Questions:* chapter 3.
6. *Frontiers:* unit 14 — Medicine.
7. *Problems of Christian Living:* chapter 3, pages 40-42.
8. *Teacher's Reference: R.E. Scheme for Secondary Schools:* Year 4: pages 57-63; Year 5: pages 32-37.

4.2 MARRIAGE

(A) THE SACRAMENT OF MARRIAGE IN THE ROMAN CATHOLIC CHURCH

'The love of man and woman is made holy in the Sacrament of Marriage, and becomes the mirror of your everlasting love.' (Preface of the Wedding Mass)

This quotation from one of the prefaces for the Wedding Mass summarises what marriage is, and what the sacrament of marriage is for. Marriage is a solemn contract between a man and a woman who love each other. The marriage contract is made holy in the sacrament. A Christian marriage reflects God who is love. The love of God is shown in the life of Jesus who gave his life for God's people. St Paul compared the love of a man for his wife with the love of Christ for his Church: *'Husbands, love your wives just as Christ loved the Church and gave his life for it.'* (Ephesians 5:25)

The rite, or ceremony, of marriage develops the idea that the couple express their love and service of God through their love and service for each other: *'...this love can lead the spouses (the couple) to God with powerful effect and can aid and strengthen them in the sublime office of being a father or a mother.'* (Constitution of the Church in the Modern World — Para 48)

The ceremony of marriage is basically very simple. Ideally, it will take place as part of the Mass, as do other sacraments.

The Greeting

The bride and groom are welcomed by the priest before the Mass begins. It is a sign that the whole congregation and parish want them to know that they share in the joy of the happy occasion. After the Mass has begun, the priest will welcome the congregation to join in the celebration of the marriage.

The Homily (Sermon)

There is a homily at a wedding Mass. The priest will talk about the meaning of Christian marriage. He will mention the dignity of married love and how this will help the couple to grow closer to God through each other. The priest also talks about the responsibilities of marriage.

The Marriage Ceremony

After the homily, the marriage takes place. The priest questions the couple individually. The purpose of this questioning is to make sure that the bride and groom understand the responsibility they are about to accept:
1. 'Have you come to give yourself to each other, freely and without reservation?'
2. 'Will you love and honour each other for life?'
3. 'Will you accept children lovingly from God?'

These questions mean that the couple publicly declare that they understand what the responsibilities of marriage are, and that they are free to undertake them.

The Marriage Vows

This is the actual moment of the Sacrament. The couple make vows to each other. Each says in turn:

I (name) do take thee (name) to be my lawful wedded wife/husband, to have and to hold from this day forward, for better for worse, for richer, for poorer, in sickness and in health, to love and to cherish, till death do us part.

Acceptance of Consent and Blessing

It is essential in the Catholic marriage ceremony that a priest is present. He represents the people of God, the Church, and accepts a mutual consent of the bride and groom with these words:

'You have declared your consent before the Church. May the Lord in his goodness strengthen your consent and fill you both with his blessings. What God has joined together let no man put asunder.'

Exchange of rings

The rings are blessed with the words:

'May the Lord bless these rings which you give to each other as a sign of your love and fidelity.'

The bridegroom places the ring on his wife's finger and says:

'Take this ring as a sign of my love and fidelity in the name of the Father and of the Son and of the Holy Spirit.'

The ring is 'a sign of love and fidelity'. The couple have promised themselves to each other in love as a permanent and exclusive (admitting no other partners) relationship. The ring is a token of their promise to each other.

The Marriage (Nuptial) Blessing

The blessing is given after the 'Our Father' of the Mass has been said. The priest approaches the bride and says:

'Let us pray that God will bless this woman, give her love and peace, may her husband recognise that she is his equal and be the heir with him to the life of grace. May he always honour her and love her as Christ loves his bride the Church. Keep them faithful to you and to each other and let them be living examples of Christian life.'

The ideas in this blessing bring out the two important themes of Catholic marriage:

1. That a husband's human love for his wife is a model of the love which Christ has for God's people — the Church.
2. That marriage is a relationship based on a faithfulness which is plain for all to see.

Signing of the Marriage Register

There are civil requirements for a marriage. A register must be signed, a marriage certificate given. The priest may be an authorised registrar. If not, the Registrar must be present.

The meaning of the Sacrament of Marriage

▶ **marriage is a sign for all to see**
▶ **marriage involves a life-long relationship**
▶ **marriage is exclusive — it demands faithfulness to one person**
▶ **marriage is life-giving and it involves responsible parenthood**

A marriage is a public affair, because marriage is lived out in the local community. Marriage is a *sign* (sacrament) for the Church because God's love is reflected in the love which husband and wife have for each other.

Marriage in the Christian tradition is a *life-long commitment* of one partner to the other, and is based on the teaching of Jesus about the permanence of marriage. In the Catholic Church, only an annulment, or death of one partner, frees a person to marry again. Marriage is *life-giving* because love is life-giving. When a person is loved and praised he or she grows in self-confidence; when a person is criticized, he or she shrinks in character, and becomes aggressive or loses confidence. The love exchange in sex is life-giving because it has the potential to create new human life. Sex promotes the growth of the human race. Families develop from the loving relationship of married couples.

The signs in the marriage ceremony itself are the *marriage vows*, the *exchange of rings*, and the *blessing*. These signs underline the meaning of a Catholic marriage:

▶ **sacrament**
▶ **permanent** (indissoluble)
▶ **exclusive** (faithful)
▶ **life-giving** (fruitful)

(B) THEMES AND PROBLEMS RELATING TO MARRIAGE

New Testament Teaching

The teaching contained in the New Testament about marriage was given to two different groups of people:

1. To *Jews* who already had definite laws concerning marriage.
2. To *New Christians* whose background might be pagan and whose customs concerning marriage were different from Christian values.

Jesus was questioned on the subjects of divorce and adultery in Jewish society, with reference to the law of Moses. In the Sermon on the Mount, he teaches the way of love which is his life's work, so when he talks about the Commandments and Jewish Law, he shows the people how they can do better than just keep the Law:

> *'You have heard that it was said, ''Do not commit adultery.'' But now I tell you: anyone who looks at a woman and wants to possess her is guilty of committing adultery with her in his heart. So if your right eye causes you to sin, take it out and throw it away! It is much better for you to lose part of your body than to have your whole body thrown into hell. If your right hand causes you to sin, cut it off and throw it away! It is much better for you to lose one of your limbs than for your whole body to go into hell.'*
>
> *Matthew 5:27-30*

© Carlos Reyes

This does not sound very loving! But the Jews would be used to the exaggeration of the rabbis' style of argument. What is understood by the argument Jesus uses here, is that nothing ought to be allowed to break the **faithful** and **exclusive** bond of married love. The teaching brings out the fact that adultery begins in very little ways, even by a look.

Concerning divorce, Jesus taught:

> *'It is also said, "Anyone who divorces his wife must give her a written notice of divorce." But now I tell you: if a man divorces his wife, for any cause other than her unfaithfulness, then he is guilty of making her commit adultery if she marries again; and the man who marries her commits adultery also.'*
>
> *Matthew 5:31-32*

Jesus underlines in these words the **permanence** of marriage. By contrast, although Jesus condemns unfaithfulness and divorce in his teaching, his attitude towards those who are unfaithful illustrates another aspect of Jesus' ministry which was to preach **the way of forgiveness**.

John 8:1-11

'Then everyone went home, but Jesus went to the Mount of Olives. Early the next morning he went back to the Temple. All the people gathered round him, and he sat down and began to teach them. The teachers of the Law and the Pharisees brought in a woman who had been caught committing adultery, and they made her stand before them all. "Teacher," they said to Jesus, "this woman was caught in the very act of committing adultery. In our Law Moses commanded that such a woman must be stoned to death. Now, what do you say?" They said this to trap Jesus, so that they could accuse him. But he bent over and wrote on the ground with his finger.

As they stood there asking him questions, he straightened himself up and said to them, "Whichever one of you has committed no sin may throw the first stone at her." Then he bent over again and wrote on the ground. When they heard this, they all left, one by one, the older ones first. Jesus was left alone, with the woman still standing there. He straightened himself up and said to her, "Where are they? Is there no one left to condemn you?"

"No one, sir," she answered.

"Well, then," Jesus said, "I do not condemn you either. Go, but do not sin again".'

Jesus clearly does not condemn the woman but he adds: *'Go, but do not sin again.'* His judgement of the woman does not contradict his teaching about adultery.

In the early Church, Paul had to encourage new Christians who were struggling with the high moral values of their new religion. His teaching on marriage and family life, however, is not out of place even after twenty centuries of Christianity.

Paul knew that Corinth, a Greek city, was famous for its immorality, so he reminded the Corinthian Christians that they were baptized and the Spirit of God was with them.

> *'Avoid immorality. Any other sin a man commits does not affect his body; but the man who is guilty of sexual immorality sins against his own body. Don't you know that your body is the temple of the Holy Spirit, who lives in you and who was given to you by God? You do not belong to yourselves but to God; he bought you for a price. So use your bodies for God's glory.'*
>
> *1 Corinthians 6:18-20*

Paul warns the people against sexual immorality because they have a new status as Christians. In Chapter 7 of his first letter to the Corinthians, Paul emphasises the **exclusiveness** of marriage.

> *'Every man should have his own wife, and every woman should have her own husband. A man should fulfil his duty as a husband, and a woman should fulfil her duty as a wife, and each should satisfy the other's needs. A wife is not the master of her own body, but her husband is; in the same way a husband is not the master of his own body, but his wife is.'*
>
> *1 Corinthians 7:2-4*

He goes on to say that within a marriage, sexual activity is not only normal, but necessary and human:

> *'Do not deny yourselves to each other, unless you first agree to do so for a while in order to spend your time in prayer; but then resume normal marital relations. In this way you will be kept from giving in to Satan's temptation because of your lack of self-control.'*
>
> *1 Corinthians 7:5*

Paul also comments on divorce:

> *'For married people I have a command which is not my own but the Lord's: a wife must not leave her husband; but if she does, she must remain single or else be reconciled to her husband: and a husband must not divorce his wife.'*
>
> *1 Corinthians 7:10-11*

Finally, he deals with a local problem about married people who find their lives difficult because one has become a Christian and the other is still a pagan. He makes it clear, however, that he is not quoting the teaching of Jesus, but giving his own opinion:

> *'To the others I say (I, myself, not the Lord): if a Christian man has a wife who is an unbeliever and she agrees to go on living with him, he must not divorce her.'*
>
> *1 Corinthians 7:12*

Paul mentions the marks of a Christian household and family life when he writes to the Christians of Colossae (the Colossians).

> *'Wives, submit to your husbands, for that is what you should do as Christians. Husbands, love your wives and do not be harsh with them. Children, it is your Christian duty to obey your parents always, for that is what pleases God. Parents, do not irritate your children, or they will become discouraged.'*
>
> *Colossians 3:18-21*

The teaching of Paul echoes the work of Jesus clearly when he emphasises the love of the Christian household and the love and forgiveness of family life.

Summary of New Testament Teaching

Teaching on personal relationships, marriage and family life is positive. It emphasises:

▶ **the way of love**
▶ **the way of forgiveness**

Problems and breakdown of marriage

Problems about the breakdown of marriage reflect the values of the sacrament in the following way:

▶ marriage is a *permanent* relationship but *divorce* occurs;
▶ marriage is an *exclusive* relationship but *adultery* occurs;
▶ marriage is *life-giving* relationship but *contraception* and *abortion* occur.

Breakdown of marriage, and divorce

> *'We must reach out with love — the love of Christ — to those who know the pain of failure in marriage; to those who know the loneliness of bringing up a family on their own; to those whose family life is dominated by tragedy or by illness of mind or body.'*
>
> *Pope John Paul II*
> *— In York on May 31st 1982*

The Pope outlines the main causes of breakdown in marriage. They are:

▶ **failure** — meaning breakdown in communication caused by selfishness, argument, neglect, resentment etc.
▶ **tragedy** — accidents or sudden death, loss of income, redundancy, unemployment etc.
▶ **illness** — when one partner may become a real burden to other, either physically or mentally.

The Divorce Law Reform Act of 1969 said that 'irretrievable breakdown' was sufficient for a civil divorce to be granted. The breakdown could be shown by adultery, unreasonable action (violence etc.), desertion or separation. The civil divorce is not recognised by the Catholic Church. There is sometimes misunderstanding about annulment in the Catholic Church. An enquiry into the marriage may show that there was no real marriage made in the first place e.g. one partner may have had no intention of having any children, and the marriage was never fully consummated after the ceremony. Annulment is the result of a very specialised form of enquiry into marriage.

The reason for the Catholic insistence on the permanence of marriage can be found in these words:

> *'Let us not forget that God's love for his people, Christ's love for the Church, is everlasting and cannot be broken and the covenant between a man and a woman joined in Christian marriage is as indissoluble and irrevocable as this love.'*
>
> *Pope John Paul*

(*Note:* indissoluble = permanent;
irrevocable = cannot be broken.)

Not all Christians agree with this point of view. They do agree on the serious spiritual bond of marriage, but they interpret Jesus' teaching on divorce in different ways. The Church of England recognises that divorce gives some kind of legal security to families who are divided. However, there is no general permission for people to marry again in church. Some Church of England ministers feel that they ought to be allowed to marry divorced persons in church, especially if they are the innocent party in a divorce. A general kind of solution is found by advising the divorced person to marry in a registry office and then go to church for prayers of blessing on the marriage. Divorced persons can get permission to receive Communion in some circumstances.

The Free Churches will generally allow divorced persons to marry again in church.

Sexual relations outside marriage

This includes sex before marriage, and adultery. It violates the promise of faithfulness within marriage. In the case of unmarried people it fails to be the sign of the sacrament. For these reasons, the Catholic Church and other Christian groups forbid sexual relations outside marriage. There are some Christians who would not think it was wrong for an engaged couple to have sex because they intend to marry, but the Catholic Church would not approve of this view.

Responsible parenthood

Family planning which involves artificial or chemical methods of contraception, and which includes an acceptance of the principle of abortion, is not in keeping with the Church's teaching on family life. *'The love of husband and wife in God's plan leads beyond itself and new life is generated, a family is born.'* (Pope John Paul II)

The Catholic Church encourages responsible parenthood and advises a natural method of planning the birth of children. *'The Church is certainly aware of the many complex problems which couples in many countries face today in their task of transmitting life in a responsible way.'* The Christian Family in the Modern World — Paragraph 31)

(*The particular issues of contraception and abortion are discussed in Unit 4.1 — Baptism*)

CONCLUSION

The Catholic Church takes a firm stand on many issues concerning marriage. Many people disagree with its points of view. Christian Churches as a whole are not agreed on the difficult issues of divorce, remarriage, contraception, abortion, and sex outside marriage. However, the teaching of the Catholic Church rests on the very positive teaching that:

▶ **marriage is a sign and sacrament for the world**
▶ **marriage is an exclusive relationship**
▶ **marriage is a life-long relationship**
▶ **marriage is life-giving**

QUESTIONS

Investigation

1. Write out the formula of the marriage vows.
2. Write out the nuptial blessing in your own words.
3. What are the civil requirements for a marriage?
4. Mention *three* problems which arise in marriages and select an example of each from a newspaper or magazine.
5. What is the main condition for a civil divorce described in the Divorce Law Reform Act.
6. What are the questions which the priest asks before the marriage vows are pronounced?
7. Outline the teaching of Jesus on marriage and divorce in the Sermon on the Mount.
8. Select *two* points of the teaching of Paul on sexual morality, and illustrate them with recent cases from a newspaper.
9. What is the teaching of the Catholic Church on sexual relationships outside marriage?
10. Describe the sacrament of marriage within the Mass.

Understanding

1. Suggest *two* points which ought to be part of the homily at a Wedding Mass, and explain why they are important.
2. Explain the role of the priest at a wedding in the Catholic Church.
3. What sign do the rings have at a wedding ceremony?
4. Explain the terms 'irrevocable' and 'indissoluble' as they apply to the marriage bond.
5. Explain in your own words the phrase 'responsible parenthood'.
6. What was the attitude of Jesus towards the woman caught in adultery?
7. Why do Christians consider the teaching of Paul on family life to be of importance?
8. How can failure, tragedy and illness lead to the breakdown of a marriage? Give an example of each cause of breakdown.

Evaluation

1. Develop the following opinions about marriage in your own words: Marriage is a sacrament; a life-long relationship; an exclusive relationship; and a life-giving relationship.
2. Outline the variety of Christian opinion about divorce and second marriages in Church, and then give your own conclusion with evidence to support your views.
3. What kinds of behaviour contradict the meaning and purpose of marriage?
4. In what ways do you think the ceremony of marriage supports the teaching on marriage which is given in the New Testament?

FURTHER READING

THE ROMAN CATHOLIC CEREMONY

1. *You Gather a People:* pages 86-96.
2. *Take My Hand* (Bavidge).
3. *The Illustrated Catechism:* chapters 53-58.
4. *Teacher's Reference: R.E. Scheme for Secondary Schools:* Year 5: pages 30-31.
5. *Focus on Marriage* (Wilkinson).

THEMES AND PROBLEMS RELATING TO MARRIAGE

1. *Framework:* chapters 2, 3, 6, 7, 8.
2. *Facing the Issues:* chapter 4.
3. *Christian Way:* Book 3, chapter 9.
4. *Revise Religious Studies:* pages 119-123.
5. *Real Questions:* chapters 6, 7.
6. *Frontiers:* unit 2: Love, marriage and sex; unit 3: Family; unit 4: Divorce.
7. *Problems of Christian Living:* chapter 3.
8. *The Illustrated Catechism:* supplement: pages xi, xii.
9. *Teacher's Reference: R.E. Scheme for Secondary Schools:* Year 5: pages 14-16, 23-26.

CHRISTIAN VOCATION

5.1 DISCIPLESHIP: THE SACRAMENT OF CONFIRMATION

The First Pentecost

When the day of Pentecost came, all the believers were gathered together in one place. Suddenly there was a noise from the sky which sounded like a strong wind blowing, and it filled the whole house where they were sitting. Then they saw what looked like tongues of fire which spread out and touched each person there. They were filled with the Holy Spirit and began to talk in other languages, as the Spirit enabled them to speak. (Acts 2:1-4)

Courage, strength and witness

When Jesus was crucified all his disciples fled. John came to stand at the foot of the cross with Mary, but the others stayed away. Only the women went to the tomb. It was they who found the stone rolled away and received the message that Jesus had risen from the dead. The eleven apostles (for Judas had hung himself) stayed behind locked doors because they were afraid. They were terrified that someone would recognise them and inform on them to the Jewish Sanhedrin and the Romans. Jesus appeared to them during the days between Easter and Pentecost. At this time he would say to them: *'Peace be with you' and 'Do not be afraid.'*

St Mark tells us: *'He scolded them, because they did not have faith and because they were too stubborn to believe those who had seen him alive.'* (Mark 16:14)

St Luke tells us that Jesus told the eleven: *'And I myself will send upon you what my Father has promised. But you must wait in the city until the power from above comes down upon you.'* (Luke 24:49)

On the day of Pentecost, the 'Power from on high', was sent upon the apostles. This power was the *Holy Spirit* which transformed their *fear* into *courage*. This courage gave them strength to *witness* to all the people the fact that Jesus had risen from the dead. For example, Peter said to the people on the day of Pentecost:

'Each one of you must turn away from his sins and be baptized in the name of Jesus Christ, so that your sins will be forgiven; and you will receive God's gift, the Holy Spirit.'

Acts 2:38

The Holy Spirit altered the daily lives of the apostles. It set them aside for the very special task. They suffered a great deal for taking the Good News of the resurrection to the people.

Confirmation — sacrament of initiation

Confirmation seals a Christian with the gift of the Holy Spirit, that same Holy Spirit which came down upon the apostles at Pentecost. The Holy Spirit is given to a Christian at baptism just as Peter said, and in the Sacrament of Confirmation the ceremony of initiation into the Christian family is completed. The Holy Spirit is given to set people aside for a special task to perform in life. It gives them the *strength and courage* to be a *witness* to Christ whom they firmly believe is their Saviour. They have the ability to show in their daily lives that they are convinced Jesus frees them from sin and gives them eternal life through his own resurrection.

Fulfilment of baptism

In the ceremony of confirmation, the faith which was professed in baptism is renewed. This involves a rejection of all that is evil; belief in God who is Father, Son and Holy Spirit; and belief in the main teachings of the Church concerning the Communion of Saints, the forgiveness of sin, the resurrection of the body, and life everlasting.

In baptism, the Christian is anointed twice, and in confirmation the anointing is confirmed in a special way. The anointing with chrism in confirmation strengthens a person against the temptations of evil and gives them the power to act as a witness to Christ in their daily lives. Peter and the other apostles were able to be real disciples after they received the gift of the Holy Spirit. Jesus had taught them, and given them the example they needed, through his own life and death. After Pentecost day, they had his Spirit in which to act, to speak, to suffer and eventually to die knowing that the power of his resurrection was also theirs.

This is true for every Christian who is baptized into the Christian family, fed with the bread of life in the Eucharist and confirmed in the Spirit of Jesus' love and service. The Catholic Church summarises the effect of confirmation like this:

'By the Sacrament of Confirmation, Christians are more perfectly bound to the Church, they are true witnesses to Christ, more strictly obliged to spread the faith by word and deed.'

Lumen Gentium: Vatican II

Pope John Paul II spoke about confirmation in the following way:

'You will hear the words of the Church spoken over you, calling upon the Holy Spirit to confirm your faith, to seal you in his love, to strengthen you for his service. You will then take your place among fellow Christians throughout the world, full citizens now of the People of God. You will witness to the truth of the Gospel in the name of Jesus Christ. You will live your lives in such a way as to make holy all human life. Together with all the confirmed, you will become living stones in the Cathedral of Peace. Indeed you are called by God to be instruments of his peace.'

The Sacrament of CONFIRMATION

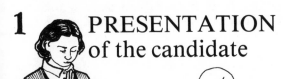

1 PRESENTATION
of the candidate

2 RENEWAL of
baptismal vows

'This is our faith. This is the faith of the
Church. We are proud to profess it in
Christ Jesus.'

3 LAYING on of HANDS

'Give them the Spirit of wisdom, courage,
understanding, right judgement,
knowledge, reverence, wonder and awe.'

4 ANOINTING
with chrism

'Be sealed with the gift
of the Holy Spirit.'

PREPARATION FOR THE SACRAMENT OF CONFIRMATION

Parish programmes in preparation for the Sacrament of Confirmation vary, but they will all include:

1. Instruction which renews the basic Christian faith professed in baptism, and prepares for the Ceremony of Confirmation. This is often given at school.

2. Meetings for parents. The purpose of these is to remind parents about the meaning of confirmation and Christian vocation. There is a renewal of their own confirmation and Christian vocation. They may be given written notes to take home and think about. Another meeting will be concerned with practical details like sponsors, details of baptism for the confirmation card, and other aspects of the ceremony.

3. Catechists. Many parishes ask for people to take small groups of young people to prepare for the Sacrament.

4. Service of Reconciliation. The parish priest will make every effort to provide the opportunity for the young people to receive the Sacrament of Penance before confirmation.

5. Day of Preparation. Sometimes it is possible to have a whole day of preparation which will include a celebration of Mass.

6. The Confirmation Card. This requires the following details:

▶ **confirmation name**
▶ **name of confirmand** (the person being confirmed)
▶ **place of baptism**
▶ **date of baptism**
▶ **name of sponsor**

THE SACRAMENT OF CONFIRMATION

Confirmation normally takes place during Mass. The Sacrament of Confirmation is given by the bishop (or a priest delegated by him) between the Liturgy of the Word and Liturgy of the Eucharist. When a number of people are going to be confirmed, the bishop will delegate a priest to assist him. A priest may confirm anyway in an emergency.

The Presentation of the Candidate
This varies from parish to parish and depends on the number of people to be confirmed. The names of the candidates for confirmation can be read out and each person answers his name by standing up so that all can see. Later, they go to the bishop for the actual Sacrament of Confirmation.

The Renewal of Baptismal Promises
There is a renewal of various aspects of baptism in this sacrament. One of these occurs when the candidates renew the promises made at baptism. There is a rejection of all that is evil and a profession of faith. These promises take the form of question and answer. It is worth comparing the questions with an outline of the Apostles' Creed. These promises at baptism and confirmation are like an enrolment into the Catholic Church.

The Laying on of Hands
This sign is an ancient form of calling down the power and blessing of God upon someone. It was often done in Old Testament times to consecrate a prophet or a

king. The laying on of hands sets the person apart for a special calling or task in life. In the Sacrament of Confirmation the candidate is given a vocation to be a witness to Christ's values and teachings. Jesus imposed his hands on people. He gave his apostles his authority to do the same. The bishop follows their example when he raises his hands over those to be confirmed.

The Anointing with Chrism

The bishop sits, wearing the mitre, and the candidate kneels before him. The confirmation card is given to the priest who reads out the name of the candidate and the confirmation name. A special confirmation name is not necessary, but it still may be taken. The candidate's Christian name is quite sufficient. The sponsor places his right hand on the shoulder of the candidate. The bishop lays his hand on the head of the candidate and then anoints with the oil of chrism, a sign of the cross on the forehead with the words, *'(Name) be sealed with the gift of the Holy Spirit.'* The response made is '**Amen**'.

The bishop then gives the Sign of Peace by saying, *'Peace be with you.'* The candidate replies '**And also with you.**'

The Mass continues with the Liturgy of the Eucharist. At the end of the Mass there is a special blessing.

Final Blessing and Dismissal

A special blessing is given, after each part of the blessing, the people answer '**Amen**'.

THE SIGNS USED IN CONFIRMATION

The Imposition (Laying On) of Hands

This is a sign that power and strength are being given. The bishop extends his hands over the candidate for confirmation, and this reminds them that the Holy Spirit will come to them in power and strength, just as he came to the apostles on Pentecost day. He says:

> *'...Send down your Holy Spirit upon them, to be their helper and guide. Give them the spirit of **wisdom** and **understanding**, the spirit of **right judgement**, and **courage**, the spirit of **knowledge** and **reverence**. Fill them with the spirit of **wonder** and **awe** in your presence...'*

These gifts are given in confirmation and the sign used is the laying on of hands.

The Oil of Chrism

The bishop signs the candidate's forehead with the sign of the cross in oil, the oil of chrism. The religious meaning of oil is very important. In the Old Testament, priests, prophets and kings were anointed. It is an important sign that a person is being set aside for a special task. Oil has healing qualities — for example, the Samaritan used oil to heal the man's wounds in the famous parable of Jesus. Oil is also used to strengthen athletes and make them supple.

In confirmation, a person is strengthened by the Holy Spirit to meet all the difficulties, dangers and challenges of Christian life. The oil of chrism is olive oil mixed with balsam, a sweet-smelling perfume. This perfume itself represents the loving relationship which a Christian has with God the Father, by having a place in his family. It is the gift of the Holy Spirit which seals this close relationship. *'Be sealed with the gift of the Holy Spirit.'*

The Sign of the Cross

The cross is the special sign of the Christian. It is the mark of ownership with which God approves a person. The sign of the cross is used in baptism and confirmation to seal the Christian in the love of God, by the power of the Holy Spirit.

The Sign of Peace

The symbol often used to represent the Holy Spirit is the dove. Doves are released on international occasions to symbolise the peace which the nations wish to express to each other. The Holy Spirit brings a person peace with God and with others. The sign of peace, using a form of words, is given immediately after the anointing with chrism. It is a reminder of the greeting which Jesus gave his apostles when they were so afraid: *'Peace be with you.'*

The Naming

In the Bible, God always called people by name before giving them a task to do. When he gave a special task, he always gave the necessary strength and talents for that task. In confirmation, at the moment of giving the sacrament, the bishop calls the candidate by name. It is a sign that a task is being given, a task to be a witness to Christ. In the scriptures, there are a number of examples of people whose names were changed after they accepted God's call. The candidate will already have a Christian name and this is sufficient, but many still prefer to choose another name for confirmation. It is not necessary, but it may be done. The name is read out to the bishop from the confirmation card.

QUESTIONS

Investigation

1. Give an account of the first Pentecost, emphasising information about the Holy Spirit and describing the nature of the change which took place among the disciples.
2. What were the signs of the Holy Spirit on Pentecost day?
3. Describe the composition of the Great Council of the Jewish Sanhedrin.
4. What were the *two* greetings which Jesus gave to his apostles when he appeared to them after his resurrection?
5. What did Peter want the people to do after he had spoken to them?
6. Describe the special blessings of the Holy Spirit in confirmation.
7. Copy the summary of the effect of confirmation from the Vatican II document.
8. What are the details required on the confirmation card?

9. Describe the *two* ingredients of chrism.
10. Write out the formula of words for the anointing in the Sacrament of Confirmation.
11. Summarise in your own words the extract from Pope John Paul II about confirmation.
12. Select and describe the most important parts of the ceremony of confirmation.

Understanding

1. Suggest *one* reason why the apostles were 'all together' on the day of Pentecost.
2. What does the word 'Pentecost' mean?
3. Explain the effect of the Holy Spirit on the apostles at Pentecost.
4. Why was the gift of tongues especially useful at the time of Pentecost?
5. Why were the apostles so frightened after the crucifixion of Jesus?
6. Explain why the apostles suffered sometimes after they had preached to the people.
7. What is the meaning of the word 'initiation' when it is used to describe a religious event.
8. Explain the purpose and importance of a catechist.
9. How did Jesus comfort his apostles after the resurrection?
10. Write an outline of Catholic faith by using the baptism promises which are renewed at confirmation.
11. Explain the significance of: i) the laying on of hands, and ii) anointing in the Sacrament of Confirmation.
12. Explain the meaning of each of the gifts of the Holy Spirit mentioned in the Sacrament of Confirmation. What other gifts of the Holy Spirit can you think of?

Evaluation

1. What is the evidence that the gift of the Holy Spirit *encouraged* the apostles; *strengthened* their faith, and made them *witnesses* to the Good News?
2. Why is it important that Christians should *live* what they *believe*? Give evidence for your answer.
3. Evaluate the life and work of a Catholic you admire, and say what gifts of the Holy Spirit they put into action. Give evidence to justify your opinion of this person.

FURTHER READING

1. *You Gather a People*: pages 29-35.
2. *Come Holy Spirit* (Bavidge).
3. *The Illustrated Catechism*: question 37: supplement pages ix, x.
4. *Focus on Confirmation* (Wilkinson).

5.2 CHRISTIAN SERVICE

> *'Surely you know that you are God's temple and that God's Spirit lives in you! So if anyone destroys God's temple, God will destroy him. For God's temple is holy, and you yourselves are his temple.'*
>
> 1 Corinthians 3:16-17

St Paul wrote these words to one of the first groups of Christians. Now that these people had become members of God's family, they were God's stewards in the world, and must act on his behalf. Paul uses two great metaphors to explain to them how God was calling them as 'fellow workers'. He calls the people *'God's field'* suggesting that they were crops which God wanted to yield a good harvest. He calls them *'God's building'* meaning that together they will do all the things God wants for his people.

Every Christian is **called** by God. Another word for a 'calling' is a 'vocation', and the Christian is given a vocation to use his/her life and talents as a member of God's family. A Christian acts like a brother or sister of Christ.

Jesus told the parable of the talents in order to explain the responsibility which each person has, and will be judged upon at the last day. In the parable, as told by Matthew (Matthew 25:14-30), the servants have to account to their master for the use they have made of the money with which they had been entrusted.

(*Note on translations:* Some translations have 'five talents', others have 'five thousand gold coins'. The translators are using either the roman coinage — talents — or the modern equivalent in gold. There is a similar parable in Luke 22:11-27 where the coinage used is minas, translated as 'pounds'. It is the meaning which matters — that the servants are trusted by the master, and given a special responsibility.)

The Parable of the Talents
(Matthew 25:14-30)
'Once there was a man who was about to go on a journey; he called his servants and put them in charge of his property. He gave to each one according to his ability: to one he gave five thousand gold coins, to another he gave two thousand, and to another he gave one thousand. Then he left on his journey.

The servant who had received five thousand coins went at once and invested his money and earned another five thousand. In the same way the servant who had received two thousand coins earned another two thousand. But the servant who had received one thousand coins went off, dug a hole in the ground and hid his master's money.

After a long time the master of those servants came back and settled accounts with them. The servant who had received five thousand coins came in and handed over the other five thousand. "You gave me five thousand coins, sir," he said. "Look! Here are another five thousand that I have earned." "Well done, you good and faithful servant!" said his master. "You have been faithful in managing small amounts, so I will put you in charge of large amounts. Come on in and share my happiness!"

Then the servant who had been given two thousand coins came in and said, "You gave me two thousand coins, sir. Look! Here are another two thousand that I have earned." "Well done, you good and faithful servant!" said his master. "You have been faithful in managing small amounts, so I will put you in charge of large amounts. Come on in and share my happiness!"

Then the servant who had received one thousand coins came in and said, "Sir, I know you are a hard man; you reap harvests where you did not sow, and you gather crops where you did not scatter seed. I was afraid, so I went off and hid your money in the ground. Look! Here is what belongs to you."

"You bad and lazy servant!" his master said. "You knew, did you, that I reap harvests where I did not sow, and gather crops where I did not scatter seed? Well, then, you should have deposited my money in the bank, and I would have received it all back with interest when I returned. Now, take the money away from him and give it to the one who has ten thousand coins. For to every person who has something, even more will be given, and he will have more than enough; but the person who has nothing, even the little that he has will be taken away from him. As for this useless servant — throw him outside in the darkness; there he will cry and grind his teeth".'

Christians who belong to the Roman Catholic Church have a choice of three ways in which to carry out the vocation they have received in baptism and confirmation. They can carry out their responsibilities as a single or married lay person; they can choose to join a religious order or congregation; or some men may be called to be a deacon, priest or bishop.

(A) LAY MINISTRIES

The term 'lay' means someone who is baptized and is a full member of the Roman Catholic Church. As a layman or laywoman, this person has responsibilities to carry out. Priests and members of religious orders have added responsibilities which are part of their particular calling. These differences do not mean that a lay person is a second class Christian! The laity have their own important calling in the Christian life. Lay people are set aside to love and serve God just as much as a religious or a priest. Their love of God is expressed in *prayer* and *service*. Lay people are called to be like Jesus so they share in the fact that he was priest, prophet and king to God's people. When a person is baptized and confirmed he/she is anointed to share in the mission or work of Jesus himself. The duties and opportunities of lay people were the topics discussed by the Synod of Bishops in 1987.

Lay people bring the word of God to others by reading in church, by catechising, by missionary work, by teaching etc. They also bring holiness to others by the example of their lives, by their prayer, by the example of their public worship — in prayer groups, or during retreat days etc.

Lay people act as stewards of the world which God has made, by using their talents to improve the world, to make it perfect. They have a duty to be aware of the world around them with all its faults, for example: unjust ways of governing, lack of human rights, crime, prejudice, violence and addiction to drugs or alcohol.

Jesus instructed his followers to be *salt*, *leaven* and *light* to the world. The sacraments help lay people to develop the love they have for God and their neighbour by bringing them close to Christ and the example he set. People need *faith* to believe that what Christ teaches through the Gospel and Church is true. They need *hope* and *trust* in the promises which Christ has made (for example, *'Where two or three are gathered...', 'Ask and you shall receive...'*)

Most of all, lay people are called to *love* God and their neighbour. The Holy Spirit strengthens a person in faith, hope and love when baptism and confirmation are received.

Everyone has their own special gifts and talents. These gifts show them the way in which their Christian vocation is likely to be fulfilled. Everyone has the *right* to use their talents. Everyone has a *duty* to use their talents, and will be judged on their responsibilities by God himself.

Honesty, *justice*, *sincerity*, *kindness* and *courage* are the characteristics of a Christian. Married people express their holiness in the quality of their married lives, or their family relationships. The same applies to a single person or a widow/widower. The example of a good life influences other people to want to share in that kind of life, and brings them to God. This good example is called being a witness to Christ. So, a Christian is called to:

▶ explain the principles which Christ taught;
▶ defend Christ's teaching;
▶ apply Christ's teachings to the problems of the modern world.

In the modern world, there are people in need of food, drink, clothing, housing, medicine, employment or education. Some may suffer great personal distress, illness, exile (e.g. refugees), or imprisonment. Christians are called to be prepared to give social assistance, publicly or in private. They are also concerned with international programmes which give aid to the weak and the poor of the world.

In a parish, there are many ways in which Christians can carry out their responsibilities by:

▶ supporting the local priest (in a variety of ways);
▶ co-operating in the way the word of God is presented to the parish;
▶ offering whatever special skills they have (whether these are professional or manual);
▶ sharing their problems and experiences (e.g. in discussion);
▶ supporting the projects which the parish has decided to undertake.

Real and practical involvement in the life of the local parish is likely to lead to a knowledge of what is going on in the diocese and of what concerns the whole Church. The lives of Christians are an important influence on the people who live near them and do not belong to any form of organised religion or 'a Church'.

The people of a parish may set up a group or society to deal with certain needs of that parish. Lay people have the right to form such groups, to join existing groups, and to control these groups (e.g. the Society of St Vincent de Paul, the Knights of St Columba, the Catholic Women's League etc.).

LAY PEOPLE ARE CALLED TO

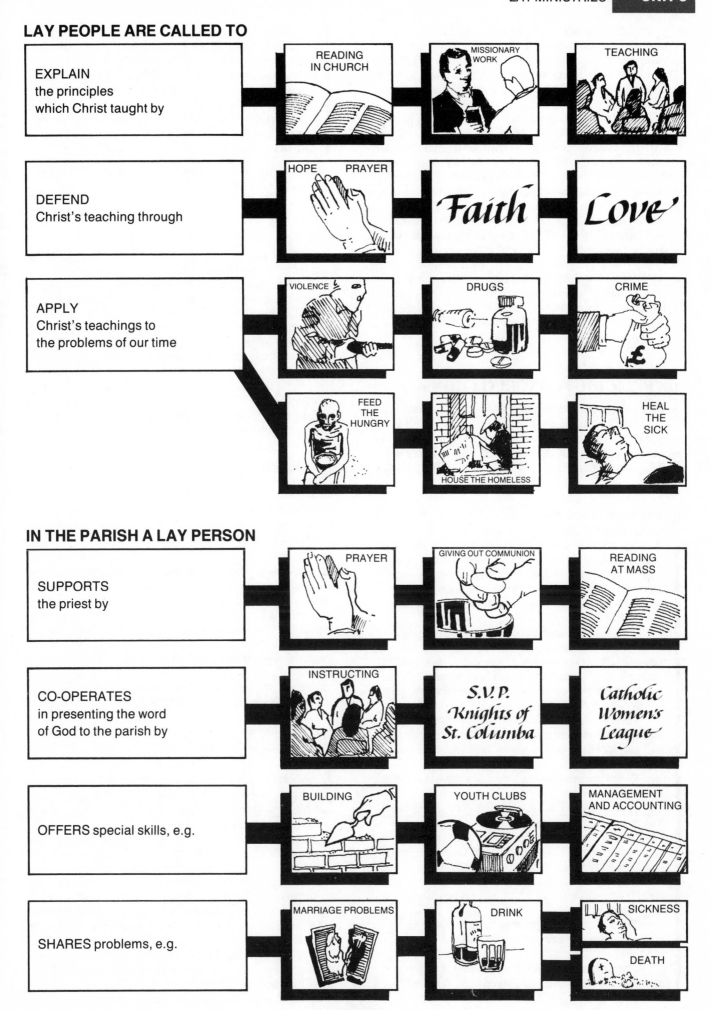

EXPLAIN
the principles
which Christ taught by

READING IN CHURCH

MISSIONARY WORK

TEACHING

DEFEND
Christ's teaching through

HOPE PRAYER

Faith

Love

APPLY
Christ's teachings to
the problems of our time

VIOLENCE

DRUGS

CRIME

FEED THE HUNGRY

HOUSE THE HOMELESS

HEAL THE SICK

IN THE PARISH A LAY PERSON

SUPPORTS
the priest by

PRAYER

GIVING OUT COMMUNION

READING AT MASS

CO-OPERATES
in presenting the word
of God to the parish by

INSTRUCTING

*S.V.P.
Knights of
St. Columba*

*Catholic
Women's
League*

OFFERS special skills, e.g.

BUILDING

YOUTH CLUBS

MANAGEMENT AND ACCOUNTING

SHARES problems, e.g.

MARRIAGE PROBLEMS

DRINK

SICKNESS

DEATH

Parish councils and diocesan councils help to improve communication, so that there is not too much overlap in the service being offered by the local Church. If they are to be effective, these councils need to be an example of the love and service to which Christ trained his disciples.

The training ground for responsible Christian living is the *home*. Parents are the first people to pass on Christian values. Schools continue to develop the qualities which Christ wanted of his followers. Later, the love and service of God is kept alive by the groups which people make for themselves or the societies already existing in the parish.

Christians cannot be effective or fulfil their calling if they do not learn the relative value of material goods. When people make an idol out of money or possessions, they are too concerned with their own needs to notice other people. On the other hand, when Christians value the teachings of Christ, they feel compelled to act on behalf of the needs of other members of God's family, as though for their own brothers and sisters.

(B) RELIGIOUS CONGREGATIONS

Some Christians are called to follow Christ by belonging to a Religious Order or Congregation. The following incident from St Matthew's Gospel contains some important clues about the life of religious congregations in the Catholic Church:

The Rich Young Man
(Matthew 19:16-30)
'Once a man came to Jesus. "Teacher," he asked, "what good thing must I do to receive eternal life?"

"Why do you ask me concerning what is good?" answered Jesus. "There is only One who is good. Keep the Commandments if you want to enter life."

"What Commandments?" he asked.

Jesus answered, "Do not commit murder; do not commit adultery; do not steal; do not accuse anyone falsely; respect your father and your mother; and love your neighbour as you love yourself."

"I have obeyed all these Commandments," the young man replied. "What else do I need to do?"

Jesus said to him, "If you want to be perfect, go and sell all you have and give the money to the poor, and you will have riches in heaven; then come and follow me."

When the young man heard this, he went away sad, because he was very rich.

Jesus then said to his disciples, "I assure you: it will be very hard for rich people to enter the Kingdom of heaven. I repeat: it is much harder for a rich person to enter the Kingdom of God than for a camel to go through the eye of a needle."

When the disciples heard this, they were completely amazed. "Who, then, can be saved?" they asked.

Jesus looked straight at them and answered, "This is impossible for man, but for God everything is possible."

Then Peter spoke up. "Look," he said, "we have left everything and followed you. What will we have?"

Jesus said to them, "You can be sure that when the Son of Man sits on his glorious throne in the New Age, then you twelve followers of mine will also sit on thrones, to rule the twelve tribes of Israel. And everyone who has left houses or brothers or sisters or father or mother or children or fields for my sake, will receive a hundred times more and will be given eternal life. But many who now are first will be last, and many who now are last will be first".'

(Note: Many translations read 'treasure in heaven' instead of 'riches in heaven'.)

Jesus springs a few surprises on several people in this incident. Quite frequently, Jesus showed people that they would have to learn to value things differently if they were going to be his followers. For example, the attitude he showed towards lepers, tax-collectors, prostitutes, Pharisees and other respected people of authority, often surprised his friends. They learned from Jesus to respect the outcasts of their society and to think of them as people who needed help or were lost: the sick need a doctor; the lost need to be found at any cost.

In the incident with the rich young man, there are four mini conversations:

1. The young man doesn't have a problem, but he feels there is something more to life than what he experiences as a good, wealthy Jew. He asks Jesus what he would have to do to win eternal life. Jesus shows him that if he is keeping the Commandments, his life as a good Jew will be sufficient.

2. The young man is inspired by the teaching of Jesus and the example of his life. He makes another enquiry: 'Is there anything else?' Then Jesus invites him to do an extra thing for God — *'to be perfect'*. It would mean becoming like the disciples of Jesus. He would have to give up the privileges of his present way of life. He must sell everything, give to the poor, let his treasure be in heaven, and follow Jesus. However, the young man had great possessions and the invitation was too much for him. He refused the invitation. He was free to do so. Jesus had *invited* — not commanded — him. Jesus made no judgement on his decision. People are quite free to refuse invitations.

3. Jesus takes advantage of the conversation to teach his disciples about the great distraction which possessions can be for a person who may set them up as a rival to God. No possessions will surround a person when they stand before God to account for the way in which they have used their talents. Notice that Jesus does not say it is wrong to be wealthy, but he points out that it is hard to find the balance between working for things and spending time helping people to come close to God. Their attention is divided, and their love is divided. However, there are many examples of very rich people who still consider that their greatest treasure is in heaven. St Thomas More is a good example of such a person. He was Lord Chancellor of England, and a very wealthy man, but he accepted no bribes, and used his position to serve God before everything else.

RELIGIOUS LIFE IN…

CONTEMPLATIVE ORDERS

LEAD A HIDDEN LIFE OF

PRAYER   WORK

IN ENCLOSED ORDERS OF
e.g.

CARMELITES,   CARTHUSIANS,
POOR CLARES   CISTERCIANS
(for women)   (for men)

ST BENEDICT
(c.480-c.550)
The people who joined him formed an Order of monks which spread throughout Europe and still exists today. The lives of members of this Order are based on **prayer** and **work**.

APOSTOLIC ORDERS

LEAD A PUBLIC LIFE OF

PRAYER

SICK   TEACHING   POOR   ELDERLY

COMMUNITY WORK

IN APOSTOLIC ORDERS OF
e.g.

NOTRE DAME   CHRISTIAN
DE NAMUR   BROTHERS
(for women)   (for men)

MOTHER TERESA
of Calcutta is an example of an *apostolic* religious, who cares for the needs of the destitute and dying.

RELIGIOUS MEN AND WOMEN
are consecrated to God
by THREE vows —

POVERTY CHASTITY OBEDIENCE

4. The conversation with Peter follows naturally because Jesus had spoken about *'treasure in heaven'*. In his reply, Jesus speaks about a *'new world'*. First he promises a reward to the twelve who were closest to him. His promise of judging the twelve tribes of Israel would be understood by them in the light of their great Jewish history (their heritage). The promise seems strange to those who are not Jews. The second promise is for everyone: *'anyone who has left houses...will be given eternal life.'*

It is a promise of a great reward and eternal life — *'treasure in heaven'*. However, in case the disciples should misunderstand and think in terms of earthly kingdoms and earthly power, Jesus reminds them: *'Many who now are first will be last, and many who now are last will be first.'*

Jesus said to the rich young man: *'If you want to be perfect, go and sell all you have, and give the money to the poor, and you will have riches in heaven; then come and follow me.'*

A man or woman may choose to belong to a *contemplative* or *apostolic* congregation.

Religious life in a *contemplative* order involves a hidden life of prayer and work. The members have *enclosure* which means that they do not normally go out of the community they have joined. Examples are Carmelites and Poor Clares for women, or Carthusians and Cistercians for men. Each day is broken, several times, by prayer together. This prayer is called the Office of the Church. Work is done on the premises of the Monastery or Convent.

Religious life in an *apostolic* congregation also involves a life of prayer and work, but the work is public — like caring for the sick, the poor, the old, the handicapped; preaching, counselling and education. Examples of apostolic orders are Sisters of Notre Dame de Namur for women and the Christian Brothers for men.

All religious men and women are consecrated to God by *three vows*. These vows are:
- **poverty**
- **chastity**
- **obedience**

The vows are called *evangelical counsels*. Not every Christian feels the special call to consecrate their lives in this way. That is why the vows are called counsels — they are not commands. They are *gifts*.

Poverty means that all personal possessions are available for the needs of the Church and especially for the *poor*. A member of a religious order is not tied down by material possessions and can quickly be available for service anywhere in the world.

Chastity — *'for the sake of the Kingdom of Heaven'* is a gift. It involves developing a personal relationship with Christ. The religious (the person) remains free to serve anyone, anywhere, without conditions and without discrimination.

Obedience involves a complete dedication to God. In the congregation to which they belong, the religious promise obedience to the work of that congregation and to those who hold special authority.

St Thérèse of Lisieux is an example of a *contemplative* nun who prayed specially for the needs of the Church and is now the patron saint of the *missions*. Mother Teresa of Calcutta is an example of an *apostolic* religious who cares for the needs of the destitute and the dying. Both these women were *consecrated* to God at their *profession*. At first, the vows are made for a limited time like a year. Then *final profession* is made. At this time, the vows are made for ever.

QUESTIONS

A) LAY MINISTRIES

Investigation

1. Describe any *three* gifts or talents which a person could use in God's service.
2. Name a parable told by Jesus about using gifts responsibly.
3. Name the sacraments which anoint a person to share in the work and teaching of Jesus.
4. Describe *five* qualities a Christian ought to have.
5. Name *two* organisations which are run by lay people in a parish.
6. Give an example of how someone could share in the work of international aid.
7. Outline the parable of the talents.
8. Describe some problems in our society which need firm action by lay people.

Understanding

1. Explain the meaning of the following phrases which Paul used to describe God's people: i) God's temple; ii) God's field.
2. What does the word 'vocation' mean?
3. Explain the following metaphors used by Jesus to describe his followers: i) salt; ii) leaven; iii) light.
4. Explain the idea that God's people are his stewards.
5. What was the purpose of the Synod of Bishops in 1987?

Evaluation

1. Write a modern story which you think follows the pattern of the parable of the talents.
2. In what sense do you think lay people are called to *explain* the teaching of Christ, to *defend* this teaching, and to *apply* this teaching?
3. Make some suggestions, with reasons, about the kind of training which lay people would need to help them live out their vocation.
4. Do you think lay people should be more active in the Church, and if so, why?
5. How can lay people: i) spread the word of God; ii) give an example of holiness; iii) be good stewards for God?

B) RELIGIOUS CONGREGATIONS

Investigation

1. Write out Jesus' words to the rich young man beginning: 'If you want to be perfect...'
2. Name the *two* main forms of religious order or congregation in the Roman Catholic Church.
3. Give *four* examples of work undertaken by apostolic religious congregations.
4. Name the *three* vows taken by members of many religious orders.
5. Outline the incident of the rich young man as far as Peter's question about the disciples.
6. What are the dangers of wealth as pointed out by Jesus after the rich young man had gone away?
7. Write a short biography of *either* a person who belongs to a contemplative order; *or* a person who belongs to an apostolic congregation.
8. Interview a member of a religious order and ask them to describe a day in their life. Make notes of your interview.

Understanding

1. What is meant by the term 'religious vocation'?
2. In the incident of the rich young man, explain the teaching given by Jesus about wealth.
3. Explain how a very rich person can also be a very good Christian. Give an example.
4. Why are the vows taken by members of religious orders sometimes called 'evangelical counsels'?
5. What does the term 'consecration' mean as it applies to religious life?
6. What does the term 'profession' mean as it applies to religious life?
7. What did Jesus mean by using the phrase 'treasure in heaven'?
8. Explain briefly the difference between a contemplative order and an apostolic congregation.
9. Explain the meaning of *each* of the *three* vows taken by religious men and women.

Evaluation

1. How important is personal wealth in society today?
2. Why do you think so many men and women follow the evangelical counsels and become members of religious orders?
3. Do you think the world needs people like Mother Teresa or Father Damien or any other famous Christian who belongs to a religious order?

FURTHER READING

1. *You Gather a People:* chapter 6.
2. *Christian Belief and Practice:* chapter 12.
3. *Real Questions:* pages 95-96.
4. *The Illustrated Catechism:* questions 98, 99.

5.3 THE SACRAMENT OF HOLY ORDERS

Jesus Calls the First Disciples
(Luke 5:1-11)

'One day Jesus was standing on the shore of Lake Gennesaret while the people pushed their way up to him to listen to the word of God. He saw two boats pulled up on the beach; the fishermen had left them and were washing the nets. Jesus got into one of the boats — it belonged to Simon — and asked him to push off a little from the shore. Jesus sat in the boat and taught the crowd.

When he finished speaking, he said to Simon, "Push the boat out further to the deep water, and you and your partners let down your nets for a catch."

"Master," Simon answered, "we worked hard all night long and caught nothing. But if you say so, I will let down the nets."

They let them down and caught such a large number of fish that the nets were about to break. So they motioned to their partners in the other boat to come and help them. They came and filled both boats so full of fish that the boats were about to sink. When Simon Peter saw what had happened, he fell on his knees before Jesus and said, "Go away from me, Lord! I am a sinful man!"

He and the others with him were all amazed at the large number of fish they had caught. The same was true of Simon's partners, James and John, the sons of Zebedee. Jesus said to Simon, "Don't be afraid; from now on you will be catching men."

They pulled the boats up on the beach, left everything, and followed Jesus.'

Jesus Calls Levi
(Luke 5:27-32)

'After this, Jesus went out and saw a tax collector named Levi, sitting in his office. Jesus said to him, "Follow me." Levi got up, left everything, and followed him.

Then Levi had a big feast in his house for Jesus, and among the guests was a large number of tax collectors and other people. Some Pharisees and some teachers of the Law who belonged to their group complained to Jesus' disciples. "Why do you eat and drink with tax collectors and other outcasts?" they asked.

Jesus answered them, "People who are well do not need a doctor, but only those who are sick. I have not come to call respectable people to repent, but outcasts".'

St Luke describes how Jesus chose his followers. In the first account, Simon the fisherman is invited to change his whole way of life in response to Jesus' words: *'Don't be afraid; from now on you will be catching men.'*

In the second account, Jesus chooses an apostle from the outcasts of his society, a tax-collector — Levi. The important fact is that once the invitation to follow him is given, Levi's whole life is changed: *'Levi got up, left everything, and followed him.'*

There are roughly four conditions to be met before a man can consider asking to be ordained as a priest. He must sincerely want to follow Christ as a priest and be prepared for the kind of life a priest leads. He must have the kind of character which can adapt to the demands of priesthood. Although a priest does not have to be a specially clever man, he must be able to understand the work involved in being a priest. Finally, he must be recommended for the priesthood by a bishop or by his religious superior if he belongs to a religious order.

These four conditions may be summarised as follows:

1. The desire to be a priest.
2. A suitable character for the priesthood.
3. The required intelligence for the studies.
4. A recommendation for the priesthood.

The Deacon (called the 'diaconate')

There is an important stage before a man is ordained to the priesthood. It is called diaconate, and the candidate for the priesthood is called a *deacon* at this stage. For some time before ordination the deacon may help in a parish in the following ways:

1. He may proclaim the Gospel at Mass.
2. He may preach the homily at Mass.
3. He may lead public prayers such as devotions or morning and evening prayer.
4. He may baptize.
5. He may assist at marriages.
6. He may distribute Holy Communion.
7. He may conduct a funeral service.

As a deacon, the candidate has already promised celibacy for life which means that he promises to remain a single man and not marry. Sometimes a married man is ordained a deacon, but most candidates for the priesthood promise celibacy for life. A deacon also has an important duty to care for the people of God. Traditionally, he assisted the bishop at services in other ways. Today, a deacon is given much more parish experience, and the local parish priest will guide his ministry.

THE PRIESTHOOD: CEREMONY OF ORDINATION

Ordination takes place during Mass. The candidate for ordination enters the church with the usual procession of clergy who are going to take part in the ordination, and the Bishop brings up the rear.

The Presentation of the Candidate

The first part of the Mass, the Liturgy of the Word, takes place and then, following the Gospel, the candidate is presented to the Bishop who then gives a homily to explain what is going to happen — *the Bishop's homily*. In this talk, the Bishop points out all the solemn duties which the priest fulfils. He will, as a priest:

1. Offer the Mass.
2. Baptize the people of God.
3. Forgive their sins in the Sacrament of Penance.
4. Anoint the sick.
5. Pray for his people.
6. Be obedient to his bishop.
7. Be a good shepherd to God's people and care for them.

Examination of the Candidate

After the homily, the Bishop examines the candidate. Some of the questions are:

— 'Will you fulfil the office of a priest, assisting the bishops, to care for God's people?'
— 'Will you celebrate the sacraments faithfully?'
— 'Will you preach the Gospel and explain the Catholic faith?'
— 'Will you consecrate your life to God for the salvation of his people?'

At this point in the ceremony, the candidate has announced publicly his intention to serve God as a priest. The candidate then places his hands between the hands of the Bishop, which is a very ancient sign of giving obedience to someone. A promise of *obedience* to the Bishop is made.

'Do you promise respect and obedience to me and my successors?'
'**I do**', is the reply.
'May God who has begun the good work in you bring it to fulfilment.'

It must always be remembered that a priest represents the Bishop in his parish and he does his work on behalf of the Bishop. The Bishop appoints him to the work he must do and gives him permission to hear confessions.

Now the congregation prays for the candidate by responding to a *litany of the saints*. A litany is a series of prayers asking all the saints to pray for a person. It means that the whole congregation is praying for the most important part of the ceremony to take place. At the end of the Litany there is a prayer to the Holy Spirit for the grace and power of the priesthood.

At this point in the ceremony, the actual *ordination* takes place. There is a solemn *action* which is followed by a *prayer*.

1. The Bishop lays his hands on the head of the candidate who kneels. This is done in silence. All the priests taking part in the ordination do the same, one by one, in silence.
2. The following prayer is said by the Bishop, while the priests stand in a semi-circle around the Bishop:

'Almighty Father, grant to this servant of yours, the dignity of the priesthood. Renew within him the spirit of holiness. As a co-worker with the order of bishops, may he be faithful to the ministry that he receives from you, Lord God, and be to others a model of right conduct.'

The Investiture

The new priest now has his stole re-arranged. As a deacon he wore the stole across the shoulder; now as a priest it is worn around the neck and hangs loose in front. It is his badge of office. For the first time also he wears the priest's Chasuble or Mass Vestment.

Anointing of hands

The Bishop anoints the hands of the priest with chrism. The oil of chrism for this man has now been used at his *baptism*, *confirmation* and his *ordination* as a priest. It has all the symbolism as on the previous occasions. The Bishop prays that the priest will persevere in his duties.

SUMMARY OF THE SACRAMENT OF HOLY ORDERS

A DEACON

The bishop lays his hands over the new deacon's head, and then he says the prayer of ordination.

The deacon is given a **stole** and a garment called a **dalmatic** to wear.

He is then given the book of Gospels.

He works in the parish, caring for God's people.

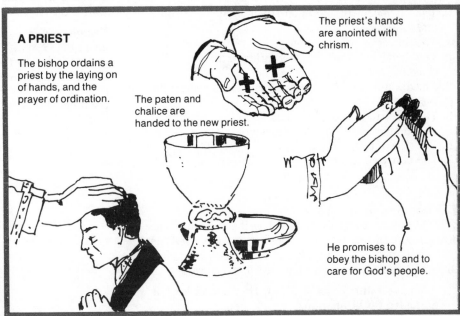

A PRIEST

The bishop ordains a priest by the laying on of hands, and the prayer of ordination.

The priest's hands are anointed with chrism.

The paten and chalice are handed to the new priest.

He promises to obey the bishop and to care for God's people.

A BISHOP

The consecrating bishop lays his hands on the head of the new bishop, or bishop-elect.

The Gospel book is placed on the new bishop's head as the consecration prayer is said.

The new bishop is anointed with chrism and given the mitre, the ring, gospel and crozier. He cares for all his people and the clergy.

Presentation of gifts

The offertory procession forms and when the paten and chalice are given to the Bishop, he hands them to the new priest who is going to consecrate the bread and wine for the very first time. (The paten is the plate on which the priest's altar-bread is placed; the chalice is the cup in which the wine is poured.)

Sign of peace

The ceremony of ordination ends with the Bishop giving the Sign of Peace to the new priest. The other priests also give the sign of welcome into the priesthood. At the end of the ceremony, the newly-ordained priest concelebrates the Mass with the Bishop and the other priests present.

SUMMARY

1. Presentation of the candidate for ordination.
2. The Bishop's homily explaining the priesthood.
3. The examination or questioning of the candidate.
4. The promise of obedience by the candidate to the Bishop.
5. The litany of the saints and the congregation's prayer.
6. The laying on of hands, in silence, by the Bishop and other priests.
7. The prayer of consecration.
8. The investiture of the new priest with stole and chasuble.
9. The anointing of the hands of the new priest by the Bishop.
10. The presentation of the bread and wine (paten and chalice) by the Bishop to the new priest.
11. The sign of peace.
12. The concelebration of Mass by the new priest with the Bishop and the other priests.

The Ordination of a Bishop

The Sacrament of Holy Orders has three stages. The deacon is admitted to certain functions of a priest. The new priest makes his promise to act as a priest to his Bishop. A Bishop is ordained in the following way:

1. After the Liturgy of the Word, the 'new Bishop' is presented for ordination.
2. There is a homily given by the Bishop who is going to ordain the 'new Bishop'.
3. The 'new Bishop' will be asked questions about his ministry.
4. There is a Liturgy asking for the prayers of all the saints.
5. The 'new Bishop' kneels and the ordaining Bishop lays his hands on his head. The other bishops present do the same.
6. The Gospel-book is placed on the 'new Bishop's' head and is held there by two deacons.
7. The Consecration prayer is said.
8. The consecrating Bishop anoints the head of the 'new Bishop' with chrism.
9. The Gospel-book and the ring are given to the 'new Bishop'. The mitre is placed on his head. The staff (crozier) is placed in his hand.
10. He is led to the Bishop's chair and the Sign of Peace is given to all the consecrating Bishops.
11. There is a special blessing at the end of the Mass.

(*Note* — In the ceremony, the 'new Bishop' is called the 'Bishop-elect'.)

The ceremony is very similar to that of ordination to the priesthood, but it is in the final stage of Holy Orders and the special signs of the Bishop are featured. These are the *Gospel-book*, the *ring*, the *mitre*, the *crozier* and the *Bishop's chair*. The chair is sometimes called the 'episcopal' chair and the office of a Bishop is called the 'episcopate', and he is a successor to the apostles. He must act like Christ, as a good shepherd to God's people.

SUMMARY OF THE SACRAMENT OF HOLY ORDERS *(See illustration on page 79.)*

Deacon — In a similar ceremony as for a priest, the Bishop lays his hands in silence, and then says a prayer of ordination. The deacon is given a stole and a garment called a 'dalmatic'. He is given the book of the Gospels. He performs certain functions of the priesthood.

Priest — A Bishop ordains a priest by the Laying on of Hands and the Prayer of Ordination. The priest's hands are anointed. He is given the chalice and paten. He promises to obey the Bishop. He is ordained to preach the Gospel, to care for the people, and to celebrate the Lord's Sacrifice.

Bishop — A Bishop is ordained by other Bishops. He is given the Gospel-book, the ring, the mitre, the crozier, and he is led to the Bishop's chair. His function is to proclaim the Gospel; to guard the faith handed down from the apostles; to act for the whole Church with all the other Bishops; to obey the successor of St Peter (the Pope); to care for his people and the clergy, and to be a good shepherd to God's people.

QUESTIONS

Investigation

1. Name the first people Jesus called to follow him.
2. Outline the *four* points which generally show that a man will make a suitable candidate for the priesthood.
3. Describe the things a deacon may do to serve his parish.
4. Describe the main parts of the ceremony for the ordination of a priest.
5. What are the promises made by a new priest at his ordination.
6. Describe the main duties of a bishop.
7. Describe an event when Jesus called people to be his apostles.

Understanding

1. What does 'celibacy' mean?
2. Explain the difference between a deacon and a priest.
3. Explain the following language and terms connected with ordination: i) a stole; ii) a homily; iii) a litany; iv) a chasuble; v) a paten; vi) a chalice; vii) a kiss of peace. (A sentence for each is sufficient.)
4. Why are the hands of a priest anointed at his ordination?
5. What does the promise of obedience mean at the ordination of a priest?
6. Explain in detail the meaning of the laying on of hands and the prayer of consecration at the ordination of a priest.
7. Explain the main differences between the ordination of a priest and the ordination of a bishop.

Evaluation

1. Give reasons why some Roman Catholics support the rule of celibacy for priests, and why some think that priests ought to be allowed to marry.
2. Explain your views on the fact that very few young men want to become priests, and make some suggestions about how the numbers of priests could be increased.

FURTHER READING

1. *You Gather a People:* pages 79-83.
2. *Called to Serve* (Bavidge).
3. *The Illustrated Catechism:* supplement page xi.
4. *Focus on Priesthood* (Wilkinson).

5.4 THE MINISTRY OF THE PRIESTHOOD

The main parts of the ceremony of ordination show the particular service which a priest gives in the Church.

1. There is an outward sign of ordination. This is the laying on of hands and the prayer of consecration.
2. The sign of ordination points to what is happening. A man is being given a special sharing in the priesthood of Christ himself. He will speak and act for the people before God.
3. The ministry of the priesthood was given by Jesus to his disciples at the Last Supper. Jesus gave them an idea of the service which they were to give when he washed their feet, and asked them to celebrate the breaking of bread 'as a memorial'.
4. The priest is anointed as a sign of strengthening so that he can carry out his duties.

The ministry of a priest may be summarised as follows:

▶ **to proclaim and preach the Gospel.**
▶ **to consecrate the bread and wine offered at Mass.**
▶ **to celebrate the sacraments in the parish.**
▶ **to care for the needs of people in the parish, especially by showing the people what they can do for each other.**

© Carlos Reyes

▶ **to assist the Bishop at confirmations.**
▶ **to assist the Bishop at ordinations.**
▶ **to consecrate himself to God, to be a holy man.**

Proclaiming the Gospel and preaching

It is important to see that a priest has a duty to study the message of Christ, to pray about this message and carefully explain the message to the people of the parish. This ministry comes before the many other tasks which priests often find they have to do — like building churches, looking after the parish funds and raising money in the parish. An important duty of a priest is to find and encourage people in the parish who can work as a team to do many of the tasks which build up a strong local Christian community.

Caring for God's people

The Bishop gives a priest the authority to hear *confessions*, and celebrate the *Sacrament of Reconciliation*. A priest has a very important task to forgive sins in the name of Christ, to bring healing to broken relationships and to restore peace when this has been lost. In a more general way he must also look for opportunities to restore peace and justice in the society in which he lives. This has often involved priests in imprisonment and even death.

A priest will always be most concerned for the sick and will anoint them with oil, and pray with them. The *Sacrament of Anointing of the Sick* is a way in which the power of Christ is brought to the people.

When couples celebrate the *Sacrament of Marriage*, the priest is essential as a witness of their marriage vows. He will frequently help them to prepare for marriage by explaining the ideal of marriage taught by Christ himself and handed down by the Catholic Church.

A priest assists the Bishop at *confirmations*. If a child is in danger of death, a priest will baptize and confirm on the same occasion. He is sometimes delegated by the Bishop to confirm, for example, when someone is received into the Catholic Church. There are other times when distance or numbers will mean that a priest, rather than the Bishop, celebrates the Sacrament of Confirmation.

The *Sacrament of Baptism* is an important parish celebration when a new member of parish is received into God's family. A deacon or a priest baptizes as a sign of the new life which Christ bought for his people with his own life, death and resurrection.

Celebration of the Eucharist

At his ordination, a priest is presented with the paten and chalice. He is given the authority in a very solemn way to do what Jesus did at the Last Supper. He will take the bread, give thanks, and say the words of consecration. He will break the bread and give the Body of Christ to God's people. He will take the wine and consecrate it with the words, *'This is my Blood...'*

The consecration of the bread and wine in the Eucharist is a very serious duty for a priest. He does this on behalf of God's people.

CONCLUSION

A priest is a man of God who is the servant of God's people. He is an assistant to the Bishop who is the successor of the apostles whom Jesus chose and taught how to serve.

The apostles watched Jesus in his ministry of teaching and healing and caring. Then Jesus invited them to serve also: *'Give them something to eat yourselves.' 'Do this in memory of me.'*

After the apostles had received the gift of the Holy Spirit at Pentecost, they were able to serve as Jesus had served. They were able to face many difficulties and dangers, and even death.

During the ceremony for the Sacrament of Holy Orders, the people pray for the gift of the Holy Spirit for their Bishop, priest or deacon who is being ordained.

Note: There are many priests who are not ordained for parish work. They may be writers or theologians, missionaries or administrators, but they will still fulfil the essential duties of a priest.

QUESTIONS

Investigation

1. Mentioning each sacrament in turn, say when a priest would celebrate the sacrament, or when he would assist the bishop to do so.
2. Describe what a priest does and says when he consecrates bread and wine at Mass.
3. Describe the religious function of a priest.
4. When did Jesus give the ministry of the priesthood to his disciples?
5. What sign did Jesus give his disciples to explain to them the spirit of service which his followers must have?
6. Mention *three* practical tasks for which a priest takes responsibility.
7. Mention *three* occupations which a priest might have besides working in a parish.

Understanding

1. Why is preaching an important part of the ministry of a priest?
2. What does the word 'ministry' mean?
3. Explain the importance of celebrating the sacraments in the ministry of a priest.
4. Explain the importance of preaching in the ministry of a priest.
5. Why do Roman Catholics call their priests 'Father'?
6. Explain the symbolism of the anointing of a priest during the ceremony of ordination.

Evaluation

1. Describe *two* occasions when you think a priest's work might lead him into danger.
2. Give *three* reasons why the description 'Man of God' should be a good one for a priest.
3. Which of the following is more important for a priest? i) to be a good organiser (administration); ii) to be a good listener and advisor. Give reasons for your opinion.
4. Describe a priest whom you think carries out his duties faithfully, and give evidence for this opinion.

FURTHER READING

1. *You Gather a People:* pages 84-88.
2. *The Illustrated Catechism:* questions 50, 51.

EUCHARIST & WORLD-WIDE FELLOWSHIP

6.1 THE MASS

The Mass is the popular name given to the celebration of the Holy Eucharist in the Catholic Church. The ceremony or liturgy emphasises the main beliefs about the Eucharist as follows: **1.** The Last Supper of Jesus is re-enacted. His words and actions are at the heart of each of the four eucharistic prayers.

2. The sacrifice of Jesus on Calvary is solemnly offered to God by the consecration of bread and wine.

3. The word 'eucharist' means 'thanksgiving' and the Mass is a great act of thanksgiving by the people of God (the Church) for what Jesus did by offering himself as the Lamb that would take away the sins of the world.

4. The Mass is also the holy meal of God's people. Jesus himself is the Bread of Life in Holy Communion, and the Christian Eucharist is food for eternal life.

These beliefs about the Mass may be summarised like this:

▶ **last supper of Jesus**
▶ **sacrifice of Calvary**
▶ **Eucharist or thanksgiving**
▶ **food for eternal life**

THE PASSOVER OF THE JEWS

The Sacrament of the Eucharist cannot really be understood without knowing something about the celebration of Passover by the Jews. Every year, the Jewish family celebrates the most important national memory of the Jewish people. In Old Testament times, when the children of Israel were slaves in Egypt, God called Moses to go to Pharoah and demand the freedom of his people. Pharoah would not release the people until the last great plague or curse. The tenth plague was the death of all the first-born of Egypt.

The Hebrews (Jews) escaped this plague by performing a special ceremony given to Moses by God. They were to slaughter a lamb, and sprinkle the doorposts of their houses with the blood. The blood of the lamb was the sign for the angel of death to *pass-over* those houses. So, the people were saved by the blood of the lamb.

Every year to this day, all Jews celebrate Passover, and during the meal in the home, the father of the family explains to the youngest child that 'on this night' God saved his people, and freed them from slavery. By saying 'on this night' the Jewish family makes the ancient memory real for the present moment. This is very important when looking at what Jesus did at the Last Supper.

THE LAST SUPPER

Jesus was a Jew and he celebrated Passover every year of his life. He shared his last Passover with his disciples. However, he did something very surprising which changed the ancient ceremony and gave it a new meaning to his friends. Gospel accounts of the Last Supper may be found in Matthew 26:26-30; Mark 14:22-26; and Luke 22:14-20.

The Gospel of Matthew explains that during the meal: *'Jesus took a piece of bread, gave a prayer of thanks, broke it, and gave it to his disciples. "Take and eat it," he said; "this is my body".'* (Matthew 26:26)

The bread of the Passover was broken among them, as the body of Jesus would be broken for the sins of the world on the cross. Jesus asked them to perform a new ceremony of deliverance from evil — the evil of sin — which was linked with himself and not an animal of sacrifice as at the Jewish Passover.

Jesus made this new ceremony even clearer: *'Then he took a cup, gave thanks to God, and gave it to them. "Drink it, all of you," he said; "this is my blood, which seals God's covenant, my blood poured out for many for the forgiveness of sins".'* (v. 27,28)

Jesus points to his resurrection and concludes: *' "I tell you, I will never again drink this wine until I drink the new wine with you in my Father's Kingdom".'* (v. 29)

By comparing this supper with the main action of the first Passover, one can see that the Old Testament sacrifice of the lamb is replaced by Jesus' own death and the offering of himself for the sin of the world. In the Eucharist, Jesus is called 'the Lamb of God'.

SUMMARY
The Passover freed the people of God from slavery. The modern Jewish Passover makes this freedom real for today. Jesus celebrated Passover every year. At the Last Supper he became the new Lamb of God whose blood would make people free from sin.

THE SACRIFICE OF CALVARY

The Mass is called a sacrifice. In the Old Testament, sacrifice was offered in the temple. A sacrifice was usually an animal or a bird. It was offered for various reasons. In the case of the Jewish Passover, a lamb was sacrificed, and its blood was the sign of God saving his people. The families at that time ate the lamb. It was their final meal before they left Egypt.

Jesus made it clear that his body and blood would be the New Covenant of God with his people. The sacrifice of his life for the forgiveness of sin only took place on Calvary when Jesus was crucified, but like the Jews, the priest at Mass repeats the offering which Jesus made as though the moment is present again. The Jewish festival of Passover is a great help in understanding the Christian celebration of the Eucharist.

EUCHARIST

The Mass is a great act of worship and thanksgiving. The first part, called the Liturgy of the Word, is a time when God is thanked and praised for showing himself to his people through Jesus as a God who is loving and forgiving. Bread and wine are offered in thanksgiving for the gifts of the earth. The first words of the offering are: *'Blessed are you, Lord God of creation...'*

This prayer of thanksgiving is like the Jewish introduction to blessing or thanking God, and is used in many of their family prayers. The preface to the eucharistic prayer is a special prayer of thanksgiving and always begins: *'we do well...to give you thanks and praise...'*

During the eucharistic prayer, the gifts of bread and wine are consecrated. When the priest repeats the words and actions of Jesus at the Last Supper, he 'gives thanks' for the bread and wine. The great prayer of thanksgiving occurs at the end of the eucharistic prayer with the words: *'Through him, with him, in him, in the unity of the Holy Spirit, all honour and glory is yours, almighty Father, for ever and ever.'*

In this prayer, thanksgiving is made to God for the gift of his Son Jesus who gives perfect worship and praise through his sacrifice for the sins of the people. At Communion time, God is thanked for the gift which he gives his people in Jesus whom they receive in Holy Communion.

SUMMARY

Thanksgiving is made for:

1. The God of love in scripture.
2. The gifts of God's creation: bread and wine.
3. The consecration of bread and wine into the body and blood of Jesus.
4. The gift of Jesus to his people in Holy Communion.

FOOD FOR ETERNAL LIFE — THE MASS AS THE HOLY MEAL OF GOD'S PEOPLE

Great events, for example birthdays, weddings etc., are often marked by a celebration meal. National events are no exception, and the coronation of a King or Queen is often celebrated by street parties. The end of a war is celebrated in this way as well.

The Mass celebrates Christ's victory over sin and evil, and his resurrection from the dead. Jesus instituted the Eucharist at the Last Supper. The Last Supper took place during Passover which was the most solemn holy meal of the Jews. Jesus speaks of himself in the Gospel of John as 'the bread of life': *'Whoever eats my flesh and drinks my blood has eternal life, and I will raise him to life on the last day.'* (John 6:54)

The Jews celebrated their freedom from slavery at Passover. Christians celebrate their salvation from sin and death in the Mass. The Mass, therefore, is the family meal of the Catholic Church, and Communion is the spiritual food which the people share.

OUTLINE OF THE MASS

The following is a simple outline of the main actions of the Mass:

1. Greeting and penitential rite.
2. Liturgy of the Word: readings and homily.
3. Creed and the prayers of the faithful (bidding prayers).
4. Offertory — bread, wine, and gifts (collection).
5. Preface and eucharistic prayer (many prefaces, and four eucharistic prayers).
6. Our Father; sign of peace; 'Lamb of God'.
7. Communion: the body and blood of Jesus Christ under the appearance of bread and wine.
8. Blessing and command to 'Love and serve the Lord'.

The Order of the Mass explained:

1. Greeting and Penitential Rite

The greeting helps the congregation to realise that Jesus promised to be with his people when they came together to pray e.g. *'The grace of our Lord Jesus Christ and the love of God and the fellowship of the Holy Spirit be with you all.'*

Between the greeting and the penitential rite, the priest may say a little about the theme of the Mass for the day e.g. it may be a Mass in honour of a particular saint.

Penitence is sorrow for sin, so the penitential rite asks for God's forgiveness. The priest may either sprinkle the people with holy water as a symbolic action of cleansing them from sin, or use a form of words asking forgiveness for the people.

2. The Liturgy of the Word

On most Sundays, and feast days of the year (excluding Lent and Advent) the *Gloria* is said. It is a prayer of worship, thanks and praise and it is followed by the opening prayer which expresses the theme of the celebration.

Readings from the Bible follow. The purpose of these readings is three-fold:

i) The Bible is the word of God to his people. It tells them that God promises to save his people and that he has kept his promise in the life, death and resurrection of Jesus.
ii) The readings are food for the spiritual life of God's people, the Church.
iii) The Church believes that Christ is always present in the words of scripture.

These readings are arranged in yearly cycles so that a great portion of the Bible is read at Mass during the year, and all four Gospels are read. Lay people sometimes read the Old Testament and the epistles of the New Testament, but the Gospel is solemnly proclaimed by the priest or deacon.

There are community responses between the readings, and the Gospel is introduced by an 'Alleluia' verse. The readings are usually explained or commented on by the priest in his homily or sermon.

3. Creed and the Prayers of the Faithful

There are two creeds which are said publicly. One is called the *Nicene Creed* and the other the *Apostles' Creed*. It is the Nicene Creed (this was agreed upon at the Council of Nicea very early in the history of the Christian Church) which is usually said at Mass. A Creed is a summary of what people believe about:

▶ **God the Father**
▶ **Jesus Christ, the Son of God**
▶ **the Holy Spirit**
▶ **the Church**

The *Prayers of the Faithful* (sometimes called 'Bidding Prayers') are a series of about five prayers asking God's assistance for the needs of the Church, the world, and the local community. e.g. *'We pray for the sick of this parish — Lord hear us.'*

1 GREETING, Penitential Rite ✝

2 Liturgy of the WORD

3 CREED, PRAYERS

4 OFFER-TORY

5 PREFACE, EUCHARISTIC ✝ PRAYER ✝

6 Our Father, SIGN of PEACE

7 COMM-UNION

8 BLESSING 'Go in peace to love and serve the Lord.' ✝

THE MASS

---

4. Offertory: bread, wine and gifts

The preparation of the gifts may include a procession when the people of the parish bring gifts of bread and wine and other offerings (usually money). The bread and wine are blessed, and the people pray that their sacrifice will be acceptable to God. The priest says a prayer over the gifts.

5. Eucharistic Prayers

There is a choice of four eucharistic prayers. They are introduced by the *preface* (which means 'introduction'). This is a prayer of thanksgiving (or 'Eucharist'). There is a short dialogue between the priest and people and then the preface generally begins (though not always): *'Father, all powerful and ever living God, we do well always and everywhere to give you thanks through Jesus Christ our Lord...'*

The next part of the prayer says why thanksgiving is being made. This depends upon the theme of the Mass or the season of the year e.g.

> *'He is the true and eternal priest who establishes this unending sacrifice. He offered himself as a victim for our deliverance and taught us to make this offering in his memory. As we eat his body which he gave for us, we grow in strength. As we drink his blood which is poured out for us, we are washed clean.'*
>
> *Preface of the Holy Eucharist*

The preface prayer is completed by a prayer of praise said or sung by the people which begins 'Holy, holy, holy...'. The *eucharistic prayers* are different from each other but they have common ideas. At the heart of the eucharistic prayer is the *consecration* of the gifts of bread and wine. The priest recites the words of Jesus at the Last Supper, and Catholics believe that Jesus Christ is then present under the appearance of the bread and wine. The consecration is followed by an acclamation made by all the people e.g.

▶ **Christ has died**
▶ **Christ is risen**
▶ **Christ will come again**

The acclamation is followed by the *memorial prayer* which asks God the Father to accept the sacrifice which is Christ himself who is present by the faith which the people have in remembering all that Jesus did. There is a prayer to ask God's blessing on the Church; a prayer for the dead, and a prayer to honour the saints. Eucharistic prayers II, III and IV have a prayer asking for the gift of the Holy Spirit. Eucharistic prayers III and IV have special openings of praise to God the Father. Eucharistic prayer I is the most distinctive and is sometimes called the **Roman Canon** (or approved prayer). It is a very old eucharistic prayer. The final prayer is in praise of God. He is praised through the offering which Jesus made, so the priest says or sings (because this is a very solemn moment in the Mass): *'Through him, with him, in him, in the unity of the Holy Spirit, all glory and honour is yours Almighty Father for ever and ever.'* The people answer *'Amen'*.

6. Our Father etc.

The congregation ask for the food of eternal life and for forgiveness in the *Lord's Prayer*. As they will share the same bread, the people offer each other a *sign of peace and unity*. This is usually a hand-shake or another expression of peace. The people remember that Jesus is the '*Lamb of God*' and they ask to receive the forgiveness won by the sacrifice of Jesus on the cross.

7. Communion of priest and people

The priest receives Communion with Christ under the appearance of bread, followed by the chalice. Each person receiving Communion will answer 'Amen' to the words 'The Body of Christ'. If Communion is being given under the appearance of wine as well, then the chalice is offered to the person with the words 'The Blood of Christ'. Communion under the appearance of both bread and wine emphasises that the Mass is food and drink for the spiritual life of God's people. It is called '*Communion under both kinds*'.

There is a special prayer before and after the Communion which brings out the meaning of what is happening.

8. Blessing and command to 'Love and serve the Lord'

The Communion of the congregation with Christ has far-reaching effects which are looked at in the next two chapters. The blessing can be special to the theme of the Mass e.g. if it is a wedding, it emphasises the marriage theme. All are sent out into the world to do good works for their neighbour, especially if he/she is in need. In this way God is loved and served by his people.

QUESTIONS

Investigation

1. When did Jesus celebrate the Last Supper?
2. What food and drink is used at Mass?
3. Describe a typical 'Preface' for Mass.
4. Give another name for the 'Prayer of the Faithful'.
5. Write out *two* forms used to dismiss the people at the end of Mass.
6. Describe the origin of the Jewish feast of Passover.
7. Describe, in detail, the words and actions of Jesus at the Last Supper.
8. Find *two* examples which show that the Mass is a thanksgiving prayer.
9. Outline the *main* contents of the Nicene Creed.
10. What happens during the Liturgy of the Word?
11. Summarise the *main* ideas of *one* Eucharistic prayer.

Understanding

1. Explain the way in which the Mass may be described as a sacrifice.
2. What does the word 'eucharistic' mean?
3. What is the meaning of the word 'covenant' as it is used in the Bible?
4. Why is Jesus called the 'Lamb of God'?
5. Explain the purpose of the 'penitential rite' of the Mass.
6. What is the purpose of the 'Gloria' prayer?
7. Why are the people's offerings included with the gifts of bread and wine?
8. What did Jesus mean when he spoke about a 'new covenant' in his blood?
9. Explain what Catholics believe about the presence of Christ in the Eucharist.
10. What is the significance of receiving Communion under both kinds at Mass?
11. Explain how the Mass recalls the Last Supper of Jesus.

Evaluation

1. Explain why some Catholics, particularly young people, find the Liturgy of the Word boring. Why does this happen, and what action can be taken to help such people?
2. Describe *two* different Masses (e.g. a wedding and a youth Mass). What would remain the same for these Masses? Do you think people should use the opportunity more often for celebrating Mass in a variety of ways?

FURTHER READING

1. *You Gather a People:* pages 36-50.
2. *Gather Round His Table* (Bavidge).
3. *The Illustrated Catechism:* questions 40-49; supplement pages x, xi.
4. *Teacher's Reference: R.E. Scheme for Secondary Schools:* Year 4: pages 65-70.
5. *Focus on the Eucharist* (Wilkinson).

6.2 THE CHURCH — THE BODY OF CHRIST

'What the faithful have received...in the celebration of the Eucharist should have its effect on their way of life...everyone who has participated in the Mass should be eager to do good works, to please God...devoted to the Church, putting into practice what he has learnt...'

Flannery, *Vatican Council II:* p.111

There is an important idea in this quotation that anyone who goes to Mass and really knows what they are doing, will want to be very practical Christians in their daily lives. Why should this be so? The answer lies in an important piece of description which Paul used to explain to the first Christians that they could not say that they loved Christ in the breaking of bread, and at the same time neglect their neighbour. In a very strong letter he made sure that they realised that belonging to Christ brought responsibilities towards each other. He wanted the people of Corinth (the 'Corinthians') to realise that their prayer meetings and Eucharist had to lead to caring for the poorer members who were there.

Paul had heard that the poorer Christians in Corinth were neglected by the wealthy. In the early days of the Church it is probable that the Eucharist was preceded by an ordinary meal. Although the people would come together for their prayers and the 'breaking of bread' or Eucharist, they would eat their own meal separately in small groups. The person who owned the house where the meeting was going to take place would not feel obliged to cater for the whole congregation. Some people, therefore, ate and drank too much before the meeting, and others were hungry. Paul was angry with them:

1 Corinthians 11:17-22
'In the following instructions, however, I do not praise you, because your meetings for worship actually do more harm than good. In the first place, I have been told that there are opposing groups in your meetings; and this I believe is partly true. (No doubt there must be divisions among you so that the ones who are in the right may be clearly seen.) When you meet together as a group, it is not the Lord's Supper that you eat. For as you eat, each one goes ahead with his own meal, so that some are hungry while others get drunk. Haven't you got your own homes in which to eat and drink? Or would you rather despise the church of God and put to shame the people who are in need? What do you expect me to say to you about this? Shall I praise you? Of course I don't!'

Paul wanted them to understand that sharing in the Body of Christ at the Eucharist was a way of becoming closer and more responsible for each other.

© Carlos Reyes

Body of Christ

1 Corinthians 11:23-25
'For I received from the Lord the teaching that I passed on to you: that the Lord Jesus, on the night he was betrayed, took a piece of bread, gave thanks to God, broke it, and said, "This is my body, which is for you. Do this in memory of me." In the same way, after the supper he took the cup and said, "This cup is God's new covenant, sealed with my blood. Whenever you drink it, do so in memory of me".'

After this description of what Jesus meant by what he had done at the Last Supper, Paul explains that to take part in the Eucharist in such a way as to dishonour Christ and the people he loved is a terrible thing:

1 Corinthians 11:26-29
'This means that every time you eat this bread and drink from this cup you proclaim the Lord's death until he comes. It follows that if anyone eats the Lord's bread or drinks from his cup in a way that dishonours him, he is guilty of sin against the Lord's body and blood. So then, everyone should examine himself first, and then eat the bread and drink from the cup. For if he does not recognise the meaning of the Lord's body when he eats the bread and drinks from the cup, he brings judgement on himself as he eats and drinks.'

Later on in the letter Paul says exactly what he means by the following teaching: *'ALL OF YOU are Christ's body and each one is a part of it.'* (1 Corinthians 12:27)

Paul is quite clear that: *'If one part of the body suffers, all the other parts suffer with it...'* (1 Corinthians 12:26)

The quotation at the beginning of this chapter emphasises that 'the Eucharist should have its effect on their way of life'. Anyone who counts himself a member of the Catholic Church, and takes part in the Eucharist, goes away from the service with clear responsibilities to contribute to the:

▶ **community life of the Church**
▶ **prayer for the whole Church**
▶ **fellowship of God's people**
▶ **action necessary to help the poor**

The Church today is in the same position as the group of Christians at Corinth with whom Paul was so angry. Christians cannot take part in the Eucharist and at the same time neglect the poor. Catholics in the rich countries of Western Europe cannot neglect the poor of the developing countries. If Paul were alive in the twentieth century, he would say it was like a person who neglected one part of his body: he would soon be sorry for it. The idea that the Church is the Body of Christ is a spiritual description, but it is a good one to illustrate the close community bond which the sacraments bring, particularly baptism and Eucharist.

The Vatican Council expressed the responsibilities of community, prayer, fellowship and action in the following: *'The joys and the hopes, the griefs and the anxieties of the men of this age, especially those who are poor or in any way afflicted, these too are the joys and hopes, the griefs and anxieties of the followers of Christ.'* (Vatican Council II)

The Vatican Council explains 'The Church' as the 'new people of God'. Jesus told a parable to explain the responsibilities of God's people towards each other:

The Final Judgement
(The Parable of the Sheep and the Goats)
(Matthew 25:31-46)
'When the Son of Man comes as King and all the angels with him, he will sit on his royal throne, and the people of all the nations will be gathered before him. Then he will divide them into two groups, just as a shepherd separates the sheep from the goats. He will put the righteous people on his right and the others on his left. Then the King will say to the people on his right, "Come, you that are blessed by my Father! Come and possess the kingdom which has been prepared for you ever since the creation of the world. I was hungry and you fed me, thirsty and you gave me a drink; I was a stranger and you received me in your homes, naked and you clothed me; I was sick and you took care of me, in prison and you visited me."

The righteous will then answer him, "When Lord, did we ever see you hungry and feed you, or thirsty and give you a drink? When did we ever see you a stranger and welcome you into our homes, or naked and clothe you? When did we ever see you sick or in prison, and visit you?" The King will reply, "I tell you, whenever you did this for one of the least important of these brothers of mine, you did it for me!"

Then he will say to those on his left, "Away from me, you that are under God's curse! Away to the eternal fire which has been prepared for the Devil and his angels! I was hungry but you would not feed me, thirsty but you would not give me a drink; I was a stranger but you would not welcome me in your homes, naked but you would not clothe me; I was sick and in prison but you would not take care of me."

Then they will answer him, "When Lord, did we ever see you hungry or thirsty or a stranger or naked or sick or in prison, and would not help you?" The King will reply, "I tell you, whenever you refused to help one of these least important ones, you refused to help me." These, then, will be sent off to eternal punishment, but the righteous will go to eternal life.'

The idea or spiritual description of the Church as the Body of Christ can be understood especially clearly in the words spoken by the king in the parable when the people ask 'When did we ever see *you* sick or in prison...?' *'Whenever you did this for one of the least important of these brothers of mine, you did it for me.'*

CONCLUSION

The ceremony of the Eucharist and its meaning is only understood if the final words of dismissal are put into practical terms by the congregation: *'Go in peace to love and serve the Lord.'*

To be counted as part of the Body of Christ and one of the people of God brings with it serious responsibilities to build up community by caring locally and in the world-wide Church for all God's people, but especially the poor and the weak. These are the subjects of the next chapter.

Work

'Body of Christ'

Prayer

Visiting the lonely

'GO IN PEACE TO LOVE AND SERVE THE LORD'

Feeding the hungry

Offering shelter

Providing love and comfort

Clothing the naked

QUESTIONS

Investigation

1. Illustrate the quotation from Vatican II about the effect which the Eucharist ought to have on the ordinary lives of people. Choose key words to highlight the illustrations you have chosen.
2. Identify *one* important difference between the Christians meeting at Corinth and the Christians who meet today at Mass.
3. Summarise the way in which Paul explained to the Corinthians their responsibilities towards each other.
4. Relate the parable of the sheep and the goats.
5. Find modern examples of those who are hungry, thirsty, naked, strangers, in prison, sick. Collect illustrations and accounts from newspapers.

Understanding

1. Explain *four* responsibilities which are accepted by a person who takes part in the Eucharist with understanding.
2. Explain what the Vatican II document (the second quotation in this chapter) says about the poor and the responsibilities of those who follow Christ.
3. What is meant by the parable-language of 'the sheep'?

4. What is meant by the parable-language of 'the goats'?
5. Explain the *main* teaching of the parable of the sheep and the goats.
6. What made Paul so angry about the way in which the Corinthians met for the breaking of the bread?
7. What did Paul mean by saying 'All of you are Christ's body'?

Evaluation

1. Suggest some ways in which people could practise the command to 'love and serve the Lord' which is given at the end of Mass. Do you think that most people take this command seriously? Give reasons for your answer.
2. Describe *two* kinds of need among God's people today, and say whether you think these needs should be met by public funds or by private charity.
3. Do you think that there are modern equivalents in the world today which match the Corinthians' neglect of the poor?

FURTHER READING

1. *Framework*: chapter 9.
2. *You Gather a People*: pages 50-54.
3. *Christian Way*: Book 3, chapter 12.
4. *The Illustrated Catechism*: questions 20, 21.
5. *Teacher's Reference: R.E. Scheme for Secondary Schools*: Year 4: pages 77, 78.

6.3 THE POOR

> '...the Council asks individuals and governments to remember the saying of the Father: "feed the man dying of hunger, because if you do not feed him you are killing him...".'
>
> Vatican II:
> *The Church in the Modern World: para. 69*

In this quotation the 'Father' refers to the early fathers of the Church who were famous bishops, writers or monks like St Augustine or St Ambrose. The Catholic Church has always taken very seriously the responsibility to care for the poor. Pope John Paul II visited Britain in 1982, and reminded the people gathered in Liverpool to keep on sending aid to the developing nations (often called the Third World):

> '*I hope that, despite all obstacles, the generosity of your hearts will never weaken. I hope that, through programmes such as the Catholic Fund for Overseas Development, you will continue to help the poor, to feed the hungry and to contribute to the cause of development. Always keep alive your gospel tradition of loving concern to others in the name of Jesus.*'
>
> *Sunday May 30th 1982*

This chapter will outline the work of the **Catholic Fund for Overseas Development** (CAFOD), but first there will be a description of the problems and the needs of the developing nations: *hunger, population, poverty, and disease.*

HUNGER

In 1980 the **Brandt Report** was published. The former Chancellor of the Federal Republic of Germany, Herr Willy Brandt, was the Chairman of an international commission which examined the needs of developing nations. The Brandt Report was called *'North-South: a program for survival'*. This report emphasises that there must be an end to mass hunger and malnutrition. In the 1980s the world has been horrified by reports from Africa which have shown films of the effects of the great droughts. People have died in their thousands every day, and the wealthy nations have been shocked into raising millions of pounds and dollars for the relief of famine. The deaths of 12 million children in one year is not a startling record in the Third World.

Two diseases afflict children when hunger is a severe problem. **Marasmus** is when, through lack of food, children become so thin that they suffer from sickness and diarrhoea and die. **Kwashiorkor** occurs when malnutrition is present through lack of protein in the diet. Pictures of children with very little hair, distended stomachs, and faces which look old are common in films of famine-stricken areas like Ethiopia and the Sudan.

The causes of food shortages in these countries are various. The country may lack money for the necessary imports of food-stuffs which it cannot produce itself. Sometimes, there is money but the wealth of the country is in the hands of a few and it is not available for the nation in general. Sometimes the food that can be grown is destroyed by pests or by long droughts. In some countries, like India for example, a valuable source of protein is lost because religion forbids the killing or eating of the sacred cows which wander in their thousands, producing nothing for the people. Sometimes it is just inexperience, lack of technology and bad organisation which means that insufficient food is produced. Above all, developing nations cannot recover from a bad year because they have no real resources to cover a natural disaster.

The Brandt Report recommended more funds for developing:

- ▶ **agriculture**
- ▶ **irrigation**
- ▶ **agricultural research**
- ▶ **crop storage**
- ▶ **fertilisers etc.**
- ▶ **fisheries**

Food aid was recommended, but not at the expense of helping the people themselves to increase their own food production. The following saying emphasises the importance of self-help aid: *'Give a man a fish and you feed him for a day; teach him to fish and you feed him for life.'*

POPULATION

Families in developing countries often have more children than families in wealthy nations. Sometimes this occurs because there is much more manual labour to be done when machinery and modern farming methods are not used. The life expectancy of babies born in developing countries is very short. Very few babies born to one couple survive to become adults who will care for their aged parents. However, the fact that disease is more easily controlled now means that there are problems of population explosion in developing countries. It can happen that a man will find himself unable to support a large family and his own elderly parents. In the country as a whole, the resources have to be shared with many more people than in wealthy countries where families are small. Statistics suggest that in the 1990s, 90% of the world population increase is likely to take place in developing countries. Solutions to the population explosion include:

- ▶ **family planning**
- ▶ **a fairer distribution of the world's resources**
- ▶ **improved trading conditions**
- ▶ **loans for improving agricultural techniques**

Family planning requires education. Ignorance and illiteracy prevent successful programmes being carried out. The Roman Catholic Church teaches responsible parenthood and recommends only natural methods of birth-control. Chemical and artificial methods are not accepted by the Catholic Church, but some countries have imposed such methods, and the Church sees this as a violation of human rights.

A fairer distribution of the world's resources could be achieved, but only if people in rich countries were prepared to lower their own consumption of food and other resources. The 'North' mentioned in the Brandt Report has a quarter of the world's population, but has

© Carlos Reyes

Mother with baby looking for blades of grass to eat in Makele, Ethiopia, November 1984.

The arms race means that the governments of developing countries spend money on tanks and military aeroplanes, so that there is no money left for social services or agricultural programmes.

Natural disasters, for example drought or pests, may destroy a crop, and there are no reserves to supply the needs of the following year. International loans from banks can keep a country in permanent poverty if it is constantly trying to meet payments with a high interest.

Education is a great need in developing countries. Children of illiterate parents may only know their local dialect and may not be able to communicate outside their own village or tribal unit. In some countries education is not available to women. Ignorance and illiteracy have serious repercussions on health, techniques of farming, industry, and trade.

DISEASE

Great progress has been made in improving standards of public health, and in the field of preventing and curing disease. Unfortunately, much modern research into disease and medical aid cannot be applied in developing countries because of the poverty which exists there. When money is spent on weapons it cannot be spent on hospitals and clinics. The pollution of rivers actively promotes disease. Poor nutrition causes many of the diseases of developing nations. Lack of housing or inadequate housing causes hardship which makes people break down in health. Lack of sanitation results in disease.

Solutions to this problem are found by the ***World Health Organisation*** (WHO) and the ***Food and Agriculture Organisation*** (FAO). There are many problems to overcome in giving medical aid. Drugs can only be taken effectively if people can read and understand how to take them, so education becomes an important factor. There is little point in curing people if the conditions they live in are only going to make them ill again. All the problems which affect the progress of developing countries are inter-linked and lead to a cycle of depression. Reports like the Brandt Report attempt to provide a balanced programme of human, agricultural, industrial, medical and economic aid.

CAFOD

Private charity and the work of CAFOD

The problems of developing countries are so vast that an individual person might well think that any personal effort to give or send aid is virtually useless. However, it is often from voluntary services and organisations that much relief from poverty is given. The Catholic Fund for Overseas Development is one such organisation. It is the United Kingdom unit of Caritas International. It was set up by the bishops of England and Wales in 1962 to express the concern of the Catholic community for the needs and problems of developing countries. CAFOD is the official agency of the Catholic Church for overseas development. It is funded from the private charity of people who feel that they cannot allow world organisations, agencies of the United Nations and governments to be the only source of help for the developing nations.

four-fifths of the world's income. Their standard of living is forty times higher than poorer nations. Ninety per cent of the world's manufacturing industry is owned by the North.

Improved trading conditions can only take place when poor countries are not exploited for their raw materials, which may become very valuable when they have been processed in the North. Often a country will depend on income from the export of one major crop such as tea or coffee-beans.

Loans for improving agricultural techniques would result in the production of more food. Unfortunately, the interest on such loans often leads to yet more poverty.

The problems of developing countries are inter-linked, and many of the facts already discussed in this chapter explain the crippling poverty of the people. The major causes of poverty are:

▶ **the arms race**
▶ **inability to recover from natural disasters**
▶ **a cycle of debt**
▶ **the population explosion**
▶ **unjust trading conditions**
▶ **ignorance and illiteracy**

CAFOD and individuals, schools and parishes

CAFOD makes the link between the continents of Africa, Asia and Latin America, and the people at home who want to send aid. A CAFOD group in a school or parish learns about the problems facing the poor, and they raise funds to support the self-help projects initiated by CAFOD. Sometimes a committee of parishioners will act as a link between CAFOD and the whole parish.

Scripture preaching and tradition about helping the poor

CAFOD asks people to remember the teaching of Jesus concerning:

- ▶ **prayer**
- ▶ **fasting**
- ▶ **alms-giving (charity)**

About *prayer*, Jesus said:

'...when you pray, go to your room, close the door, and pray to your Father, who is unseen. And your Father, who sees what you do in private, will reward you.' (Matthew 6:6)

About *fasting*, Jesus said:

'...When you go without food, wash your face and comb your hair, so that others cannot know that you are fasting — only your Father...And your Father...will reward you.' (Matthew 6:17-18)

About *charity*, Jesus said:

'...when you give something to a needy person, do not make a big show of it, as the hypocrites do...do it in such a way that even your closest friend will not know about it.' (Matthew 6:2-3)

The spirit of these words of Jesus explains the attitude of giving which is encouraged by CAFOD. Prayer, fasting and alms-giving are the three traditional ways in the Church of helping those in need, and go back to the very earliest days in the Acts of the Apostles. The CAFOD groups, therefore, are encouraged to give up something each week as a regular act of self-denial, in order to help the poor. They are reminded by Pope John Paul II:

> *'The poor of the world are your brothers and sisters in Christ. You must never be content to leave them just the crumbs from the feast. You must give of your substance, and not just of abundance in order to help them. And you must treat them as guests at your family table.'*
>
> *Pope John Paul II: New York 1979*

The projects and organisations of CAFOD

One activity of CAFOD is to supply information about the needs of the developing countries. Information packs contain the history, social conditions and development of a particular country. Films, slide-sets,

© *Carlos Reyes*

Poverty in Peru.

pamphlets, books, and posters are produced. Regular reports on the progress of development programmes are made to CAFOD groups. Communication of information is a most important function of CAFOD.

A group raises funds for a particular project. Money is generally sent on a monthly basis. Only a minimum amount is spent on the administration of funds for the various projects. The group itself has no direct link with the project, because CAFOD takes responsibility for all communication between the group and the development project so that the possibility of unanswered letters does not discourage the group. The projects of CAFOD are linked with:

▶ **community development**
▶ **food production**
▶ **water supplies and irrigation**
▶ **preventative medicine**
▶ **vocational training**
▶ **adult education**

Particular projects may include a village well; a rural dispensary; a mother and child nutrition scheme; or a latrine programme in a slum. These projects aim at developing a healthy community.

More reasons for CAFOD projects

CAFOD operates because it believes in the basic equality of all people in the sight of God. Human dignity demands a reasonable standard of living. Everyone has the same basic needs of food, clothing and shelter. All who have been baptized share in the risen life of Christ, and they try to *'bring the good news to the poor'* (Luke 4:18) as Jesus did. CAFOD is a way of being with Christ who is hungry, thirsty, and in need.

QUESTIONS

Investigation

1. Give another description for the 'Third World'.
2. Name the Catholic agency which gives aid to developing nations.
3. What funds or improvements were recommended by the Brandt Report?
4. Select and describe an example of a project to do with agricultural research in the Third World.
5. Write out the full titles for W.H.O. and F.A.O.
6. What is the link between CAFOD and CARITAS.
7. Describe some of the ways in which CAFOD receives its funds.
8. Mention *three* kinds of information supplied by CAFOD about the poor.
9. Describe *two* examples of vocational training.

10. Outline the main problems facing the developing nations.
11. Give *two* examples of problems concerning public health in the Third World.
12. Select and describe a teaching of Jesus about prayer, fasting and charity.
13. What did Pope John Paul II say about giving aid to the poor of the world?
14. Find out details of *two* projects of CAFOD and give an account of them.
15. Find out and describe the work of a parish for the CAFOD partnership scheme.

Understanding

1. What does the following sentence mean: 'If you do not feed him, you are killing him'?
2. What does the term 'Father of the Church' mean?
3. Why is irrigation important in developing countries?
4. What does the phrase 'life-expectancy' mean?
5. Explain the importance of 'literacy' in developing countries.
6. Explain the teaching of scripture which supports the activities of an organisation like CAFOD.
7. What does the term 'preventative medicine' mean?
8. Explain *two* of the major causes of poverty in the developing nations.

Evaluation

1. Do you think that people are a *resource* to a nation, or a *problem* to be solved by family planning programmes? Explain the arguments which support *both* points of view, and form your own conclusion.
2. Do you think that *voluntary* agencies ought to be necessary to give aid to the developing countries?
3. What do you think an *individual* person can do to help the developing nations, and why should a Christian consider this an important responsibility?

FURTHER READING

1. *Framework:* chapter 21.
2. *Facing the Issues:* chapter 2.
3. *Christian Way:* Book 3, pages 19-20; chapter 11.
4. *Revise Religious Studies:* pages 152-154.
5. *Real Questions:* chapter 7.
6. *Frontiers:* units 19, 20, 21, 22.
7. *Teacher's Reference: R.E. Scheme for Secondary Schools:* Year 4: pages 41-50.

RECONCILIATION — OUR WAY TO GOD

7.1 THE SACRAMENT OF RECONCILIATION (PENANCE)

When Jesus was accused of mixing with tax-collectors and sinners, his reply was that sick people need a doctor: *'People who are well do not need a doctor, but only those who are sick. I have not come to call respectable people to repent, but outcasts.'* (Luke 5:31-32)

On another occasion the Pharisees complained: *'This man welcomes outcasts and even eats with them!'*

In reply, Jesus told three parables about things and people who were lost. The most famous of these parables concerns a lost son and a most forgiving father.

On the cross, Jesus said: *'Forgive them, Father! They do not know what they are doing.'*

Sinful people, in the eyes of Jesus, were **sick or lost, or ignorant**.

Jesus wept over Jerusalem: *'Jerusalem, Jerusalem! You kill the prophets and stone the messengers God has sent you! How many times have I wanted to put my arms round all your people...but you would not let me!'* Jesus came to make the ways of God known to men. The ways which he revealed were very loving!

The sacrament of penance extends this loving attitude towards sinners through the ministers of the Church. John's Gospel records an appearance of Jesus to his disciples after his resurrection:

> *'The disciples were filled with joy at seeing the Lord. Jesus said to them again, "Peace be with you. As the Father sent me, so I send you." Then he breathed on them and said, "Receive the Holy Spirit. If you forgive people's sins, they are forgiven; if you do not forgive them, they are not forgiven".'*
>
> John 20:20-22

SIN

The Catholic Church recognises that sin shows itself in two basic ways.

a) 'Original sin' is the term used for the basic tendency of mankind to turn away from the plan for creation in which God intended that people would be good stewards of the earth and its resources. The description of sin in Genesis 3 is an early attempt to express what everyone sees is true. In this description, it was not God's intention that Adam should eat the fruit of the tree of knowledge of good and evil. The knowledge was gained, however, and so the conclusion is made that all people are born into a sinful world. They are part of it and they contribute to it in terms of local and national quarrels (war), prejudice and discrimination of all kinds, and every variety of criminal act.

In baptism, there is a promise to reject sin, and the symbol of water represents a death to sin and a new life in Christ.

b) Personal sin still occurs even after baptism. Sometimes the matter is serious and public. The label '**mortal sin**' has been attached to serious sin because 'mortis' means 'of death' and serious sin means a death to the life of Christ in which a person is baptized. There are other sins which weaken a person's promise to follow Christ, and these have often received the label '**venial**' meaning 'pardonable' from a word 'venia' which means 'pardon'. It suggests that there are some sins which are less serious, but which give a bad example in the Christian life.

All sin can be described as those thoughts which are not a reflection of God's love for people; those words which do not echo the forgiveness of Jesus; those actions which destroy the love of God for other people; and those failures to help others which neglect the love of God which Christians ought to proclaim to the world.

FORGIVENESS

God sent his son, Jesus, to be the great liberator from sin for God's people. A liberator is someone who brings freedom to people. One only needs to think of the many films of the allied armies marching through towns and cities at the end of the Second World War, to appreciate the wild joy of people who are set free.

Jesus announced the forgiveness of God to the people especially by his own innocent death on the cross. The great sign that this forgiveness was granted was the resurrection of Jesus which was a victory over the greatest human enemy — death. Death and sin are often linked together. The Genesis description of punishment for original sin was death. The resurrection reverses the pattern for human existence. Sin is defeated, and the destiny of human beings is not death but life.

The descriptions which Jesus gave of forgiveness were of:
▶ **sick people being healed**
▶ **lost people being found**
▶ **ignorant people hearing God's good news and changing their lives**

There are many incidents in the life of Jesus which illustrate these descriptions of forgiveness. Perhaps the most famous is the:

Parable of the Lost Son (or 'The Forgiving Father')
(Luke 15:11-32)

'Jesus went on to say, "There was once a man who had two sons. The younger one said to him, "Father, give me my share of the property now." So the man divided his property between his two sons. After a few days the younger son sold his share of the property and left home with the money. He went to a country far away, where he wasted his money in reckless living. He spent everything he had. Then a severe famine spread over that country, and he was left without a thing. So he went to work for one of the citizens of that country, who sent him out to his farm to take care of the pigs.

He wished he could fill himself with the bean pods the pigs ate, but no one gave him anything to eat. At last he came to his senses and said, ''All my father's hired workers have more than they can eat, and here I am about to starve! I will get up and go to my father and say, ''Father I have sinned against God and against you. I am no longer fit to be called your son; treat me as one of your hired workers.'' So he got up and started back to his father.

He was still a long way from home when his father saw him; his heart was filled with pity, and he ran, threw his arms round his son, and kissed him. ''Father,'' the son said, ''I have sinned against God and against you. I am no longer fit to be called your son.'' But the father called his servants. ''Hurry!'' he said. ''Bring the best robe and put it on him. Put a ring on his finger and shoes on his feet. Then go and get the prize calf and kill it, and let us celebrate with a feast! For this son of mine was dead, but now he is alive; he was lost, but now he has been found.'' And so the feasting began.

In the meantime the elder son was out in the field. On his way back, when he came close to the house he heard the music and dancing. So he called one of the servants and asked him, ''What's going on?'' ''Your brother has come back home,'' the servant answered, ''and your father has killed the prize calf, because he got him back safe and sound.''

The elder brother was so angry that he would not go into the house; so his father came out and begged him to come in. But he answered his father, ''Look, all these years I have worked for you like a slave, and I have never disobeyed your orders. What have you given me? Not even a goat for me to have a feast with my friends! But this son of yours wasted all your property on prostitutes, and when he came back home, you kill the prize calf for him!'' ''My son,'' the father answered, ''you are always with me, and everything I have is yours. But we had to celebrate and be happy, because your brother was dead, but now he is alive; he was lost, but now he has been found''.'

There are *four* points in the parable which illustrate the main stages in the Sacrament of Penance. When the young man was in the greatest misery *'he came to his senses'*.

The first important stage in the rite of penance is: *contrition* which means *sorrow for sin*.

The parable tells how the young man planned to say: *'Father, I have sinned against God and against you. I am no longer fit to be called your son.'* This admission of personal responsibility for having offended another person describes what happens when a person makes *confession* of their sinfulness.

The attitude of the father is one of immediate and loving forgiveness. He ran to meet the boy, and his response to the confession of sin was to honour his son and restore him to full membership of the family. The signs of this were the robe, the ring, the sandals, and the feast. The response of the father corresponds to what occurs in *absolution or forgiveness* of sin.

As part of the young man's confession of sin, he made it clear that he was prepared to work as a hired servant, and this indicates that he was prepared to do penance or make up in some way — to give *satisfaction* for what he had done.

The four stages of the young man's return to his family are a good guide to the stages of the New Rite of Penance:

contrition ★ confession
absolution ★ satisfaction

There are three ways in which the Sacrament of Penance can be celebrated:

1. Individual celebration.
2. Community celebration with individual confessions and absolution.
3. Community celebration with general absolution.

Individual celebration of penance

An individual has a choice of two ways of presenting himself for the Sacrament of Penance:

a) In the traditional screen-type of confessional where the priest cannot see the penitent or know who he is. The confession of sin is anonymous.
b) In an 'open' situation where the priest and penitent face each other in a conversational way.

Outline of the Ceremony
1. The Greeting
The new Order of the Sacrament in the documents of Vatican II, emphasises that there should be a conversation between the priest and the penitent. The priest should welcome the penitent so that an easy atmosphere is introduced.

2. Use of scripture
There ought to be a sharing of a suitable passage of scripture which speaks of the mercy of God or the sorrow of sinners, and their forgiveness. The reading helps a person to want to change his/her ways and to trust in the mercy and forgiveness of God.

3. Confession of sin with counsel from the priest
The penitent confesses his/her sins. The priest may help the person to make a complete confession. He 'urges him to repent sincerely of his offences against God; he offers him suitable advice to help him begin a new life and if necessary instructs him on the duties of the Christian life'. (Order of Penance — Para. 18).

4. A suitable 'penance' is given or discussed
The idea of a penance is to give the satisfaction which has been mentioned. A penance is a prayer or an action which will act as a remedy for the main fault of the person. For example, a visit to an elderly grandparent might help a person to overcome his/her selfish ways. A penance may be any of the following:

▶ **a prayer**
▶ **an act of self-denial**
▶ **service of a neighbour**
▶ **works of mercy (visit the sick etc.)**

5. A prayer for pardon (Act of Contrition)
The penitent is invited by the priest to express that he is genuinely sorry for his sins and that he is determined to change to a better way of acting. '...a prayer composed of the words of scripture' is recommended. An example of such a prayer would be: *'Father, I have sinned against you. I am not worthy to be called your son.'*

The Sacrament of PENANCE

1 GREETING
'In the name of the Father and of the Son and of the Holy Spirit.'

2 USE OF SCRIPTURE

3 CONFESSION of sin with counsel from the priest

4 PENANCE is given
A prayer. Service of a neighbour. Self denial. Visits of mercy.

5 PRAYER for pardon

6 ABSOLUTION
'I absolve you from your sins.'

7 PRAYER & PRAISE
'Praise the Lord for he is good.'
'Go in peace.'

---

6. Absolution (Forgiveness)
After the prayer for pardon, the priest 'extending both hands, or at least his right hand', says a set prayer of forgiveness, or absolution. The essential words of this prayer are: *'I absolve you from your sins, in the name of the Father, and of the Son, and of the Holy Spirit.'*

As he says these words, the priest makes the sign of the cross over the penitent. The familiar prayer of absolution is: *'God the Father of mercies through the death and resurrection of his Son has reconciled the world to himself, and sent the Holy Spirit amongst us for the forgiveness of sins; through the ministry of the Church, may God give you pardon and peace, and I absolve you from your sins, in the name of the Father, and of the Son, and of the Holy Spirit.'*

7. Prayer of praise and final blessing
The penitent makes a prayer of praise and thanksgiving, for example: *'Praise the Lord for he is good and his mercy lasts for ever.'* The priest will tell the penitent to *'go in peace'*.

There are circumstances when this fairly long ceremony would have to be shortened because of an emergency or illness. In this case, the following points are made:

▶ **confession of sins**
▶ **penance**
▶ **act of contrition**
▶ **absolution**
▶ **prayer of blessing and dismissal**

The examination of a person's conscience is part of a private preparation before going to the priest.

Community celebration with individual confession and absolution
The ceremony is called 'Order for the Reconciliation of a Number of Penitents, but with Individual Confession and Absolution'. An outline for this kind of celebration for a group would be:
— opening hymn
— a Liturgy of the Word (scripture on the theme of penance)
— homily (sermon on the purpose of sacrament)
— examination of conscience
— general prayer of confession ('I confess')
— prayer or hymn of sorrow
— the Lord's Prayer
— individual confessions (there would be several priests)
— absolution during individual confessions
— community thanksgiving
— final blessing and dismissal

The community celebration of the Sacrament of Penance emphasises the social aspects of sin. Sin affects the whole Church just as pain in one part of the body affects the whole person. It is, therefore, to express not only the desire to be reconciled with God but also with each other.

Community celebration with general absolution
There are circumstances when there are not enough priests to hear the confessions of a large number of people properly, in the time available. If this meant that large numbers of people had to go without Absolution or Holy Communion for a long time, then a service with

general absolution for all the people could he held: *'This can happen on the missions especially, but also in other places, in any gathering where the need arises.'* (Order of Penance — para. 31) Permission for such a celebration is given by the Bishop of the diocese.

The ceremony is similar to that described in *'Community celebration with individual confession and absolution'.* There is a special instruction to be given. The people must be sorry for their sins, and if they have any serious sins they must intend to confess them individually when the opportunity arises. No one could receive a general absolution if they intended to go on leading a sinful life. It is the spirit of the sacrament which is important, not just the carrying out of a ceremony.

A penance is given to the whole group. Before the general absolution is given, some sign is given by those who want absolution. For example, the people might bow their heads, or kneel. There is a community prayer of confession (the 'I confess' for example). This is followed by prayers or a hymn of sorrow. The Lord's Prayer is said, and the general absolution is given by the priest. The ceremony ends with thanksgiving.

CONCLUSION

The Sacrament of Penance celebrates the loving forgiveness of God to his people. It confirms the faith of the people in the fact that Christ died for the forgiveness of sins. It expresses the belief that through the power of the Holy Spirit and the minister of the Church (the priest) forgiveness may be given. In the Church, there is a reconciliation with God and with each other. Also, 'baptism for the forgiveness of sin' is made real in the Sacrament of Penance. Forgiveness is given through the confession of sin, through sorrow and good resolution, and by absolution.

QUESTIONS

Investigation

1. Write out a famous saying of Jesus about forgiveness.
2. Write *two* names for the sacrament in which the Church continues to practise the loving forgiveness of Jesus towards sinners.
3. In which sacrament is original sin forgiven?
4. Give *two* examples which show that the world is not a perfect place to live in.
5. What was the special way in which Jesus announced God's forgiveness to people?
6. Describe briefly *three* methods of celebrating the Sacrament of Penance.
7. What choice does a person have about the way they go to individual confession?
8. Copy the words of absolution.
9. Choose and describe examples of Jesus referring to sinful people as sick, lost or ignorant.

10. Describe an occasion when Jesus gave his followers the authority to forgive sins.
11. Summarise in your own words the parable of the forgiving father (the 'prodigal son').
12. Outline the ceremony for individual confession.
13. What are the special conditions for receiving general absolution?

Understanding

1. What is meant by personal sin?
2. What does the term 'mortal sin' mean?
3. What does the term 'venial sin' mean?
4. What does the word 'prodigal' mean?
5. How is original sin explained in Genesis 3?
6. Explain the idea of sin as Christians understand it.
7. Why do Christians say that the resurrection of Jesus is so important for human beings?
8. Show how the following ideas are contained in the parable of the prodigal son: sorrow, confession, absolution and satisfaction for sin.

Evaluation

1. What do you understand by the phrase 'all people are born into a sinful world'? What evidence would you give to illustrate this?
2. What are the particular advantages of the community celebration of penance with individual confession and absolution? Why do you think some people might prefer this method of celebrating the sacrament?

FURTHER READING

1. *You Gather a People:* pages 55-68.
2. *Real Questions:* chapter 1.
3. *Come Back To Me* (Bavidge).
4. *The Illustrated Catechism:* questions 75-82; supplement pages xii, xiii.
5. *Teacher's Reference: R.E. Scheme for Secondary Schools:* Year 4: pages 72-76.
6. *Focus on Penance and Reconciliation* (Wilkinson).

7.2 RECONCILIATION IN SOCIETY

The Sacrament of Reconciliation (Penance) asks a person to have second thoughts about their lives, to confess their sins and to reform their lives for the future. These ideas also have an application to the problems faced by modern society:

> '...the reconciliation between man and man which means the elimination of every kind of injustice and oppression, the eradication (wiping out) of ideological and nationalistic hatreds, the destruction of every kind of barrier that divides men from men, and men from God.'
>
> J.D. Crichton, *Christian Celebration.*
> G. Chapman, 1973

The group celebration of the Sacrament of Reconciliation draws out the idea that sin damages the relationship between one person and another, and one group with another in society. A healing (reconciliation) of relationships is needed by:

▶ an individual
▶ a group
▶ a nation

This chapter explores three aspects of broken relationships in the world and their healing:
A. Crime and punishment
B. Prejudice and discrimination
C. War and peace

(A) CRIME AND PUNISHMENT

The purpose of law and order

Laws are made to protect the common good of the people. It is the function of the law to define a crime, that is to say when someone has acted against the common good. Breaking the law of the country could be a trivial matter like parking for too long in a place restricted to 30 minutes parking only. On the other hand, it could be something very serious like murder or rape. Police try to prevent crime and to make sure that the law is kept. They also detect crime when it has been committed, and try to bring the offender to justice. Anyone who breaks the law is considered to have committed a criminal act and they are dealt with by the various courts. *'An offender needs to be reconciled with the society whose law has been broken.'*

There are different kinds of courts to deal with an offender. The main ones worth some investigation are:

CRIMINAL COURTS	CIVIL COURTS
Magistrates Court	County Court
Juvenile Court	
Crown Court	High Court
Court of Appeal (Criminal)	Court of Appeal (Civil)

These courts decide the guilt or innocence of a person, and then a punishment or sentence is given and the criminal begins to repay society for crime which has been committed.

Causes of Crime

A person may break the law for a number of reasons. Some of the causes of crime today are:
▶ **greed**
▶ **personal revenge**
▶ **unemployment and boredom**
▶ **influence of newspapers and television** (e.g. violence in popular programmes)
▶ **the demands of drug addiction**
▶ **poor environment**
▶ **careless neglect**

(See illustration on page 99.)

These conditions lead to crimes of violence, theft, sexual assault, breaking and entering, mindless vandalism and destruction of property, and sometimes murder.

Punishment

The types of punishment given by the courts varies. The following are most common:

▶ **attendance centres**
▶ **community service**
▶ **probation**
▶ **fines**
▶ **imprisonment**
▶ **capital and corporal punishment**

(See illustration on page 100.)

Attendance Centre: Young offenders may be required to go to an attendance centre for two hours at a time over a set period. There is an opportunity here for reforming the attitudes which have led to crime in the past.

Community Service: Sometimes the offender is ordered to do a specific number of hours of community service, perhaps in an old-persons' home. The idea of this form of punishment is that the offender has a chance to make up for what he/she has done by giving a positive service to the community. It is aimed at giving the offender an opportunity to reform.

Probation: The offender is allowed to return home provided that certain conditions are kept. No further offence must be committed, and the person must report on a regular basis to his/her probation officer who will help and give counsel. This kind of punishment allows people to realise the seriousness of their crimes and reform their lives with help.

Fines: These are 'heavy' or 'light' depending on the seriousness of the offence. Fines usually prevent a person from wanting to do the same thing again. They may also act as a deterrent to others.

Imprisonment: The criminal is deprived of his/her freedom for a time. There are different kinds of prisons in which the degree of security varies. Prisons for serious crime and for the criminally insane have very tight security. Some others are called 'open prisons' because the prisoners can be given a degree of trust, and the security of these prisons is less formal. On the continent, experiments have been made with the idea of 'part-time' imprisonment. Offenders are allowed to

Causes of crime

Violence & hooliganism

The influence of TV and newspapers

Bad housing

Boredom and unemployment

The demands of drugs

---

keep their jobs but are deprived of their freedom at other times, and return to prison.

There is an element of revenge in imprisonment because the prisoner loses many of the normal privileges of life such as home, employment, friends and privacy. As such, it can act as a great deterrent to the prisoner and to others. On the other hand, open prisons and part-time imprisonment give a prisoner a chance to show that he/she can be trusted, and there is an opportunity for reform of life.

Capital and corporal punishment: Capital punishment involves the death sentence. When a particularly shocking crime has been committed, some people call for the law to allow the death penalty. In some parts of the world, the death penalty is imposed for murder or drug-trafficking. The death penalty is a constant topic for debate. Arguments for and against this form of punishment are well worth considering in detail, because they raise the question of the reasons why people want criminals to suffer for what they have done. The most common forms of administering the death penalty are hanging and electrocution, although the injection of a fatal drug is also used. In the past, there have been more brutal and painful forms of the death penalty, mainly to deter others from crime, but sometimes in order to take revenge.

Corporal punishment involves physical forms of punishment other than the death penalty (e.g. the cane, or a form of mutilation such as the amputation of

a hand or ear, or branding parts of the body). There is no agreement about the value of these punishments, although it is often claimed that they are a great deterrent to the offender and to others.

SUMMARY

Some forms of punishment have the idea of revenge attached to them. It is as though society wants to retaliate for the crime which has been committed. These punishments make the offenders 'pay' for what they have done. Such punishments do not necessarily help the offender give up committing crimes, but they make sure that society is satisfied for the time being. It is possible that the criminal will become bitter, and be much worse as a result of such punishments. Other punishments frighten the offender so much that they, and others, will think twice before committing the same crime again. These punishments deter crime. However, there is a move towards finding suitable forms of punishment which help offenders to see and understand what they have done, reform their ways, and help them in the future. Punishment, therefore, may:

▷ **take retaliation and revenge**

▷ **deter the criminal and others**

▷ **assist in the process of reform**

The teaching of the New Testament

In the Sermon on the Mount, Jesus commented upon the commandment, *'You shall not kill'*:

Matthew 5:21-26

'You have heard that people were told in the past, "Do not commit murder; anyone who does will be brought to trial." But now I tell you: whoever is angry with his brother will be brought to trial, whoever calls his brother "You good-for-nothing!" will be brought before the Council, and whoever calls his brother a worthless fool will be in danger of going to the fire of hell. So if you are about to offer your gift to God at the altar and there you remember that your brother has something against you, leave your gift there in front of the altar, go at once and make peace with your brother, and then come back and offer your gift to God.

If someone brings a lawsuit against you and takes you to court, settle the dispute with him while there is time, before you get to court. Once you are there, he will hand you over to the judge, who will hand you over to the police, and you will be put in jail. There you will stay, I tell you until you pay the last penny of your fine.'

In this passage Jesus looked at the cause of anger which leads to murder. He said that the lack of forgiveness in the home, and broken relationships there, make a mockery out of any sincere attempt to worship God: *'...leave your gift...make peace...then come back.'*

Next, Jesus suggested that disputes with neighbours ought to be settled privately before public cases are made and long-lasting bitterness is established.

Jesus also said something about revenge:

'You have heard that it was said, "An eye for an eye, and a tooth for a tooth." But now I tell you: do not take revenge on someone who wrongs you. If anyone slaps you on the right cheek, let him slap your left cheek too. And if someone takes you to court to sue you for your shirt, let him have your coat as well.

And if one of the occupation troops forces you to carry his pack one kilometre, carry it two kilometres. When someone asks you for something, give it to him; when someone wants to borrow something, lend it to him.'

Matthew 5:38-42

Retaliation was limited in Jewish Law to 'an eye for an eye'. The teaching Jesus gave suggests that there is an even better way. The temptation to retaliate can be resisted. To respond with the same kind of violence as the offence does not solve any problems. It is more likely that the offender will be won by forgiveness. Some modern forms of punishment aim at the correction of the criminal and the opportunity to begin again. Jesus' own life and his treatment of outcasts and sinners helps to deepen an understanding of this teaching which at first sight seems so hard.

Philemon

Paul wrote to Philemon who was the master of the slave Onesimus. Onesimus had committed the greatest crime possible for a slave. He had run away from his master. The punishment for this crime was death. Paul asked

Punishment

1 ATTENDANCE CENTRE

2 COMMUNITY SERVICE

3 PROBATION

4 FINES

5 IMPRISONMENT

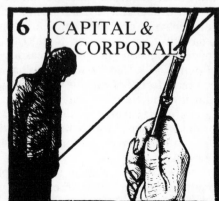

6 CAPITAL & CORPORAL

Philemon to receive the slave back and give him a second chance on the basis that he was now a fellow Christian and a brother in the family of God. This early example of Christian teaching about the right of the master to punish, but the duty of the Christian to forgive, emphasises the purpose of punishment as reform rather than revenge.

CONCLUSION

The healing of relationships between the criminal and society depends on two factors which are closely related to the meaning of the Sacrament of Reconciliation:

1. A change of mind on the part of the criminal; sorrow for past crime and some making up for that crime; and the determination to do better in the future.
2. An intention on the part of society to punish, with an opportunity for a reform of life.

(B) PREJUDICE AND DISCRIMINATION

Prejudice and discrimination divide groups of people from each other. Individuals learn to hate each other as a result of active prejudice or personal suffering from discrimination.

The main forms of prejudice arise through:

▶ **colour**   ▶ **class**
▶ **religion**   ▶ **race**

(See illustration on page 102.)

The main forms of discrimination occur through:

▶ **racial inequality**
▶ **sexual inequality**
▶ **mental handicap**
▶ **physical handicap**
▶ **the generation gap**

Prejudice and discrimination cause major breakdowns in relationships, and in society. There is a great need for reconciliation.

Prejudice
Colour: Some people have no experience of living with others who are different because of the colour of their skin. These people can easily be led to positions which develop a prejudice against people of a different colour. The prejudice involves making a decision about others simply because of their colour. The usual ways in which friendships develop do not apply. An example of the effects of colour prejudice might be detected if a white person reading about a mugging by black youths were to develop a fear of any black person. This fear, combined with ignorance of the person behind the black skin, leads to a judgement which is not based on good reasons. The same person might be aware of a violent crime committed by white youths, but he/she would be able to distinguish between one white person and another, because the person does not have a white-prejudice. Colour prejudice is a very complex human problem today. There are no simple descriptions of the problem and no simple answers.

Class: God made man to be a social person. It matters very much that a person is made to feel that they belong. Wealth, and traditional social classes divide people from each other. The difference between the social classes used to include the advantages which a good education gives. Free education for all has cancelled the idea that some people must be better than others because they are educated.

Even so, a strong regional accent in speech can still cause prejudice because, in some circles, a particular kind of class-accent is considered acceptable and another is not. In the east, the Hindu caste system was an example of class prejudice. Although such a system does not officially exist now, there are still old fears and superstitions concerning the classes.

Race: Different races pass on fear and ignorance of each other. Racial prejudice does not necessarily involve colour at all. The prejudice and brutality practised by the Nazis against the Jews in the Second World War, did not happen because of a colour-prejudice. Jews were thought by the Nazis to be 'vermin' regardless of who they were, or what talents and skills they possessed.

Sometimes racial minorities feel that they are victims of the racial majority, and sometimes the opposite occurs as, for example, in South Africa where government is exercised by a racial minority. These situations feed attitudes caused by racial prejudice.

Religion: Many wars have been fought over religion or in the name of religion. The strongest feelings can be generated by religious hatred between, for example, Israelis and Arabs. The Israelis are Jews, the Arabs are Muslim. Often, the most ignorant of opinions can be passed on from generation to generation. This has frequently happened between Catholics and Protestants. Religious customs can be easily misunderstood, and the misunderstanding can be turned into an outright lie, and the lies are passed on without any second thought or real search for the truth. Fortunately, there are groups of people who work hard to overcome religious prejudice, and the Ecumenical movement among Christians is an example of this.

Discrimination
A person can discriminate in favour of another, or against another. Discrimination involves making a choice on the grounds of colour, race, nationality or ethnic or national origins. It can be applied in the case of a person's education or employment. The 1976 Race Relations Act makes this illegal. The provision of housing, goods, facilities and services is also protected by the Act. The Commission for Racial Equality makes sure that the Act is carried out; it promotes good relations, and equal opportunities for all.

Sexual inequality: Discrimination can occur in favour of men, or in favour of womem. It used to be thought that a man could not be a good nurse: the nursing profession was dominated by women. Equally, it was thought that women could not be good doctors, or lawyers or politicians. It still remains true that most famous artists are men! In a male-dominated industry, women may be sexually harassed with no hope of protection because they fear they will lose their jobs. Sometimes, even when sexual equality is claimed, it is found that men are more frequently favoured for jobs, or the opposite occurs.

Main forms of prejudice

Mental handicap: Mentally handicapped people often look different from 'normal' people, and yet they might be perfectly capable of carrying out some tasks. Yet they often experience discrimination from people who would describe themselves as intelligent. Sometimes it is assumed that the mentally handicapped cannot succeed when really they are never allowed to try.

Physical handicap: The same kind of discrimination can be experienced by people with a physical handicap. They may be better qualified and more proficient, and still suffer discrimination in favour of the physically strong. During the Second World War the Nazis despised any kind of physical blemish and they felt that they were doing a service to the human race by exterminating people with mental or physical handicap.

The generation gap: The struggles between the old and the young cause great quarrels in families and in society as a whole. The young feel that they are not understood, or that their parents are 'old-fashioned'. The older generation think that the standards of their youth have sadly dropped away in today's society. On these grounds, young or old may find themselves discriminated against. Examples of discrimination against the young can still be found in cruel jokes played on a new apprentice in a trade.

Reconciliation

When prejudice and discrimination exist, relationships cannot be healed until people:
1. Stop and have second thoughts about their prejudice.

2. Genuinely regret the bad relations their prejudices have caused.
3. Admit that they have been wrong in some of their opinions.
4. Ask for forgiveness and a new beginning to the relationship.
5. Make up in some way for the damage they have already done by their prejudice or discrimination against others.
6. Begin to build better relationships.

These steps closely follow the pattern set for Catholics by the Sacrament of Reconciliation. If this sacrament is lived out in society, then one could expect such reconciliation between people to occur more often.

OUTCASTS IN THE NEW TESTAMENT

Lepers

Leprosy was one of the most dreaded diseases of the society in which Jesus lived. There was no cure for it, and sufferers were isolated from the rest of society as soon as possible. Prejudiced views about leprosy often condemned people who were not infected, but had a temporary skin complaint. Like the modern scare of AIDS, people thought of leprosy as a great curse which was in some way the fault of the sufferer. One form of leprosy shows itself in a skin eruption like a boil, so ordinary mild skin infections were sometimes mistaken for leprosy which can be a fatal disease unless treated. Judgement without knowing all the facts (prejudice) was often made. There were very strict rules to be followed before a suspected leper could be allowed back into the community.

Whole families were divided from each other because of leprosy, but the fear of the real disease often isolated people when they were suffering from something else. The priestly rules found in the book of Leviticus (chapters 13 and 14) are very detailed, and a person had to be declared 'clean'. They were forbidden to return home because they themselves *thought* they were well: they needed official recognition that they were cured.

Given the terrible fear which people had of leprosy, it was one of the sensational aspects of Jesus' miracles that he healed the ten lepers. The ten lepers, mentioned by Luke, were outcasts on two counts, because it is likely that they were a mixed group containing people who were outcasts for a different reason. There were *Samaritans* in the group: *'As Jesus made his way to Jerusalem, he went along the border between Samaria and Galilee.'* (Luke 17:11)

Samaritans

Samaritans were people of mixed race but descended from the original Israelites who were deported during the period of the exile in Old Testament times. Some Israelites had remained in the country and had married into the foreign families who were sent by the Assyrians and Babylonians to occupy Palestine. The Jews could not forgive them for two things:

1. Marrying into foreign families, many of whom worshipped gods of other religions. They were racially impure.
2. Building a temple for worship on Mount Gerizim. The Jews thought it was impossible to sacrifice to Yahweh (the name for God in the Old Testament) in any place but Jerusalem.

The hatred between Jews and Samaritans was probably the best example of broken relationships between people known in Jesus' day. Jesus taught that love was the most important quality to have and to practise. There could be no greater act of love for a Jew than to accept the company of a Samaritan and treat him as a brother. In the miracle, the ten lepers shout out for help:

> *'He was going into a village when he was met by ten men suffering from a dreaded skin-disease. They stood at a distance and shouted, ''Jesus! Master! Take pity on us!'' Jesus saw them and said to them, ''Go and let the priests examine you.'' On the way they were made clean. When one of them saw that he was healed, he came back, praising God in a loud voice. He threw himself to the ground at Jesus' feet and thanked him. The man was a Samaritan.'*
>
> *Luke 17:12-16*

Jesus remarks on the lack of gratitude of the other ni men:

> *' ''Why is this foreigner the only one who came back to give thanks to God?'' And Jesus said to him, ''Get up and go; your faith has made you well''.'*

Tax-collectors

The Romans occupied Palestine during the time of Jesus. They imposed taxes on the Jews for the upkeep of the Roman Empire, and for the maintenance of the Roman forces in the land. The taxes were collected by Jews. These Jews were hated for two reasons:

1. To collect taxes was collaboration with the enemy. Such men were traitors.
2. They collected more than was necessary, and made a profit for themselves. Their dishonesty was protected by the Roman officers at hand.

Tax-collectors were not acceptable in Jewish company. The teaching of Jesus on brotherly love also included these tax-collectors. It is no wonder that Jesus soon became a controversial figure with law-abiding Jews. The example of Zacchaeus made Jesus the centre of disputes about this particular social issue of the day.

Zacchaeus was the chief tax-collector of Jericho. He was rich, which branded him as one of those who made money on the job. Luke's account is told with good humour. Zacchaeus is a little man, curious to see Jesus. To the horror and dismay of the local people, Jesus chooses to stay with him. Zacchaeus is transformed by the experience, and reforms his way of life.

Jesus and Zacchaeus
(Luke 19:1-10)

'Jesus went on into Jericho and was passing through. There was a chief tax collector there named Zacchaeus, who was rich. He was trying to see who Jesus was, but he was a little man and could not see Jesus because of the crowd. So he ran ahead of the crowd and climbed a sycamore tree to see Jesus, who was going to pass that way. When Jesus came to that place, he looked up and said to Zacchaeus, ''Hurry down, Zacchaeus, because I must stay in your house today.''

Zacchaeus hurried down and welcomed him with great joy. All the people who saw it started grumbling, ''This man has gone as a guest to the home of a sinner!''

Zacchaeus stood up and said to the Lord, ''Listen, sir! I will give half my belongings to the poor, and if I have cheated anyone, I will pay him back four times as much.''

Jesus said to him, ''Salvation has come to this house today, for this man, also, is a descendant of Abraham. The Son of Man came to seek and to save the lost''.'

Prostitutes

Luke delicately refers to the woman in Simon the Pharisee's house as *'a woman who lived a sinful life.'* Women in any age or generation who make their living by prostitution are not considered socially acceptable. Often, in the twentieth century, they are not given the same consideration as 'respectable' women if they are attacked or cheated.

Jesus had been invited to the home of Simon the Pharisee. The woman came in. Jesus had not been given the usual hospitality of water to wash his feet. The woman did not have water and towel, but she had one of the tools of her trade — expensive perfume. She expressed sorrow for the life she led. She cried, and let the tears wash the feet of Jesus. She used her long (and probably beautifully kept) hair to dry his feet. After this, she used the perfume to pour on them.

Simon was shocked that Jesus let the woman touch him. Jesus had a reputation as a holy man. Jesus pointed out two things to his host:

1. He had not given him the usual signs of hospitality, a kiss of greeting and olive oil for his head. (These are eastern customs which are difficult for Westerners to appreciate.)
2. Jesus told him the parable of the two debtors. One owed a little, the other owed a great deal. Both were forgiven their debts. It is likely that the most grateful was the one who was heavily in debt.

> '"I tell you, then, the great love she has shown proves that her many sins have been forgiven. But whoever has been forgiven little shows only a little love." Then Jesus said to the woman, "Your sins are forgiven".'
>
> *Luke 7:47,48*

Simon's guests are horrified that Jesus absolves her in this way. Jesus lived out his message that God is love. When this teaching on love cut across the prejudice and discrimination practised in his society, he became a very suspicious character in the eyes of 'respectable' citizens.

Romans
The Romans were:
> ▶ **conquerors**
> ▶ **foreigners**
> ▶ **heathens**
> ▶ **polytheists**

As *conquerors*, the Romans were hated because of their cruelty. The Jews had painful memories of their punishments for rebellion. As *foreigners*, the Romans were hated because their style of life was very different from that of the Jews. Their physical features were different. Their social customs horrified the Jews.

As *polytheists*, the Romans worshipped many gods. Their religion was so different as to be a constant example of the worst kind of blasphemy. Romans were unacceptable targets for love and service of one's neighbour.

The general prejudice against Romans is shown by the way a Roman officer, who wanted Jesus to heal his servant, sent a deputation of the Jews to Jesus who would vouch for his character.

> 'A Roman officer there had a servant who was very dear to him; the man was sick and about to die. When the officer heard about Jesus, he sent some Jewish elders to ask him to come and heal his servant. They came to Jesus and begged him earnestly, "This man really deserves your help. He loves our people and he himself built a synagogue for us".'
>
> *Luke 7:2-5*

Jesus agreed to go, but the Roman, conscious of what a visit to his house might do to the reputation of Jesus, declared that his home was socially unacceptable, but that he had faith in the fact that Jesus had power to heal which did not need his physical presence.

> 'So Jesus went with them. He was not far from the house when the officer sent friends to tell him, "Sir, don't trouble yourself. I do not deserve to have you come into my house, neither do I consider myself worthy to come to you in person. Just give the order, and my servant will get well. I, too, am a man placed under the authority of superior officers, and I have soldiers under me. I order this one, "Go!" and he goes; I order that one, "Come!" and he comes; and I order my slave, "Do this!" and he does it".'
>
> *Luke 7:6-8*

There is a sense in which Jesus himself displays the prejudice of a Jew towards a Roman when he expresses amazement that a Roman could have more faith in God than his own countrymen: *'Jesus was surprised when he heard this; he turned round and said to the crowd following him, "I tell you, I have never found faith like this, not even in Israel!"'* (Luke 7:9)

SUMMARY
The prejudice and discrimination practised in the twentieth century is paralleled by the kinds of prejudice and discrimination found in Jesus' day which involved:
> ▶ **lepers**
> ▶ **Samaritans**
> ▶ **Tax-collectors**
> ▶ **prostitutes**
> ▶ **Romans**

(C) WAR AND PEACE

Reconciliation between nations
In every age there is a struggle for power, between the nations of the world. The twentieth century is different from all the others because now human beings have the power to destroy themselves and the planet Earth. This is called 'genocide'. There is a need for reconciliation between the nations in a way which is unique in the history of the world.

Causes of War
A war may be caused by any of the following:

> ▶ **greed for power**
> ▶ **the desire to rule by force**
> ▶ **revenge for some offence**
> ▶ **defence of the nation**
> ▶ **injustice to others**
> ▶ **to acquire necessary resources for the people**

The first and last of these motives for war are closely linked. If a nation needs land or other resources for the survival of the people, a small group may fight for those resources. However, success can lead to greed for the power which a victory may bring. Empires have been won and lost in this way. There may be a desire to rule another people by force so that they may be useful in manpower and services for the dominant race. A single incident between two nations may cause one of them to make war on the other in revenge. If a nation feels its freedom or land is being threatened, it may go to war in defence of its people. In countries where governments deny the basic human rights of its citizens, other nations may go to war against them to overcome the injustice of the situation.

A 'Just War'

The following conditions are necessary for a war to be justified in the eyes of the Church:

1. It must be waged by a legitimate authority i.e. by those with the right to make decisions on behalf of the nation.
2. The cause must be serious enough to justify the amount of killing and suffering which a war causes.
3. It must be undertaken with the right intention of producing a just and lasting peace.
4. War should only be a last resort when all other peaceful methods have been exhausted.
5. There should be a reasonable hope of success.
6. The methods used in the war must be morally legitimate.
   a) The innocent must not be killed by indiscriminate slaughter.
   b) It must not result in disproportionate evils to the enemy population, to the home population, or to the international community.

Nuclear war

> *'In this age, which boasts of its atomic power, it no longer makes sense to maintain that war is a fit instrument with which to repair the violation of justice.'*
>
> Pope John XXIII *'Pacem in Terris'*
> *(Peace on Earth)*

In the twentieth century, nuclear arms are used as a deterrent by one nation against another. *Nuclear strategy* means that weapons are placed as a threat to another nation. As long as there are an equal number of effective weapons threatening the major cities of the world, peace is maintained because no one nation could win the war — all would be destroyed.

The Bettman Archive/BBC Hulton Picture Library

U.S. atomic bomb test, central Pacific Ocean, 1946.

The basic effects of nuclear war are the immediate destruction of vast areas of land and population; and long term effects include the pollution and radiation of the planet. This is quite different from the many wars already being waged with conventional weapons like guns and tanks. Conventional weapons depend to a large extent on the personal responsibility and skill of an army. They involve a certain amount of hand-to-hand fighting. In the event of a nuclear war, however, the ultimate responsibility for the destruction of millions of people would be a most impersonal affair.

Disarmament

There are two suggestions for disarming nuclear weapons in the world:

Unilateral disarmament: This requires the courage of one nation to destroy all its nuclear weapons, thus withdrawing the threat of war to any other nation. The hope of such a nation is that all the others would follow suit. The plan would depend on trusting other nations. Some people honestly think that this would work, and they actively campaign for unilateral disarmament.

Multilateral disarmament: This would mean a gradual reduction of nuclear weapons in equal proportions by the most powerful nations. Such disarmament could only be achieved by agreement and special treaties. Some people are convinced that the huge amounts of money spent on defence are justified until these treaties for disarmament are successfully made.

The arms trade

The actual manufacture of weapons and nuclear devices is an important part of the wealth and economy of some nations. Reduction in the manufacture of arms would go hand-in-hand with unemployment and poverty — or so some people think. Alternative economies for such nations would have to be planned.

The New Testament

In the Sermon on the Mount, the message of love taught by Jesus reflects upon the treatment of enemies:

> *'You have heard that it was said, "Love your friends, hate your enemies." But now I tell you: love your enemies and pray for those who persecute you, so that you may become the sons of your Father in heaven. For he makes his sun to shine on bad and good people alike, and gives rain to those who do good and to those who do evil. Why should God reward you if you love only the people who love you? Even the tax collectors do that! And if you speak only to your friends, have you done anything out of the ordinary? Even the pagans do that! You must be perfect — just as your Father in heaven is perfect!'*
>
> *Matthew 5:43-48*

This passage makes a plea for reconciliation between enemies. *'Love your enemies'* suggests that reconciliation begins with the individual person. The reason for loving enemies is given as being because God treats the whole world in this way. Good and evil people alike enjoy the good things of creation: *'he makes his sun to shine...and gives rain to those who do good and those who do evil.'* Jesus adds that even tax-collectors are good to each other. There is no virtue in being generous only to those who will return the compliment! The teaching is that all people ought to reflect the Father who loves the world.

Paul spoke strongly to the Christians in Rome about how they should treat those who persecuted them:

> 'If someone has done you wrong, do not repay him with a wrong...Do everything possible on your part to live in peace with everybody. Never take revenge...Do not let evil defeat you; instead, conquer evil with good.'
> *Romans 12:17,18,19,21*

On the other hand, James speaks to the early Christians about making positive attempts to be peacemakers:

> '...wisdom from above is...peaceful, gentle and friendly...goodness is the harvest that is produced from the seeds the peacemakers plant in peace. Where do all the fights and quarrels among you come from?...You want things but you cannot get them, so you are ready to kill...'
> *James 3:17,18; 4:1,2*

The teaching of Paul and James echoes the teaching of Jesus.

Many people argue that the teaching of Jesus leads to pacifism, or the refusal to fight. Others say that justice in the New Testament is a very strong theme, and that to fight in the cause of what is right is justified.

CONCLUSION

The need for reconciliation between the nations is urgent in the twentieth century. The pattern of the Sacrament of Penance suggests the following stages to peace in the world:

1. Examination of the present nuclear defence programmes (i.e. more international meetings).
2. Recognition and regret for the division of nations and the nuclear threat.
3. Honest declaration of good will for the future.
4. Practical measures towards nuclear disarmament.

None of these stages would ever be easy to undertake, which accounts for the deadlock in nuclear talks today. The abolition of intermediate range missiles was a landmark in progress towards disarmament.

The Christian point of view gives every hope, and the World Council of Churches is active in encouraging Christians to be involved in the current debate about defence and disarmament. The Catholic Church is also deeply involved in peace-making attempts. The letter of Pope John XXIII *Peace on Earth* urges that every effort should be made to reduce the threat of race-suicide to which the nuclear arms race is leading.

Pope John Paul II said to the people of Coventry in May of 1982:

> 'The voices of Christians join with others in urging the leaders of the world to abandon confrontation and to turn their backs on policies which require the nations to spend vast sums of money for weapons of mass destruction...Mistrust and division between nations begin in the hearts of individuals. Work for peace starts when we listen to the urgent call of Christ — "REPENT AND BELIEVE IN THE GOSPEL".'

QUESTIONS

A) CRIME AND PUNISHMENT

Investigation

1. Make a collection of newspaper articles about individual crimes and the punishments given for those crimes. Select *three* types of crime and describe the examples you have of them.
2. What is the purpose of a law?
3. Investigate and give examples of *three* causes of crime today.
4. Name *three* kinds of court set up to deal with offenders and find out more about *one* of them. Describe this type of court.
5. Describe *three* styles of prison.
6. What are the conditions of probation?
7. Describe the difference between capital and corporal punishment.
8. Give examples of the following kinds of punishment: i) intending to take revenge (retribution, retaliation); ii) intending to deter from further crime; iii) intending to reform the offender.
9. Summarise the teaching of Jesus on anger and revenge.
10. Tell the story of Onesimus, the runaway slave.

Understanding

1. Explain the purpose of a fine.
2. What is the function of an attendance centre?
3. What do you understand by the term 'society'?
4. Explain some of the reasons why people steal, or commit acts of violence.
5. What is the point of giving an offender a community service order?
6. Explain the purpose of *either* capital *or* corporal punishment.
7. Explain the Christian attitude towards offenders, using the teaching of Jesus to illustrate your answer.

Evaluation

1. Which do you think is a more severe punishment: a heavy fine, or imprisonment? Give some evidence to justify your conclusion.
2. Do you think the process of forgiveness which is shown in the Sacrament of Reconciliation is a good guide towards finding a solution to crime and its punishment in society today? Give reasons for your answer.
3. Which form of punishment do you think is most Christian? Are there ways of making up for wrong-doing which are hard but still imply forgiveness? Give some evidence for your opinion.

B) PREJUDICE AND DISCRIMINATION

Investigation

1. Collect newspaper articles which show that some form of prejudice is at work. Arrange these into the types discussed in this chapter: colour; class; race; religion. Describe *two* examples from your collection.
2. Describe *two* groups of people who are frequently discriminated against.
3. Describe *two* clear cases of discrimination.
4. Relate the incident of Jesus curing the ten lepers.
5. Relate an incident involving Jesus and a prostitute.
6. Relate an incident involving a Roman.

Understanding

1. Why are prejudice and discrimination wrong for a Christian?
2. What was the cause of the hatred between Jews and Samaritans?
3. What is the difference between prejudice and discrimination?
4. Explain the causes of *two* types of prejudice.
5. Explain the importance of an 'equal opportunity' clause in an advertisement.
6. What is meant by the 'generation gap'?

Evaluation

1. What stages are necessary for solving the problems caused by prejudice and discrimination? Find out about a group which works to heal the damage caused by prejudice (e.g. Corrymeela) and say how far you think they succeed in their aim.

C) WAR AND PEACE

Investigation

1. Outline *three* major effects of a nuclear attack.
2. Describe the conditions for a 'just war'.
3. Summarise in your own words the teaching of Jesus, Paul and James on the treatment of enemies.
4. What advice did Pope John Paul II give to the people of Coventry about the role of Christians in working for world peace?
5. Name an encyclical which is concerned with promoting peace in the world.

Understanding

1. Explain some of the causes of war between nations.
2. Why did Pope John XXIII think that war was no longer an appropriate way to settle disputes?
3. Outline the way in which the Sacrament of Reconciliation can suggest ways of solving the difficulties between nations.

4. Explain the term 'strategy' when it is applied to war.
5. What does the term 'unilateral disarmament' mean?
6. What does the term 'multilateral disarmament' mean?
7. Explain some of the reasons why a pacifist will not take part in violence or war.

Evaluation

1. Do you think a nuclear war could ever be justified? Give evidence for your opinion.

FURTHER READING

CRIME AND PUNISHMENT

1. *Framework:* chapters 16, 17.
2. *Revise Religious Studies:* pages 139-142.
3. *Real Questions:* chapter 8, pages 64-66.
4. *Frontiers:* unit 11.
5. *Problems of Christian Living:* chapter 5.

PREJUDICE AND DISCRIMINATION

1. *Framework:* chapter 11.
2. *Facing the Issues:* chapter 3.
3. *Christian Way:* Book 3: pages 31-34; chapter 10.
4. *Revise Religious Studies:* pages 153-159.
5. *Real Questions:* chapter 2.
6. *Frontiers:* unit 9.
7. *Problems of Christian Living:* chapter 4.

WAR AND PEACE

1. *Framework:* chapter 20.
2. *Facing the Issues:* chapter 6.
3. *Christian Way:* Book 3: pages 22-25.
4. *Revise Religious Studies:* pages 142-144.
5. *Real Questions:* chapter 8, pages 60-63.
6. *Frontiers:* unit 18.
7. *Problems of Christian Living:* chapter 6.

7.3 ANOINTING OF THE SICK

> 'Extreme unction which may also and more fittingly be called Anointing of the Sick is not a sacrament for those only who are at the point of death. . .as soon as anyone of the faithful begins to be in danger of death from sickness or old age, the fitting time for him to receive this sacrament has certainly already arrived.'
>
> *The Constitution on the Sacred Liturgy*
> *— para. 73*

SHORT HISTORY OF THE SACRAMENT OF THE SICK

In this chapter so far this Sacrament has been given three titles:

▶ **Extreme Unction**
▶ **Anointing of the Sick**
▶ **Sacrament of the Sick**

The first of these titles needs some explanation because it is linked with a custom which grew up in the Middle Ages. The tradition for Christian ministers to lay hands upon the sick, pray for them and anoint them with oil, goes back to the New Testament times. In the time of Jesus, diseases and sickness were closely linked with sin. Jesus first forgave the sins of the paralysed man in Mark 2:1-12. Then, as a sign that he had power to do this, Jesus healed the man. On other occasions, he healed first and then said, *'Your sins are forgiven.'* Healing and forgiveness of sin are the two main themes in the Sacrament. In the letter of James, instructions are given about the sick members of any Christian community:

> 'Is there anyone who is ill? He should send for the church elders, who will pray for him and rub olive-oil on him in the name of the Lord. This prayer made in faith will heal the sick person; and the Lord will restore him to health, and the sins he has committed will be forgiven.'
>
> *James 5:14-15*

Because forgiveness of sin was linked with the Sacrament of the Sick, and in the early centuries of the Church severe penances were attached to the Sacrament of Penance, people used to leave the confession of their sins to the last minute when they were on their death bed. They confessed their sins as part of the Sacrament of the Sick. This sacrament was connected more and more with preparation for death. It was called *extreme* (meaning 'at the last moment') *unction* (meaning 'anointing'). In the same way, the idea of the sacrament being a comfort to those who were ill, and a help to their recovery, was lost.

In the Church today the care of the sick and the care of the dying are carefully distinguished. There are instructions for:

For the sick
{
1. Visiting and giving Communion to the sick.
2. The Sacrament of Anointing.
   i) Outside Mass e.g. in the home.
   ii) During Mass.
   iii) With great crowds e.g. on pilgrimage.
}

For the dying
{
3. Viaticum (Holy Communion for a dying person).
4. Penance, Anointing and Communion (Three Sacraments).
5. Confirmation in danger of death.
}

The anointing of the sick can only be understood properly if it is remembered that there are other ceremonies for the dying. Many Catholics still associate the sacrament with the last moments before death.

THE CEREMONY

The stages of the ceremony (rite) for the Anointing of the Sick are:

1. There is a greeting given by the priest to the sick person. At this time, he may sprinkle holy water and give a blessing. The priest explains a little about the anointing of the sick and he will read the instruction of James about sick people (see above).

2. The sick person may go to confession. Sometimes this has been done before the anointing ceremony.

3. There is a reading from scripture. A passage describing Jesus healing sick people is suitable. The priest will give a brief homily (sermon) on the reading.

4. A litany (prayers of intercession) follows. These prayers are for the patient and for those who take care of the sick.

5. The priest lays his hands on the sick person. This is done in silence and it is a powerful symbol of calling down the power of the Holy Spirit to heal the sick person.

6. The priest says a thanksgiving prayer for the oil he is going to use. The oil has been blessed by the bishop of the diocese on Maundy Thursday at the Mass of Chrism (a morning service). If there is no blessed oil available, the priest himself will bless olive oil.

7. The sick person is anointed on the forehead and on the hands with the words:
   Priest: Through this holy anointing may the Lord in his love and mercy help you with the grace of the Holy Spirit.
   Answer: **Amen.**
   Priest: May the Lord who frees you from sin save you and raise you up.
   Answer: **Amen.**

8. The prayer after the anointing should be a suitable one taken from a selection provided in the rite. It may be one for an elderly person, for example, or a sick child.

9. The ceremony ends with everyone joining in the *Lord's Prayer.* The priest gives a blessing.
   (Communion may be given after the Lord's Prayer and before the last prayer and blessing.)

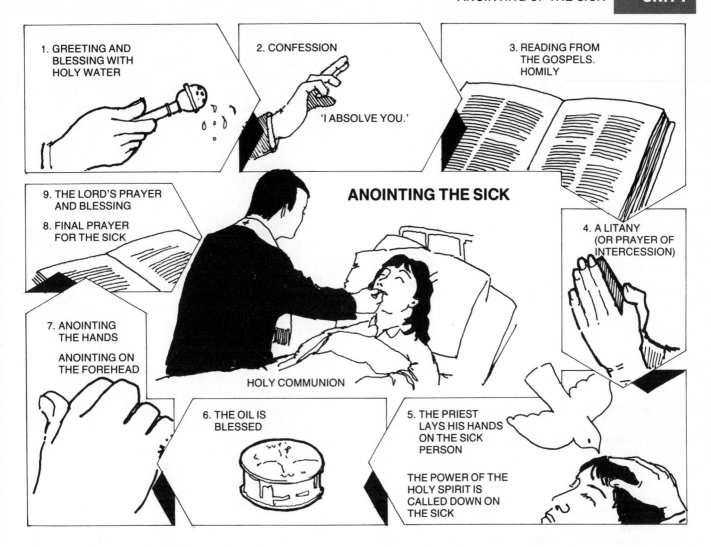

ANOINTING THE SICK

1. GREETING AND BLESSING WITH HOLY WATER

2. CONFESSION — 'I ABSOLVE YOU.'

3. READING FROM THE GOSPELS. HOMILY

4. A LITANY (OR PRAYER OF INTERCESSION)

5. THE PRIEST LAYS HIS HANDS ON THE SICK PERSON — THE POWER OF THE HOLY SPIRIT IS CALLED DOWN ON THE SICK

6. THE OIL IS BLESSED

7. ANOINTING THE HANDS — ANOINTING ON THE FOREHEAD

8. FINAL PRAYER FOR THE SICK

9. THE LORD'S PRAYER AND BLESSING

HOLY COMMUNION

OCCASIONS WHEN A REQUEST FOR THE SACRAMENT SHOULD BE MADE

> *'The faithful should be taught in public and in private to ask for anointing...All who have the care of the sick should be taught the meaning and purpose of anointing.'*
> *Introduction to the Rite of Anointing and to the Pastoral Care of the Sick, Para. 13*

The following occasions are times when the Sacrament of Anointing should be requested:

1. When a person is dangerously ill. The sacrament may be given again if the person recovers on that occasion. If the danger becomes greater in the same illness, the sacrament may be given a second time, and so on. A person may be anointed several times in his/her life.
2. A sick person should be anointed before surgery if the operation is a serious one.
3. Elderly people may be anointed because of their weakness and not necessarily for any dangerous illness.
4. Sick children may be anointed if they would be comforted by the sacrament.
5. Unconscious people who would have asked for the sacrament if they could.

Note: A person who is already dead is not anointed. The priest will say prayers for the dead, asking God to forgive him/her and to receive him/her into his kingdom.

EFFECTS OF THE SACRAMENT

The idea of the Sacrament of Anointing is that, through the Church, Christ continues to care for, to heal, and to forgive sins. Jesus is recorded in Mark's Gospel as saying to his disciples after his resurrection: *'Go throughout the whole world...Believers will be given the power to perform miracles...they will place their hands on sick people, who will get well.'* (Mark 16:15-18)

The Church expects the same effects for the Sacrament of Anointing, as those seen in the life of Jesus in the Gospel. The following effects can be expected:

1. The sick person receives the grace (love and power) of the Holy Spirit of God.

2. The sick are given strength and courage to accept illness. They may completely recover their health.

3. They are not anxious about death. When this fear is lifted, people often get well again.

4. There is forgiveness of sin for the sick person.

5. The prayer of faith has a most important effect for the sick person. James' words are 'The prayer made in faith, will heal the sick person.' Healing in this sense is to be understood as strengthening of the whole person in body and mind. The healing is a spiritual victory over sickness.

CONCLUSION

Illness often brings a crisis in a person's life. For Catholics, the Sacrament of Anointing is a ceremony which gives them spiritual comfort and often recovery of health. The reason for this sacrament is found in the life of Christ who had a special care for the sick and told his followers to have the same concern. The effects of the sacrament are summarised as:

▶ **spiritual comfort**
▶ **forgiveness of sins**
▶ **strengthening to face illness**

A note on Viaticum

It has been noted that there are special rites for people who are dying. Viaticum is Holy Communion given to a dying person. The Latin word suggests that this Communion is *'food for the journey'*. This means the journey or pilgrimage which all Christians make to be like Christ and so enter into the glory of eternal life. (See Unit 7.4, page 112.)

QUESTIONS

Investigation

1. Describe *two* occasions, with examples, when a request should be made for the sacrament of the sick.
2. Write out the *three* titles by which the sacrament is known.
3. Copy what James wrote about the care of the sick, and give an example of how this could happen today.
4. When are the oils used in the sacraments blessed by the bishop of the diocese?
5. Write out the words used for anointing a sick person.
6. Describe briefly the spiritual care provided for the sick and the spiritual care provided for the dying.
7. Describe the ceremony for the anointing of the sick, selecting the most important moments and illustrating them.
8. Relate an incident when Jesus healed a sick person.

Understanding

1. Explain the *two* main themes of the sacrament of the sick.
2. What do the two words 'extreme' and 'unction' mean?
3. What does 'viaticum' mean?
4. Explain why people, in the early days of the Church, often left the confession of their sins to the time of their death.
5. What are the main effects of the sacrament of the sick?

Evaluation

1. Do you think forgiveness and healing are a spiritual comfort to sick people? Do you think some Catholics have the wrong ideas about anointing? Give evidence for your opinions.

FURTHER READING

1. *You Gather a People:* pages 70-75.
2. *His Healing Touch* (Bavidge).
3. *The Illustrated Catechism:* questions 83, 84, 85; supplement page xiii.
4. *Focus on Anointing of the Sick* (Wilkinson).

7.4 FURTHER THEMES

(A) SICKNESS AND HEALING

Sickness is a great sign

Sickness is a great sign of a world which is *imperfect*. The description of sin in Genesis 3 points to a world which is cursed by pain, hard work and death, and tries to find an explanation for it. The conclusion which the writer comes to is that man himself is responsible for the imperfect state of affairs because he makes a faulty response to God's goodness in the simple Genesis account.

Sickness is a great mystery

There are certain kinds of suffering, particularly those which affect children, which are much too heart-rending to be understood. It would be wrong to think that people were ill because they had sinned, like some Jews thought in the time of Christ. Illness is a fact of human existence.

Jesus, the Son of God, transformed human suffering

One of the titles of Jesus is *Messiah*. The Messiah was announced by the prophets of the Old Testament as the *Saviour* of God's people. Isaiah pointed out that the Messiah would reverse the signs of the imperfect world.

> *'Wolves and sheep will live together in peace. ...Even a baby will not be harmed if it plays near a poisonous snake...there will be nothing harmful or evil...'*
>
> *Isaiah 11:6-9*

The greatest impact made by Jesus was through his miracles which defeated the great evil of disease and sickness. The blind were able to see, the lame were able to walk, the deaf were able to hear.

Jesus himself suffered mental and physical pain

Jesus suffered anguish in the Garden of Gethsemane when he pleaded in prayer to be able to escape the suffering which was coming. He also suffered a Roman crucifixion.

The resurrection was a great victory over suffering and death, God raised Jesus from the dead. Jesus promised that all who believed in him would also have *life everlasting*. The Christian faith, therefore, teaches that a person has *value* and *dignity* because of what they are, not because of what they do. Old age and sickness do not devalue a person in the Christian faith. Sick people are a constant reminder to the Church of this truth, and they have a special and positive role in the Church.

> *'Sick people have this role in the Church; to put others in mind of the essential, the higher things...'*
> *Introduction to the Rite of Anointing and to*
> *Pastoral Care of the Sick. Para. 3*

Communion for the sick

In the Catholic Church, the care of the sick is the responsibility of:

1. **The Christian community** — Jesus said in the parable of the sheep and the goats (Matthew 25:31-48), *'I was sick and you visited me.'*
2. **The family and friends of the sick.**
3. **Priests.**

Infirm people do not have to keep the usual fast of one hour before Communion. Their fast is limited to about a quarter of an hour's abstinence from food and alcoholic drink. Communion in the home may be given by a priest or a eucharistic minister (a person commissioned by the bishop to distribute Holy Communion).

Pilgrimages for the sick

There are places such as *Lourdes* where there is a special care of the sick. The sick are prayed for, anointed, and taken to the baths which are connected with many miraculous cures. In the Catholic Church, one of the processes before a saint is publicly proclaimed concerns an examination of miracles of healing attributed to that person. *Healing* is a great sign of God's action in the Church.

Blessing of the sick in Lourdes.

Euthanasia

Euthanasia is sometimes called mercy-killing. It means to hasten the death of a person by drugs, neglect, suffocation, or some other method.

It also means that someone makes a decision that life should end. Christianity teaches that life is a gift from God, and that it is God who decides the moment of death. *Natural* death may be allowed to occur. *Compulsory euthanasia* was practised by the Nazis in World War II when they terminated the lives of physically and mentally disabled people. *Voluntary euthanasia* is encouraged by a society called EXIT, but the Bill proposing voluntary euthanasia has been defeated in the House of Commons whenever it has been discussed (1935, 1950 and 1969). Anyone who helps another person to end his life is liable to a criminal charge of murder or manslaughter.

(B) DEATH AND ETERNITY

Christian teaching on death

The Creeds of the Church contain the phrase: *'I believe ...in the resurrection of the body, and life everlasting.'* This phrase summarises the fact that Christians are people who believe that if a person belongs to Jesus Christ (by baptism) he/she will have eternal life after their death.

'The importance of this final article of the baptismal Creed is obvious: it expresses the goal and purpose of God's plan.' (The Reality of Life after Death: A Post-Conciliar document of the Church)

The Church believes that the resurrection refers to *the whole person* and that it is an extension to human beings of the *resurrection* of *Christ himself*. There is a belief that people who have lived according to law of Christ will be happy and will one day be with Christ.

'There will be eternal punishment for the sinner, who will be deprived of the sight of God.' (Ibid)

The Church believes that there is a 'purification' for good people before they see God. This 'purification' is not like the punishment of the damned. The 'purification' of good people is called *purgatory*. The punishment of the damned is called *hell*. The happiness of being with God is called *heaven*.

The Christian hope concerning life after death is that:
▶ there is a *continuity* between the present life and the future life. The measure for this future life is the *love* shown in life to others. *('Charity is the law of the Kingdom of God'.)*
▶ there is a radical *break* between the present life and the future life. In the present life, the Christian has faith, and lives this faith through the *sacraments*. In the future life, *'we shall see God.'* (I John 3:2)

Scriptural images and human imagination about eternity

The Church teaches that a proper picture of life after death cannot be realised by the descriptions given in the Bible, or by what can be imagined: *'What no one ever saw or heard, what no one ever thought could happen, is the very thing God prepared for those who love him.'* (I Corinthians 2:9)

Care of the dying

Christian death follows the pattern of the example of Christ. A great proportion of each of the four Gospels is concerned with the:

▶ **suffering** (Passion)
▶ **death and**
▶ **resurrection of Jesus**

Therefore, the care of dying people is most important in the Catholic Church.

Viaticum

Viaticum is the sacrament for people who are facing death. Viaticum is Holy Communion. It is a way of strengthening the faith of the dying person because they are joining Christ in his own journey through suffering and death to resurrection. *'Whoever eats my flesh and drinks my blood has eternal life, and I will raise him to life on the last day.'* (John 6:54)

Having received viaticum, the dying person may receive Holy Communion on other visits before death actually occurs. There is a Mass of Viaticum if the person is well enough to attend.

Anointing of the Dying

There is a special rite of anointing for the dying. The Anointing of the Sick is the sacrament of forgiveness and healing, so the separate anointing for the dying person preserves the meaning of the sacrament.

Commendation of the Dying

Jesus said on the cross: *'Father! In your hands I place my spirit.'* (Luke 23:46) Other translations say 'I *commend* my spirit.'

The commendation of the dying is a series of prayers and readings which help and comfort a dying person. They help that person to place their lives trustingly into the loving hands of God who is their Father, their creator, and one who loves them.

The Hospice Movement

Medical care of the dying has sometimes been unhelpful in that it concentrated on nursing the body of a sick person, but did not look at the needs of the whole person and their family.

The Hospice Movement is dedicated to dying people and their families. It makes a special study of the control of pain so that the person can remain conscious but free of pain. It helps families to understand what is happening to the person they love, and to care for the dying in their own homes. In this connection, the example of Mother Teresa caring for the dying people of Calcutta and throughout the world is an outstanding witness to Christian values concerning death.

QUESTIONS

Investigation

1. Name *four* kinds of disease and illness cured by Jesus.
2. Describe *two* cases when some people think that euthanasia ought to be allowed.
3. Describe, in detail, *one* occasion when Jesus suffered *either* physically *or* mentally.
4. What do Christians believe about death and eternity?
5. Describe the spiritual care of the dying provided by the Catholic Church.
6. Describe the work of the hospice movement, and find out about the work of one *named* hospice in the area where you live.
7. Describe a place of pilgrimage for sick people, and some of the activities which take place there.

Understanding

1. Explain what is meant by *voluntary* euthanasia.
2. Explain what might be involved in carrying out *involuntary* euthanasia.
3. Explain the function of a eucharistic minister in the Catholic Church.
4. What does the term 'purgatory' mean?
5. Explain the way in which sickness is a sign and a mystery.

Evaluation

1. What are the arguments used by some people to show that the old, the sick and the handicapped are of no use to society?
2. Write out your own thoughts on euthanasia and give reasons for your opinions.
3. What is your opinion of places like Lourdes where sick people are taken on pilgrimage and where they ask for healing?
4. What evidence is there that sick people benefit from the prayers and other practices of a pilgrimage?
5. If you were sick, would you ask to be taken on a pilgrimage? Give reasons for your answer.

FURTHER READING

SICKNESS AND HEALING

1. *Framework:* chapter 22.
2. *You Gather a People:* pages 76-78.
3. *The Illustrated Catechism:* question 86.
4. *Frontiers:* unit 15.
5. *Real Questions:* pages 86-89.

DEATH AND ETERNITY

1. *Framework:* chapter 25.
2. *Christian Way:* Book 3, chapter 14.
3. *Revise Religious Studies:* pages 150-152.
4. *Real Questions:* chapter 3.
5. *Problems of Christian Living:* page 130.
6. *Teacher's Reference: R.E. Scheme for Secondary Schools:* Year 4: page 26.

THE PERSON & MINISTRY OF JESUS — ST MARK'S GOSPEL

UNIT 8 The Gospel of Mark

8.1	*Social, political and religious background*	**117**
8.2	*The making of Mark's Gospel*	**120**
8.3	*The structure of Mark's Gospel*	**124**

UNIT 9 Christianity in Mark's Gospel

9.1	*'Who do people say I am?'*	**128**
9.2	*Disciples of Jesus*	**132**
9.3	*The Kingdom of God*	**136**
9.4	*Parable and allegory; miracle and sign*	**140**
9.5	*Opposition and conflict*	**146**
9.6	*The suffering, death & resurrection of Jesus*	**151**

THE GOSPEL OF MARK

8.1 SOCIAL, POLITICAL AND RELIGIOUS BACKGROUND

SOCIAL BACKGROUND

The people who appear in the Gospel come from three kinds of background: ▶ old Jewish towns ▶ Roman centres ▶ rural areas. Jesus himself lived in the Old Testament town of Nazareth. When he taught the crowds, they came from: 'Galilee, from Judaea, from Jerusalem, and from the territory of Idumea, from the territory on the east side of the Jordan, and from the region around the cities of Tyre and Sidon.' (Mark 3:8)

These regions represent every area of Palestine from the deep south to the northern cities in Phoenicia. Jerusalem had a strong Roman presence: the Roman fort and Praetorium was adjacent to the temple buildings. The great trade routes from Egypt came through Idumea.

The ten Greek towns (*The Decapolis*) were on the east side of the Jordan. The people who lived in this region were mainly Gentiles, and generally cut themselves off from Jewish people and their ways. The man who lived in the region of Gerasa, and was cured of the evil spirit, 'Mob', later went '...all through the Ten Towns, telling what Jesus had done for him.' (Mark 5:20) The cure of the deaf and dumb man (Mark 7:31-36) is only recorded by Mark, and it took place in the Decapolis region. Mark says, '...they kept talking about it...' (v.36).

The shepherds, farmers and fishermen came from the rural areas around the Sea of Galilee. The crowds which followed Jesus, therefore, represented every type of social grouping in Palestine in the first century AD.

The Roman way of life was unacceptable to the Jews. Jews would not mix with Romans on a social level for three reasons:

▶ **religious:** Romans were polytheists. Jews were monotheists.
▶ **dietary:** Jews ate only permitted foods and meat prepared according to the law.
▶ **political:** The Romans were conquerors. The Jews resented the taxes they paid to Rome for the up-keep of the army of occupation.

For these reasons racial prejudice was very strong among the Jews. (See Unit 7.2)

There were great contrasts between the wealthy and the poor. The wealth of the Roman cities built in the Greek style in the Decapolis region was a source of wonder and suspicion to the Jews. Any Jew who co-operated with the Romans or adopted their customs was considered a traitor and was despised by his own people. When Jesus mixed with 'tax-collectors and sinners' he risked his own reputation.

Social life and customs

Social customs concerning home life, weddings and death are illustrated in Mark's Gospel. The healing of the paralytic in Chapter 2 notes that the four men 'made a hole in the roof' which refers to the houses of the poor which had flat roofs. These roofs had rough rafters with a covering of branches plastered with mud and straw. The simple houses and the lives of the poor contrasted strongly with the wealth of the Roman houses and their way of life.

When Jesus wanted to contrast his disciples with those of John the Baptist, he described his presence among them as being *a bridegroom among his wedding guests*: *'Do you expect the guests at a wedding party to go without food? Of course not!'* (Mark 2:19) Jesus refers to the lavish hospitality of a Jewish wedding feast.

When Jairus' daughter died, Mark says: *'Jesus saw the confusion, and heard all the loud crying and wailing.'* (Mark 5:38) This verse refers to the Jewish custom of hiring **professional mourners** to **weep** and **wail** for a dead relative.

The imagery of the parables

Jesus taught a great deal in parables. He used everyday examples in his illustrations. When he spoke of the different behaviour of his disciples, he talked about the effect of **new cloth** as a patch on an **old cloak** (Mark 2:21), and the necessity of **fresh wineskins** for **new wine** (Mark 2:22).

He used imagery of the fields and agricultural life: the farmer *'scatters'* his seed. The seed falls on the **path, rocky ground**, and **among thorn bushes**. He speaks of **lamps** and **sickles**. He tells his disciples to be on their guard against the *'yeast of the Pharisees and the yeast of Herod'*. He teaches his disciples about faith and prayer from the parable of the **fig-tree** (Mark 11:20-26). The parable of the tenants in the vineyard reflects the typical **vineyard** with its **wine press** and **watch tower** (Mark 12:1-8).

Other references to everyday life

Jesus speaks of the **salt** of the sacrifice (Mark 9:49), referring to the salting of meat to make it kosher. When the woman in Bethany poured perfume on the head of Jesus, he said, *'She poured perfume on my body to prepare it ahead of time for burial'*. Behind this remark lay the customs of the Jews for preparing bodies for burial by anointing them. The linen sheet brought by Joseph of Arimathea also reflects the way in which the dead were buried.

SUMMARY

The social background to Mark's Gospel illustrates the following aspects of life in Palestine at the time of Christ:

▶ **types of people**
▶ **city life**
▶ **town life**
▶ **the agricultural community**
▶ **social customs**
▶ **houses: food: domestic utensils**
▶ **village crafts**

POLITICAL BACKGROUND

Rome

At the time of Christ, Palestine was part of the Roman province of Syria. The country was riddled with the activities of a people who hated the army of occupation. They looked forward to their idea of the Messiah who would be a great national leader and *liberator* of the people. Heavy taxes were taken from the people to pay for the upkeep of the Roman Empire.

Roman Inspector of Taxes, c. AD30.

Herod

Herod the Great had been allowed by Rome to govern Palestine with the title *'King of the Jews'*, even though he was an *Idumean* and not a Jew at all. Herod the Great died in 4BC so by the time of Christ, Palestine had been divided between his three sons:

- ▷ **Herod Archelaus**
- ▷ **Philip**
- ▷ **Herod Antipas**

Herod Archelaus was deposed for his incompetence and cruelty, and the region of Judaea and Samaria was governed by a *procurator* sent from Rome. Pontius Pilate was sent to fulfil this duty.

Philip governed land to the north-east of Galilee. Herod Antipas governed Galilee and Peraea which was land to the east of the Jordan. The Jews hated the sons of Herod and also the Roman procurator. However, a few people, called Herodians, felt that the return of one Herodian king to rule Israel would solve their political problems.

The Publicans/Tax-Collectors

All countries conquered by Rome became part of the Empire and paid tribute (taxes) to Rome and those employed by Rome in the provinces. Palestine came under the province of Syria and the army of occupation came from there. Tax-collectors were people employed by the Romans to collect the tribute. There would be taxes for an individual's property, so they kept a census of the people as well as collecting the taxes for public amenities like roads and bridges. The people hated the men employed locally to collect taxes for their masters. It was well known that these people became rich themselves by collecting more than was due to the Roman overlords. They were hated by the people, and if they were Jews, they were seen as traitors to the nation.

Zealots

The Zealots were deeply religious Jews who thought that violence was justified if it was in defence of the Jewish religion. They were loyal to the law of Moses and the worship of the Temple in Jerusalem. In Mark's list of the apostles, he names Simon 'The Patriot' or Zealot. The Zealots were Jewish patriots who caused a great deal of unrest among the people, and Jesus was suspect when he had a Zealot among his closest followers. The political charge which was brought against Jesus was 'King of the Jews'.

Samaritans (See Unit 7.2)

It is worth noting that, politically, Samaria was part of the province of Judaea. However, the bitterness and resentment which existed between the Jews and the Samaritans was so great that Jews travelling south to Jerusalem would cross the Jordan rather than travel through Samaria. There is a suggestion that sometimes Jesus did this: *'Then Jesus left that place, went to the province of Judaea and crossed the River Jordan.'* (Mark 10:1)

Luke, however, records a specific incident when the disciples were very angry because a Samaritan village would not receive their company because they were going to Jerusalem (Luke 9:52-56). It is clear that the religious struggles between the Jews and the Samaritans, and the political consequences, are reflected in the life of Jesus.

RELIGIOUS BACKGROUND

It is quite clear that there comes a point when the political and religious background of Mark's Gospel becomes so inter-related that the two cannot be separated. The Zealots, for example, were deeply religious Jews who became political agitators simply because of their religious convictions. This same situation applies to the relationship of the Pharisees, the Sadducees and the Essenes, to the Roman authorities. It is important to realise that the Jews felt that God ruled their people, so law and order in the nation had both religious and political significance.

The Sanhedrin

The Council of the Sanhedrin was led by the High Priest and seventy elders. Members of the council included Pharisees and Sadducees. The Sanhedrin was a court of law for the Jews, and had its own guards or police officers. It was allowed by the Romans to punish offenders, but only the Roman authorities could give the death penalty. When the Sanhedrin passed the sentence of death on Jesus (Mark 14:64) they had to refer his case to the governor, Pontius Pilate. Although the Sanhedrin condemned Jesus on the religious charge of blasphemy (*'Are you the Messiah, the Son of the Blessed God?'*), the charge brought before Pilate was a political one: *'Are you the king of the Jews?'* (Mark 15:2)

Sadducees

This powerful group of men are a good example of the combination of religious and legal authority among the Jews. They were very wealthy, probably descended from the priest-class of the nation, and the equivalent of the aristocracy in western society. The Romans allowed

Arthur Baker

them authority among the Jewish people. It was one of the Roman methods of government to allow conquered peoples to have local officials who acted under the authority of Rome. The Sadducees were very conservative Jews who followed the Law of Moses in the **Pentateuch** (the first five books of the Bible) exactly. They did not recognise the authority of the **oral tradition** of the Jews, which explained the way in which the **Torah** (the Law) was to be kept. They also rejected developments in Jewish theology like belief in resurrection. Their interpretation of the Jewish religion brought them into conflict with the **Pharisees**, and kept the judgements of the Council of the Sanhedrin divided.

Pharisees

Whereas the Sadducees were remote from the Jewish people as a whole, the Pharisees were the great interpreters of the Jewish religion to the people. They believed that, from the time of Moses, God had given the people an **oral tradition** which explains how the great written law of Moses must be lived in daily life. They were concerned with keeping the rituals of the Jewish religion exactly. They attended the full temple services. They fasted twice a week. They were not priests, but their way of life set them apart from the people, and marked them as a professional religious group. They were very influential, and many of the great council (the Sanhedrin) were Pharisees. Sometimes, their religious fanaticism hid the true spirit of Judaism, and this is reflected in the criticisms made by Jesus and recorded in Mark's Gospel. An example would be when Jesus said to them: *'You have a clever way of rejecting God's law in order to uphold your own teaching...'* (Mark 7:9)

Scribes

This group of men were extremely well educated. They were experts in the scriptures and the writings of the Jewish religion. As the scriptures contained the laws by which the people lived, the scribes were the interpreters of the law as well. They were very influential, and their knowledge meant that they were closely connected with the Pharisees. It was a scribe who asked Jesus: *'Which commandment is the most important of all?'* (Mark 12:28) Mark called the scribe *'A teacher of the Law'*.

Essenes

The discovery of the Dead Sea Scrolls has revealed the existence of religious groups who are not explicitly mentioned in the New Testament but whose way of life helps to explain the writings of the New Testament. The Essenes lived in communities, and kept themselves apart from the public form of the Jewish religion which was expressed by members of the Sanhedrin and trusted by Rome. These communities probably influenced the religion of the ordinary people, and it has been suggested that the work and life of John the Baptist reflects the Essenes' way of life. An example of this would be the emphasis which the Essenes placed upon the importance of ritual bathing. John baptized people in the river Jordan. He also *'appeared in the desert'* (Mark 1:4) and the Essenes settled in remote places like Qumran where the Dead Sea Scrolls were found.

The religious background of Mark's Gospel also includes the importance of Temple worship, the observance of the Sabbath and the expectation of the Messiah. However, these aspects will be discussed in the themes of Mark's Gospel in Unit 9.

CONCLUSION

The social, political and religious background of the Gospel of Mark illustrates the life and ministry of Jesus. Jesus was a Jew, living in an occupied country, and deeply influenced by the culture and traditions of his own people. His interpretation of the Jewish religion and the traditions of the Pharisees brought him into conflict with the authorities.

The purpose of the Gospel of Mark is to proclaim that Jesus was the Christ, the anointed Messiah, of the Jewish people: *'This is the Good News about Jesus Christ, the Son of God'* (Mark 1:1)

QUESTIONS

Investigation

1. Find out all you can about *four* places from which people came to listen to Jesus.
2. Which region of Palestine contained one of the main trade routes from Egypt?
3. Write down *four* daily objects or sights which Jesus spoke about in his parables.
4. To which province of the Roman Empire did Palestine belong?
5. Name the *three* sons of Herod the Great.
6. What were the taxes of the Jewish people used for?
7. Give another name for a Jewish patriot at the time of Jesus.
8. Describe the membership of the Sanhedrin.
9. Who were the scribes?
10. State *one* place where the Essenes lived.
11. Find out all you can about the Dead Sea Scrolls.
12. Give examples from Mark's Gospel which tell us something about home-life, weddings, and funerals in the time of Jesus.
13. Who was Herod the Great and what happened to his kingdom when he died?
14. Write about some of the ways in which ordinary people would have been affected by the Roman occupation of Palestine.

Understanding

1. What does the word 'Decapolis' mean, and explain why it would be unusual for a Jew to have a great influence there.
2. Explain why some Jews would not mix socially with Romans.
3. Explain the importance of knowing something about the way houses were constructed in the time of Jesus. (Refer to the miracle in Mark 2:1-12.)

4. What does the word 'kosher' mean, and what is its importance in the daily life of a Jew.
5. Why did Jews often cross to the east of the Jordan when they travelled from the north to the south of Palestine?
6. Explain why law and order had both religious and political importance for the Jews.
7. Why did the Sanhedrin have to send Jesus to Pilate after they passed the death sentence?
8. Explain *two* items of belief on which the Sadducees and Pharisees disagreed.
9. What was the purpose and the importance of the oral tradition of the Jews?
10. In what ways do the parables reflect the social life of Palestine in the first century?
11. Explain why the Zealots might have had great hope in Jesus.

Evaluation

1. If a person is not interested in history or sociology, they might find studying the background of a Gospel boring. How would you persuade this person that the background brings the Gospel to life?
2. What is the evidence in the Gospels that Jews and Samaritans hated each other?
3. Do you think ordinary people would have found Jesus' teaching very different from that of professional religious people (teachers of the law, Pharisees)? Give the evidence for your answers.

FURTHER READING

1. *According to Mark:* A6, A7.
2. *The Gospel in the Making:* pages 31-34.
3. *Revise Religious Studies:* pages 1-12.
4. *A First Gospel Commentary:* pages 1-6.
5. *Setting the Foundations:* chapters 3, 4, 5.
6. *Jesus* (Chichester Project Book 4): chapters 2, 3.

8.2 THE MAKING OF MARK'S GOSPEL

In this chapter a series of simple questions will be asked. The answers to these questions are far from simple because one can only use the suggestions made by scholars, or guess the answers from the clues that lie in the Gospel itself. However, by attempting an answer to the questions, an idea of the making of Mark's Gospel begins to emerge.

The questions:
▶ **Who is Mark?**
▶ **When did Mark write his Gospel?**
▶ **Why did Mark write a Gospel?**
▶ **Who did Mark write for?**
▶ **What did Mark want his readers to know?**
▶ **What were the sources of Mark's information?**
▶ **Who else wrote for the early Christian Church?**

Suggested outlines to help find the answers:

Who is Mark?
The bishop, Papias, in the second century, said that he knew of a good authority which claimed that Mark was the interpreter of Peter, but that he was not an eye-witness to the ministry of Jesus. *'Neither did he hear the Lord, nor did he follow him',* says the authority quoted by Papias.

Most scholars agree that the author of Mark's Gospel was the John Mark mentioned in the New Testament (Acts 12:12; Colossians 4:10; Philemon v.24; 2 Timothy 4:11; 1 Peter 5:13). Mark is certainly an author who is close to the earliest preaching and teaching about Jesus. There is no certain answer about his identity. There would be many people in the early Christian communities of the Roman Empire who were called 'Marcus'. It was a common name at the time.

When did Mark write his Gospel?
There is a general agreement that the Gospel was written sometime between AD65 and AD75. In this ten year period the early Christian Church experienced persecution by the Romans. In AD64 Nero made the Christians a scapegoat for the burning of Rome, and many were tortured and executed. In AD70, Jerusalem was completely destroyed. There are suggestions that Mark refers to this persecution and destruction in the Gospel, especially in chapter 13. He seems to hold out hope for those who are suffering: *'...before the end comes, the gospel must be preached to all peoples.'* (Mark 13:10)

It would seem quite sensible to record what was preached about Jesus by eye-witnesses if those same eye-witnesses either died or were put to death during the time of persecution.

Why did Mark write a Gospel?
It has been suggested that Mark wrote to comfort the Christians in Rome who were facing all kinds of problems, including the death penalty, for practising an illegal religion. In the very early days after Pentecost, Christians were thought by the Romans to be just another kind of Jew, and they allowed the Jews to practise their religion. Soon, the message and good news about Jesus Christ was taken to Gentiles (non-Jews)

who did not want to be practising Jews as well as Christians. The Christian faith became much more independent, and recognisable as a separate religion. Christianity lost the protection which the Jewish faith had given it. The Christians in Rome, after AD64, were crushed by persecution. The writing of Mark's Gospel did four things:

1. **Preserved** the first-hand preaching about Jesus after the apostles died.
2. **Encouraged** the Christians in Rome by showing that Jesus was misunderstood and rejected, just as they were.
3. **Pointed to the future** and emphasised the coming of the Kingdom of God. '...*there are some here who will not die until they have seen the Kingdom of God come with power.*' (Mark 9:1)
4. **Answered** some important questions for the Christian community.

The last point is very important. There are about sixty questions asked in the Gospel. A selection of them will show that Mark has the same cares and concerns as a pastor and a theologian. The answers to the questions raised in the Gospel emphasise Mark's message for his readers:

A – that God is victorious over all evil in the world through the work of Jesus, 'the Christ'.
B – that the message of Jesus was for all people, not just the Jews.
C – that the kingdom of God would be known when God's ways were followed by his people, and they accepted personal responsibility for the growth of the Kingdom, (see the purpose of the parables in Unit 9.3).
D – that Jesus was the Messiah (Christ) who suffered in the service of God.
E – that the practical problems of Christian living in the first century AD could be solved by careful attention to the teaching of Jesus.

A

▶ evil spirits ask Jesus: *'Have you come to destroy us?'*
— Mark shows that this is certainly true and a sign of the coming of God's Kingdom.

B

▶ some people ask: *'What is this? A new teaching?'*
— Mark shows the new people of God that Jesus' life and ministry is for all, not just the Jews.
▶ the teachers of the law ask: *'Who can forgive sins but God alone?'*
— Mark wants his readers to know that Jesus is the Christ, the Son of God, and that God's work is done in him.
▶ Jesus asks: *'What does our Law allow us to do on the Sabbath?'*
— Mark knows of the struggle in the early Church to distinguish the duties of the Jewish converts from the *new* religious practices of the Christian community, which did not involve the *old* law. The 'Sabbath' was kept by Christians on Sunday, not from sunset on Friday to sunset on Saturday.

C

▶ Jesus teaches: *'What shall we say the Kingdom of God is like?'*
— It is very important to Mark that his readers understand the nature of God's Kingdom, as a growth in faith. (See Unit 9.3)

D

▶ Some questions refer to Jesus himself. Mark emphasises the innocence of Jesus at the time of his trials. The Messiah is the servant of God who suffers for what is right:

'Isn't this the carpenter?'
'You have eyes. Can't you see? You have ears. Can't you hear?'
'Who do people say I am?': 'What about you?'
'By what authority are you doing these things?'
'How can the teachers of the law say that the Messiah will be the descendant of David?'
'Did you have to come with swords and clubs to capture me, as though I were an outlaw?'
'Have you no answer to the accusation they bring against you?'
'Are you the Messiah, the Son of the Blessed God?'
'Why do we need any more witnesses? What do you think?'
'Are you the King of the Jews?'
'What crime has he committed?'

E

▶ Some questions refer to the life of the Christian community, and they are given answers which are in keeping with Jesus' ministry and teaching:

'Who are my mother and my brothers?'
'Why are you so afraid? Do you still have no faith?'
'Why is it that your disciples do not follow the teaching handed down by our ancestors?'
'Don't you understand? Nothing that goes into a person from the outside can really make him unclean.'
'Does a person gain anything if he wins the whole world but loses his life?'
'Why couldn't we drive the spirit out?' (of the epileptic boy)
'Does our Law allow a man to divorce his wife?'
'What must I do to inherit eternal life?'
'Who then can be saved?' (after Jesus' teaching on wealth.)
'Is it against our Law to pay taxes to the Roman Emperor?'
'When all the dead rise to life on the day of resurrection, whose wife will she be?'
'Which commandment is the most important of all?'

There are other questions which hint at the temptations facing the early Christians to betray their friends, and give up their faith. Peter is given as the example of one who denies Jesus.
▶ the disciples ask in desperation: *'Teacher, don't you care that we are about to die?'*
— Mark's answer to this question is one of the great themes of his Gospel. The Christian community is given proof after proof that God's plan is safe, and that they are following his path.

Themes of Christian living covered by Mark include:

▶ **Wealth, charity and fellowship**
▶ **Ambition and promotion**
▶ **Christian mission and service: being a witness**
▶ **Trials, temptation and betrayal**
▶ **Coming to terms with fear**
▶ **Bereavement and resurrection**
▶ **Christian marriage**
▶ **Prayer**

Briefly, Mark wrote a Gospel because he wanted to give 'glad tidings' to his Christian community. What he wrote was good and welcome news which explained the ministry of Jesus, encouraged the people and showed the way for the future.

Who did Mark write for?

It is important to realise that Mark does not actually say to whom he is writing. There are clues in the Gospel which lead to the conclusion that it was written in Rome. Mark describes the problems and situations which the Christians in Rome experienced. Papias thought that Mark was Peter's companion and tradition says that Peter died in Rome. Mark wrote for Christians suffering persecution. He also wrote for the future of Christianity.

An old ending to the Gospel, sometimes thought to have replaced a lost, original ending, says:

> *'Go throughout the whole world and preach the gospel to all mankind. Whoever believes and is baptized will be saved; whoever does not believe will be condemned.'*
>
> *Mark 16:15,16*

Whoever Mark wrote for, and whatever difficulties they had, he saw a future for them and for the Christian message.

What did Mark want his readers to know?

Unit 9 will look at the themes of Mark's Gospel, but a simple outline is as follows:

1. Mark shows that Jesus is the Son of God (Unit 9.1).
2. Jesus is a human person who acted with great power (Unit 9.4).
3. Jesus is the Messiah but not the popular idea of a Messiah which most Jews expected (Unit 9.1).
4. Mark wants his readers to know about the Kingdom of God (Unit 9.3).
5. Mark emphasises what it means to be a disciple of Jesus (Unit 9.2).
6. Mark shows an understanding of persecution through the conflict of Jesus with the Jews and Romans (Unit 9.5).
7. Mark wants to answer some important questions about the death and resurrection of Jesus, the final judgement and the end of time (Unit 9.3 and 9.6).
8. Mark wants to point the way to some answers for difficult decisions which Christians face in trying to follow the teaching of Jesus.

What were the sources of Mark's information?

Papias, who died about the year AD130, knew 'John the Elder' and was familiar with the very earliest Christian communities. He had it on good authority that Mark was the 'interpreter of Peter', and his companion. Papias said that Mark wrote carefully about the words and deeds of the Lord (Jesus) but that he had not himself heard Jesus. The suggestion is that Mark was close to Peter, and he passed on the information which Peter used in his sermons. There is evidence that some of Mark's information seems to come from an eye-witness of the events, but it is not certain that this person was Peter.

The main message about Jesus given by the apostles to the early Church is called by scholars the ***kerygma*** (a Greek word meaning ***proclamation***). The teaching of the apostles on the Christian way of life is called the ***didache*** (a Greek word meaning ***teaching***).

The preaching and teaching in the early Church is called the ***oral*** (by word of mouth) ***tradition***.

(Summary: *preaching + teaching = oral tradition*).

In order to write his Gospel, Mark used every source of information which was available to him. It has been suggested that some of the words and actions of Jesus could have existed in a written form. Mark probably used this information.

Note: the oral tradition of the early Church ought not to be confused with the oral tradition of the Pharisees concerning the Law of Moses.

The clues which lead to an explanation of the sources of Mark's Gospel may be summarised as follows:

1. Mark may be close to the teaching and preaching of Peter.
2. Mark knows about the teaching and preaching of the other apostles.
3. Mark probably had access to written collections of sayings and actions of Jesus.

Having explored the probable sources of the Gospel, it is important to recognise that Mark is an independent author with a unique message of his own about Christ and the Christian life.

Who else wrote for the early Christian Church?

In the New Testament there are the letters of Paul and other apostles, and as well as the other Gospels of ***Matthew***, ***Luke*** and ***John***. The three Gospels of Matthew, Mark and Luke are called the ***synoptic gospels***. There are various theories about their relationship to each other. It is the opinion of many scholars that Mark's was the first Gospel to be written and that Matthew and Luke knew of his Gospel and used his information. All three Gospels have written information which is special to them. It also looks as if Matthew and Luke knew of some information which was not available to Mark. The diagram on page 123 is a popular way of showing how the Synoptic Gospels are related to each other. In addition, it is likely that the Gospel writers used the ***oral tradition*** about the ministry of Jesus.

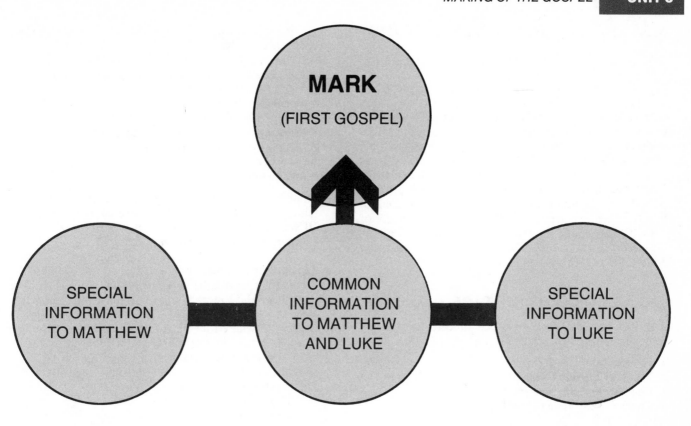

QUESTIONS

Investigation

1. What did the authority quoted by Papias say about the identity of Mark?
2. What happened in Rome in AD64 which caused the Christians to be persecuted as scape-goats?
3. Investigate and make notes on the probable sources of Mark's information.
4. Describe some of the other writings of the New Testament.
5. Name the Synoptic Gospels.
6. Find an example of an incident which could provide evidence for a connection between the three Synoptic Gospels.
7. Select *four* questions from Mark's Gospel and identify the points he wants to make in the answers.

Understanding

1. Explain why Christians were allowed to practise their religion at first, and then were persecuted by the Romans.
2. Explain the term 'Gentile'.
3. What is meant by the 'oral tradition' of the early Church?
4. What does the word 'Kerygma' mean?
5. What does the word 'Didache' mean?
6. Explain the importance of this Gospel for people who are suffering persecution for their beliefs.
7. Explain how the kerygma and didache could have helped Mark to write his Gospel.
8. Explain the importance of 'eye-witness' accounts and give an example of an eye-witness account in Mark's Gospel.
9. Explain the term 'Messiah'.
10. Explain *one* belief which Mark writes about, and say how it applies to Christians today (e.g. 'any one who gives you a drink of water because you belong to me will certainly receive his reward').

Evaluation

1. Find as much evidence as you can for the date at which Mark wrote his Gospel. Why are scholars concerned about this kind of research? Do you think this date could be of importance for understanding the Gospel message?
2. What is the value of the themes of Christian living in Mark's Gospel for Christians today (e.g. wealth, ambition, Christian service, betrayal of friends etc)?

FURTHER READING

1. *Witness in a Pagan World:* chapters 1, 2, 3, 4.
2. *According to Mark:* A3, A4.
3. *Revise Religious Studies:* pages 12-15.
4. *A First Gospel Commentary:* pages 7, 8 with references; page 13, 14.
5. *St Mark's Gospel* (Price): pages 1-4.
6. *Investigating Jesus:* chapter 2.
7. *What Manner of Man?:* pages 1-5.

8.3 THE STRUCTURE OF MARK'S GOSPEL

GOOD NEWS BUT NOT A BIOGRAPHY

If a biography, a story of a life, is being written, it usually begins with some account of birth and childhood. The first thing one notices about Mark's Gospel is that it begins with John the Baptist announcing Jesus as a man who *'will baptize you with the Holy Spirit.'* Even though the incidents of the Gospel are all concerned with the adult life of Jesus, they do not seem to link together very well if the Gospel is read as a life of Jesus Christ. Mark himself introduces the style of the Gospel with the words: *'This is the Good News about Jesus Christ...'* (Mark 1:1)

THE GEOGRAPHY OF MARK'S GOSPEL

The structure of Mark's Gospel appears to take the form of geographical scenes in:

1. **Galilee** (Mark 1—7:23)
2. **Territory outside Galilee** (Mark 7:24—9:50)
3. **The journey to Jerusalem** (Mark 10)
4. **Times in Jerusalem** (Mark 11—16)

BAPTISM: The ministry of Jesus is introduced by events at the River Jordan describing a kind of initiation and dedication to his work. Mark 1:1-14 describes the preaching of John the Baptist who says, using the words of the prophet Isaiah: *'Get the road ready for the Lord.'* (Mark 1:3)

Jesus is baptized by John and a voice from heaven says: *'You are my own dear Son.'* (Mark 1:11) After baptism, Jesus is tempted by the devil. The temptations of Jesus are a time of preparation for him, before he returns to Galilee for the opening of his public life. Mark makes the point that it is the Spirit of God which *'made him go into the desert'*, and that during this time of trial *'angels came and helped him.'* (Mark 1:12,13)

1. Galilee

The rest of chapter 1 describes the calling of the disciples (Mark 1:14-20) and a day in the town of Capernaum when Jesus casts out demons and heals *'many who were sick with all kinds of diseases'*, and teaches in the synagogue. The pattern of his ministry is set during this day. Jesus:

▶ **casts out demons**
(he has power over evil)
▶ **cures all kinds of diseases**
(a sign of the Messiah)
▶ **teaches the people**
(but not like the teachers of the Law)

In chapter 1:38, Jesus announces his mission: *'We must go on to other villages round here. I have to preach in them also, because **that is why I came.'***

The incident of the leper (verses 40-45) completes the opening portrait of Jesus' growth in fame and popularity:

> *'He (the leper) talked so much that Jesus could not go into a town publicly...he stayed out in lonely places, and people came to him from everywhere.'*
> *Mark 1:45*

Having set out the popularity of Jesus, Mark's next two chapters describe the growth of opposition and conflict with the religious leaders of the Jews. The issues which cause criticism, complaint and *'plans to kill Jesus'* (Mark 3:6) include the following:
▶ **blasphemy** (ch.2:7)
(because Jesus forgives sins)
▶ **breaking of Sabbath customs** (ch.2:24)
▶ **mixing with outcasts** (ch.2:13-17)
(he makes a disciple of a tax-collector)
▶ **fasting** (ch.2:18)

Finally, Jesus is accused of having the power of Satan. (ch.3:22) These criticisms are answered by the teaching: *'Whoever does what God wants him to do is my brother, my sister, my mother.'* (ch.3:33-35)

Teaching in parables: The teaching of Jesus in parables is contained in chapter 4. There are other parables. The Parable of the Vineyard occurs in the Temple in Jerusalem, so it is in 12:1-12. There are two parables in chapter 13 where Mark includes an account of the end of time, and a time of persecution followed by judgement. These are the Parable of the Fig-Tree (ch.13:28-31) and the Parable of the Absent Householder (ch.13:34-37) The parables of chapter 4 are:

> **The sower**
> **The lamp**
> **The measure**
> **The seed growing secretly**
> **The mustard seed**

The parables are followed by four works of power; they include:

4:35-41	A nature miracle ('The stilling of the storm')
5:1-20	A conquest of Satan ('The madman in Gerasa')
5:21-24,35-43	A victory over death ('Jairus' daughter')
5:25-34	A reward for faith ('The woman with the haemorrhage')

Ministry: The next part of the ministry of Jesus in Galilee begins with a return from Capernaum to Nazareth where he is rejected by his own village. He sends the twelve apostles out to try their own ministry without him. It is probable that Mark uses his knowledge of the early missionaries of Christianity when he describes the instructions given by Jesus to his disciples (Mark 6:6-12).

The identity of Jesus: There are rumours about the identity of Jesus which say he is:
▶ **John the Baptist, returned from the dead**
(Herod is convinced of this — 6:16)
▶ **Elijah**
(Who was supposed to return to announce the coming of the Messiah)
▶ **A prophet**
(With the status and importance of an Old Testament prophet)

At this point in the Gospel, Jesus is at the height of his popularity. The apostles return from their ministry but, despite an attempt to be alone with them, Jesus is followed by crowds of people and the following incidents occur:
▶ **The feeding of the five thousand** (Mark 6:30-44)
▶ **The stilling of the storm** (Mark 6:45-52)

These two miracles show how Jesus does what God did for his people in the Old Testament. Under the leadership of Moses, God fed the people in the desert with manna, and he rescued them from the Egyptian army at the waters of the Red Sea.

▶ **More healings** (Mark 6:53-56)

Opposition and conflict: There is more bitter opposition from the Jewish religious leaders who see that Jesus' way of life prevents him from keeping the religious customs exactly. The teaching on religious purity points out that people are not made religiously unclean by things but by evil thoughts leading to evil actions.

2. Territory outside Galilee (Mark 7:24—9:50)
The journeys which Jesus makes outside Galilee take him to:

Tyre (Mark 7:31)
Sidon (Mark 7:31)
The Decapolis (Mark 7:31)
Caesarea Philippi (Mark 8:27)

Mark makes a point in this section of the Gospel of emphasising the lack of faith of the Jews and the great faith of Gentile people like the Syro-Phoenician woman. There are miracles of healing — a deaf man, and a blind man in Bethsaida.

Those who cannot hear properly and those who cannot see clearly symbolise the Jews who are deaf to the mission of Jesus and blind as to who he is. Comments about this from Jesus include: *'You have eyes — can't you see? You have ears — can't you hear?'* (Mark 8:18)

Peter's declaration that Jesus is the Messiah occurs outside Galilee at Caesarea Philippi which is a thoroughly Roman and Gentile area (Mark 8:27-31). The incident is followed by the first prediction by Jesus of suffering and death, and the teaching on the cost of discipleship (Mark 8:34—9:1).

The incident of the transfiguration finally resolves the question about the identity of Jesus. A voice says: *'This is my own dear Son — listen to him.'* (Mark 9:7)

The healing of the epileptic boy is an occasion when Jesus again comments on the lack of faith of his own people: *'How unbelieving you people are!'* (Mark 9:19)

Jesus predicts his death a second time, and the ministry in Galilee ends with teachings on discipleship which must have given great comfort to the people for whom Mark was writing. These teachings are in chapter 9:33-50:

PALESTINE IN THE TIME OF JESUS

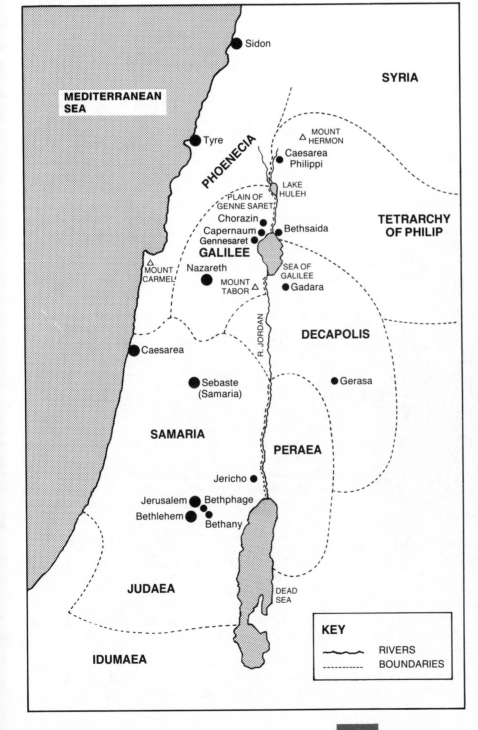

'Whoever wants to be first must place himself last of all and be the servant of all.' (Mark 9:35)
'Whoever welcomes me, welcomes not only me but also the one who sent me.' (v.37)
'Whoever is not against us is for us.' (v.40)
'Anyone who gives you a drink of water because you belong to me will certainly receive his reward.' (v.41)

There are also warnings about failure in faith:

'If anyone should cause one of these little ones to lose his faith in me, it would be better for that person to have a millstone tied round his neck and be thrown into the sea.'

Mark 9:42

3. The journey to Jerusalem (Mark 10)
The incidents which cover the journey to Jerusalem concern:
▶ **religious controversy** (A question on divorce — Mark 10:1-12)
▶ **receiving the Kingdom of God like a child** (Mark 10:13-16)
▶ **the cost of discipleship** (Jesus and the rich young man — Mark 10:17-31)
▶ **true greatness** (The request of James and John — Mark 10:35-44)
▶ **the healing of blind Bartimaeus** (Mark 10:46-52)

The themes of these incidents include rejection of Jesus because of his attitude to the way in which the Pharisees interpreted the Law of Moses. He accused them of neglecting the intention that God had for marriage. The rich young man does not reject Jesus but he cannot pay the price of discipleship which Jesus offered him. Jesus talks to Peter about the rewards of those who persevere in following him, even if they have to suffer persecution. The readers of Mark's Gospel in the Church at Rome would find great comfort in the teaching on discipleship: *'Many who now are first will be last and many who now are last will be first.'*

Jesus speaks of the rejection by his people which will cause his death (Mark 10:33-34). The question put to Jesus by James and John illustrates the misunderstanding of his Messiahship by his own close friends. Jesus was the servant Messiah and not the popular idea of a warrior king: *'If one of you wants to be great, he must be the servant of the rest.'* (Mark 10:43)

Finally, Bartimaeus calls him by one of the titles by which the Messiah would be known. This time Jesus does not silence the man. The fact that Jesus is the Messiah is out in the open. Bartimaeus shouts: *'Jesus! Son of David! Take pity on me!'* (Mark 10:47)

In summary, the themes of the journey are:
▶ **rejection by the Jews**
▶ **misunderstanding of the true nature of the Messiah**
▶ **misunderstanding of true discipleship**
▶ **public announcement of the Messiah**

4. Time in Jerusalem (Mark 11—16)
After the entry of Jesus into Jerusalem (Mark 11:1-11) Jesus begins a period of his ministry in the temple. The great Temple in Jerusalem was the religious centre for his people.

He continues to reject the way in which the religious leaders of the Jews interpret the law of Moses. He announces:

'It is written in the scriptures that God said, "My temple will be called a house of prayer for the people of all nations, but you have turned it into a hideout for thieves".'

Mark 11:17

Jesus rejects the authority of the Pharisees and they look for some way to kill him (Mark 11:18).

Jesus tells the parable of the tenants in the vineyard and the Jewish leaders try to arrest him *'because they knew that he had told this parable against them'* (Mark 12:12).

The questions put to Jesus in the temple are an attempt to trap him into exposing himself as either a political agitator or a false teacher. The teaching which Jesus does give in Jerusalem emphasises:

▶ **the law of love** (The great Commandment — Mark 12:28-34)
▶ **the importance of faith and prayer** (Mark 11:22-26)
▶ **the law of forgiveness** (Mark 11:25-26)
▶ **sincerity in prayer and charity** (Mark 12:38-44)

The last days: The ministry of Jesus in the temple is completed by the chapter in which Mark introduces a description of the disasters which will overcome the temple, the nations, and the followers of Jesus. Jesus describes a time of terrible persecution and tells them to be on their guard for the coming of the Son of Man. The chapter is an important one. The style of writing is called *'apocalyptic'* which means that it describes a final period of world history. Some scholars think that Mark was writing after the destruction of Jerusalem by the Roman General, Titus, in the year AD70, and attempt to date the Gospel after AD70. Others think that Mark is describing the events which led up to that destruction.

Suffering and crucifixion: The events leading up to the crucifixion of Jesus include plans for his betrayal and an incident when he is anointed *'for burial'* (Mark 14:8).

Jesus eats the Passover meal with his disciples during which he speaks of his own body in terms of the broken bread, and his own blood *'poured out for many'* (Mark 14:12-26). The scene in Gethsemane illustrates his human dread of suffering, and his arrest emphasises the *non-violent* way in which he saw his ministry.

The trials of Jesus show that the accusations against him are:
— **religious** (before the Jewish people), and
— **political** (before the Romans).
The disciples run away, and Peter denies that he knows Jesus.

Jesus is sentenced to death as a political agitator (he is 'King of the Jews'), and he suffers a Roman crucifixion. He is challenged to reveal himself as the Messiah while he is dying. At the time of his death the temple curtain is torn from top to bottom. Only the High Priest might enter the Holy of Holies behind the veil of the temple. Mark makes the point that after the death of Jesus, all men may approach God.

The Gentile army officer announces: *'This man was really the Son of God.'* (Mark 15:39)

Joseph of Arimathea buries the body of Jesus in *'a tomb which has been dug out of solid rock'* and a large stone is rolled across the entrance.

Resurrection of Jesus: The resurrection of Jesus in chapter 16 is announced by a young man wearing a white robe who says that Jesus has been raised and *'is going to Galilee ahead of you.'* (Mark 16:6,7) In the earliest manuscripts of Mark's Gospel, the chapter breaks off at verse 8 where the women say nothing to anyone *'because they were afraid'*. There are alternative endings which will be discussed in Unit 9 but which appear to be a summary of resurrection appearances which are mentioned in the other Gospels. One of the reasons suggested for the last section of the Gospel is that the ending might have been lost and the last verses added to give a more satisfactory conclusion. The last verses, in any case, have been the traditional ending of the Gospel since the earliest times.

CONCLUSION

Mark selects units of information about the ministry of Jesus which suit the purpose of his Gospel. The structure of the Gospel appears to take the form of:

▶ **a prologue in Judaea — the Baptism and temptations of Jesus**
▶ **a ministry in Galilee and the neighbouring countryside**
▶ **a journey to Jerusalem**
▶ **a ministry in Jerusalem itself**

(and an account of Jesus' arrest, trial, crucifixion, and resurrection.)

It is to Galilee that Jesus says he will return after rising from the dead. The structure of the Gospel supports the theory that Jesus broke with the Jewish practices of the religious leaders. The structure also supports the idea that Mark wanted to comfort Christians who were suffering persecution.

QUESTIONS

Investigation

1. Describe *two* accusations made against Jesus by Jewish religious leaders.
2. List the parables contained in chapter 4 of Mark's Gospel.
3. Name *four* places outside Galilee which Jesus visited.
4. Write out the words of the voice which spoke at Jesus' baptism.
5. Jesus is described as the Son of God on *three* important occasions. Say when these three occasions occurred.
6. Describe the way in which the content of Mark's Gospel seems to be arranged according to the regions in which Jesus worked and taught.
7. Outline the incidents which occur on the journey to Jerusalem (chapter 10).
8. What did Jesus tell Peter about the rewards for disciples who remained faithful to his teaching?
9. Outline the major events which occur in Jerusalem.
10. Describe the events in chapter 16 and the suggestions which have been made about verses 9-20.

Understanding

1. Explain the purpose of a biography.
2. Explain the purpose of a Gospel.
3. Explain the suggestion that chapter 1 of the Gospel contains a kind of summary of the whole of Jesus' ministry.
4. Why was it important that Jesus should answer those who criticised him for breaking Sabbath laws?
5. What are the themes of the Gospel as Jesus journeys towards Jerusalem (chapter 10)?
6. Explain the main ideas of the Last Supper and the events in the Garden of Gethsemane.
7. What is the religious importance of the temple veil being torn in two after the death of Jesus?

Evaluation

1. What is the evidence that the structure of Mark's Gospel follows his understanding of God's plan for Jesus and his followers?
2. Do you think it is important that Mark deliberately included mention of Gentile areas and Jesus' influence in them? Give your reasons.
3. Peter confessed that Jesus was the Messiah near Caesarea Philippi. Examine the position of this incident in the Gospel story and decide whether you think Mark had a plan in writing about the incident at this point.
4. Give some reasons why Mark included chapter 13 in his Gospel. Consider some of the arguments for dating the Gospel from the contents of this chapter.
5. Outline *two* events which you think would support the idea that Jesus broke away from the religious practices of the Jewish leaders.
6. Look for *two* pieces of evidence which support the idea that Mark wanted to comfort Christians who were suffering persecution, and say why you come to this conclusion.
7. For what reasons do you think: i) Jesus is rejected by people today. ii) People today misunderstand who Jesus is. iii) Christians today misunderstand what it means to be a follower of Jesus?

FURTHER READING

1. *According to Mark:* A5, B2.
2. *Revise Religious Studies:* pages 15-17.
3. *A First Gospel Commentary:* page 106 — follow up page references for a commentary on the content of the Gospel.
4. *The Life and Teachings of Jesus Christ:* page 183 — follow up the page references for Mark's Gospel.

CHRISTIANITY IN MARK'S GOSPEL

9.1 WHO DO PEOPLE SAY I AM?

The Christian statements of belief about Jesus (the Creeds) make several important points (see Unit 2.1). Christians not only *say* that they believe these statements — they *live* as though the purpose of their lives and their destiny after death is ruled by them.

1. Jesus was a human being — born of a woman, a virgin called Mary.
2. Jesus was conceived by the Spirit and power of God.
3. Jesus is given the title 'Christ' because he is God's anointed one, or Messiah.
4. Jesus is the Son of God. He called God his 'Father'.
5. Jesus is the Lord and Saviour of all people.
6. Jesus suffered at the hands of the Romans, was crucified, died and was buried.
7. Jesus rose from death on the third day.
8. Jesus returned to 'God, the almighty Father'.
9. Jesus will come to judge all people, the living and the dead.
10. The reign of Christ at the end of time will be for ever. 'His Kingdom shall have no end.'

Christians believe that they will be judged on their faithfulness to Jesus Christ and his teaching. Many people live good lives for all sorts of reasons both religious and non-religious. It is important to realise that Christian behaviour is influenced by the life and teaching of Jesus, his death and resurrection. The Gospels are one of the foundations for Christian belief, so they are sacred texts which have meaning for every generation of Christians.

This chapter looks at what Mark's Gospel says about the identity of Jesus.

THE MESSIAH

The word 'Messiah' is Hebrew. The word 'Christ' is Greek. They both mean the same:

'The Anointed One'

Mark's first sentence talks about the Good News he wants people to know about: JESUS and CHRIST.

'Christ' is not Jesus' surname, like 'Smith' or 'Jones'. Christ is the *title* which Mark gives to Jesus, the man, who has a family mentioned in chapter 3:31-34: *'Then Jesus' mother and brothers arrived. They stood outside the house and sent in a message.'*

The title Christ, or Messiah, is a very complicated one to follow in the Old Testament, but it is important to know something about it, because the Gospel cannot be properly understood otherwise. Mark writes for Christians whose way of life (a life of persecution) depends upon the truth of their faith in **Jesus as a human being and Jesus as God's anointed One.**

The complete opening sentence of the Gospel is: *'This is the good news about Jesus Christ the Son of God.'*

Some old manuscripts of the Gospel do not have 'Son of God' in the sentence. Perhaps the writer thought that 'Christ' said all that needed to be said!

The title 'Messiah' (Christ) is very important because Christians believe that Jesus was also God's Son, and that he saves God's people from sin, and offers them eternal life.

What did the Jews expect of their Messiah? By the time that Jesus was born, most of them thought that the Messiah would:

1. Overcome the power of the Romans.
2. Establish a wonderful new kingdom for the Jewish people.

The ministry of Jesus is a great disappointment to anyone who thinks like this. Jesus was not a great warrior-king, and his teaching about the Kingdom of God was not about a wonderful new Jewish State.

THE MAIN FEATURES OF THE MINISTRY OF JESUS IN MARK'S GOSPEL

The first chapter is a model for what happens in the rest of the Gospel.

1. Jesus does not teach like the Jewish religious leaders (Mark 1:21,22).
2. Jesus has power over evil (the man with an evil spirit) (Mark 1:23-28).
3. Jesus heals the sick (Peter's mother-in-law) (Mark 1:29-32).
4. Prayer is an important feature of his life. (Mark 1:35).
5. The spirit of service. The ministry of Jesus is for others (Mark 1:38).

These features of the ministry of Jesus show that he is the Messiah. He does save God's people. He does announce the Kingdom of God, but not in the way that the Jewish people of the time expected.

The people were amazed that Jesus did not just repeat the teachings about the Mosaic law with which they were familiar. He was prepared to comment on religious practices in an entirely new way: *'He wasn't like the teachers of the Law; instead he taught with authority.'* (Mark 1:22)

The man with the evil spirit recognised Jesus: *'I know who you are — you are God's holy messenger!'*

The Greek words make it quite clear that Jesus is being called 'The Holy One'. The people admire the power that accompanies the 'new teaching': *'This man has authority to give orders to the evil spirits and they obey him.'* (Mark 1:27)

One healing, that of Peter's mother-in-law, is given as a sample of the many cures given by Jesus in Capernaum: *'All the people of the town gathered in front of the house. Jesus healed many who were sick with all kinds of diseases and drove out many demons.'* (Mark 1:33-34)

The power and authority which Jesus plainly showed was never something which Jesus claimed for himself. He frequently went away to be alone so that he could pray:

'Very early the next morning, long before day-light, Jesus got up and left the house. He went out of the town to a lonely place, where he prayed.'
Mark 1:35

The first cures in Capernaum established a popular reputation for Jesus as a wonder-worker. However, he made it quite clear that his ministry was one which involved the service of others: *'We must go on to the other villages around here. I have to preach in them also, because that is why I came.'* (Mark 1:38)

These features of Jesus' ministry were signs that the time of the Messiah had arrived. The first readers of Mark's Gospel would understand why there was no political power attached to the Christian ministry, but that God's work was being done. The features of *teaching* on the authority of Christ, *miracle*, *prayer*, and *service of others* can be clearly seen in the Christian religious tradition throughout the centuries, down to the present day.

THE 'SECRET' MESSIAH

Jesus continually tells people not to talk about him in Mark's Gospel:

'He would not let the demons say anything because they knew who he was.'' (Mark 1:34)

'Whenever the people who had evil spirits in them saw him, they would fall down before him and scream, "You are the Son of God!" Jesus sternly ordered the evil spirits not to tell anyone who he was.' (Mark 3:11,12)

After Jairus' daughter was restored to life, Jesus *'gave them strict orders not to tell anyone...'* (Mark 5:43)

After curing the deaf-mute, Jesus *'ordered the people not to speak of it to anyone; but the more he ordered them not to, the more they spoke.'* (Mark 7:36)

After curing the blind man at Bethsaida, *'Jesus sent him home, with the order, "Don't go back into the village".'* (Mark 8:26)

When Peter declared that Jesus was the Messiah near Caesarea Philippi, Jesus said, *'Do not tell anyone about me.'* (Mark 8:30)

After the transfiguration of Jesus, he ordered Peter, James and John: *'Don't tell anyone what you have seen.'* (Mark 9:9)

There are many suggestions as to why Jesus wanted his identity to be kept a secret. One of the suggestions is that Jesus did not want people to welcome him with a false idea of who the Messiah was going to be. He waited until someone recognised the true pattern of the Messiah's life, and the true Kingdom of God. Peter eventually managed to do this near Caesarea Philippi when he said: *'You are the Messiah.'* (Mark 8:29)

After this, Jesus tried to show the disciples that the Messiah would be the suffering servant of God. He warned them three times of what was going to happen when he went to Jerusalem. The teaching about suffering, death and rising to life was beyond Peter's understanding: *'...Peter took him aside and began to rebuke him.'* Jesus replied: *'Your thoughts don't come from God but from man.'* (Mark 8:32,33)

Another suggestion which is made about the 'secret' Messiah is that the Romans would have instantly arrested anyone who claimed the title because, at that time, the title was political. The Messiah would be a Jewish King, and a threat to Roman power. The title 'King of the Jews' was the cause of his sentence to be crucified, even though Pilate was not convinced that Jesus was a political leader.

WHAT JESUS SAYS ABOUT HIMSELF

In Mark's Gospel, Jesus says things about himself and what he is doing.

1. **Jesus says he is a preacher.** In chapter 1, he leaves Capernaum for the villages round about because he has a sense of mission to preach in them. (Mark 1:38)
2. **Jesus calls himself 'the Son of Man'** frequently. He uses the title fourteen times in the Gospel, and usually it is a way of referring to himself as people might say 'I'. e.g. *'...the Son of Man has authority on earth to forgive sins.'* (Mark 2:10) On one occasion, he uses the title in a more mysterious sense. During his trial before the Jewish Great Council, the Sanhedrin, he was asked if he was the Messiah. He quoted the vision of Daniel about the court of God: *'...you will see the Son of Man seated at the right hand of the Almighty and coming on the clouds of heaven.'*
3. **Jesus is the bridegroom.** When his disciples are criticised for not fasting, Jesus says that his presence among them is a cause for rejoicing. The idea of the wedding banquet of God and his people was an important theme in the Old Testament. *'Do you expect guests at a wedding party to go without food? As long as the bridegroom is with them they will not fast.'* (Mark 2:19)
4. **Jesus is Lord of the Sabbath.** Many of the early Christians were Gentiles, and there were difficult decisions to be made about how far these Christians should keep Jewish law and ritual. Mark chooses to include an incident where Jesus' disciples are criticised for not keeping the Sabbath laws. The reply which Jesus gave to the Pharisees shows that he is the reference for what Christians should or should not do. His was a new teaching given with authority. *'The Sabbath was made for the good of man...the Son of Man is Lord even of the Sabbath.'* (Mark 2:28)
5. **Jesus belongs to a family.** It is quite clear in the Gospel that Jesus was a Galilean, well known in Nazareth, and belonging to a family who were concerned about his activities and his fame. Christians firmly believe in the humanity of Jesus and have always rejected groups of Christians who have tried to deny that he was truly human. However, he claims that all those who do what God wants them to do, are also his family. (Mark 3:31-35)
6. **Jesus recognises the authority of God.** When James and John ask for places with Jesus in the Kingdom, Jesus tells them that God himself will award places in the Kingdom. Jesus is God's servant. He does not have the role of a great general who might well have rewarded the disciples in the way they were asking: *'It is God who will give these places to those for whom he has prepared them.'* (Mark 10:40)

Preacher 1:38

The Master 11:3

Anointed One 14:3-9

The Messiah 14:61

WHO DO PEOPLE SAY I AM?

The Son of Man 2:10,28

The Bridegroom 2:19

The Son & heir 12:1-9

Lord of the Sabbath 2:28

JA

---

7. Jesus calls himself the Master (or Lord). Jesus sent his disciples to collect a colt for his entry into Jerusalem. He claims the animal as an owner would: *'...tell him that the Master needs it and will send it back at once.'* (Mark 11:3)

8. Jesus is the Son and heir (see the Parable of the Tenants in the Vineyard — Unit 9.4). Jesus told the Pharisees a parable which was in many ways familiar to them. God had spoken of his people as his vineyard in the Old Testament. Jesus made it quite clear that he was the owner's son whom they (the Pharisees) were rejecting (Mark 12:1-9). Mark expresses the relationship of the 'new' people of God to the old. Jesus is the key figure who must be recognised as God's Son.

9. Jesus is the Anointed One. Jesus allowed the sinful woman to anoint him with precious perfume, as a sign of his approaching death and burial (Mark 14:3-9). The incident was important to the first Christians. Mark chooses it for readers who were preparing for violent deaths themselves.

10. Jesus admits that he is 'the Messiah, the Son of the Blessed God.' At his trial before the Sanhedrin, Jesus is asked openly if he is the Messiah. His answer shows that he is now ready to accept this title.

It is worth noting that Jesus does not claim that he is the Messiah until his trial before the Jewish authorities. However, he says a great deal about himself which means the same thing, but he tries to educate people about the real purpose of the Messiah sent by God.

WHAT OTHER PEOPLE SAY ABOUT JESUS

There is a gradual realisation about the identity of Jesus in Mark's Gospel. The last statement made about him in the Gospel is: *'This man was really the Son of God.'* (Made by the Roman army officer — Mark 15:39)

The following statements are made about the identity of Jesus in Mark's Gospel:

1. John the Baptist says he is the one who *'will baptize you with the Holy Spirit.'* (Mark 1:8)
2. The voice says *'my own dear Son.'* (Mark 1:11)
3. The people say he is someone who had authority. (Mark 1:22)
4. The man with the evil spirit says Jesus is *'God's holy messenger.'* (Mark 1:24)
5. Jesus is called a devil by the teachers of the Law. (Mark 3:22)
6. The man at Gerasa says Jesus is *'Son of the Most High God'* (Mark 5:7).
7. Jesus is called *'the teacher'* (Mark 5:35).
8. Jesus is the carpenter, *'the son of Mary'* (Mark 6:3).

9. Herod says Jesus is the *'John the Baptist come back to life'* (Mark 6:14).

10. Jesus is Elijah (Mark 6:15). The Jews expected the second coming of Elijah as a preparation for the coming of the Messiah.

11. Jesus is a *'prophet'* (Mark 6:15). Some people welcomed the activities of Jesus as those of one of the prophets. The prophets of the Old Testament had also been great teachers and wonder-workers.

12. For some people Jesus was just a wonder-worker. In the first century this would not have been an unusual gift to witness. The following are taken from chapter 6.
'How does he perform miracles?' (v.2)
'John the Baptist has come back to life. That is why he has this power to perform miracles' (v.14)
They would *'beg him to let them at least touch the edge of his cloak; and all who touched were made well.'* (v.56)

13. Peter says *'You are the Messiah'* (Mark 8:29).

14. Jesus is called *'Master'* (Mark 11:3).

15. Blind Bartimaeus calls Jesus *'Son of David'* (Mark 10:47).

16. Jesus is given the title *'King of the Jews'* by the Romans as a form of mockery (Mark 15:2,9,12,18).

CONCLUSION

The way in which Jesus speaks about himself, and the way in which others speak to him, gradually reveals the truth of Mark's opening sentence: *'This is the Good News about Jesus Christ, the Son of God.'* (Mark 1:1)

The actions of Jesus chosen by Mark reveal that he is a very human person (see Mark 3:5; 6:34; 8:2,12; 10:14,16,21; 14:41).

The answer to the question, *'Who do people say I am?'* is still an important one for Christians to think about, because Christianity is about people who believe that Jesus was the Son of Mary, and Jesus is the *Son of God*.

QUESTIONS

Investigation

1. Give *two* names which mean 'the Anointed One'.
2. Copy the first sentence of Mark's Gospel.
3. Which king did the Jews remember as an ideal monarch?
4. Select *two* occasions when Jesus asked someone to keep his identity a secret.
5. On what occasion did Jesus claim to be the Son of the Blessed God?
6. What title did Jesus give himself most frequently?
7. Who was Elijah?
8. Mention *two* occasions when Jesus' reaction to events was very human.
9. Give *three* examples of occasions when people recognised Jesus as the Messiah.
10. Describe the incident when Jesus asked the question 'Who do people say I am?'

Understanding

1. Why is 'Christ' a title and not a surname?
2. Explain some of the differences between
   a) the Messiah expected by most Jews, and
   b) the Messiah Jesus actually was.
3. Give an explanation for the 'Messianic Secret' in Mark's Gospel.
4. Why would the religious leaders be afraid of anyone who claimed to be the 'king of the Jews'?
5. Why did Peter argue with Jesus when he spoke of being put to death by the Jewish leaders?

Evaluation

1. How would a Christian today expect to witness the power of Christ over evil, and over sickness and disease? Give some evidence to support your opinion.
2. 'The Gospels are sacred texts which have meaning for every generation of Christians.' Does the picture of Jesus in Mark's Gospel provide an image of a Saviour for people today?

FURTHER READING

1. *Witness in a Pagan World:* chapters 8, 14.
2. *According to Mark:* B10.
3. *The Gospel in the Making:* pages 39-40 (Messianic Secret).
4. *Jesus* (Chichester Project Book 4): chapters 1, 9; *see also* pages 22, 23.
5. *A First Gospel Commentary:* pages 53, 59, 62.
6. *Investigating Jesus:* chapters 1, 8.
7. *Setting the Foundations:* chapters 2, 29.
8. *The Life and Teachings of Jesus Christ:* chapter 5.
9. *What Manner of Man?:* chapter 8 (Peter's Confession), pages 44, 45.
10. *Real Questions:* chapter 10, pages 82-84.

9.2 DISCIPLES OF JESUS

A Christian disciple is a person who follows the way and teaching of Jesus Christ. Mark encouraged his own Christian community by showing them the way of a disciple of Jesus. He selected incidents from the ministry of Jesus which would help people to understand what it meant to be a Christian. Although Mark was familiar with the life of the early Church, the guidance he gives in the Gospel presents a challenge to Christians today. This is because he uses Jesus himself as the example for them to follow. Mark shows that anything Jesus asked his disciples to do, he put into practice himself.

JESUS AS THE EXAMPLE TO BE FOLLOWED

Jesus set out to preach *'the Good News from God'*. (Mark 1:14) The way in which he did this was to teach people to turn away from sin (Mark 1:15), and to believe in the message he brought from God.

Jesus acted with power and authority. He performed many miracles, and had power over the spirit of evil. What he did caused the Jewish religious leaders to criticise him and to plot against him. The result of what he did was that the Sanhedrin (the great council of the Jews) condemned him to death. The charge against him was a religious one. Jesus claimed the title 'Messiah, son of the Blessed God'. He was crucified by the Romans on the political charge of being the 'King of the Jews'.

Jesus suffered because he could not go back on the ministry (work) he had been given to do by God. He did not want to suffer, but he was convinced that what he preached was right. He prayed *'not what I want, but what you want'*. He rose from death, and this is what he promised his disciples he would do. Mark shows that the life and work of Jesus were for all people who could take the consequences. Being a Christian involves great sorrow and great joy as well.

SUMMARY
▶ **Jesus had a task given to him by God;**
▶ **he acted with great power and authority;**
▶ **his work caused great trouble for him;**
▶ **he suffered and died;**
▶ **he was raised to life.**

THE TEACHING OF JESUS ABOUT DISCIPLESHIP IN MARK'S GOSPEL

Mark describes how Jesus chose a small group of men and taught them his way. He began by calling four fishermen with the promise: *'Come with me, and I will teach you to catch men.'* (Mark 1:17)

He called Levi, the tax-collector, who also changed his way of life to follow Jesus (Mark 2:13-17). Jesus chose people who were part of the main industry of the area (the fishermen), or who were civil servants (the tax-collector).

Jesus chose twelve men *'whom he named apostles'*. He said to them: *'I have chosen you to be with me. I will also send you out to preach, and you will have authority to drive out demons.'* (Mark 3:14,15)

Among the twelve there were:
▶ **fishermen**
▶ **a tax collector**
▶ **a zealot (patriot)**

Jesus instructed the twelve and sent them out to do the work that he had done. Mark describes a typical wandering preacher of his own time when he includes these instructions. They were to travel in twos. They were to be poor people:

    ▶ **no bread**   ▶ **no beggar's bag**
    ▶ **no money**   ▶ **no extra clothing**

They were to accept any hospitality that was offered, and leave if they were not welcome.

The disciples began to copy the life-style of Jesus and they went out to do his work. They:
▶ **preached**
▶ **drove out demons**
▶ **anointed the sick**
▶ **healed people** (see Mark 6:6-13)

When people decided to follow Jesus, they became members of a new family. Jesus claimed as his family, anyone who followed God's way as he did: *'Whoever does what God wants him to do is my brother, my sister, my mother.'* (Mark 3:33)

The Christians whom Mark knew often had to make difficult decisions about leaving their pagan or Jewish families. The life-style demanded by Jesus often separated people from their own relatives.

MISUNDERSTANDINGS ABOUT DISCIPLESHIP

A few incidents in the Gospel seem to be there in order to clear up some misunderstandings in the early Church about being a follower of Jesus. It is clear that the Jewish religious leaders were made very angry by his attitude towards the religious customs which they thought were very important. Mark, however, shows that the disciples were slow to understand the teaching which Jesus was giving them.

1. One of the things Jesus tried to teach the disciples was that God's work did not depend on their own human strength. At the feeding of the five thousand, the disciples first of all ask if they should buy bread for the people. Jesus showed them what they should do to rely upon God: He
    ▶ **takes what they have,** (which is five loaves)
    ▶ **looks up to heaven,**
    ▶ **gives thanks to God.**

After this, he broke the bread and gave it to his disciples to give to the people. There were twelve baskets of scraps left after the meal. The demonstration given by Jesus showed the disciples that the feeding was God's work, and they were to be his followers, his workmen, his disciples.

2. It is fairly obvious in Mark's Gospel that the disciples are not sure who Jesus is. At Caesarea Philippi, the question is asked: *'Tell me, who do people say I am?'*

The disciples know what the people think: Jesus is perhaps John the Baptist (come back from the dead), or Elijah, or one of the prophets. Peter declares that Jesus is the Messiah. This is a big step because Jesus does not appear to be the kind of Messiah which the Jews expected (see Unit 9.1). The disciples grow into an

THE TWELVE FOLLOWERS OF JESUS

PHILIP

THADDAEUS

JUDAS ISCARIOT

ANDREW the brother of SIMON PETER

SIMON THE ZEALOT

BARTHOLOMEW

JAMES
Son of Alphaeus

THOMAS

JAMES the brother of JOHN

LEVI (MATTHEW)
Son of Alphaeus

THEY WORKED IN TWOS AND WERE POOR

NO BREAD   NO BEGGING BAG
NO MONEY   NO EXTRA CLOTHES

THEY MINISTERED TO THE PEOPLE

PREACHED   ANOINTED THE SICK
                HEALED PEOPLE
                DROVE OUT DEMONS

understanding of who Jesus is, so it is not surprising that they frequently misunderstand what it means to be a follower of this new Messiah. Some of them would have found it much easier to follow the popular warrior Messiah who would overthrow the Romans.

3. Mark showed his readers that being a disciple of Jesus would make great demands on their faith. After Peter had declared that Jesus was the Messiah, Jesus told the disciples on *three* occasions that he would be rejected by his own people, put to death and rise to life three days later (Mark 8:31; 9:30-32; 10:32-34). This was not Peter's idea of the person he knew, and he argued with Jesus. Jesus pointed out his lack of understanding: *'Your thoughts don't come from God but from man.'* (Mark 8:33)

When Peter saw the suffering of Jesus, his courage and his faith in Jesus failed him, and he denied any knowledge of him. Mark gives some comfort to Christians who had weakened under the Roman persecution of the early Church.

Jesus explained that his disciples would be treated no better than their master: *'If anyone wants to come with me...he must forget self, carry his cross, and follow me.'* (Mark 8:34)

The follower of Jesus would have a cross of suffering just as Jesus did. *'Whoever wants to save his life will lose it; but whoever loses his life for me and for the gospel will save it.'* (Mark 8:35)

This teaching on discipleship was just what the readers of Mark's Gospel needed, and it is emphasised by the following words of Jesus:

> *'Does a person gain anything if he wins the whole world but loses his life? Of course not! There is nothing he can give to regain his life. If a person is ashamed of me and of my teaching in this godless and wicked day, then the Son of Man will be ashamed of him when he comes in the glory of his Father with the holy angels.'*
>
> *Mark 8:36-38*

(*Note:* A strange verse follows when Jesus says *'there are some here who will not die until they have seen the Kingdom of God come with power.'* This is perhaps a reference to the fact that the first Christians expected the second coming of Christ and the end of the world within their own life time).

4. Importance of prayer and humility: Mark describes a very distressing episode when the disciples fail to cure a boy with epilepsy. No doubt there had been similar episodes in the early Church when it looked as though the confidence which Christians had in their ability to cure the sick was misplaced. Mark emphasises two points in what Jesus did for the boy: his father was asked if he *believed* the boy could be cured. Jesus said to him:

> *'"Everything is possible for the person who has faith." The father at once cried out, "I do have faith, but not enough. Help me to have more".'*
>
> *Mark 9:23,24*

The disciples were told that **prayer** was the important factor in the life of a disciple of Jesus: *'Why couldn't we drive the spirit out? "Only prayer can drive this kind out," answered Jesus, "nothing else can".'* (Mark 9:28,29)

On another occasion, the disciples argued about who was the greatest among them. Jesus replied: *'Whoever wants to be first must place himself last of all and be the servant of all.'* (Mark 9:35)

The important lesson which the disciples were very slow to learn was that there would be no particular status attached to following Jesus. The disciples had to learn that they would be treated no better than their master.

Jesus frequently used picture-language to show what he meant, so he took a child, and said that they would have to be as simple and trusting as a child. Jesus also said that his followers had to have the quality of salt, and make life 'taste good' for other people: *'Have the salt of friendship among yourselves, and live in peace with one another.'* (Mark 9:50)

5. The request of James and John (Mark 10:35-45): James and John asked Jesus if they might have seats on his right and left hand in the Kingdom. They misunderstood what Jesus was trying to do. A disciple must have the attitude of a servant. These two still had the popular idea of the Messiah as a conquering King, and saw themselves as victorious warriors of the Messiah. Jesus told them:

> *'If one of you wants to be great, he must be the servant of the rest; and if one of you wants to be first, he must be the slave of all.'*
>
> *Mark 10:43,44*

> *'Even the Son of Man did not come to be served; he came to serve and to give his life to redeem many people.'*
>
> *Mark 10:45*

1. The poor widow in the temple was pointed out by Jesus as an example of his teaching:

> *'...a poor widow came along and dropped in two little copper coins, worth about a penny..."I tell you that this poor widow put more in the offering box than all the others. For the others put in what they had to spare of their riches; but she, poor as she is, put in all she had — she gave all she had to live on".'*
>
> *Mark 12:42-44*

2. Peter asked Jesus about the reward of a disciple. After the rich man had left Jesus, Peter said: *'Look we have left everything and followed you.'* This statement would mean a great deal to Mark's readers because they must have wondered sometimes if their hard lives were worth anything in the end. Jesus' reply to Peter would make good sense to them:

> *'He will receive a hundred times more houses, brothers, sisters, mothers, children and fields — and persecutions as well; and in the age to come he will receive eternal life.'*
>
> *Mark 10:30*

The first Christians supported each other like brothers and sisters. When they became Christians it was as though they had gained a new family. There were great joys and great sorrows attached to being a Christian. Their treasure was in heaven, and they could look forward to everlasting life, even if the Romans could destroy them in large numbers.

3. A disciple must be a good steward of all God trusts him/her with. This includes personal wealth. One incident gives an example of the cost of following Jesus. It is the incident where the rich man asked Jesus: *'Good Teacher, what must I do to receive eternal life?'* (Mark 10:17-31)

(A commentary on Matthew's account of this incident, which is almost identical to Mark's may be found in Unit 5.2 — Vocation)

CONCLUSION

One of the important features of Christianity is the way in which Christians follow the example set by Jesus:

▶ **Jesus is the example of living in God's way**
▶ **Jesus trained his disciples to follow him**
▶ **they had to consider what this would mean for their families, careers, and personal wealth**
▶ **the way taught by Jesus was often misunderstood by the disciples**
▶ **discipleship would involve self-sacrifice, careful stewardship, humility, and service**

QUESTIONS

Investigation

1. What kind of 'ordinary' people did Jesus choose to be his closest friends?
2. Name *two* people today who are worthy to be called modern disciples of Jesus.
3. Write an account of the call of the first *four* disciples.
4. What instruction did Jesus give to the twelve when he sent them out to imitate his own work and teaching?
5. Give an example, with details, of an occasion when Jesus made the Jewish religious leaders angry.
6. Outline the incident when Jesus taught that prayer was a very important part of the power to heal.
7. What lesson about discipleship did Jesus teach James and John?
8. Describe the invitation which Jesus gave to the rich man, and his refusal of this invitation.
9. Describe a well-known Christian who has shown the following qualities: i) self-sacrifice; ii) responsible stewardship; iii) humility and service.

Understanding

1. How could people tell that Jesus had authority?
2. What did Jesus mean when he said that the disciples would 'catch men' instead of fish?
3. Suggest a reason why Jesus did not include any Jewish religious leaders as his closest friends.
4. What did Jesus mean by saying that his followers must be like salt?
5. What was important about the poor widow's offering in the temple?
6. How did Jesus show the disciples that the feeding of the five thousand was God's work?
7. Explain the answer Jesus gave to Peter when Peter said '…we have left everything to follow you'.
8. Why did Jesus put a child forward in order to explain the qualities of discipleship?
9. Why did the rich man turn away from Jesus? Explain with reference to Mark's account of the incident.
10. Suggest *two* reasons why people today might find it hard to follow the teaching of Jesus.

Evaluation

1. Think of *two* people you know who have authority. Would you praise or criticise this service of others? Give reasons for your answer.
2. Why do you think Jesus chose a tax-collector to be one of his apostles? What criticism would this receive from the average Jewish citizen?
3. Why do you think 'persecutions' are mentioned in connection with following Jesus?
4. What challenges to their discipleship do Christians experience today?
5. How might a person's Christian values affect their family life and personal wealth?

FURTHER READING

1. *Witness in a Pagan World:* chapter 6.
2. *According to Mark:* C1, C2, C3, C4, C5.
3. *The Gospel in the Making:* pages 40, 41 (The Apostles).
4. *Revise Religious Studies:* pages 26-33 (selections referring to Mark).
5. *Jesus* (Chichester Project Book 4): chapter 5.
6. *A First Gospel Commentary:* pages 22, 27.
7. *The Life and Teachings of Jesus Christ:* chapter 6.
8. *What Manner of Man?:* pages 8, 46, 20, 33 and following.

9.3 THE KINGDOM OF GOD

'The right time has come...and the Kingdom of God is near!' (Mark 1:15)

These words show that Mark's Gospel begins in an atmosphere of great excitement! The urgency of the message is at the heart of what Christians believe about God as creator and human beings as responsible members of God's family. Christians prepare themselves personally for living as though this world was the Kingdom, and they try to make the world a place fit for people to live in as intended by God. This is why many Christians become involved in working in areas of great deprivation, or in situations of great injustice. In Unit 1 it was noted that the Society of Friends and the Salvation Army are deeply committed to social justice. This is also true of other Christian denominations.

The opening of the Gospel describes how Jesus called the first citizens of the Kingdom, the four fishermen, and then showed the truth of his message about the Kingdom by casting out evil spirits and healing the sick.

▶ **The teaching and the actions of Jesus were signs that the reign of God had begun upon the earth.**

The first chapter ends with the words: *'People came to him from everywhere.'*

IDEAS WHICH DESCRIBE THE KINGDOM OF GOD

There is no single idea which describes what Jesus meant by the Kingdom of God. There are several ideas which can be illustrated from Mark's Gospel. The teaching about the Kingdom includes the following:

▶ **the Kingdom is near**
▶ **the Kindom has arrived — it is in the present time**
▶ **the Kingdom is a mystery**
▶ **the Kingdom is a reward — it will come in the future, and will be eternal**
▶ **the Kingdom demands a new set of human values**

All these ideas were present in the words and actions of Jesus. The very fact that Mark was using the oral tradition of the early Church shows that these ideas were part of the faith of those first Christians. It is important to understand that the same beliefs are true of the Christian Church today, and that they influence the way Christians worship God and relate to each other as brothers and sisters in Christ.

1. THE KINGDOM IS NEAR

Jesus used the phrase 'Kingdom of God' to his own people, the Jews. The Jews always thought of God as their king. No other ruler could have absolute power over his people. The kings which the Jews had in Old Testament times were only servants of God. Kings like David and Solomon acted on God's behalf.

During the long years of exile and under the government of the armies of occupation, the Jews had begun to look forward to a golden age when God would once again come with power to rule his people. Perhaps the Messiah would be a new David who would free the people from the Romans.

Against this background, the people would be most excited by the message which Jesus began to preach: **'the time has come'**. The Greek word which Mark uses for 'time' means an era, a season, or a period of time. Unfortunately, people thought that this period would be one when the Jews recovered the promised land for themselves. It is not likely that Jesus meant this, because his words and actions pointed to a time when people would live as God wanted them to live, with values of justice, true worship and love of their neighbour. God's Kingdom, in the Christian faith, is not measured by political control, but by the way people live with each other. This message would console the Christian community of Mark's day.

It was the whole ministry of Jesus which explained the way in which the power and the reign of God among his people was about to take place: **'the Kingdom of God is near.'**

2. THE KINGDOM OF GOD HAS ARRIVED — IT IS IN THE PRESENT TIME

There are references to the Kingdom of God in Mark's Gospel which seem to declare that the rule or reign of God has already begun. In the ideal world, there would be no evil, sickness or death, and in the ministry of Jesus:

▶ **evil spirits are overcome**
▶ **every kind of disease is cured**
▶ **nature is controlled**
▶ **death is overcome**

It seems that God has begun his reign on earth in the person of Jesus himself! In Unit 9.2 it was noted that the disciples were trained to do exactly what Jesus was doing, and in Mark's Gospel there is a special teaching for the disciples about the Kingdom of God. This is contained in chapter 4, where Jesus tells three parables about growth:

▶ **the sower** (Mark 4:3-9,13-20)
▶ **the seed growing secretly** (Mark 4:26-29)
▶ **the mustard seed** (Mark 4:30-34)

These parables emphasise that the appearance of God's Kingdom depends upon the response which people make to his word. The Kingdom grows without people being able to measure its growth, but it becomes a splendid place where people may find their home and their shelter in difficult times.

Jesus tells the twelve and some others who came to enquire about the parables: *'You have been given the secret about the Kingdom of God.'*

The parable of *the sower* concerns the seed which comes successfully to the harvest despite the fact that some is lost. The *seed growing secretly* also survives all the hazards and difficulties of growth. These two parables are images of the success of God's work in the world, and the final 'harvest' is the arrival of the rule of God, his Kingdom.

The parable of the *mustard seed* is about the unlikely result of what seems at first to be such an insignificant seed. There was great comfort in Mark's choice of this teaching for the early Christian community. People today are impressed by the continuous growth of the Christian Church over the centuries despite persecution and internal quarrels. The parable

THE KINGDOM IS NEAR

The right time has come

Turn away from your sins

Believe the Good News.

THE KINGDOM IS A MYSTERY

'The seed of faith grows secretly.'

THE KINGDOM HAS ARRIVED

Nature is controlled

Death is overcome

every kind of disease is cured

evil spirits are overcome

IN JESUS

THE KINGDOM DEMANDS A NEW SET OF VALUES

'YES' to:	'NO' to:
faithfulness	adultery
honesty	deceit
purity	indecency
joy in the achievements of others	jealousy
truth	slander
humility	pride

THE KINGDOM IS A REWARD IN THE FUTURE

"... in the age to come he will receive eternal life."

---

also contains the promise for the first Christians, who were struggling, that their faithfulness would be rewarded. The first readers of Mark's Gospel would find great encouragement in the teaching on the Kingdom contained in these parables.

There are four other references in which Jesus shows the qualities of character required here and now for those who are citizens of the kingdom. These people allow God to rule their hearts and lives:

i) Nothing must be allowed to weaken a person's faith in Jesus. Great efforts are required to have *'the salt of friendship'* (Mark 9:47-50).
'It is better for you to enter the Kingdom of God with only one eye than to keep both eyes and be thrown into hell. Everyone will be purified by fire as a sacrifice is purified by salt...Have the salt of friendship among yourselves and live in peace with one another.'

ii) The Kingdom of God must be received with the simplicity of a child, because the Kingdom belongs to the poor and the lowly, and to those who suffer. (Mark 10:14,15)

iii) Wealth and ambition must be sacrificed if it is an obstacle to allowing God to rule the heart and mind. (Mark 10:23)

iv) The teacher of the law is *'not far from the Kingdom of God'* because he recognises that love of God and one's neighbour is more important than the sacrifices of animals. (Mark 12:34,35)

'Man must love God...and he must love his neighbour...It is more important to obey these two commandments than to offer animals and other sacrifices to God.' (Mark 12:33)

3. THE KINGDOM IS A MYSTERY

The mystery of the Kingdom of God was spoken about in the parables of growth. These parables apply to preaching about the Kingdom and the growth of Christianity in any age. The variety of people who hear the word of God guarantees a variety of responses, but the parables emphasise the final and certain harvest despite troubles. Again, the first readers of Mark's Gospel needed some explanation of the mysterious nature of God's Kingdom, because they were living in such difficult times, and must have experienced discouragement. Christians today can learn exactly the same lessons about the mysterious nature of the growth of God's rule among his people.

4. THE KINGDOM IS A REWARD — ETERNAL LIFE

There are incidents in his ministry when Jesus speaks of the Kingdom as still to come.

i) After his teaching on the cost of discipleship, Jesus says: *'I tell you, there are some here who will not die until they have seen the Kingdom of God come with power.'* (Mark 9:1) The first Christians expected the second coming (of Christ and God's Kingdom) during their own life time. The next passage of chapter 9 describes the Transfiguration of Jesus before his disciples. Mark describes Jesus in shining splendour talking with Moses and Elijah. It is as though Peter, James and John witness the end of the former rule of God among the Jews, and see the new rule beginning in the person of Jesus. The voice from the cloud says: *'This is my own dear Son — listen to him.'* (Mark 9:7)

ii) When James and John ask for places on the right and left of Jesus in the Kingdom, Jesus says: *'It is God who will give these places, to those for whom he has prepared them.'* (Mark 10:40) This teaching seems to speak of the Kingdom as a reward for those who follow God's way.

iii) At the Last Supper, Jesus speaks of the Kingdom as a future banquet: *'I will never again drink this wine until the day I drink the new wine in the Kingdom of God.'*

   Jesus spoke of himself as a bridegroom at the beginning of his ministry (Mark 2:19-21). The heavenly wedding banquet was a popular way of thinking about the reign of God in the Old Testament.

iv) Joseph of Arimathea is described as a member of the Council, *'who was waiting for the Kingdom of God'* (Mark 15:42,43). Mark wants his readers to know that the Kingdom has yet to come. The Kingdom theme in Mark emphasises the belief of Christians in eternal life.

5. THE KINGDOM DEMANDS A NEW SET OF HUMAN VALUES

When Jesus announced that 'the Kingdom of God is near' he added: *'Turn away from your sins and believe the Good News!'* (Mark 1:15) His message was an urgent one: *'the right time has come.'*

   Whenever Jesus preached, people had to do something about their own lives. He taught with authority and he forgave sins: *'...Jesus said to the paralysed man, "My son, your sins are forgiven".'* (Mark 2:5)

   Jesus met with opposition from the Jewish leaders because he taught that outward observances of religious customs did not necessarily touch a man's heart. Prayer might be insincere even though it looked right.

> *'...from a person's heart, come the evil ideas which lead him to do immoral things, to rob, kill, commit adultery, be greedy and do all sorts of evil things; deceit, indecency, jealousy, slander, pride, and folly...'*
>
> *Mark 7:21,22*

A brief survey of the daily newspapers illustrates all the sins which show that God's rule is not accepted in the world.

The disciples had to be taught what true discipleship meant. It did not mean greatness in the usual sense of being important, but it did mean being ready to serve others, to forgive others and to be ready to follow the example of suffering which was set by Jesus himself:

If the Kingdom of God is for the poor and the lowly and those who suffer for their Christian values, it appears to be quite the opposite of popular human values. Mark emphasises the personal effort required to gain entry into such a Kingdom.

CONCLUSION

The Kingdom of God is seen in the words and deeds of Jesus himself, where evil is overcome and disease and death are conquered. Forgiveness of sins and reconciliation are signs of the Kingdom. The teaching of Jesus on the Kingdom of God has more than one meaning. The Kingdom is a mystery. It is present in the lives of those who believe, but it is also a future reward and a future event. Jesus is the bridegroom who looks forward to the Messiah's banquet in the Kingdom of God.

The Kingdom of God is significant for each person because it is a way in which they will find God, by allowing him to reign in their hearts.

The Kingdom of God is also important for society as a whole because, as the parables of growth point out, the gradual transformation of the human race takes place secretly, but finally reaches a time of good harvest.

QUESTIONS

Investigation

1. Write a short definition of a disciple.
2. What was the occupation of the first *four* disciples?
3. Relate the parable which describes the growth of the Kingdom of God from a small beginning.
4. Which disciples asked for places on the right and left hand of Jesus in the Kingdom of God? Describe the occasion.
5. Name the member of the Sanhedrin who was waiting for the Kingdom of God. What else does Mark tell us about this person?
6. Describe, and give examples of, *three* qualities of true discipleship.
7. Describe the life and work of *one* Christian who could be said to work for the Kingdom of God on earth.
8. Summarise the teaching of Jesus about religious purity.
9. Describe *three* occasions when Jesus spoke about the Kingdom of God.

Understanding

1. Explain a sign which showed that the reign of God had begun with the ministry of Jesus.
2. What is meant by talking about 'values' in human behaviour?
3. Why did the Jews think of their king as a servant of God in the Old Testament times?
4. Why did the Jews think that the Messiah would be another King David?

5. What is meant by a 'mystery' in a religious tradition?
6. Explain the way in which Jesus showed that his authority came from God.
7. Explain how the life of Jesus acts as an example (a model) for all his followers.
8. Why did Jesus train his disciples to do exactly as he did, including the miracles?
9. In what ways did the behaviour of the disciples prevent the true character of the Kingdom of God from being shown?
10. Explain how the Kingdom of God is:
    i) present but still to come in the future;
    ii) a reward.

Evaluation

1. Examine a daily newspaper and say which stories prevent the Kingdom of God from being established in society, and which items show that God reigns in the lives of some people. Give reasons for your choice of stories.
2. What is the evidence in Mark's Gospel that the Kingdom of God is a reward which involves eternal life? Describe the arguments for and against people wanting such a reward today, and give your own opinion with reasons.
3. Is the teaching of Jesus on the Kingdom of God important for people today? Give reasons for your answer.
4. Describe changes which you think would make an ideal world. Compare your list with the changes which Mother Teresa would like to make. Comment on any similarities or differences in the two lists.

FURTHER READING

1. *Revise Religious Studies:* pages 33-40 (Parables).
2. *Jesus* (Chichester Project Book 4): page 21.
3. *A First Gospel Commentary:* pages 85-86.
4. *The Life and Teachings of Jesus Christ:* pages 87-88, 91-92.
5. *Setting the Foundations:* chapter 19.
6. *What Manner of Man?:* chapter 4.

9.4 PARABLE AND ALLEGORY; MIRACLE AND SIGN

PARABLES — A METHOD OF TEACHING

One of the teaching methods used by Jesus in his ministry was the Jewish custom of parable story and parable language. The Jewish rabbis often explained one thing by talking about something else which explained its meaning clearly. It might involve telling a story, or there might be a simple comparison of one thing with another. Jesus wanted to preach the good news about the Kingdom of God. The people had to prepare themselves for the coming of God's Kingdom by turning away from sin and making ready for the reign of God. Parable-talk was a good way of delivering his message.

PARABLES IN MARK'S GOSPEL

The teaching of Jesus in parables is mostly found in chapter 4 of Mark's Gospel, although there are three other parables later in the Gospel (the tenants in the vineyard, Mark 12:1-9; the fig-tree, Mark 13:28-31; absent householder, 13:34-37).

In chapter 4 there are three parables which teach something about the Kingdom of God. They are:

▶ **the sower** (Mark 4:1-9; 13-20)
▶ **the seed growing secretly** (Mark 4:26-29)
▶ **the mustard seed** (Mark 4:30-32)

The teaching about the Kingdom in these parables has been mentioned in Unit 9.3.

Jesus also uses parable-language which sometimes seems like talking in riddles. Examples of this are the lamp under the bowl, and the measure.

The Lamp Under the Bowl

> *'Does anyone ever bring in a lamp and put it under a bowl or under the bed? Doesn't he put it on the lampstand? Whatever is hidden away will be brought out into the open, and whatever is covered up will be uncovered.'*
>
> *Mark 4:21-25*

Mark's choice of this teaching is clever. The Christians in Rome were forced to hide all traces of their worship. They had to put the 'light of the good news' under the 'bed' for the time being. But there is a clear promise in the parable that such times would come to an end and then the light of the Gospel would be clearly shown to the world.

The Measure (The Judgement)
(*Note:* The *Good News Bible* paraphrases the parable of the measure, and only gives its meaning.)

The Greek used by Mark compares the 'measure' used in the market place for weighing out quantities, with the fair judgement of others. It is interesting to note that Matthew repeats himself and includes the market, parable-language, and also the plain words about judging others (Matthew 7:2). The market language is very effective because fairness in trading was strictly controlled by instruments which measured an exact amount. Mark's readers would find the comparison a very clear one. The modern equivalent of the 'measure' would be an accurate pair of scales.

Other examples of parable-language
In chapter 2, Jesus spoke about his teaching as being like new cloth which could not be used to patch up an old coat, and like wine which could not be poured into old wine-skins (Mark 2:21-23). In chapter 8, Jesus spoke about the 'yeast' of the Pharisees, meaning their influence upon the people.

In this kind of language a comparison is being made:

1. A lamp should give light.	The good news should be made known.
2. A measure or scale used for serving others may be used for you also.	A person is judged by the standards he uses to judge others.
3. New cloth is not used for patching old clothes.	Jesus' teaching is not a repetition of old Jewish law.
4. New wine will spoil old wine skins.	The good news might upset the traditional religious customs of the Jews.

ALLEGORY AND PARABLE

There are two parables which are given the meaning of allegory in Mark's Gospel. Allegory is a particular style of writing in which each detail of a story represents a detail of a second story or lesson. Jesus explains the parable of the sower in Mark's Gospel as an allegory.

The seed =	*God's message*
The birds =	*Satan*
Seed on the path =	*people who allow Satan to take away God's message immediately*
Seed on rocky ground =	*people who give up God's message as soon as troubles arise*
Seed among thorn bushes =	*people who let worries and love of money choke God's message*
Seed in good soil =	*people who hear and act on God's message*

The parable of the Tenants in the Vineyard (Mark 12:1-12) is also given an allegorical meaning:

The vineyard =	*God's people, Israel*
The tenants =	*Jewish religious leaders*
The owner =	*God*
The slaves =	*God's messengers, the prophets*
The owner's son =	*Messiah*
New tenants =	*Gentiles (non-Jews)*

The story of the Jewish people and their relationship with God is told in the parable. Jesus knew that the Pharisees and those listening to him would know the Old Testament parable about the vineyard of the House of Israel. The extra details about God's Son and heir being sent and rejected by the people would not have

Allegory and parable

The seed growing secretly (4:26-29); The sower (4:1-9, 13-20); The fig-tree (13:28-29); The absent householder (13:32-36)

been wasted on his audience: *'The Jewish leaders tried to arrest Jesus, because they knew that he had told this parable against them.'* (Mark 12:12)

This parable, however, can just as easily be given the simple interpretation that if religious people will not accept God's message, it will be given to the tax-collectors and sinners instead. Mark's Christian community would also understand that the way taught by Jesus was now open to the Gentiles. The Pharisees were often angry with Jesus because he seemed to favour the company of outcasts.

Two parables of growth

'The seed growing secretly' — Mark 4:26-29
'The mustard seed' — Mark 4:30-32

These parables compare the mystery of natural growth with the gradual nature of the growth of God's Kingdom. The Christians in Rome would be glad of the message contained in these parables because, for them, it seemed as if their way of life was being crushed. The parables pointed to a bright future for Christianity despite their present suffering.

Christians today might well be discouraged by their apparent failure to hold up Christian values to a world where material values and prosperity matter more than justice. These two parables contain a promise that the Kingdom of God grows and comes to a harvest in spite of set-backs.

Two parables about Judgement Day

In chapter 13, where Jesus speaks about persecution and the end of time, there are two parables which teach about the end.

The parable of the *fig-tree* compares the natural signs which trees show in the summer (leaves etc) with the signs which will show people that the end of time is near. The *absent householder* story compares the need for the doorkeeper to keep watch for the master coming at any time, with the need for God's people to keep alert for the end of time and the coming of God's Kingdom.

THE PURPOSE OF PARABLES IN MARK'S GOSPEL

Between the parable of the sower and its allegorical meaning, Mark has a few verses in which Jesus explains why he teaches in parables. Jesus says to his followers: *'You have been given the secret of the Kingdom of God.'* He says that other people will only hear the parable story, and not be able to see or understand the teaching. Later, in verse 34, Mark says: *'He would not speak to them without using parables, but when he was alone with his disciples, he would explain everything to them.'*

It certainly looks as though Mark is saying that only the disciples knew the meaning of the parables which Jesus taught them personally. However, another explanation links the parables with the reason for the Messianic secret (see Unit 9.1). Perhaps Jesus was anxious not to announce publicly a teaching which might be understood as political. This would have put an end to his teaching straight away because the Romans would have arrested him. The Christians in Rome had to leave messages for each other in signs and symbols for fear that they would be discovered, so the idea of a hidden teaching would not have appeared strange to them.

Understanding the parables now

Christians today have certain problems about appreciating the parables. They are not always familiar with the comparison Jesus makes. For example, language describing life in first century Palestine: the sower, the lamp, the measure, the wineskin, the mustard seed, the doorkeeper, the fig-tree. However, the teaching contained in the parables of Mark's Gospel is often as suitable for Christian life now as it was in his day:

1. Faith grows gradually, and becomes strong enough to support others. Consider, for example, the work and teaching of Mother Teresa.
2. The teaching of Christ has something new to say to every generation.
3. God's message is received by a variety of people, some of whom do great work for God's Kingdom on earth.
4. God's people have a responsibility for which they will have to give an account at the time of judgement.

MIRACLES AS SIGNS OF THE KINGDOM

An important feature of the ministry of Jesus was the remarkable number of miracles he performed. He also taught his disciples to expect the same power of healing if they took up his message of the good news about the reign of God in the world (the Kingdom of God). Healing and miracles have been a feature of the truth of the Christian message throughout the centuries, and the twentieth century is no exception to this. The marvellous things which happened during the ministry of Jesus were signs that God was at work among the people.

The main kinds of miracle are:
> **healing of illness and disease**
> **casting out of evil spirits**
> **nature miracles**

Examples of the healing of illness and disease in Mark's Gospel are:

Peter's mother-in-law (Mark 1:30)
The leper (Mark 1:40-45)
The paralytic (Mark 2:1-12)
The man with a withered (paralysed) hand (Mark 3:1-6)
The woman with the haemorrhage (Mark 5:25-34)
Jairus' daughter (Mark 5:21-24,35-43)
The deaf and dumb man (Mark 7:31-37)
The blind man at Bethsaida (Mark 8:22-26)
Blind Bartimaeus (Mark 10:46-52)

Examples of Jesus casting out evil spirits are:

The demoniac in the synagogue (Mark 1:21-28)
The madman in Gerasa (Mark 5:1-20)
The Syro-Phoenician woman's daughter (Mark 7:24-30)
The epileptic boy (Mark 9:14-29)

Mark records only *examples* of Jesus' miracles. He constantly says that there were many more.

'*...people brought to Jesus all the sick and those who had demons. Jesus healed many who were sick with all kinds of diseases and drove out many demons.*' (Mark 1:32,34)

'*...he travelled all over Galilee preaching in the synagogue and driving out demons.*' (Mark 1:39)

'*He had healed many people, and all those who were ill kept pushing their way to him in order to touch him.*' (Mark 3:10)

In Nazareth, '*he was not able to perform many miracles ...he placed his hands on a few sick people and healed them.*' (Mark 6:5)

In the region of Gennesaret, '*wherever they heard he was, they brought to him sick people lying on their mats.*' (Mark 6:55)

'*...everywhere Jesus went, to villages, towns or farms, people would take those who were ill to the market places and beg him to let them at least touch the edge of his cloak; and all who touched it were made well.*' (Mark 6:56)

Examples of the power of Jesus over natural forces and multiplication of food are:

Calming of the storm (Mark 4:35-41)
Walking on the water (another storm) (Mark 6:45-52)
Transfiguration of Jesus (Mark 9:1-8)
Curse of the fig-tree (Mark 11:12-14,20-26)
Feeding of 5,000 people (Mark 6:30-44)
Feeding of 4,000 people (Mark 8:1-21)

All the miracles are *signs of victory* over an imperfect world and the evil which separates people from God and his Kingdom. They are not just 'proof' that Jesus was God's Son. Each miracle is carefully chosen by Mark in order to illustrate particular aspects of what it means to be a Christian.

The miracles:
> **tell the reader what God is like**
> **show that Jesus is Lord**
> **emphasise the importance of faith**
> **give hope to those in despair**
> **emphasise the power of prayer**
> **show that the followers of Jesus can do what he did**

1. GOD: Some of the miracles remind Mark's readers of basic Jewish beliefs about the relationship which God had with his people in the Old Testament. For example, the calming of the storm (Mark 4:35-41), and the feeding of the 5,000 (Mark 6:30-44), remind them of how God saved and fed his people after the Exodus from Egypt at the time of Moses. God rescued his people at the waters of the Red Sea. God had fed his people in the desert.

2. JESUS IS LORD: Jesus repeats the basic saving acts of God in the miracles. Mark tells his readers that by looking at the saving acts of Jesus, they will know more about the nature of God himself. God is the one who saves his people and shows them the way. Jesus points to what God is like. Jesus is compassionate to ordinary human needs in the miracles. He does not reject anyone because they are outcasts. He has authority to forgive sin. He defeats evil in any form. He calls God 'Father' and shows in the miracles that God cares as a Father cares for his children. Jesus is aware of his people's needs, and particularly of their distress: '*Courage. It is I. Don't be afraid.*' (6:50)

Main kinds of miracle

HEALING OF ILLNESS AND DISEASE

Woman with the haemorrhage

Peter's mother-in-law

The leper (1:40-45)
Blind man at Bethsaida (8:22-26)

Man with the withered hand

Jairus' daughter

The paralytic (2:1-12)
Deaf and dumb man (7:31-37)

Blind Bartimaeus

CASTING OUT EVIL SPIRITS

Madman in Gerasa

Syro Phoenician woman's daughter

Demoniac in the synagogue

Epileptic boy

POWER OVER NATURAL FORCES AND FOOD

Calming of the storm

Walking on the water

Transfiguration of Jesus

Feeding of the 4,000 & 5,000 people

Curse of the fig tree

3. THE NATURE OF CHRISTIAN FAITH: Mark tells his readers that they must demonstrate what it means to be a Christian. Their faith should never fail, even in the most difficult circumstances. For example, Mark shows the faith of the men who could not get the paralytic near Jesus, but who were certain that he could cure the man (Mark 2:1-12). The persistence of their faith is illustrated by the removal of the roofing on the house so that they could lower the man down. The father of the epileptic boy (Mark 9:14-29) is in despair about his son's condition, but his faith saved the boy. There are lessons for Christians in every age in Mark's message through the miracles.

4. HOPE FOR THOSE IN DESPAIR: The disciples are sometimes seen in a great state about their powerlessness: they are caught in a storm on the sea of Galilee; they don't know how to deal with the crowds which follow Jesus; they fail to cure the epileptic boy. On each occasion, Mark shows that they must trust in the power of Jesus. The first readers of the Gospel needed this kind of reassurance. So do Christians today.

5. THE POWER OF PRAYER: Mark emphasises the importance of prayer in the Christian life. He portrays Jesus as finding a lonely place to pray in before and after he has performed miracles (Mark 1:35; 6:46; 9:29).

6. THE FOLLOWERS OF JESUS CAN DO WHAT HE DID: Jesus makes it clear that the miracles are God's work, and the disciples share in this work when they, too, realise that it is not they themselves who heal:

> *'He gave them authority over the evil spirits... They drove out many demons, and rubbed olive-oil on many sick people and healed them.'*
> *Mark 6:7,13*

> *' "Why couldn't we drive the spirit out?" "Only prayer can drive this kind out," answered Jesus; "nothing else can".'*
> *Mark 9:28,29*

The greatest sign of victory over evil which is shown by Jesus' miracles is the **victory over death** itself. Two incidents in Mark's Gospel illustrate this sign: the raising of Jairus' daughter by Jesus, and the greatest miracle of all, the resurrection of Jesus himself.

The miracles of Jesus in this Gospel have certain important features:

1. The miracle must be kept secret
2. Faith is essential
3. Physical touch is sometimes important
4. Miracles support the authority of Jesus

1. Secrecy

The fact that Jesus wanted his identity to be kept secret is a mysterious aspect of Mark's Gospel (see Unit 9:1). After at least four major miracles, Jesus asked for the miracle to be kept a secret. There could be a simple explanation. Mark records that Jesus and his disciples were besieged by people night and day. They had no time to eat. In these circumstances Jesus might ask for secrecy as he did in the following miracles:

a) The leper (1:40-45) was warned by Jesus to be silent about his cure, but: *'he talked so much that Jesus could not go into a town publicly.'*
b) When Jesus raised Jairus' daughter back to life, he *'gave them strict orders not to tell anyone.'* (5:43)
c) After the healing of the deaf and dumb man, Jesus *'ordered the people not to speak of it to anyone; but the more he ordered them not to, the more they spoke.'* (7:36)
d) The blind man at Bethsaida is sent home with the order, *'Don't go back into the village.'* (8:26)

Jesus also asked for secrecy after his transfiguration.

2. Importance of faith

Examples of the importance of the faith of the people in the power of Jesus is an even more common feature of the miracles. At least seven miracles mention the importance of faith as in the case of the woman with the haemorrhage; or the friends and relations of the sick person have great faith, as in the case of the father of the epileptic boy:

> *' "Everything is possible for the person who has faith." The father at once cried out, "I do have faith, but not enough. Help me to have more"'!*
> *Mark 9:23,24*

When the paralysed man's friends brought him to Jesus, *'Seeing how much faith they had, Jesus said...'* (Mark 2:5)

The Syro-Phoenician woman's daughter was healed from a distance by the faith that her mother showed in Jesus. Jesus told Bartimaeus that it was his faith which had healed him. Belief in the truth of the Good News and the coming of God's Kingdom brought about the great works of power in Jesus' ministry which were also passed on to his disciples (Mark 6:13).

3. Importance of physical touch

'All those who were ill kept pushing their way to him in order to touch him.' (Mark 3:10) Sometimes the sick people themselves were convinced that they only had to touch Jesus to be healed (e.g. the woman with the haemorrhage).

Mark reveals the attitudes of first century people to the wonder-workers of the age. They thought there might be power in the clothes they wore. Mark even quotes the healing phrases used by Jesus in the original Aramaic, as though power was contained in the formula used:

▶ **'Talitha cum'** ('Arise little girl!') was the command given to Jairus' daughter.
▶ **'Ephphatha'** ('Open up!') was the command made when Jesus healed the deaf mute.

Sometimes Mark describes Jesus deliberately healing by physical actions:
a) Jesus touched the leper.
b) Jesus put his fingers into the ears of the deaf mute and spat and touched the man's tongue.
c) Jesus spat on the blind man's eyes in Bethsaida, and placed his hands on him. The miracle in this case was gradual. The man was able to see in stages.

4. Miracles support the authority of Jesus

When the teachers of the Law were scandalised because Jesus forgave the sins of the paralysed man, the miracle followed as a proof of his teaching:

> '"I will prove to you, then, that the Son of Man has authority on earth to forgive sins!" So he said to the paralysed man, "I tell you, get up, pick up your mat, and go home"!'
>
> *Mark 2:10,11*

When the Pharisees are angry with Jesus for not keeping the Sabbath customs, Jesus heals the man with a paralysed (withered) hand to support his teachings:

> *'Jesus said to the man, "Come up here to the front." Then he asked the people, "What does our Law allow us to do on the Sabbath? To help or to harm? To save a man's life or to destroy it"?'*
>
> *Mark 3:3,4*

The authority of Jesus to command the evil spirits also illustrates the power and truth of his teaching about the Kingdom of God.

CONCLUSION

Mark's Gospel is packed with miracles and accounts of what Jesus did. There is less of his teaching than in the other Gospels although Mark gives a sample of his parables. The vivid accounts of the powerful works of Jesus are Mark's way of emphasising the ministry of Jesus which was to preach the Good News. The miracles are signs of the Kingdom, and contain powerful information for Christians today:

▶ **to know what God is like, by looking at Jesus**
▶ **to realise that, through the miracles, faith is strengthened**
▶ **to know that they can call on God even in impossible circumstances, when all human hope is gone**
▶ **to be confident that all forms of evil are overcome**
▶ **to realise that they share in the work of God on earth**

QUESTIONS

PARABLES AND ALLEGORY

Investigation

1. Give an example of a parable-story.
2. Name the parables about Judgement Day.
3. What are the parables with an allegorical explanation in Mark?
4. Tell the parable of the sower in your own words.
5. Select *two* kinds of people mentioned in the parable of the sower, and say what their response is to the word of God.
6. Which parables teach something important about the Kingdom of God?

Understanding

1. Explain the meaning of an allegory.
2. What is the allegorical explanation of the parable of the sower?
3. How would the religious leaders have understood the parable of the vineyard?
4. Give *two* examples of parable-language in Mark's Gospel, and explain their meaning.
5. Why did Jesus teach in parables?
6. Why were parables a familiar way of giving a religious teaching among the Jews?
7. Explain the moral issue which is raised in the parable of the tenants in the vineyard. (Include the kind of responsibilities which a tenant may have.)
8. Suggest a reason why parables might be a kind of secret teaching.

Evaluation

1. Consider the meaning of some of the parables in Mark's Gospel, and say whether they are helpful for Christians today.
2. Do you think the Pharisees were justified in being angry with Jesus when he told the parable of the tenants in the vineyard? Give reasons for your answer.
3. Do you think that the parable of the seed growing secretly and the parable of the mustard seed would have given some encouragement to Mark's first readers, and if so, why?

MIRACLES AS SIGNS OF THE KINGDOM

Investigation

1. Select and write out the title of *one* healing miracle, *one* exorcism (casting out of evil spirits), and *one* nature miracle.
2. Give *one* example of the fact that Jesus performed many other miracles besides the ones Mark chose to record.
3. What did the father of the epileptic boy say about his own faith in Jesus?
4. Give an example of Jesus *touching* people in order to heal them.
5. Describe a miracle which Jesus performed in order to show that he had authority.
6. Describe *one* miracle of healing in detail.
7. Describe *one* miracle of exorcism in detail.
8. Describe *one* nature miracle in detail.

Understanding

1. Explain the term 'miracle'.
2. How would a person today explain what Mark meant by being 'possessed by evil spirits'?
3. In what way do the miracles explain what God is like?
4. Jesus is Lord. How do the miracles help the reader to understand this statement?
5. Why is the importance of faith emphasised in the miracles?

6. In the miracles, the lame walk, the blind see, the deaf hear. Explain why these are signs that God has come to reign among his people.
7. What is the importance of prayer in relation to the miracles performed by Jesus and his disciples?
8. Suggest a reason why Jesus asked people to keep quiet about miracles he performed.

Evaluation

1. What problems do people have about believing in miracles?
2. Do you think the miracles described in Mark's Gospel were helpful for the particular difficulties which faced the Christians in Rome? Give reasons for your answer.
3. Do you think the miracles are an obstacle for Christians today, or a support for their faith? Give reasons for your answer.

FURTHER READING

1. *Witness in a Pagan World:* chapters 9, 10 (Miracles); chapters 11, 12 (Parables).
2. *According to Mark:* B3 (Parables).
3. *The Gospel in the Making:* pages 42-44 (Parables); pages 44-50, 52-56, 60-62 (Miracles).
4. *Revise Religious Studies:* pages 33-40 (Parables); pages 40-47 (Miracles).
5. *Jesus* (Chichester Project Book 4): chapter 6.
6. *St Mark's Gospel* (Price): pages 14-18.
7. *A First Gospel Commentary:* pages 94, 95.
8. *Investigating Jesus:* chapter 3.
9. *What Manner of Man?:* chapters 4, 5, 8.
10. *The Life and Teachings of Jesus Christ:* chapters 8, 9.
11. *Setting the Foundations:* chapters 15, 17, 18, 28.

9.5 OPPOSITION AND CONFLICT

'How does he dare to talk like this? This is blasphemy!' (Mark 2:7)

The ministry of Jesus quickly brought him into conflict with the religious leaders of his people. (See Unit 8.1 for an identification of Pharisees; Sadducees; Scribes.) The scribes, or teachers of the Law, were experts on the oral tradition of the *Torah*, or Law of Moses. Some of them were afraid, puzzled and angry when Jesus clearly demonstrated his authority over:

▶ **sin** (He forgave people's sins — Mark 2:5)
▶ **evil** (He 'drove out many demons' — Mark 1:34)
▶ **nature** (Mark records four nature miracles)
▶ **disease** (He 'healed many who were sick with all kinds of diseases' — Mark 1:34)

Mark records the opposition of the Jewish religious leaders towards Jesus on the following issues:

    1. **Sabbath law and customs**
    2. **Fasting**
    3. **Religious purity**
    4. **Jewish faith and practice**

(See illustration on page 147.)

1. SABBATH LAWS AND CUSTOMS

Two incidents in which Jesus broke the Sabbath law led to plans being made by the Pharisees and Herodians to kill Jesus. *'...the Pharisees left the synagogue and met at once with some members of Herod's party, and they made plans to kill Jesus.'* (Mark 3:6).

The first incident which provoked the Pharisees involved his disciples picking ears of corn on the Sabbath day. This action was counted as reaping the corn, which was forbidden on the Sabbath. The penalty for breaking the Sabbath was death by stoning. Jesus defended their actions by quoting the incident of the great King David breaking a law in a time of need. Jesus' conclusion must have frustrated the religious experts even more:

> *'The Sabbath was made for the good of man; man was not made for the Sabbath. So the Son of Man is Lord even of the Sabbath.'*
> *Mark 2:27,28*

It was not usual for a Jewish teacher to interpret the Law himself. He would normally repeat the Jewish oral tradition concerning the law of Moses. Jesus was teaching a new way, and his teaching was considered unorthodox. This was a dangerous thing for him to do.

The second incident involved healing a man on the Sabbath day. The man had a paralysed hand. The only kind of healing permitted on the Sabbath was when someone's life was in danger. Jesus openly rejects the oral tradition by healing in a less serious case.

> *'What does our Law allow us to do on the Sabbath? To help or to harm?...he felt sorry for them, because they were so stubborn...he said to the man "stretch out your hand." He stretched it out, and it became well again.'*
> *Mark 3:3-5*

Opposition and conflict

The Sabbath laws

...Why are they doing something on the Sabbath day that is forbidden? (2:23-28) (*Jerusalem Bible*)

...What does our Law allow us to do on the Sabbath? To help or to harm? To save a man's life or to destroy it? (3:1-5)

Fasting

...Why is it that the disciples of John the Baptist and the disciples of the Pharisees fast, but yours do not? (2:18-21)

Religious practices

...Why is it that your disciples do not follow the teaching handed down by our ancestors, but instead eat with ritually unclean hands? (7:1,2,5)

...Why does he eat with such people? (tax collectors and outcasts) (2:15-17)

Faith & practice

...Does the Law allow a man to divorce his wife? (10:2-12)

...Now, when all the dead rise to life on the day of resurrection, whose wife will she be? (12:18-27)

...Which commandment is the most important of all? (12:28-34)

2. FASTING (see Unit 8)

Fasting was a regular religious duty which was kept strictly and publicly by the Pharisees particularly. Jesus was asked why his disciples were not fasting. He answered simply by saying that it would not be appropriate. Jews did not fast at weddings and Jesus implied that he was the bridegroom of Israel and his followers were as guests are at a wedding. Jesus' teaching was a new one, and the old ways would not necessarily fit in well with his teaching. *'Do you expect guests at a wedding party to go without food? Of course not!'* (Mark 2:19)

Mark's choice of this incident was very important for his first readers. One of the earliest problems of the Christian Church was about how much of the Jewish religion should be preserved and practised by Gentiles (non-Jews) who became Christians. (The parable of the new patch and the new wine-skins could be Mark's way of showing his readers that the teaching of Jesus himself supported the move away from Jewish religious practice.) Fasting became important in the Christian tradition, but for different reasons. It is still important in the Christian tradition today.

3. RELIGIOUS PURITY

There were many external religious practices which marked a person as a good Jew. A Jew's religious purity was easily spoiled by forgetting to perform a custom like the ritual washing of hands before eating, or by mixing with sinners and foreigners who might lead the person away from their religious duties. Jesus offended the religious leaders of his people in both these ways:

▶ Jesus ate with outcasts and tax collectors. Mark records a meal in the house of Levi, the tax-collector:

'...A large number of tax-collectors and other outcasts were following Jesus, and many of them joined him and his disciples at the table...Pharisees...asked his disciples, "Why does he eat with such people?" Jesus heard them and answered, "People who are well do not need a doctor, but only those who are sick. I have not come to call respectable people, but outcasts".'

Mark 2:15-17

▶ The disciples of Jesus did not perform the ritual washing:

'They noticed that some of his disciples were eating their food with hands that were ritually unclean — that is, they had not washed them in the way the Pharisees said people should.'

Mark 7:2

The criticism led to the following:

Jesus' teaching on Jewish oral tradition (Mark 7:6-23)
Jesus was not afraid to challenge the 'teaching of our ancestors'. The Pharisees and teachers of the Law asked him: *'Why is it that your disciples do not follow the teaching handed down by our ancestors, but instead eat with ritually unclean hands?'* (Mark 7:5)

Jesus' reply contains four points:
i) The Pharisees could be hypocrites.
ii) The Pharisees are examples of what Isaiah said: *'They teach man-made rules as though they were God's laws.'*
iii) Jesus gave one example of this: The law of **Corban** which said that if a man dedicated his possessions to God he could make it an excuse to neglect the needs of his parents.
iv) Jesus teaches that real sin comes from the heart: *'It is what comes out of a person that makes him unclean.'*

The teaching on the oral tradition was most important for Mark's readers. The Christians in Rome, many of whom were Gentile converts, did not observe the Jewish religious customs any more.

There were still a number of Jewish Christians who needed the teaching that what is pleasing to God does not concern what someone eats but the way they think and behave towards others. Jesus' teaching points to the importance of the *spirit* of religious observance, not the letter of the law. Christians today sometimes deserve criticism for being very observant of Sunday worship but neglecting the needs of their neighbour. The opposite may also be true, that they are generous towards their neighbour, but neglect their duty to God.

Jesus taught the disciples:

'...from a person's heart come the evil ideas which lead him to do immoral things, to rob, kill, commit adultery, be greedy, and do all sorts of evil things; deceit, indecency, jealousy, slander, pride, and folly — all these evil things come from inside a person and make him unclean.'

Mark 7:21-23

Christian behaviour (morality) arises from the observance of the great commandments of **love of God and of neighbour**. To follow the teaching of Jesus which means being good from the heart demands more than the mere observance of external rules of religious purity.

The issue of religious purity points to conflict experienced by Jesus himself, but it also points to problems faced by Mark's readers, and Christians of any generation.

4. JEWISH FAITH AND PRACTICE (MORALS)

Jesus was challenged by the Jewish religious leaders to declare his teaching on basic points of Jewish faith and practice. The following incidents are examples of this:
i) Jesus' teaching on divorce (Mark 10:1-12). (See Unit 1.4)
ii) His teaching on what to believe about resurrection (Mark 12:18-27).
iii) His teaching on the two great Commandments of God (Mark 12:28-34).

Caution!
It would be wrong to imagine that Jesus thought that all Pharisees, Sadducees, Teachers of the Law (Scribes) and Herodians were bad Jews who did not please God by their practice of religion. Joseph of Arimathea was one member of the great council (Sanhedrin) of the Jewish people who is favourably mentioned in Mark's

Gospel. The teacher of the Law who questioned Jesus about the most important Commandment is told by Jesus: *'You are not far from the Kingdom of God.'* (Mark 12:34) However, Jesus taught one parable against the religious leaders who led people astray from God's way.

The Parable of the Tenants in the Vineyard
Mark 12:1-12
The image of the Jewish people as the *vineyard of God* was quite familiar to the Jews in the time of Jesus. The religious leaders knew what Jesus meant by telling the parable. The parable is told in stages which could be recognised as referring to the responsibilities of the Jewish leaders.

1. The vineyard was a good one — it belonged to the owner.
2. The tenants are responsible for the vineyard.
3. The tenants ill-treat the slaves sent for the master's share of the harvest.
4. They reject and kill the owner's son.
5. The owner is likely to give the vineyard to others who will please him.

The message of the parable tells the Jewish leaders that they have neglected their responsibilities towards God's people. *'The Jewish leaders tried to arrest Jesus because they knew he had told this parable against them.'* (12:12)

In this parable, Mark comments on the conflicts going on in his own Christian community about the relationship of Jewish practice to the new 'Way' taught by the first Christians.

The parable also comments on the responsibility which Christians have in the Kingdom of God, because they are the tenants of the 'new vineyard of God'.

JESUS' ENTRY INTO JERUSALEM
(Mark 11:1-11)

The incident looks like the arrival of a political leader. The shouts of the people are a welcome for the Messiah. This is not necessarily so for two reasons:
i) It is suggested that Jesus merely joined in the usual pilgrims' procession for the festival.
ii) He rides on an animal of peace, not a war-horse.

However, this does not stop a growing fear on the part of Jewish leaders, that Jesus might upset the delicate political peace they enjoyed with the Romans.

JESUS IS QUESTIONED ON THE AUTHORITY OF THE STATE (Mark 12:13-17)

The Herodians particularly would fear any popular religious leader who might rouse the people to rebel against the Romans. They had seen frightening examples of the Romans' power to crush any revolt. They had a fairly satisfactory agreement about taxes for the Empire. The religious leaders of the Jews were also allowed the Temple-tax for the upkeep of their religious practices. They were very nervous of anyone upsetting the peace of the arrangement. Such a man would be dangerous. They put this question to Jesus: *'...is it against our Law to pay taxes to the Roman Emperor? Should we pay them or not?'* (12:14)

The answer which Jesus gave provided no excuse for them to condemn him as a political agitator of the people: *'...pay the Emperor what belongs to the Emperor, and pay God what belongs to God.'* (12:17)

JESUS' CONFLICT WITH EVIL IN MARK'S GOSPEL

One of the great messages of Mark's Gospel is to reassure the early Christians that the difficulties and trials they were suffering were not unusual. People who had accepted the teaching and values of Jesus could expect persecution because their way of life was a challenge. Added to this, the wars between Rome and the Jews caused great suffering at the time that Mark was writing.

Some people were delighted with the success of Jesus' ministry in Galilee. Others were alarmed by the extent of his popularity, and the threat he became to the spiritual leaders of his people. They could see that Jesus and his disciples had no time to eat. His family thought he had gone mad: *'They set out to take charge of him, because people were saying, "He's gone mad!"'* (Mark 3:20)

The spiritual leaders thought it was just possible that Jesus' power was a sign of evil among the people. The teachers of the law say: *'He has Beelzebul in him! It is the chief of the demons who gives him the power to drive them out.'* (Mark 3:22)

Jesus' reply to this accusation is in the form of two short parables about the effect of a country divided against itself. He teaches that it is not Satan's power but God's spirit which enables him to cast out the evil spirits. Mark records four main instances of Jesus' power over evil spirits:

1. **The demoniac in the synagogue** (Mark 1:21-28): this man was probably a well-known religious eccentric in Capernaum.
2. **The madman in Gerasa** (Mark 5:1-20): this man's frightening behaviour is easily recognised as a form of severe mental illness. Such people can be treated with drugs today or, if they are dangerous, they are kept in secure hospitals.
3. **The Syro-Phoenician woman's daughter** (Mark 7:24-30): the nature of the girl's illness is not clear, only that she *'had an evil spirit in her'*. Here was a mother having trouble with her daughter — a common state of affairs in any age!
4. **The epileptic boy** (Mark 9:14-29): the father's love for his son reminds one of the complete dedication of some parents to their handicapped children.

There are two references to the disciples and others who cast out 'demons' in the name of Jesus:

1. When Jesus sent out the twelve, *'they drove out many demons.'* (Mark 6:13)
2. John complained to Jesus that they had caught a man casting out demons in his name. On this occasion, Jesus says, *'no one who performs a miracle in my name will be able soon afterwards to say evil things about me.'* (Mark 9:38-40)

In the Gospel, the people with evil spirits are usually examples of people who cause great anxiety to their families and their local religious and civic communities. People's understanding of the power of Satan in the time of Jesus and in the early Church was different from today. Their understanding included all kinds of behaviour (the symptoms of epilepsy, for example) which was frightening. However, the basic victory of Jesus over evil is not necessarily diminished by this fact. People today still recognise the power of evil, as can be seen by the popularity of the theme in the media of T.V., radio and science fiction.

JESUS' TEACHING ABOUT PERSECUTION (Mark 13)

This chapter is important for an understanding of the fact that Mark wrote his Gospel for a particular Christian community who were suffering a time of great persecution. Jesus is portrayed as the Son of God, but as one who faced rejection by his own people. He suffered opposition to his teaching, and death for remaining faithful to the ministry given him by God. The outcome of the life and teaching of Jesus was as miserable on the face of things as that of the early Christian community. But the whole point of the Gospel is that Jesus conquered evil, sin and death itself by his resurrection. Mark lets his people see that they follow the way of Jesus himself.

The following points from chapter 13 would have given great encouragement to these first Christians:

▶ Jesus describes the persecution that his followers will face (13:9-13) and concludes: *'Everyone will hate you because of me.'*

▶ There will be a time which will seem like the end of the world (13:14-23): *'The trouble of those days will be far worse than any the world has ever known from the very beginning...until the present time.'* (13:19) Today, this reads like a description of the nuclear threat!

▶ The Son of Man will come *'with great power and glory, and all God's people will be gathered together'* (13:26-27).

▶ No-one knows when the second coming will happen. They must read the signs of the times (13:28-31). They must constantly watch and pray for that time (13:32-37).

CONCLUSION

Mark presents a great struggle taking place — a struggle between good and evil in all kinds of forms. Jesus meets opposition from the Jewish religious leaders. The parable of the tenants in the vineyard warns the Jewish leaders about their responsibility and tells them that the owner's son is Jesus.

Jesus is not a political agitator. He is frequently in conflict with evil (disease, sickness, evil spirits) but overcomes it by the power of God on every occasion, and teaches his disciples to do the same.

Finally, Jesus is the model of the servant of God who suffers for his faithfulness to the ministry given to him. Mark uses the example of Jesus himself to explain the mystery of persecution to the early Church. The solution to their trials lay in the message of the Gospel that Jesus rose from the dead, and that God's plan gave them victory, not defeat.

QUESTIONS

Investigation

1. Give examples of *three* issues on which Jesus offended against Jewish belief or religious customs.
2. Give *two* examples of the way in which Christians today are persecuted.
3. What did King David do which broke a religious law?
4. Copy out the answer Jesus gave to the teacher of the law about the most important Commandment (Mark 12:29-31) and learn this answer by heart.
5. Which parable did Jesus tell to point out to the Jewish leaders that they had neglected their responsibilities towards God's people? Summarise the *main* points of the parable.
6. Write a list of names by which Beelzebul is called.
7. What answer did Jesus give to those who asked him about paying taxes to Rome?
8. Give an account of the time when Jesus was challenged about the Jewish laws concerning fasting.
9. Describe the occasion when Jesus condemned the religious customs of the Pharisees.

Understanding

1. Why was it wrong for the disciples to pick ears of corn on the Sabbath day?
2. Copy out what Jesus said about the purpose of the Sabbath day and explain what he meant.
3. What did Jesus mean by referring to himself as the 'bridegroom'?
4. Explain how Jesus answered his critics when they accused him of breaking Sabbath laws.
5. Why was there a problem among the first Christians about keeping *Jewish* religious customs?
6. Explain what Jesus meant by saying that evil comes from the heart.
7. Why were the questions about divorce (Mark 10:2-12), resurrection (Mark 12:18-27), and taxes to Rome (Mark 12:13-17), difficult for Jesus to answer without getting into trouble?
8. How did Jesus answer those who accused him of healing by the power of Beelzebul?

Evaluation

1. Why did some people welcome Jesus to Jerusalem, and some people get alarmed at his coming? Which group would you join, and why?
2. Imagine you were one of Mark's Christian community in Rome. Would you agree with Mark's reply to your complaints about the suffering of the Christians? Do you think Mark gives some comfort in the Gospel?

FURTHER READING

1. *Witness in a Pagan World:* chapter 7.
2. *According to Mark:* B6.
3. *The Gospel in the Making:* pages 34-36, 58, 81-85.
4. *Revise Religious Studies:* pages 61-65.
5. *A First Gospel Commentary:* pages 92-93.
6. *The Life and Teachings of Jesus Christ:* chapter 10.
7. *Setting the Foundations:* chapter 33.
8. *What Manner of Man?:* chapters 2, 3, 7, 10, 12, 14.
9. *Real Questions:* chapter 1, pages 7-13.

9.6 THE SUFFERING, DEATH AND RESURRECTION OF JESUS

> '*I believe...in Jesus Christ...who suffered under Pontius Pilate, was crucified, died and was buried. He descended into hell. The third day he rose again from the dead. He ascended into Heaven.*'

These words are part of the Apostles' Creed which is one of the common statements about what Christians believe. (See Unit 3.1)

In Mark's account, the suffering, crucifixion and resurrection of Jesus takes up one third of the Gospel. It is important for Christians to be clear about the following:

▶ **why Jesus suffered for others**
▶ **in what way Jesus overcame death for all people**
▶ **what is meant by the second coming of Christ and the judgement of the world**
▶ **what is meant by the Christian belief in life after death**

The account of the death and resurrection of Jesus is the basic document for exploring these fundamental beliefs of Christian people.

Outline of Mark's account of the suffering, death and resurrection of Jesus (see illustration on p.153.)

1. Plans for betraying Jesus (14:1-2,10-11).
2. Anointing of Jesus by the woman at Bethany (14:3-9).
3. The Last Supper of Jesus with his disciples (14:12-26).
4. Peter's denial is foretold by Jesus (14:27-31).
5. Events in the garden of Gethsemane (14:32-52).
6. The trial of Jesus before the Great Council of the Jews (14:53-65).
7. Peter denies any knowledge of Jesus (14:66-72).
8. The trial of Jesus before the Romans (15:1-15).
9. The Romans mock Jesus as King of the Jews (15:16-20).
10. The crucifixion of Jesus (15:21-41).
11. The burial of Jesus by Joseph of Arimathea (15:42-47).
12. The women find the tomb empty (16:1-8).
13. Appearance of Jesus after the resurrection and his return to heaven (16:9-20).

These events form six stages in which Mark emphasised two distinct and important Christian beliefs: that Jesus was a human being, rejected and put to death; that Jesus was revealed as the Son of God by his resurrection appearances and ascension into heaven. The six stages are as follows:

Stage 1 events leading up to the arrest of Jesus (1-5 above)
Stage 2 the two main trials of Jesus (6,8)
Stage 3 Peter's denial of Jesus (4,7)
Stage 4 the physical suffering and death of Jesus (9,10)
Stage 5 burial of Jesus and finding of an empty tomb (11,12)
Stage 6 resurrection appearances and the return of Jesus to heaven (13)

Stage One: Events leading to the arrest of Jesus

Mark constructed his Gospel in a geographical pattern (see Unit 8.2). The journeys in the ministry of Jesus lead up to one final week in and around Jerusalem, Jesus had spoken about what would happen three times. The content on each occasion was:

▶ the Son of Man would be rejected by the Jewish religious leaders;
▶ the Son of Man would be put to death;
▶ the Son of Man would rise to life three days later.

In the events which lead up to his arrest the following facts become clear:

i) **Jesus is occupied with the thought of his death.** (He accepts the anointing by the woman as a preparation *'ahead of time for burial'* — Mark 14:8)
ii) **He is saddened by the knowledge that he will be betrayed and denied by friends.** (He talks about it at the Last Supper, and in Gethsemane)
iii) **Jesus dreads his 'cup of suffering'.** (In Gethsemane he is frightened of physical pain)

Note on the Last Supper

The reason why Jesus' ministry ends in suffering and death is contained in his words and actions at the Last Supper:

> *'Jesus took a piece of bread, gave a prayer of thanks, broke it and gave it to his disciples. "Take it," he said, "this is my body." Then he took a cup, gave thanks to God, and handed it to them; and they all drank from it. Jesus said "This is my blood which is poured out for many, my blood which seals God's covenant. I tell you, I will never again drink this wine until the day I drink new wine in the Kingdom of God".'*
>
> *Mark 14:22-26*

The words and actions occur at, or before, the feast of **Passover**. At Passover, the Jewish people remember how God saved his people from slavery in Egypt at the time of the Exodus. The sign that the Hebrew people would be spared was the lamb which was sacrificed (see Unit 6.1). The lamb was the sign of the **covenant** (agreement) between God and his people. At the Last Supper, Jesus says that his blood will be poured out 'for many', as a sign of God's covenant. This kind of sacrificial suffering is called **vicarious** (done for another person). Jesus understood that his death would be a covenant sign that all his people would be saved from sin and death. This is God's plan as Mark sees it, and he presents it in his Gospel for the Christian community in Rome, many of whom would need to understand covenant teaching in the Jewish tradition and its importance for the Christian tradition.

Stage Two: The two main trials

Jesus was given no basic human rights at his trial. He was arrested by night. This is a common feature of societies and forms of government which will not allow freedom of speech and action.

The charges brought against Jesus, and the witnesses who were produced, did not agree. Finally, he was condemned to death on a charge of blasphemy. The charge was a **religious** one:

> *'"Are you the Messiah, the Son of the Blessed God?"*
> *"I am," answered Jesus, "and you will see the Son of Man seated on the right hand of the Almighty and coming with the clouds of heaven".'*
>
> *Mark 14:62*

The death sentence could only be passed by the Roman authority, so the Jewish leaders took Jesus to Pilate. The charge is now a **political** one: *'Are you the king of the Jews?'* (Mark 15:2)

Again Jesus is given no basic human rights. The judge, Pontius Pilate knows *'that the chief priests had handed Jesus over to him because they were jealous.'* (Mark 15:10) Knowing that Jesus has committed no real crime, Pilate condemns the innocent man to crucifixion.

Stage Three: Peter's denial of Jesus

In the garden of Gethsemane *'all the disciples left him and ran away.'* (Mark 14:50) The role of Peter in Mark's Gospel is important because it is probable that the writer knew of Peter's preaching first-hand. The account of Peter's denial has all the evidence of personal confession of failure to live up to brave words of loyalty. The story may have given comfort to the first readers of the Gospel who knew what fear could do to a man in a time of interrogation. In any case, there must have been a strong tradition of Peter's account of the Gospel among the Christians in Rome.

Stage Four: The physical suffering and death of Jesus

The political prisoner is first of all tortured by his guards. One is reminded of the accounts of torture circulated by Amnesty International today. Jesus is taken to **Golgotha** (the place of the skull) and crucified. He has no privileges. His clothing is gambled for by the soldiers. The challenges given to Jesus were to show himself as the Messiah by saving himself. A Messiah who was a servant and a sacrifice for the people was not the popular image which people expected. Mark adds that when Jesus died, the curtain hanging in the temple was torn in two. Perhaps Mark wanted to impress on his readers that the death of Jesus marked the end of the old covenant and the beginning of the new covenant sealed in the blood of Jesus. Another explanation is that the curtain separated the people from the holiest part of the temple where God was thought to be present. The sacrifice of Jesus took away any barrier between God and his people for ever.

Stage Five: Burial of Jesus and finding of an empty tomb

Pilate's surprise that Jesus was dead so soon is perhaps a way of underlining that the Gospel account is certain that Jesus really died. There is an account of the officer's report that Jesus was indeed dead, and Joseph of Arimathea is allowed to bury him in a *'tomb which had been dug out of solid rock.'* (Mark 15:46)

The Sabbath day passes, and when it would be permissible to anoint the body, the women (Mary Magdalene, Mary the mother of Jesus, and Salome) go at sunrise to the tomb. The stone is rolled away; a young man wearing a white robe announces that Jesus of Nazareth has been raised. The women are told to give a message to the disciples that Jesus will be seen in Galilee as promised. The women are terrified and they say nothing because they are afraid.

Mark's account of the passion & resurrection

1. Plans for betraying Jesus

2. Anointing of Jesus

3. The Last Supper

4. Peter's denial foretold

5. Garden of Gethsemane

6. The trial of Jesus

7. Peter denies Jesus

8. The trial of Jesus by the Romans

9. The Romans mock Jesus as King of the Jews

10. The crucifixion of Jesus

11. Burial of Jesus

12. The tomb is found empty

13. Resurrection

Stage Six: Resurrection appearances and the return of Jesus to heaven

The oldest manuscript of Mark's Gospel ends with the women saying nothing because they are afraid. There are some verses in later manuscripts which give a sort of summary of the occasions on which Jesus appeared to people. It is the witness of people who saw Jesus after his resurrection which is the foundation of the belief that Jesus really was raised from death. With that conviction, Christians claim that there is a resurrection and life for ever, for all who follow Christ and his teaching. The last verses of the Gospel (Mark 16:9-20) contain the following information:

▶ The disciples do not believe Mary Magdalene when she tells them that Jesus has risen.

▶ Jesus appears to the disciples outside Jerusalem.

▶ Jesus appears and gives instructions to the eleven.

▶ Jesus 'was taken up to heaven' after the appearances, and the disciples carried on his ministry. The signs that their preaching was true, were the miracles which happened.

There is another ending to the Gospel which says:

'Jesus himself sent out through his disciples from the east and the west, — the sacred and everliving message of eternal salvation.'

The mission of all Christians is made clear in this ancient ending to the Gospel.

MARK'S CHURCH AND GOD'S PLAN SHOWN BY JESUS

The Christians known to Mark were under great pressure. Sometimes the persecution they suffered was beyond their ability to endure. They despaired of life itself: *'Teacher, don't you care that we are about to die?'* They experienced the sentence of death every day under the Romans.

Mark's message tells these Christians, and the Christians of all time, that they must rely on God who raises the dead.

In Mark's Gospel, Jesus raised the dead (Jairus' daughter). Then he himself rose from death. The message is that God has *saved* his people: *'Why are you frightened?' Have you still no faith?'* (Mark 4:40). *'Courage. It is I. Don't be afraid!'* (Mark 6:50)

Mark makes it quite clear that the people must set their hope in God. They must give him thanks (another strong theme in the Gospel). They must pray, and know that their prayers are heard, just as the people in the time of Moses called to God and were saved by him (the Passover theme).

Conflict and rejection are to be expected. Mark shows his readers that people who do not accept the Spirit of God think that those who do are fools, because they cannot understand the challenge of discipleship.

Jesus is portrayed as a man who was brutally treated. He blessed when others cursed him. He endured persecution. He answers in a kindly way when others slander him. At his crucifixion, he became the scum of the earth, the refuse of the world.

In God's plan, anyone who asks in the name of Jesus will be saved. Christians may approach God as 'Father'. Jesus prepared God's people for works of service to others, so that his plan could be completed (the Kingdom of God theme).

God is with Jesus. Mark shows his readers that God is with those who are with Jesus (the disciples do and say the same wonderful things as Jesus does — Mark 6:13).

CONCLUSION

The ministry of Jesus was to preach the truth about the Kingdom of God. In doing so, Jesus came into conflict with the religious leaders of the Jewish people. He taught that God's way was one of self-sacrifice and service of others. The way into God's Kingdom required personal effort (see Unit 9.2, 9.3). Jesus himself was the model of the way. The death and resurrection of Jesus was the cost of discipleship and its reward. All Christians take the example of Jesus as their own model:

▶ **Christians follow the teachings of Christ**
▶ **they accept the cost of following (the 'cross')**
▶ **they believe that death is overcome in the resurrection of Jesus**
▶ **they believe that judgement will be according to the law of love, service and forgiveness taught by Christ**
▶ **they believe that life in God's Kingdom is their reward.**

QUESTIONS

Investigation

1. What *three* things did Jesus predict would happen to him in Jerusalem?
2. What is a covenant?
3. What is sacrifice?
4. Describe the *religious* charge brought against Jesus.
5. Describe the *political* charge brought against Jesus.
6. What do Christians say they believe about the death and resurrection of Jesus?
7. Outline the *main* words and actions of Jesus at the Last Supper.
8. Describe the trial of Jesus before the Jews.
9. Describe the trial of Jesus before the Romans.
10. Give *two* examples to show that Jesus was denied basic human rights at his trial.
11. Describe the occasion on which Peter denied that he knew Jesus.
12. Give an account of the crucifixion in your own words, including the remarks of people who passed by.
13. Name those who went to the tomb on the third day.
14. Describe the events on the morning of the resurrection as told by Mark.
15. What other appearances of Jesus after his resurrection are mentioned in Mark's Gospel?
16. What is the name of the Christian festival which marks the time when Jesus 'was taken up to heaven'?
17. What instructions did Jesus give the disciples during the days after the resurrection?

Understanding

1. What did Jesus mean by 'this cup of suffering' when he prayed in Gethsemane?
2. What does the word 'vicarious' mean?
3. Why was the lamb of the Passover slaughtered on behalf of the people?
4. What was the importance of the torn temple-veil for the readers of this Gospel?
5. Explain why Pilate was surprised that Jesus had died so quickly.
6. Why was Passover time chosen in God's plan for the time that Jesus would offer his life?
7. What did Jesus mean when he said that his blood 'seals God's covenant'?
8. Why do Christians believe that the suffering of Jesus is of benefit to them?
9. Explain why Mark saw the suffering and death of Jesus as part of God's plan for his people.
10. Why is the Christian tradition of the empty tomb important?

Evaluation

1. Do you think the evidence against Jesus at his trial was convincing? Would you have found him guilty or innocent?
2. Compare the techniques of interrogation used at the trial of Jesus with the techniques of interrogation used on political prisoners today. Do you think a society like Amnesty International is necessary?
3. Suggest some reasons why the account of the suffering, death and resurrection of Jesus takes up so much of Mark's Gospel.
4. Consider the issues facing Pilate as the Roman Governor, and say what choice Pilate had in judging Jesus.

FURTHER READING

1. *Witness in a Pagan World:* chapter 13.
2. *According to Mark:* B7, B8.
3. *The Gospel in the Making:* chapters 8, 9.
4. *Revise Religious Studies:* pages 49-61.
5. *Jesus* (Chichester Project Book 4): chapters 7, 8.
6. *Investigating Jesus:* chapters 5, 6, 7.
7. *First Gospel Commentary:* page 95.
8. *St Mark's Gospel* (Price): chapters 14, 15, 16.
9. *The Life and Teachings of Jesus Christ:* chapters 11, 12.
10. *Setting the Foundations:* chapters 35-45, pages 190-252.
11. *What Manner of Man?:* chapters 14, 15, 16.
12. *Real Questions:* chapter 11, pages 86-89; chapter 12, pages 92-94.

APPENDIX A: SHORT TESTS ON SOME RECOMMENDED TEXTS

The Ten Commandments — Exodus 20:1-17

1. How does God describe himself in v.2? What does this refer to?
2. How does God compare his relationship with the gods of other nations in vv.3-6?
3. How could a person use the name of God for an evil purpose?
4. What reason does God give for the people to rest on the Sabbath day and do no work?
5. What promise does God attach to respect for father and mother?
6. What is murder? Would this command include anything else?
7. What is adultery, and why do you think God includes this command to his people?
8. Why is theft a great weakness in a society which is trying to begin a new life as the people of God?
9. What do you think is included in 'Do not accuse anyone falsely'?
10. Why do you think envy of other people's possessions is one of the Commandments given to Moses at this time?

The Beatitudes — Matthew 5:1-12

1. What is the popular title given to the teaching of Jesus which begins with the Beatitudes (i.e. the sentences on true happiness)?
2. The Kingdom of heaven belongs to the 'spiritually poor'. What does this mean?
3. What promise is made to the mourners?
4. How would you describe a humble person?
5. What promise is given to people whose greatest desire is to do what God requires?
6. Give an example of an occasion when mercy ought to be shown.
7. What do you think is meant by 'the pure in heart'?
8. Give examples of modern people who work for peace.
9. Give an example of religious persecution.
10. Why are people who are persecuted for the sake of Jesus told to be happy?

The Rich Young Man — Matthew 19:13-30

1. What question did the man ask Jesus?
2. What did Jesus tell him to do?
3. Which Commandments did Jesus mention that the man should keep?
4. When the young man wanted to do more, what did Jesus reply?
5. What was the reaction of the young man?
6. What remark did Jesus make to his disciples about the Kingdom of heaven after the young man had gone away?
7. What did Jesus mean by saying 'This is impossible for men; but for God everything is possible'?
8. Peter pointed out that the disciples had accepted Jesus' invitation to follow him. What question did he ask Jesus?
9. What did Jesus say about the New Age?
10. What did Jesus mean by 'many who now are first will be last, and many who now are last will be first'?

Parable of the Talents (Pounds) — Matthew 25:14-30

1. What was Jesus referring to when he said '*It* will be like...'?
2. Why did the man call his servants?
3. What did the man give to each servant?
4. What did the first and second servants do with their money?
5. What did the third servant do with his money?
6. When the master returned what did the first servant say to him?
7. What was the master's reply?
8. How did the third servant explain what he had done with his money?
9. What was the main *reason* for what the third servant had done?
10. What did the master tell the servant that he should have done with the money?
11. What decision did the master make about the lazy servant?
12. How does Jesus expect people to understand the parable with reference to the Last Judgement?

The Final Judgement: The Parable of the Sheep and the Goats — Matthew 25:31-46

1. How does Jesus describe the scene of the nations coming for judgement?
2. What comparison does Jesus use for the division of the good people from the bad?
3. Are sheep and goats important in this parable?
4. Are good and bad people important in this parable?
5. What is meant by 'righteous people'?
6. What reward does the King offer the righteous people?
7. Name the six signs of love which the righteous had shown.
8. Why were the righteous people surprised?
9. What answer did the King give them?
10. What punishment is threatened to the people on the left?
11. What were the signs of neglect which they had shown?
12. What is the conclusion of this parable?

The Parable of the Sower — Mark 4:3-8
The Sower explained — Mark 4:13-20

1. What method of sowing seed was being used in the parable of the sower?
2. What happened to the seed which fell on the path?
3. Why did the seed on the rocky ground grow so quickly?
4. Why did these plants dry up in the sunshine?
5. Why couldn't the plants among the thorn-bushes survive?
6. Describe the progress of the seed which fell on good soil.

(Jesus explains the parable.)

7. What does the sower in the parable represent?
8. What happens when God's message is given to people who are like the seed that falls on the pathway?
9. Why do people give up God's message so easily when they are like the seed in rocky ground?
10. What chokes God's message for people who are like seed among the thorn-bushes?

11. What is the clue that shows how people, who are like the seed in good soil, respond to God's message according to the talents which they have?
12. When a parable is given an allegorical explanation, it is a special method of teaching. Do you think it is a good method of teaching about the message of God?

Feeding of the Five Thousand — Mark 6:30-44

1. Why were the apostles reporting back to Jesus, and what had they been doing?
2. Why hadn't Jesus and the apostles enough time to eat?
3. What suggestion did Jesus make to them?
4. What did the people do when Jesus and the apostles went off in the boat?
5. What is meant by the phrase 'They were like sheep without a shepherd'?
6. When it got late the disciples made a suggestion to Jesus. What was the suggestion?
7. When Jesus told them to give the people something to eat, what question did they ask?
8. How much food had they already got?
9. What instructions did Jesus give his disciples about organising the crowd?
10. Describe in detail what Jesus did with the bread.
11. When everyone had finished eating, what did the disciples do?
12. How many men had been fed?

The Transfiguration of Jesus — Mark 9:2-14

1. Name the disciples Jesus took with him 'up a high mountain'.
2. Describe the change which came over Jesus.
3. Who was Elijah?
4. Who was Moses?
5. What was Peter's reaction to the scene?
6. What did the cloud and the voice mean in this incident?
7. Write out the message given by the voice.
8. What order did Jesus give the disciples as they came down from the mountain?
9. What did Jesus refer to when he said 'the Son of Man will suffer much and be rejected'?
10. When Jesus said that Elijah had already come a second time, who do you think he meant?

The Parable of the Tenants in the Vineyard — Mark 12:1-12

1. Describe the vineyard which the man in the parable owned.
2. What are the duties of a tenant?
3. What happened to the slave sent for the man's share of the harvest?
4. What happened to the second slave?
5. Were these two slaves the only ones sent to the tenants?
6. 'I am sure they will respect my son.' What response did the tenants make when the man's only son was sent for the harvest?
7. What judgement did Jesus say would be given to those tenants?
8. What do you think Jesus meant by the text of scripture which he quoted to the Jewish religious leaders? (vv.10,11).

9. In what way did the Jewish leaders realise that Jesus had told the parable against them?
10. Why couldn't the Jewish leaders arrest Jesus straight away?

The Passover Meal and the Lord's Supper — Mark 14:12-26

1. What did the disciples ask Jesus on the first day of the Festival of Unleavened Bread?
2. What question did Jesus tell the two disciples to ask the man with the jar of water?
3. What did Jesus say the man would show them?
4. What did the disciples prepare when everything happened just as Jesus had said?
5. At what time of day did Jesus come to eat the meal?
6. What did Jesus tell the disciples which upset them?
7. What did Jesus say about the man who would betray him?
8. What did Jesus do and say with the bread?
9. What did Jesus do and say with the wine?
10. Explain what Jesus meant by:
    a) 'my blood which seals God's covenant.'
    b) 'the day I drink new wine in the Kingdom of God.'

The Good Samaritan — Luke 10:25-30

1. What question is put to Jesus by the teacher of the Law?
2. What answer does the man make when Jesus asks him a question instead?
3. What was the man's second question?
4. Jesus answers the man by telling him a parable. What is this parable about? *(in one sentence)*
5. What journey is the man in the parable making?
6. Describe what happened to the man.
7. What did the priest and the Levite do when they saw the man?
8. Describe each detail of the Samaritan's action.
9. What did the Samaritan tell the inn-keeper?
10. Describe the conversation of Jesus with the teacher of the Law after he had finished the parable.

The Parable of the Forgiving Father (the Lost Son) — Luke 15:11-32

1. Why did the man in the parable divide his property between his two sons?
2. What did the younger son do a few days later?
3. How did the younger son spend his money?
4. What result did the severe famine have for the younger son?
5. Why would looking after pigs be a terrible thing for a Jew particularly?
6. What did the boy decide to say to his father when he went home?
7. Describe the actions of the father when he saw his son in the distance.
8. Write out what the father said to his servants.
9. What did the elder son hear as he returned from the field?
10. How did the elder son answer his father when he begged him to go in to the feast?
11. What did the father mean by 'everything I have is yours'?
12. What reason did the father give his son for the celebration?

Paul's Letter to Philemon

1. Mention two things which Paul praises Philemon for. (vv.4-7)
2. How did Paul describe his living conditions at the time?
3. What is the name of the runaway slave?
4. In what way does Paul describe the fact that the slave has become a Christian?
5. Why do you think the slave was no use to Philemon before he ran away?
6. Copy verse 12.
7. What attitude is Paul taking to the favour he is asking of Philemon? (v.14)
8. How does Paul describe the slave in v.15?
9. In what way should the slave be a 'brother in the Lord'?
10. How does Paul ask Philemon to take the slave back? (v.17)
11. What guarantee does Paul give? (vv.18,19)
12. What is Paul's hope for himself in the near future? (v.22)

The First Account of the Institution of the Eucharist — I Corinthians 11:17-29

1. What is Paul's mood as he speaks to the Christians at Corinth?
2. What was happening when the Christians at Corinth met together?
3. Who is Paul's authority for his teaching about the Lord's Supper?
4. What were the actions of Jesus at the Last Supper?
5. What were the words of Jesus at the Last Supper?
6. What did Paul say that these actions and words meant when Christians performed them?
7. If a person dishonours the Lord's Supper, what is he guilty of?
8. Why does Paul say that everyone should make sure that they understand the 'meaning of the Lord's body'?
9. In what way do you think the people of Corinth had failed to understand the true meaning of the Lord's Supper?
10. Why should there be no distinction between the wealthy and the poor at a meeting of Christians?

Paul's Teaching on Love — I Corinthians 13

1. Name the three talents which Paul says are no use unless they are accompanied by love.
2. Complete this saying: 'I may give away everything I have...'
3. Make two columns (1) of what love is, and (2) of what love is *not*. (vv.4-7)
4. Mention three human gifts which Paul declares are only temporary compared with love which is eternal.
5. How does Paul compare the change from childhood to adulthood with the change from knowing God now and in the next life?
6. What do you think Paul meant by the phrase: 'What we see now is like a dim image in a mirror'?
7. What does Paul mean by faith?
8. What does Paul mean by hope?
9. Why does Paul insist that love is the greatest gift of all?

APPENDIX B: 'WHAT THE CHURCH SAYS'

A series of relevant conciliar and post-conciliar documents in outline. Also: an outline of *Peace on earth* (Pacem in Terris) Pope John XXIII.

Documents

1. The Dogmatic Constitution on the Church *(Lumen Gentium)*, 1964.
2. The Constitution on the Sacred Liturgy, 1963.
3. The Pastoral Constitution on the Church in the Modern World *(Gaudium et Spes)*, 1965.
4. Decree on the Apostolate of the Laity, 1965.
5. Decree on the Appropriate Renewal of the Religious Life, 1965.
6. Decree on Priestly Formation, 1965.
7. The Christian Family in the Modern World, 1981.
8. Encyclical Letter on the Regulation of Births *(Humanae Vitae)*, 1968.
9. Apostolic Constitution on the Sacrament of the Anointing of the Sick, 1972.
10. The Reality of Life after Death, 1979.
11. Declaration on Euthanasia, 1980.
12. Peace on Earth *(Pacem in Terris)*, 1963.
13. Respect for Human Life in its Origin and the Dignity of Procreation, 1987.

Note: the texts of these documents (with the exception of *Peace on Earth*) may be found in *Vatican Council II*, volumes 1 & 2, edited by Austin Flannery (Pub. Fowler Wright).

---

1. Dogmatic Constitution on the Church ('Lumen Gentium') (1964)

Part One: The Mystery of the Church

God the Father planned that all people should share in his life. God sent his Son, so that all people could be his adopted children. The Holy Spirit brings people to God. All people who accept the teaching and work of Christ are part of the Kingdom of God.

The Church is described as:

a sheepfold
a land (cultivated by God)
the building of God
the temple of God
God's holy city
the bride of Christ
the body of Christ

The different gifts which people have are used to serve the Body of Christ. The Church is people who have **faith**, **hope**, and **charity**. The people of God are **one**, **holy**, **catholic** (worldwide) and **apostolic** (they tell other people about their faith). The Church is governed by the **pope** and the **bishops**. God's people love the **poor** and **suffering**. The Church **welcomes** and **cares** for **sinners**.

Part Two: The People of God

God chose Israel to be his people. Christ made a new covenant with God for his people. The Church is the **new people of God**.

a) The people of God have a **priesthood**.
They join in offering the **Eucharist** which shows their unity.
They receive the **sacraments**:
Baptism consecrates them to proclaim their faith.
Confirmation strengthens them to spread and defend the faith.
Penance reconciles them to God and to each other.
Anointing of the Sick asks them to join their suffering with the suffering of Christ which saves God's people.
Holy Orders brings God's word and love to his people.
Matrimony reflects the love of Christ for his people.
b) The people of God are **prophets**.
They have talents and gifts which help them to take the teaching of Christ to the world.
c) The people of God have a **kingship** with Christ. They are citizens of the Kingdom of Heaven. They have a **mission** to tell others about Christ. If they do this in charity and have faith, they are saved by Christ. All Christians can baptize. They pray and work so that the whole world can become the People of God.

Part Three: The Structure of the Church

There is a variety of service in the Church. Jesus sent the apostles to do his work. Bishops are the successors of the apostles. Jesus made Peter the leader of the apostles, and this gave them unity. The Pope is the successor of Peter. The Pope is called the Vicar of Christ. He is the visible head of the whole Church. Bishops act with the Pope for the good of all God's people. This joint decision-making is called the 'College' of Bishops. The power they have is 'Collegiate power'.

An individual bishop cares for his own diocese. The Pope is infallible (is correct) when he gives a teaching which cannot be changed. Priests make their bishop present in the local congregation. Deacons are ordained to a ministry or service in the Church.

Part Four: Lay People

Lay people are those who are not in Holy Orders or members of the religious life. Their Christian vocation is followed in the ordinary circumstances of family and social life. They make Christ known to others and they consecrate the world to God — a **priestly** work.

Lay people **witness** to God in the ordinary surroundings of the world, especially in marriage and family life — a **prophetic** work. Lay people resist sin themselves and lead others to the Kingdom of God — a share in the **Kingship** of Christ.

Part Five: Vocation to Holiness

Holiness is expressed in different ways. Everyone is called to holiness. Jesus asked everyone to be perfect like the Father. This is done by loving God and serving their neighbour. **There are many ways of becoming holy**. It happens when people use the gifts they have and fulfil their duties e.g. a bishop, priests, deacons, lay people. Loving others, the sacraments, worship, prayer, self-denial are important channels to holiness.

Martyrdom is a special sign of love, and so are the evangelical counsels (poverty, chastity and obedience).

Part Six: Religious Men and Women

Poverty, chastity and obedience are gifts received from God. There are many forms of solitary and community life. There are many religious families or congregations. Religious life includes both clergy and lay people. It is a particular gift in the life of the Church. Vows dedicate a person to God — they continue the baptismal consecration.

Religious men and women are devoted to the welfare of the Church by *prayer* and *good work*. They are witnesses to the truth of new life through Christ. They show the power and strength of Christ working in the Church. Religious life helps a person to develop in a fully human way.

Part Seven: The Church on a Journey of Faith

The Church makes Christ active in the world. The sacraments and customs of the Church are part of the journey of faith. All members of the Church are in communion with each other whether they are alive or dead. Therefore the people pray for the dead, and honour the saints. This communion enriches the worship of God.

Part Eight: The Blessed Virgin Mary

Mary is honoured as the *Mother of God* and *Mother of the Redeemer*. The Son of God took a human nature from *Mary*, and she freely became the mother of Jesus. Mary appeared in the public life of Jesus. She was with the apostles on Pentecost day. Mary was taken up body and soul into heaven at the end of her life, and she intercedes for all people before God. Mary is a sign of the Church who is a mother to all who are baptized. Mary is honoured by the Church, but not adored as Christ is. Images of Christ, Mary and the Saints are used in prayer and devotion.

2. Constitution on the Sacred Liturgy (1963)

Liturgy means 'worship'.
Worship:
1. Helps to strengthen the Christian life.
2. Needs to be adapted to suit the present time.
3. Ought to encourage unity among Christians.
4. Strengthens the Church's mission to teach all people.

Part One: The Importance of Worship

Priests must be well instructed in worship and they must instruct and encourage people to *take part* in worship. The regulations surrounding public worship are controlled by the Pope and the bishops. Scripture is important in public worship and a love for scripture ought to be encouraged. Acts of public worship are celebrations of the *whole Church* and participation by everyone is the method most preferred. Worship teaches people about the gospel and how to express their faith. Public worship must allow for the differences found in groups, regions and peoples.

Part Two: The Eucharist

The Eucharist was introduced by Christ at the Last Supper. It also continues the saving power of the sacrifice of the cross. The Eucharist is:
- *a sacrament of love*
- *a sign of unity*
- *a bond of charity*
- *a gift of grace*
- *a pledge of future glory*

People ought to be fully informed about the Mass; take part with devotion, knowing what they are doing.
People are: instructed by God's Word,
           nourished by the Lord's Body.
People — give thanks to God
        — offer themselves, through Christ, to God
        — develop their love for God and for each other.
Communion under both kinds is strongly recommended.
Concelebrations are encouraged on certain occasions.

Part Three: Other Sacraments and Sacramentals

Purpose of the Sacraments:
— to make people holy
— to increase membership of the Body of Christ
— to give worship to God.
Sacraments: *teach*, *strengthen* and *express faith*. The love and gifts of God are given through the sacraments.
Sacramentals — make the ordinary events and actions of life holy.
Sacraments: *baptism*
               confirmation
               penance
               anointing of the sick
               ordination
               marriage
Other public acts of worship include: *consecration of virgins: religious profession: burial of the dead*.

Part Four: The Divine Office

— is the daily praise of God in the name of the Church. The *laity* are encouraged to say the *divine office*.

Part Five: The Liturgical Year

The Church's year 1. Recalls the life and work of Christ and Mary.
                   2. Remembers the saints and martyrs.
Sunday is most important.
There are special seasons of preparation for great feasts. *Lent* is a preparation for baptism and for the festival of *Easter*.

Part Six: Sacred Music

Music is very important in public worship. Choirs should be trained but *everyone* should join in singing — it is a special form of prayer. There is a special form of singing in the Catholic Church called *Gregorian Chant*. All kinds of musical instruments may be used in public worship. Composers of good church music should be encouraged.

Part Seven: Sacred Art

All kinds of art are approved of. Poor art should not be displayed in churches. Art-work may be regional and suitable for the culture of the people.

3. Pastoral Constitution on the Church in the Modern World ('Gaudium et Spes') (1965)

Introduction

Key questions today:
— what is man?
— sorrow, evil, death?
— cost of progress?
— what can man offer to society?
— what can he expect from it?
— what follows this life?

Part One: The Church and Man's Calling

1. The dignity of the human person

Human dignity: *Freedom*: *Conscience*. These are very important. Atheism works for good projects but says that religion deceives people. This can only be overcome if the Church's teaching is presented properly.

2. The community of mankind

The great Commandment is love for God and neighbour. The social order of the nations is for the benefit of the human person. This means *reverence* for:
• the old and abandoned
• the foreign labourer
• the refugee
• the illegitimate child
• the hungry.
There must be *basic equality* and all *discrimination* is to be rejected.

3. Human activity throughout the world

Christians *build up the world* — they unfold what God has done in creation. Ordinary circumstances provide the opportunity for activities which are for the good of the human race. On this earth, the Kingdom of God is present in mystery when human progress is being made.

4. The role of the Church in the modern world

The Church insists on the rights of man, and values the way these rights are being developed today. There should be no division between faith and daily life.

Part Two: Some Problems of Special Urgency

1. The need to foster the beauty (nobility) of marriage and the family

Marriage is threatened by polygamy, divorce, free love, the worship of pleasure. Sometimes society and civil authorities put great pressure on family life. The purpose of marriage, and the work of parents ought to be understood. Difficulties about the size of families are not solved by methods of birth control which are against the teaching of the Church. Children need the security of the complete family. Other people with special skills can help the family.

2. The proper development of culture

There has been a change in modern times caused by
• *industrialisation*
• *urbanisation*
• *mass culture*
• *uses of leisure.*

God's people have the task of building a better world based on *truth* and *justice*. God's command is that his people should *subdue the earth*, *perfect creation* and *develop themselves*. For this task, people have *freedom of enquiry* and *freedom of expressing their mind*.

3. Economic and social life

Today, great extravagance and wretchedness exist side by side. But every person has the right to work and society must help people to find sufficient work. Pay and conditions must be fair. All have a right to share in the use of property. The hungry must be fed. Social services should provide for the needs of the family.

4. The life of the political community

This exists for the common good of all and citizens have a right to take part in choosing their leaders and the structures of authority in their community.

5. The fostering of peace and the promotion of a community of nations

Peace is based on justice and love. Peace is *not* absence of war, or a balance of power between nations. Peace cannot be brought about by a dictatorship.
a) *The avoidance of war.* International agreements are important. People in military service are agents of security and freedom. 'Any act of war aimed indiscriminately at the destruction of entire cities...is a crime against God and man himself...' The arms race is not a safe way to keep peace. Extravagant sums of money are spent on arms. *'The arms race is an utterly treacherous trap'*. War must be outlawed by international agreements.
b) *Setting up an international community*
The causes of war need to be rooted out. International co-operation is important for serious problems of *population*: *wealth*: *aid*. Christians ought to belong to international groups. The Church is a sign of *brotherhood*.

4. Decree on the Apostolate of Lay People (1965)

(*Note:* The content of this document is contained in **Unit 5.2 — Christian Service**. Below is the formal layout of this document in outline.)

Introduction — the importance of the lives of lay people as a witness to the world today.

Chapter 1: The Vocation of Lay People to the Apostolate

Lay people share in the mission of the Church to spread the Kingdom of God all over the earth. There is one mission in the Church but many ways in which it is carried out. (2)

Foundations of the lay apostolate. Every person is an apostle because of their relationship with Christ. In addition, each person has their own gifts to offer in service. (3)

The spirituality of lay people takes its character from the ordinary circumstances of their lives i.e. married, single or widowed; from their health; from their professional and social duties. (4)

Chapter 2: Objectives of Lay People
(the way in which they follow Christ)

Evangelization and sanctification. Lay people bring others to God by the example of their own lives and by their good deeds for others. They also spread God's word to others. (6)

Renewal of the Temporal Order. This means that lay people make good use of all that God has created. (7)

Charitable works and social aid. Kindness and love to others is the point on which all people will be judged: 'When you showed it to one of the least of my brothers here, you showed it to me' (Matthew 25:40).

Lay people share in international schemes to help the poor. (8)

Chapter 3: The Various Fields of the Apostolate

Church Communities. Lay people offer their services in the parish, and the diocese to which they belong and make missionary work a special priority. (10)

The family is the unit of society, and among the things the family can do are: care for abandoned children, hospitality to strangers, help with schools, support young people, help engaged couples, instruct people in the faith, help other families. (11)

Young people are very important in modern society. (12)

The surroundings in which people live provide their opportunity to live the values of Christianity. (13)

National and international levels of involvement in public life are important so that a way is prepared for the good news of Christ. Lay people are 'travelling messengers of Christ'. (14)

Chapter 4: The Different Forms of the Apostolate

Individual Apostolate. A person's own life is the point from which Christ's message is brought to others. (16)

Special circumstances mean that some people have to live their Christian faith under persecution, or in places where there are not many Christians. (17)

Group Apostolate. When people work together they are strong. (18)

Types of group apostolate concentrate on different needs e.g. of instruction in the faith, or assistance for the poor. (19)

Catholic Action groups take the Gospel spirit to others; investigate the conditions for the work of the Church; act with the strength of a group; and co-operate with their bishops. (20)

International associations of Catholics, and voluntary service by Catholics are praised. (21, 22)

Chapter 5: The Order to be Observed

Rivalry is to be avoided. The work of lay people fits into the total pattern of the work of the Church. (23)

Relations with the bishops. Parish and diocesan groups help in the bishops' work in a special way. (24)

Lay groups ought to receive encouragement from priests and religious men and women. (24, 25)

Communications are improved by parish and diocesan councils. (26)

Lay people work with other Christians and non-Christians. (27)

Chapter 6: Training for the Apostolate

Lay people need training. (28) This includes spiritual preparation and particular practical preparation. (29)

This training begins in the home. It is continued in schools, colleges etc. Groups in the parish also help. (30)

Fields calling for specialised training

a) Materialism is a special threat to Christ's message.

b) The social teaching of the Church is another important area.

c) Aid for the poor. (31)

Help available: conferences, retreats, meetings, books. There are centres for training lay people. (32)

Exhortation. Lay people should be involved in the work of the Church. 'It is the Lord who is again sending them into every town and every place where he himself is to come.'

---

5. Decree on the Appropriate Renewal of the Religious life (1965)

TYPES OF RELIGIOUS COMMUNITIES

1. Completely contemplative communities
2. Apostolic (Active) communities
3. Monastic communities
4. Religious life lived by lay people
5. Secular institutes

The Three Vows

chastity is a gift which reflects God's love. Religious should care for their health in mind and body. Community life lived in charity helps in keeping this vow.

poverty: religious must be poor people in their daily lives and in their attitudes. They use their possessions for the needs of the Church and the poor. They avoid the appearance of luxury.

obedience: in the religious life, superiors hold the place of God, but these superiors should act in a spirit of service.

The Common Life — includes prayer and a sharing of the same family spirit. There should be equality among the members of the community.

The Religious Habit — This should be simple and modest, poor and becoming, suited to health and circumstances (e.g. work).

General Points — A good education is important for religious. Independent institutes and monasteries form federations. Major superiors meet at conferences.

The Encouragement of Vocations

1. Priests should preach about religious vocations.
2. Religious communities should tell others about their life and work.
3. Religious should give good example and attract vocations that way.

6. Decree on Priestly Formation (Decree on the Ministry and Life of the Priests) (1965)

I *The Priesthood in the Ministry of the Church*

Priests are given the power in the Sacrament of Holy Orders:
1) To offer the sacrifice of the Mass
2) To forgive sins

Priests serve God's people publicly in the name of Christ. They work with their bishop to do Christ's work in the world. Like Christ, they work for the glory of God the Father.

II *The Ministry of Priests*

1. They proclaim the Gospel of God, and they preach the word of God.
2. They have sacred duties: ***worship, baptism, penance, anointing the sick, celebrating Mass.***
   Priests make the bishop present in every congregation.
3. They offer Mass and say the Divine Office.
   They care for the church (God's house of prayer).
4. They educate others in the faith. They look after the poor and the weak. They look after the needs of young people, married people and parents. They help religious men and women. They visit the sick and the dying.

The Holy Eucharist is the basis and centre of the Christian community which a priest helps to form.

A priest must:
1. Support and be loyal to his bishop.
2. Help other priests especially when they have difficulties. Older priests should accept and support younger priests. Younger priests should respect the age and experience of older priests.
3. Trust lay people with duties in the church, and encourage them to develop their own ideas for the parish.
4. Not forget the needs of other Christians and non-Christians.

Vocations to the priesthood should be encouraged.

III *The Life of Priests*

A priest is called to be holy by his baptism, but particularly by being consecrated to act in the place of Christ himself. A priest who performs his duties in the spirit of Christ becomes holy. A priest:
1. Celebrates Mass daily
2. Makes himself available to hear confessions
3. Recites the Divine Office
4. Gives up his personal convenience for the service of the people

Spiritual Qualities:

- ***obedience:*** He must be obedient to God by carrying out the orders of the Pope, the bishop and other people with authority over him.
- ***celibacy:*** The Church accepts the married priests of the Eastern Orthodox Church, but celibacy is required for a priest of the Latin Church (*Roman* Catholic Church).
- ***voluntary poverty:*** Priests care for the possessions of the Church with the help of lay people. They must never give bad example which would turn the poor away. They must be approachable.

Help for Priests

1. ***spiritual help:*** Scripture and the Eucharist, spiritual reading, devotion to Mary, a daily time of prayer with Christ in the Eucharist, retreats and spiritual direction help to strengthen a priest spiritually.
2. ***study:*** Priests must be well-informed, and able to discuss human affairs. They must attend courses to increase their knowledge of the teaching of the Church, and the care of God's people.
3. ***finance:*** The people have a duty to provide for their priest. Each priest should have a suitable holiday every year. There should be equal care for all priests. The diocese should have a fund to help a poor parish. Wealthier dioceses should help poorer ones.

God is always with his people and a priest is never alone in his work — he must have faith in God.

7. The Christian Family in the Modern World (1981)

Part One: Bright Spots and Shadows

Parents have the gift of the sacrament of matrimony to help them:
1) to develop their personal relationship with each other.
2) contribute to promoting the dignity of women.
3) co-operate in responsible parenthood.
4) give a good education to their children.

Shadows — in society we see:
1) mistaken ideas of independence in marriage.
2) a breakdown of authority between parents and children.
3) Christian values are difficult to pass on to children.
4) a growing number of divorces.
5) abortion and sterilization.
6) 'a contraceptive mentality' — this means that contraception is favoured as a solution to problems in personal relationships.
7) countries in the Third World are at a particular disadvantage, although these countries often give the best example of family life.

Part Two: The Plan of God

Married people reflect the kind of love which God has for his people. The sacrifice of Christ shows this love at its best — his love was ***total***, and ***life-giving***. Marriage should be like this. A good marriage is the foundation for family life. The family is a community of life and love.

Part Three: The Role of the Christian Family

The family has four tasks:
1. To form a community of persons.
2. To serve life.
3. To have a social and political role in society.
4. To share in the life and work of the Church.

1. The family forms a community of persons — this means that parents ought to be *loving, united and faithful.* (20) Good relationships include:
a) parents with their children.
b) brothers and sisters with each other.
c) the family with other relatives.

The family is a place where there is:
a) care and love for the children;
b) care and love for the sick;
c) care and love for the old;
d) service and sharing with each other. (21)
In the family *women* have equal dignity and responsibility with men. (22) The place and work of the *father* in a Christian family is most important. (24)
Children must be accepted, loved and valued. There must be great care for their material, emotional, educational and spiritual development. (26) The *old* often have the gift of bridging the generation gap. 'How many children have found understanding and love in the eyes and words and caresses of the aging!' (27)

2. The family serves life. The passing on of human life is 'a most serious responsibility'. The 'anti-life' mentality in our society is condemned.
> *'The Church firmly believes that human life, even if weak and suffering, is always a splendid gift of God's goodness.'* (30)

Public authorities have no right to force contraception, sterilization, or abortion on the people. Natural rhythms are the responsible way of spacing the births of children. Married people are called to holiness and anyone who has a care for them (priests, religious and lay people) must help them to follow this call. (34)

The education of children by their parents begins with *love.* 'Man is more precious for what he is than for what he has.' Sex education begins with the practice of love and generosity. Sex education is the basic right and duty of parents, and moral education is part of sex-education. Parents should:
> *pray* with their children.
> *read* the Bible with them.
> *introduce* them to the life of the Church. (39)

A Christian family helps and encourages other families, and sometimes fosters and adopts other children.

3. The family has a social and political role in society by:
a) good example
b) care of the poor
c) hospitality
d) making sure that the law of the country does not weaken or threaten family life.
The State has a duty to support the rights of the family (*see especially* §46 page 854 Vatican Council II volume 2 Flannery).

4. The family shares in the life and work of the Church.
1) In its own practice of the faith. It takes part in fulfilling the command of Jesus 'Go into all the world and preach the Gospel to the whole creation.' Children should be encouraged towards missionary vocations. (54)
2) The family is called to be holy by celebrating the sacraments and by prayer. (55-62)
3) The family is a community at the service of others, by loving especially the *poor* and the *weak*, those who *suffer* and those who are *unjustly* treated.

Part Four: Pastoral Care of the Family

1. Stages of pastoral care
Marriage preparation is very important — it must include all aspects e.g. doctrinal, legal and medical. Couples who are getting married must understand the meaning of the sacrament. Young families must be cared for.

2. Structures of Family Pastoral Care include the parish and the diocese, priests and religious with specialised training, married couples themselves, other groups and movements devoted to family life.

3. People involved in the Pastoral Care of the Family include — bishops, priests and deacons, lay people, theologians and experts in family matters. (73)
Religious men and women care for the abandoned, unwanted, orphaned, poor, and handicapped children. They visit families and look after the sick. They help one-parent families and counsel young people. (74)
Doctors, lawyers, psychologists, social workers give expert care. (75)
The media (TV, radio etc.) have a great influence over family life. (76) Special care must be taken of families divided because of working conditions. (77)
Difficult situations include: mixed marriages: trial marriages: free unions (living together) caused by poverty or injustice: Catholics in a civil marriage who have delayed or rejected a religious marriage: separated or divorced people who have not remarried: divorced people who have remarried. Some people live in the sort of poverty which makes it impossible for them to belong to a true family. (85) 'No one is without a family in this world: *the Church is a home and family for everyone.*'

Conclusion

The future of humanity depends upon the family. The family is often discouraged. The Holy Family is an example.
> St Joseph — a tireless worker, guardian of those entrusted to his care.
> Mary — humble and generous, and a mother who suffered.
> Christ — blessed the family in Cana.

'I entrust each family to him, to Mary and to Joseph.'

---

8. Encyclical Letter on the Regulation of Births. Paul VI 'Humanae Vitae' (1968)

This letter contains the teaching of the Catholic Church on *contraception* and *birth control.* Modern society has experienced many changes, and there are serious questions being asked about the way in which married people co-operate with God to transmit (pass on) human life. The Church cannot ignore factors which affect the life and happiness of people. (1)

Part One looks at the fact that there are problems today concerning *population, housing, money, education.* Large families are difficult to provide for. Women have a different place in society. Medical science has progressed so that it can control the conception of human life.

The question is being asked whether people ought to decide for themselves if they will allow conception to occur. (3) The Church has the authority to teach about marriage and the duties of husbands and wives. (4) A Commission was set up by Pope John XXIII to advise about the matter. In this letter, the Pope says that some of the conclusions of this Commission were not in keeping with the teaching of the Church on marriage. (5)

Part Two discusses the meaning of marriage and the sacrament of marriage.
- *marriage is a sacrament* — it reflects God's love for his people. (8)
- *marriage is a total, faithful and exclusive relationship*.
- *children are the outstanding gift of marriage*. (9)
- *responsible parents co-operate with God's plan for creation*. (10)
- *human life is sacred*.

Marriage is a gift which must not be deprived of its meaning and purpose. (11-14)
Unlawful ways of regulating birth:
i)   direct abortion
ii) interruption of the marriage act
iii) direct sterilization
iv) contraception. (14)
However, the means 'necessary to cure organic diseases' are not unlawful 'even though they also have a contraceptive effect.' (15)
Infertile periods are a natural way of spacing births. (16)
Artificial birth control could have serious results (17):
i)   The faithfulness of married love is threatened.
ii) The dignity of women may be forgotten.
iii) Public authorities may force people to be childless as a way of solving population problems.
The teaching of the Church on this matter interprets what is *natural* and what is 'loyal to the example and teaching of the divine Saviour.' (18)

Part Three explains how the teaching of the Church on the regulation of births is to be put into operation *(pastoral directives)*.
People need God's help in marriage. (20) Married people need self-discipline in many ways and not just in the spacing of their children. (21)
Teachers, *the media* and *governments* are asked not to give people false values. (22, 23)
Scientists are asked to research the *natural rhythms* of human fertility. (24)
Married people are asked to remember that their love is a reflection of Christ's love for his people, the Church. (25) Example given to other married couples is important. (26)
Doctors and nurses are asked to *support* this teaching. (27)
Priests are asked to help married couples in prayer, and to encourage them to approach the sacraments of the *Eucharist* and of *Penance* more often. (28)
Married couples must never despair because of their weakness. (29)
Bishops are asked to safeguard the holiness of marriage. (30)
The final appeal. (31) True happiness cannot be found unless people keep the *natural Law of God*. 'These laws *must be wisely and lovingly observed.'*

9. Apostolic Constitution on the Sacrament of the Anointing of the Sick (1972)

Scripture
Mark 6:13, James 5:14, 15.

Purpose of the sacrament

Anointing removes any remaining sin:
— gives comfort and strength;
— the sick can bear their illness better;
— they are able to resist temptation to sin.

General points

Once called *extreme unction*: now to be called *'anointing of the sick'*.
Anyone in danger of death from sickness or old age may be anointed. The sick person is asked to accept their suffering as part of Christ's suffering. The anointing is on the forehead and hands with olive oil. The sacrament may be repeated if the sick person recovers and then becomes ill again. Also, if the danger becomes worse during the same illness, the anointing may be given again.

INTRODUCTION TO THE RITE OF ANOINTING AND TO THE PASTORAL CARE OF THE SICK

The Meaning of Human Sickness

Suffering is *not* a punishment for sins. Suffering is a *preparation for eternal life*.
Christ suffered, and he continues to suffer in his people. Illness should be overcome if possible, and good health should be wanted. Doctors, and those who care for the sick fulfil the command of Christ to *visit the sick*.

The Sacrament — essentials are:
- *laying on of hands*
- *prayer of faith*
- *anointing with blessed oil*.
Faith is an important factor in saving those who are ill.

People to be anointed

1. Those who are dangerously ill through sickness or old age.
2. The sick person may be anointed again in the same illness after a relapse, or for another illness after recovery.
3. Before surgery for a dangerous illness.
4. Elderly people who are weak, but not dangerously ill.
5. Children if they will be comforted by the sacrament.
6. Sick people who are unconscious, if they would have asked for the sacrament when they were conscious.

Dead bodies are not anointed. The prayers for the dead are said instead. If there is any doubt about death, a conditional anointing may be given. People should be taught to *ask for the sacrament*, especially those who care for the sick.

VIATICUM is given when a person is in danger of death. It is *Holy Communion* given by a priest or a person commissioned to distribute the Eucharist.

Ministry for people who care for the sick

Efforts are made to prolong life. Love and kindness is shown to sick people. Family and friends have a special share in this ministry.
1. they offer comfort and prayer;
2. they 'urge the sick to associate themselves with the passion and death of Christ', for the sake of God's people;
3. they inform the priest if the sick person gets worse.

During the sacrament, the priest has a choice of prayers appropriate for the particular person he is anointing.

10. The Reality of Life after Death (1979)

Everlasting Life

There is an article of the Creed which is about everlasting life. This life is the purpose of God's plan for his people.

If there is no resurrection, the whole structure of the Christian life collapses.

Questions which people ask —
• Is there really anything after death?
• Does anything remain of us when we die?
• Is there a nothingness before us?
• What happens between the death of a Christian and the general resurrection?

The Teaching of the Church

1. The Church believes in the resurrection of the dead.
2. Resurrection is an extension to human beings of the resurrection of Christ.
3. The name given to the spiritual part of people which survives after death is called the *soul*.
4. Any way of thinking or speaking which would make the ceremonies, prayers and religious acts offered for the dead, seem like nonsense, is rejected by the Church.
5. Explanations of life after death must not take away from the meaning of the Assumption of the Virgin Mary's body and its glory.
6. The Church believes that there will be eternal punishment for the sinner, who will be deprived of the sight of God — *hell*. The Church believes that there is a possibility that good people go through a time of purification before they see God — *purgatory*.

Essential Points About Life After Death

1. Our present life is continued into the next one by the power of the *Holy Spirit*.
2. There is a radical break between our present life in Christ (through the sacraments) and the future life.
3. What life after death means is beyond our imagination.

Theologians must be cautious about spreading ideas which might upset the faith of ordinary people.

11. Declaration on Euthanasia (1980)

Introduction

Progress in medicine means that doctors are able to *cure more illness* and *people live longer*. Old people wonder about asking for an 'easy death' so that they can keep their human dignity. The life, death and resurrection of Christ has given a new meaning to death for a Christian. This declaration is about the human rights of a person concerning their death.

The Value of Human Life

God's people see life as a gift of his love. Therefore —
1. No-one ought to make an attempt on the life of an innocent person.
2. Life is a trust given to a person, a talent meant to increase.
3. Intentional suicide is as wrong as murder. It is a rejection of God's plan of love. It is a refusal to love oneself and others, but sometimes there is no responsibility when the person's mental state diminishes their blame.

Euthanasia — means 'easy death' without severe suffering. Today, the word is used to mean 'mercy killing' for the following reasons:
• to put an end to extreme suffering.
• to prevent abnormal babies growing up.
• to end the life of the mentally ill.
• to prevent the incurable from having a miserable life.
No-one can permit the killing of an innocent human being whether a foetus or an embryo, an infant or an adult, an old person or the incurably ill and dying.

The Meaning of Suffering for Christians and the Use of Pain-killing Drugs

Pain and suffering often come before death itself. The Christian faith teaches that suffering has a special place in God's plan. It is a share in the suffering of Christ and a part of the sacrifice which saves God's people. For this reason, some people will refuse pain killers, but not all people are called to this kind of suffering.

Pain ought to be controlled. However, addiction to drugs ought to be avoided. As long as death is not intended, drugs may be given. *Warning:* 'It is not right to deprive the dying person of consciousness without a serious reason.' *(Pope Pius XII).*

Due Proportion in the Use of Remedies

Everyone has the right *to die peacefully with human and Christian dignity*. Everyone has a duty to care for personal health. Doctors have a duty to give remedies — *but* sometimes a judgement needs to be made about the remedies given:
1. A patient can accept a treatment which is still in an experimental stage.
2. Such treatment may be interrupted if the cost is too much or the suffering of the patient becomes unbearable.
3. The normal means offered by medicine are enough. A person may refuse other techniques without being accused of suicide.
4. Treatment may cease when death is near, but normal care must still be given.

Conclusion

Life is a gift from God. Death is unavoidable. Death ought to be accepted with dignity and responsibility. Death opens the door to immortal life. Doctors ought to do all that their skill allows, but *kindness* and *charity* are even more important. Christ said:

'As you did it to one of the least of my brethren, you did it to me.' (Matthew 25:40)

12. Peace on Earth
(Pacem in Terris) Pope John XXIII (1963)

God puts into the hearts of his people *intelligence* and *freedom*. With these gifts they can create a peaceful world.

Part One: Human Rights

The basic needs of people are *food, clothing, shelter, rest, medical care*. People need *security* in case of sickness, the inability to work, widowhood, old age, unemployment. Every person has a right to a *good reputation*, the right to *honour God*, the right to choose *marriage, the priesthood* or *the religious life*. People may:
— form associations
— emigrate or immigrate
— take part in public affairs (political rights).
Each person ought to *respect the rights* of another. Changes in the twentieth century include a different working class, a change in the position of women, and the growth of independent nations.

Part Two: Individuals and Public Authorities

Civil authority comes from God. People have a right to take part in choosing this authority. Civil authorities must work for the material (e.g. roads, housing etc.) and spiritual (freedom to worship) needs of the people.

Part Three: Relations Between States

All authority must respect the *personal dignity* of the people. All nations have the right to exist and develop. Minority groups must be given respect concerning their language, natural gifts, ancestral customs and economic progress. Land should be properly distributed according to the population. Political exiles and refugees have the right to be accepted as immigrants into another country.

Disarmament

Countries which are wealthy spend huge amounts on armaments. Poorer countries, therefore, do not get the help they need. Some people say that there cannot be peace without an equal balance of armaments. If one country increases its armaments, another country must do the same. If one country has nuclear weapons, another country develops them. The world lives under the threat of terrible violence. A nuclear war would be fatal for life on earth.

Justice demands that the arms race should cease. Stockpiles of arms should be reduced equally and at the same time.

Nuclear weapons should be banned

Peace exists at the moment *only* as a *threat* of war. True peace depends upon *mutual trust*. Peace will exist as a result of *truth, justice and sincere co-operation*.
Pius XII: 'Nothing is lost by peace; everything may be lost by war.'

Part Four: Co-operation in the World Community

The world must respect the human rights of each person. A world-wide authority like the UN provides the right atmosphere for individual nations to tackle their own problems. It maintains peace, encourages equality and mutual respect. The *Universal Declaration of Human Rights* (1948) ought to be respected by all people.

Part Five: Pastoral Requests About Peace

Ordinary people ought to contribute to the *economic, social, cultural* and *political* aspects of life. Spiritual values are important when this is done.

Scientific training and religious instruction should be given in equal proportion. When injustice is found, it must be met without violence. Peace among people depends upon peace with the individual person. Peace on earth reflects the peace of the Kingdom of God. Christ is the Prince of Peace:

'Peace I leave with you, my peace I give to you; not as the world gives do I give to you.'

13. Respect for Human Life in its Origin and the Dignity of Procreation (1987)

Issued by the Congregation for the Doctrine of the Faith: March 1987.

This instruction is about the kind of moral problems which medical progress has brought concerning methods of conception and how human life is transmitted other than by sexual intercourse. The instruction recognises that science and technology can change the world, but that it should be used in a responsible way.

Science must not be free to act *without conscience*. Biology and medicine must not be applied without considering that a human being is a whole person. This should be specially recognised with regard to human reproduction.

The important point to remember is that: *everyone has a right to life from the moment of their conception to the moment of their death*.

The fact that reproduction is now *possible* without sexual relations does not mean that it must be *right*. The Church teaches that:
a) Human beings share in the creative action of God.
b) Marriage is the setting for this partnership with God in creation.

Introduction

The application of scientific research and technology to the beginning of human life must respect the basic right which every person has to his/her life.

Human beings have a spiritual soul and a moral responsibility. The instruction is to help people to recognise: their rights as human beings; their duties as human beings.

Science and technology must always be at the *service* of human beings — they must never *control* the life and death of others.

Part One

1. What respect is due to the human embryo?

Human beings must be respected from the very first instant of their existence. Any kind of procured abortion is condemned.

2. Is pre-natal diagnosis permissible?

— as long as this process is directed towards safeguarding the embryo, or part of a treatment for healing. It should not be applied with a view to abortion should the foetus be abnormal or not the sex which was wanted.

3. Are therapeutic procedures carried out on the human embryo permissible?

— as long as the treatment is for healing, improving the condition of its health, or ensuring its survival.

4. Is it right to research and experiment on human embryos and foetuses?

— such experimentation should not cause harm to the life or integrity of the unborn child or its mother. Parents must give *consent*. Any experimentation on a dead foetus should be the same as for any dead person.

5. Is it right to use embryos which have been fertilized 'in vitro' for research?

— human embryos *in vitro* are human beings — they are not disposable biological material.

6. What about procedures which control the destiny of the embryo or change it?

— these procedures do not respect the human dignity of the embryo. Every person has a right to be conceived and to be born within marriage. The instruction condemns *cloning* and parthenogenesis**.

The freezing of embryos is an offence against the respect due to human beings. Attempts to control the chromosomes or genes, when they are not for therapeutic reasons, are forbidden.

*cloning = making an exact copy of another
*parthenogenesis = reproduction without sexual intercourse

Part Two

1. Why is it necessary that human procreation should take place within a marriage?

— it emphasises that children are a gift and a blessing from God. It reflects faithfulness in marriage.

2. Does IVF* and ET* involving a third person — a donor — reflect the dignity and truth of marriage?

— relying on the gametes of a third person is a violation of the essential character of marriage which required the faithfulness of the couple to each other. It also violates the rights of the child.

3. Is surrogate motherhood permissible?

— This is against the unity of marriage and the dignity which is due to the human person.

4. What connection is necessary, then, between the married couple and sexual relationship?

— no one should subject the coming of a child into the world to conditions of technical effeciency at the expense of the partners' love.

5. Is IVF and ET which involves a man and his wife permissible?

— this could be an aid or a form of therapy which is acceptable, providing that embryos are not destroyed. But the marriage act is considered the only setting which is worthy of procreation. *In vitro* fertilization is against this dignity. However, babies born by this method must be considered a gift of God's goodness, and be brought up with love.

6. How is IVF and ET involving a man and his wife to be considered from a moral point of view?

— if technology can assist the natural marriage act it is acceptable, but it must not *replace* the act of sexual intercourse itself. Artificial insemination as a substitute for the marriage act is not acceptable.

7. What rights do doctors have with regard to procreation?

— a doctor does not have the authority to dispose of people or to decide what kind of human being will be born. Medical intervention in procreation must *assist* the marriage act and its results — it must not take over the function of procreation.

8. What about the suffering caused by infertility in marriage?

— the desire for children can sometimes be even greater for couples who know that they are not fertile. Marriage gives a couple the right to sexual intercourse, but not necessarily the *right* to have children. A child is not an object to which others have a right. A child is a *gift* of marriage. Scientists are encouraged to continue their research into *preventing the causes* of sterility.

*IVF = *In vitro* ('test-tube') fertilization
*ET = embryo transplant

Part Three

Moral and civil law

It is the task of civil law to guard the common good of people by recognising and defending their fundamental rights, by promoting peace, and providing for public behaviour.

Civil law cannot take the place of conscience.

The human rights of a child do not depend upon individuals, or on parents. Human rights are not the gift of society or of the state, they belong to an individual because the creative act has brought them to life. These rights are:

a) the right to life and physical wholeness from the moment of conception to the moment of death.

b) the rights of the family:

— marriage as an institution.

— a child's right to be conceived, and be brought up by its parents.

The law must expressly forbid that human beings should be treated as objects of experimentation, be mutilated or destroyed because:

a) they are superfluous *or*

b) they are incapable of developing normally.

Civil law cannot legalise the donation of gametes between persons who are not legitimately united in marriage.

Legislation must also forbid:
* *embryo banks*
* *post-mortem insemination*
* *surrogate motherhood*

Civil law must respect:
* *human rights*
* *human life*
* *the institution of the family.*

Where laws exist which violate these rights 'conscientious objection' must be supported and recognised.

Conclusion

The purpose of the instruction is to protect and defend Christian teaching. The instruction is for:
* people responsible for the formation of conscience and of public opinion.
* scientists and medical professionals
* jurists and politicians
* theologians
* moralists

The instruction is not meant to prevent the efforts of the medical profession. It is meant to give guidelines on the application of scientific progress. Medical progress must be faithful to the teaching of the Church.

'What you do to one of the least of my brethren you do unto me.' (Matthew 25:40)

APPENDIX C: GLOSSARY OF RELIGIOUS TERMS AND VOCABULARY

abortion: a miscarriage of birth; **procured abortion** — a deliberate termination of a pregnancy.

acclamation: a joyful prayer, honouring God or Christ.

agricultural: where the way of life is mostly from the cultivation of the land.

annulment: a declaration that a marriage is invalid, i.e. the marriage was never really made.

anointing: when oil is applied in a symbolic way as part of a religious ceremony, e.g. baptism or ordination.

apostles: the twelve close followers of Jesus who were sent out by him to preach, teach and heal.

article of faith: a belief which is held by all Christians on the authority of the whole Christian Church.

Ascension: the return of Jesus to his Father in heaven, forty days after his resurrection from death.

authority: the power to settle a question, particularly in religious matters, e.g. the meaning of scripture.

baptism: the rite or sacrament of initiation into the Christian Church and the family of God.

baptistry: a place for baptism; the actual tank for baptism in a Baptist church.

beatitude: one of the eight blessings spoken by Jesus in the Sermon on the Mount, e.g. 'blessed are the poor in spirit.'

belief: faith in a teaching of the Christian Church, e.g. an article of the Creed.

biography: the story of a person's life written down.

blasphemy: irreverent or false speech about holy things, e.g. swearing or cursing.

carol: a hymn or song for Christmastide.

catechumen: a person who is being instructed in the basic teaching of the Christian faith, and is preparing for baptism.

celebration: a public service, e.g. of the Christian Eucharist.

celibacy: a decision not to marry — a solemn promise in the case of a Roman Catholic priest.

ceremonial: a formal order of service, with ritual actions, e.g. ceremony of a sacrament.

chancel: the sanctuary, or eastern end of a church reserved for the clergy and choir.

charismatic: a person who has the gifts of the Holy Spirit, e.g. tongues, healing, prophecy, teaching etc.

chrism: a mixture of olive oil and balsam used in the ceremony of sacraments, e.g. baptism, confirmation.

Christian Church: all people baptized into the Christian religious tradition.

citadel: the place of worship used by the Salvation Army; also a small fortified city.

commandments: usually refers to the laws given by God to Moses for the good of the chosen people.

concelebration: the ceremony of Mass or Holy Communion where there is more than one priest or minister consecrating the elements of bread and wine.

conception: life-giving result of sexual intercourse: to become pregnant.

congregation: a group of people gathered together for worship of God.

consecration: to set apart for a sacred use e.g. the bread and wine at Holy Communion; a person in the religious life. *Note:* Roman Catholics believe that Christ is present under the appearance of bread and wine after the consecration of the Mass.

conventional weapon: a weapon used in the kind of war which involves hand to hand combat e.g. tanks, guns but not forms of war carried on by remote control.

course-work: a piece of continuous writing, based on the individual research of the student.

covenant: an agreement made by God with his people. e.g. with Noah or Abraham in the Old Testament, or by Christ's sacrifice in the New Testament.

creed: a summary of basic religious teaching, agreed upon by a trusted authority e.g. a council of religious leaders, as for the Apostles' Creed or the Nicene Creed.

crib: a rack holding food for animals — used as a cradle for the infant Jesus.

crozier: a shepherd's crook used as a symbol for the loving service and authority of a local bishop for his people.

crucifixion: a form of punishment given by the Romans. The victim is nailed to a cross beam, or tree.

dedication: an act which makes a building or a person sacred to God: a solemn offering.

demoniac: a person possessed by evil spirits. In the New Testament this was often a person with epilepsy or a mental illness.

denomination: a group of Christians with their own individual tradition of prayer, worship and charity, e.g. Roman Catholics; Baptists.

diaconate: a stage in Holy Orders where a man is set apart for service in the Church under the guidance of the bishop.

diocese: an administrative area of the Church, in the charge of a bishop.

disciple: someone who follows the teaching of another, e.g. the followers of Jesus in the New Testament.

divorce: the dissolving of a marriage by civil law, not accepted as a religious fact by the Roman Catholic Church and some other Christians.

early Church: the first communities of Christians, mentioned in the New Testament, and in the earliest writings of Christian authors.

empire: usually refers to a powerful nation which has conquered other nations. In the New Testament, the Roman Empire is frequently referred to.

enclosure: usually refers to an area set aside for the exclusive use of a particular group. In the Roman Catholic tradition, an area in a convent or monastery.

Epiphany: a season in the Christian calendar which celebrates the 'showings' of Jesus as the Son of God, e.g. the worship of the Magi; the baptism and transfiguration of Jesus.

eucharistic prayer: the main part of a Catholic Mass in which the bread and wine is consecrated by a priest; a thanksgiving prayer for Christ's sacrifice.

Eucharist: a service of thanksgiving. Sometimes another name given for the Lord's Supper, or Holy Communion.

euthanasia: an easy death. Sometimes used for bringing about the death of someone with incurable or painful disease.

Extreme Unction: the name for the Sacrament of the Sick, sometimes called the Anointing of the Sick.

eye-witness: a person who sees something happen, and is prepared to confirm the happening before others.

fasting: deliberately going without something, for a spiritual benefit or in order to give charity to others; a Christian custom inspired by the temptations of Jesus.

festival: a celebration of a Christian feast, sometimes as a holiday.

foetus: a fully developed embryo in the womb, dependent upon the mother for life, but independent as to its human right to life.

font: a place reserved for the baptism of infants in the Christian church, but also for adults where it is not the custom to baptize by full immersion.

fundamentalist: a person who accepts and lives by a literal interpretation of the truth of the Bible (or a holy book in a religious tradition other than Christianity).

genealogy: a family tree, a list of ancestors, a family line, e.g. in Matthew 1, the genealogy of Christ.

Gentile: a person who is not a member of the Jewish race or religious tradition.

god-parents: persons who undertake to make baptismal promises on behalf of an infant in the Christian religious tradition.

Gospel: the good news about God, brought by and taught by Christ and his followers.

harvest: a gathering together of the fruits of the earth, or the fruits of a good life in a metaphorical sense; an image used by Jesus in his teaching.

hell: the eternal punishment for a person who rejects God.

heretic: a person who holds a belief which is not in agreement with the Christian creed.

Herodian: a person who supported the reign of Herod the Great or his successors. These were appointed by the Romans as Kings of Palestine at the time of Christ.

Holy Saturday: the day in Holy Week when Christians remember Christ in the tomb before his resurrection.

homily: a sermon or talk given usually on a text from scripture in a Christian act of worship.

House of David: the family or people who claim King David from the Old Testament in their ancestry, e.g. Jesus, through Joseph.

human rights: basic conditions of existence to which every person has a claim, e.g. life, food, housing, freedom.

hypocrite: a person who pretends by an outward show, e.g. of holiness.

Immanuel: a name meaning 'God with us', and one of the titles for the Messiah.

Incarnation: the act by which God became a human person in Jesus Christ.

incense: a pleasant smelling gum or spice which is burned as a sign of devotion in a religious ceremony.

initiation: a ceremony which admits a person to a group, e.g. baptism is a sacrament of initiation.

inspiration: the influence of God's spirit upon a writing or a saying in a religious tradition.

intercession: a form of prayer where the worshipper asks for a favour from God.

investiture: a clothing with symbolic or ceremonial garments, e.g. a priest's investiture at ordination.

Kingdom of God: the rule of God in the minds and hearts of his people as preached by Jesus Christ.

laity: members of the Christian Church who are not in Holy Orders or consecrated in the religious life.

Lamb of God: a reference to Jesus as a sacrifice for the forgiveness of sin and the saving passover of God's people to new life.

Last Judgement: a verdict, passed by God at the end of time, on the way a person has lived.

Last Supper: the meal eaten by Jesus with his apostles on the night before he died, at which he spoke of his death as the New Covenant.

lectern: a stand or desk from which the Bible is read in a religious service.

Lent: a period of 40 days' preparation for the Christian festival of Easter.

litany: a series of short intercessions (prayers) to which there is a response made by the congregation, e.g. during the sacraments.

liturgy: an act of worship, from a Greek word meaning service.

malnutrition: insufficient and unhealthy diet, causing weakness and disease.

manuscript: a hand-written document; in the Christian tradition it usually refers to an early hand-written book of the Bible.

Mass: the service of Last Supper and the sacrifice of Christ as it is celebrated in the Roman Catholic Church.

Maundy Thursday: Thursday of Holy Week, when sacred oils are blessed and the Lord's Supper is celebrated in the Roman Catholic Church.

Messiah: the Saviour sent by God to save his people from their sins; the one who would preach the Kingdom of God. The word means 'anointed one'.

ministry: a task performed as a service to God and his people, e.g. the lay ministry.

miracle: an extraordinary cure or event which cannot be naturally explained and is attributed to the power of God.

missal: a book containing the order of service, and prayers for Roman Catholics.

mitre: a bishop's head-dress, a tall hat, deeply cleft at the top, which is a symbol of his ministry.

monastery: a place where monks live a community life of prayer and work.

mourner: a person who is sorrowful about the death of someone they love; sometimes used in a symbolic way in scripture.

mystery: a truth which is beyond human intelligence but is made known to people by God.

nave: main part of a church from the door to the chancel usually separated by pillars from the side aisles.

nuclear weapon: an armament which has a nuclear warhead capable of great destruction, e.g. a nuclear missile.

Old Testament: the portion of the Bible which deals with the covenant of God with the Jewish people.

ordination: the act or sacrament by which a person is admitted to the rank of clergy in the Christian Church.

Our Lady: a term of devotion used by Roman Catholics for the Virgin Mary, mother of Jesus Christ.

palms: a branch of the palm-tree, used as a symbol of victory in the religious service which marks the triumphal entrance of Jesus into Jerusalem.

parish: a territorial division of a diocese with its own priest who serves in the name of his bishop.

paschal: symbols or events which refer to the covenant of the Jewish passover. In the Christian tradition it refers to anything connected with Easter.

penance: the sacrament for the forgiveness of sins in the Roman Catholic Church; an act of self-denial performed as a sign of sorrow for sin in the Christian tradition.

penitent: a person presenting themselves for the Sacrament of Reconciliation (penance), or taking part in a penance celebration.

pentateuch: the first five books of the Bible which form the Torah or scriptures of the Jewish people.

persecution: a form of enmity or injury to others with a different view-point or belief, in order to prevent a movement from spreading.

Pharisee: a member of a strict sect of people who observed all the Jewish laws and customs, but often it is a word applied to self-righteous people.

pollution: the spoiling of the earth, sea or sky by waste products.

polytheist: a person who believes and worships more than one god.

preaching: the act of explaining the word of God or teaching of a religion, which also urges people to action.

profession: the act of consecration of a religious, usually by the pronouncement of vows.

prophet: a person who interprets what is happening in society according to God's laws and commandments.

publican: another name for a tax-collector in New Testament times.

pulpit: a raised platform in a prominent place in a church which is closed in and often has a flight of steps leading up to it. It is used by a clergyman for preaching the sermon.

reconciliation: the healing of a broken relationship: a making up of friendship.

redeem: the purchasing of freedom for another person; used of Christ who saved the human race from sin.

Reformation: a period in the history of Christianity when the Protestant churches were formed.

religious controversy: a debate based on the questioning of an established religious belief or custom.

religious custom: the usual practice of performing a religious act of worship or devotion.

repentence: an act of sorrow or regret for an action. In a religious context, it refers to a turning away from sin.

resurrection: a rising from death to life. It refers to the events of Easter Day in the Christian religion.

rite: a fixed order of service, or a religious ceremony.

Sabbath: the seventh day of the week, and a day of rest for the Jews; often the Christian Sunday is called the Sabbath.

sacrament: an outward religious act which has a spiritual meaning given to it by the words and actions of Jesus, in which a Christian grows in love of God.

sacred: something or someone set apart for the service of God.

sacrifice: the offering of a person or thing to God, often to make up for sin, and sometimes involving death, e.g. the crucifixion of Christ.

Sadducee: a member of a group of Jews who belonged to the ruling class; Jewish aristocrats.

saint: a holy person recognised by the Church as having a place in heaven because of their service to God and neighbour.

sanctuary: a portion of a church for the use of clergy and choir, sometimes closed off by a rood-screen.

Sanhedrin: the Jewish Great Council, made up of Sadducees, Pharisees and teachers of the law.

Satan: a word meaning 'enemy' and referring to the Devil or Lucifer.

saviour: a person who saves another — usually referring to the promised Messiah and to Jesus Christ.

scribe: one of the teachers of the law, an expert in the Jewish religion entrusted with the keeping of Jewish scripture.

scripture: the sacred writings of a religion, e.g. the Bible.

second coming: a reference to the coming of Christ at the end of time.

sign of peace: a handshake or suitable action which expresses Christian fellowship, often performed during an act of worship.

sin: a thought, word or action against the love of God: the neglect of God's law.

symbolism: the outward objects and actions which contain in themselves the meaning of a religious act, e.g. water in baptism is a symbol of life and death.

synagogue: a place of worship for Jews, and sometimes a name for the Jewish congregation itself.

tabernacle: a place for the reservation of the Eucharist, usually a box of precious metal.

talent: a personal aptitude or gift to be used for the service of others.

temple: a place of religious worship; in the New Testament, the great temple of the Jews in Jerusalem.

temptation: an attraction towards a sinful thought, word or action.

tenant: someone who cultivates land for another, or a person who is trusted with the property of another.

tomb: a hole in the earth or rock in which a dead person can be buried.

Torah: the Jewish law contained in the pentateuch and thought to have been given to Moses by God.

tradition: a belief or a custom handed down from generation to generation, e.g. the oral tradition of Jews concerning religious observances.

transept: the two 'arms' of a church which makes the shape of a cross.

transfiguration: the change in the form and appearance of Christ before Peter, James and John, when he spoke with Moses and Elijah.

transubstantiation: the belief in the Roman Catholic Church that the elements of bread and wine are consecrated into the Body and Blood of Christ.

tribe: usually refers to the descendants of one of the twelve families of the sons of Jacob, e.g. Judah.

Trinity: the Christian belief in God as Father, Son and Holy Spirit: the doctrine of three Persons in one God.

unleavened: something e.g. bread, made without yeast so that the dough will not rise, often used for a Communion service.

vestment: the ceremonial robe of a Christian minister e.g. the chasuble of a Roman Catholic priest.

Viaticum: Holy Communion given to a person who is dying.

village craft: work which supports and maintains the daily life of a village, e.g. blacksmith, carpenter, potter etc.

vineyard: a plantation of grapevines.

Whitsun: Pentecost Sunday — a day on which newly baptized persons wore their white baptismal garments which represented their new faith.

Zealot: a member of a Jewish sect which opposed Roman rule in a fanatical way.

BIBLIOGRAPHY

Details of books referred to in the Further Reading lists.

Bavidge, N. — seven booklets on the Sacraments, Kevin Mayhew Publishers.

Brady, R. *The Christian Way. Book 3*, Veritas, 1983.

Brown, Alan. *The Christian World (Religions of the World Series)*, Macdonald, 1984.

Chappell, K.R. *Investigating Jesus*, Edward Arnold, 1982.

Chignell, M.A. *What Manner of Man?* Edward Arnold, 1979.

Chignell, M.A. *Framework (Christianity and Life)*, Edward Arnold, 1987.

Chichester Project. Lutterworth, 1982:
　Rankin, J. *Christian Worship (Book 1)*
　Erriker, C. *Christian Experience (Book 3)*
　Shannon, T. *Jesus (Book 4)*
　Curtis, P. *The Christians' Book (Book 6)*
　Shannon, T. *Christmas and Easter (Book 7)*
　Erriker, C. *Christian Ethics (Book 8)*
　Rankin, J. *The Eucharist (Book 9)*

Christian Denominations Series. Religious and Moral Education Press — 13 titles cover all the main denominations.

Duckworth, R.T. *The Gospel in the Making*, Macmillan, 1986.

Field, D. *and* Toon, R. *Real Questions*, Lion Pub., 1982.

Gower, R. *Frontiers,* Lion Pub., 1983.

Greville, B. *You Gather a People*, Veritas, 1983.

Grills, J.C.M. *The Life and Teachings of Jesus Christ*, Oxford University Press, 1985.

Herod, F.G. *The Gospels — a first commentary*, Methuen, 1976.

Johns, E. *and* Major, D. *Witness in a Pagan World*, Lutterworth Press, 1980.

Kendrick, R.A. *Setting the Foundations*, Hulton, 1983.

Mackney, J.P. *Revise Religious Studies*, Letts Study Aids, 1984.

Meeting Religious Groups Series. Lutterworth, 1982:
　Visiting an Anglican Church; Visiting a Community Church; Visiting a Methodist Church; Visiting a Roman Catholic Church; Visiting a Salvation Army Citadel.

Price, N. *St Mark's Gospel*, Religious and Moral Education Press.

Redemptorist. *The Illustrated Catechism*, 1980.

R.E. Scheme for Secondary Schools. Years 4 & 5. St Paul, 1980.

Richards, C. *According to Mark*, Blackie, 1987.

Simmonds, D. *Believers All (a book of six world religions)*, Blackie, 1984.

Taylor, E.J. *Problems of Christian Living*, Blackie, 1970.

The Westhill Project: Christianity R.E. 5-16: Garth Read, John Rudge, Roger B. Howarth — *Teacher's Manual, and Pupils' Books 1-4*, Mary Glasgow Pub. Ltd., 1986.

Thompson, J. *Christian Belief and Practice*, Edward Arnold, 1982.

Thompson, J. *The Christian Faith and its Symbols*, Edward Arnold, 1979.

Thorley, S. *Christianity in Words and Pictures*, Religious and Moral Education Press, 1984.

Whiting, R. *Religions of Man*, 2nd ed., Stanley Thornes Pub. Ltd., 1987.

Wilkinson P. *Focus on the Sacraments*, Kevin Mayhew Publishers, 1987. (Also: *Focus on Baptism, Focus on Confirmation; Focus on the Eucharist; Focus on Penance and Reconciliation; Focus on Anointing of the Sick; Focus on Marriage; Focus on Priesthood* — seven booklets extracted from *Focus on the Sacraments.*)

Wintersgill, B. *Facing the Issues*, Macmillan, 1987.

Vatican II — outlines and some quotations are from:

Flannery, Austin (editor). *Vatican Council II: the Conciliar and Post-Conciliar documents*, Fowler Wright, 1981. (Vol. 2, 1982)

INDEX

Words which are also included in the Glossary (Appendix C) are marked*. Page numbers in italics indicate that the word appears in a *question*; page numbers in bold type refer to the word in an **Appendix**.

A

*abortion, 6, 60-62, 66, **163**, **164**, **168**
absolution, 94-97, *97*
adultery, 30, 47, 61, 64, 65, 66, *67*, 74, **156**
Advent, 9, *15*
A.I.D. (Artificial Insemination by Donor), 53
allegory, 140, 142, **145**, **157**
altar, 18, *21*, 23, *26*, 31, 35
Anglican Church (Church of England), 16, 21, 30, 35
*anointing, 29, 30, *33*, 57, 58, *62*, 68, *76*, 78, 152
*Anointing of the Sick (Sacrament), 82, 108-110, *110*, 111, **165**
apostles, 68, 69, 70, 71, *71*, 132-135
see also discipleship
*Apostles' Creed, 31, *33*, 37-38, *40*, 41-43, *43*, 58, 69, 84, 128, 151
*Ascension, 37

B

*baptism, 8, 23, *26*, 28, *32*, *33*, 57-59, *62*, 68-69
and confirmation, *33*
believers' baptism, 29, *32*
baptism of Jesus, 11, 29, 32, *32*, 124, *127*
ceremonies/rites, 20, 24, *33*, 57, 78
infant baptism, 19, 29, 32, *33*, 58, *62*
in the early Church, 16, 29, 32, *33*
promises, *71*
Sacrament of Initiation, 57
signs/symbolism, 58, 59
Baptist Church, 26, 27, 29, 32, 35
*baptistry, 20, *22*
see also font
Beatitudes, 49, *50*, **156**
Bible, 6, 16, 19-27, *26*, 34, 35, 41, 44-45, *45*, 53, *62*, 84
see also Scripture
bishop, 69, 72, 80, *80*
Body of Christ, 8, 30, 87-89, *89*, **158**, **159**, **160**
see also Mass *and* Eucharist
Brandt Report, 90, *93*
breaking of bread, 24, 81
burial, 24, 28, 32, *33*
of Jesus, 151, 152

C

CAFOD, 90-93, *93*
candle, 21, 25, 31, 32, *33*, 58, 59
baptismal, 58, 59
general use, 9
paschal, 58, 59, *62*
catechist, *71*

*catechumen (baptism), 57
cathedral, 16-17, *21*
Catholic Church, 57, 60, 61, *62*, 66, 72, 74, *77*, 82, 83, 88, 94, 106, *113*, **160**, **164**
ceremonies *see* Anointing of the Sick, baptism, confirmation, Eucharist, Holy Orders, marriage, penance
chalice, 35, 79, 80, 85-86
*chancel/chancel rail, 19
chapel, 16, 19, 32
charity, 11, 51, *89*, 91-93, *93*, 112, 125, **159**, **162**, **167**
choir/choir stalls, 19
*chrism, 30, 58, 59, 68, 70, 78
chrismation, 29, 30, *33*, 35
Christian Festivals, 9-15, *15*
see also Advent, Christmas, Epiphany, Lent, Holy Week, Easter, Ascension, Pentecost
Christian unity, *26*
Christmas, 8, 9, 10, *15*
Church, 8, 16, *40*, 58, 59, **159**
church buildings, 16-21
Church of England, 23, 27, 31, 35, 42
see also Anglican Church
Church of Scotland, 23, 27
*citadel, 16, *21*
Commandments, 57, 74, 121, 147, 149, *150*, **156**
see also Ten Commandments
Communion of Saints, 28, 38, *40*, 58, 68
Communion table, 20
community, 8, 16
confession, 21, 82, 94-97, *97*, 108
see also penance
confirmation, 28, 29, 30, *33*, 57, 58, 68, 69, *70*, *71*, 108
ceremony/rite, 69
sign/symbolism, *33*
conflict, 125, 146-150, *150*, 154
Congregational Church, 22, 27, 32, 35
contemplation, 25, 26, *28*, *76*, **162**
see also prayer
contraception, 60-62, *62*, 66, **163**, **164**
contrition *see* penance
convention, 24
1 Corinthians 11:23-26, 87-88, **158**
1 Corinthians 13, 50, **158**
Creed, *40*, 84
see also Apostles' Creed
crime (and punishment), 72, 98-101, *106*
cross, 21, 23, 34, 37, 57, 59, 70, 83, 96, **160**
crowns, 31
crucifix, 21, *21*
crucifixion, 23, 37, *40*, *71*, 126, 154, *154*
customs, 49
Advent, 9, *15*
Christmas, 10, *15*
Easter, 14, *15*
Lent, 11
others, *150*

D

*deacon/diaconate, 72, 78, *80*
death, 32, *33*, 59, 111-112, *113*, 144, 151, **161**, **166**, **167**
of Jesus, 151-154, *154*, *155*
deterrence, 99, *106*
see also crime
developing nations/Third World, 52, 90-93, *93*, **163**
Devil, 149
see also Satan
disarmament, 105-106, *107*, **167**
multilateral, 105
unilateral, 105
discipleship, 68, 74, 122, 125, 132-135, *139*, 154, **156**
see also apostles
discrimination, 98, 101-104, *107*, **161**
see also prejudice
disease, 52, 90-91, *93*, *113*, 124, 136, 142, 143, 146
*divorce, 30, 31, 64, 65, 66, *67*, **161**
documents of the Church, 5, *70*, 95, **159-169**

E

Easter, 8, 9, 11, 12, 14, *15*, 58, 68, **160**
Eastern Orthodox Church, 12, 14, 17, 20, 22-23, 25, *28*, 29-32, *32-33*, 35, *36*
ecumenism (Christian unity), 26, *26*, 101
*Epiphany, 11, *15*
episcopal, 80
see also bishop
Essenes, 119, *119*
eternal life, 28, 31-32, *33*, 38, 42-43, 68, 88, 134, 136, 138, **165**, **166**
ethics, 44
*Eucharist, 8, 12, 23, 30, 32, 35, 36, *36*, 37, 57, 68, 69, 70, **158**, **159**, **160**
ceremonies/rites, 35, 82, 83-86
scripture, 87
see also Mass
*euthanasia, 112, *113*, **166**
evil, 39, 57, 94, 105, 111, 121, 128, 136, 138, 142, 143, *145*, 150, **161**
exorcism (baptismal), 57, 58, *62*
Exodus 20:1-17 (The Ten Commandments), 47, **156**

F

faith, 12, 29-30, *33*, 37-38, 41, *43*, 44, 50, 57-59, 103, 126, 142, 144, *146*, **158-162**
*fasting, 11, *15*, 92-93, *93*, 124, 146, 147, 148, *150*
fellowship, 34, 88
*festivals, 8, 9-15, *15*, 35, *36*, 154, **157**
*font, 19, 20, *21*, 29, 57
forgiveness of sins, 28, 29, 30, 34, 37, 38, 39, *40*, 58, 65, 83, 94-97, *97*, 104, 108, 109, 124, 138, *145*, 146, **163**
*Fundamentalist, 41-43, 53
funeral, 31, 32, *33*, 78

G

gifts, 23, 27, 70, *76*, 85, **160**, **168**
God, 8, 24-26, 37-40, *40*, 41-44, 47-50, *50*, *51*, 57, 104, 136-139, 142, 154, **159**, **161**
*god-parents, 57, *62*
Good Friday, 12, *15*
good works, 11, *15*
*Gospels, 12, 17, 38, 41, 42, 44, 79, 122, 123, *127*, *131*, 145

H

high altar, 18
Holy Communion, 12, 14, 19, 23, 30, 34, 35, *36*, 66, 78, 85, *86*, **165**
  see also Eucharist
Holy Mass *see* Mass *and* Eucharist
Holy Orders (Sacrament), 72, 77-80, *80*
  ceremony, *80*
  *deacon/diaconate, 72, 78, *80*
  duties of a priest, 78, *80*, 81, *82*
  ministry of a priest, 81-82, *82*, **163**
  sign/symbolism, 81, *81*, *82*
*Holy Saturday, 12, *15*, 58
Holy Spirit, 9, 14, 20, 23, 24, 25, *26*, 27, 28, 29, 30, 38, *40*, 45, 60, 68-70, *70*, *71*, 94, 124, **166**
Holy Trinity, 8, 37, *40*
  see also Trinity
Holy Week, 13, *15*
House Church Movement, 24, *26*
human life, 32, 53, *54*, 60, 61, 62, *62*, **164**, **167-169**
*human rights, 72, 152, *154*, **166**, **167**, **168**, **169**
hunger, 90-93, *93*, **161**
hymn-singing, 23, 24, 27, 31, 32

I

icon, 9, 17, *22*, 25, *26*, *28*
iconostasis, 17, *21*
imposition (laying on) of hands, 23, 24, 30, *33*, 70, 80, **165**
in vitro fertilisation, 53, *54*, **168**
*incarnation, 9, *15*, 37
incense, 32, *33*
*Initiation (Sacraments of), 30, *33*, 35, *62*, 68
*inspiration (of Bible), 44, 45, *45*, 50
  see also Scripture
interpretation (of Bible), 44, *45*, *46*
  see also Scripture

J

James, 106, *107*, 109, *110*, **165**
Jesus Christ, 8, 11, 25, 30, 34, 37-40, *40*, 44, *54*, 57, 59, 64, 78, 84, 121, 124, 128-131, 142
  Messiah, 58, 111, 122, *131*, 134, 136, *139*, 140
  Son of God, 9, 11, *15*, 16, 37, *40*, 41, 84, 111, 121, 122, *127*, 128, 130, 131, 150, 151
  Son of Man, 74, 129-130, 134, 145, 146, 150, 152

Jew, 103, 104, 118-119, *119*, *120*, 124, 126, 128, 136, 140, 146-150, *150*, 152
  see also Judaism
John the Baptist, 28, *32*, 124, 130, 131, 132
Judaism, 119
judgement, 38, 88, 100, 142, **156**

K

*Kingdom of God, 39, 42, 48, 49, 50, 74, 121, 122, 126, 128, 134, 136-139, *139*, 145, *145*, 154, **156**, **157**, **161**, **167**

L

Last Supper, 12, 19, 22, 34, 35, 36, *36*, 81, 82, *86*, 88, *127*, 138, 152, *154*, **158**
lay ministry, 72, 73, *76*, **159**, **161**, **162**
laying on of hands *see* imposition of hands
*lectern, 18, 19, 31
*Lent, 11, *15*, **160**
lepers, 52, 74, 102-103, *107*, 124
life after death (world to come) *see* eternal life
liturgical year (Christian calendar), 9, 14, **160**
*liturgy, 12, 26, 45, **160**
  The Liturgy (Orthodox), 34, 35
Lord's Prayer, 24, 37, 38, 39, *40*, 41, 49, 63
Lourdes, 111, *113*
love, 48, 50, *50*, *51*, 52, *54*, 60, 63, 64, 72, 89, *89*, 94, **158**, **161**, **166**

M

Mark's Gospel (Units 8 & 9, pages 117-155)
  customs, 117, *119*
  Judaism, 119
  making of the Gospel, 120-123, *123*
  oral tradition, 119, 122, 146, 148
  political background, 118, *119*, *120*
  religious background, 118, *119*, *120*
  social background, 117, *119*
  St Mark, 5, 68
  structure of the Gospel, 124-127, *127*
Mark 12:28-31, 48
marriage, 30, 53, 61, 63, **161**, **164**, **167**
  annulment, 64, 66
  ceremony/rite, 24, 31, *33*, 63, *67*, 78
  Christian forms of marriage, 30, 31, *33*, 121
  civil requirements, 31, 63
  divorce, 30, 31, 64, 65, 66, *67*, **161**
  meaning of the sacrament, 63, 64
  nuptial blessing, 31, 63, *67*
  parenthood, 60, 64, 66, *67*
  permanence, 64, 65
  rings, *67*
  sign/symbolism, 31, 64, 66
  vows/promises, 31, 63, 64, *67*
Mass (R.C.), 16, 20, 34, 36, 57, 58, *67*, 69, 78, 83-86
  ceremony/rites, 84
  eucharistic prayers, 85
  meaning, 78, 84-86, 87
  sacrifice of Calvary, 83, *86*
  sign/symbolism, 84-86, *86*

matrimony *see* marriage
Matthew 5:1-12, 49, **156**
*Maundy Thursday, 12
Meeting House, 16, 20, 32
*Messiah, 9, 10, 12, 59, 111, 118, 121, 122, 126, *127*, 128, 130, 131, *131*, 134, 149
  see also Jesus Christ
Messianic secret, 129, *131*, 141
Methodist Church, 23, 26, 27, 30, 35
*ministries, 71-76, *76*, 81-82, **163**
*miracle, 125, 131, 142-145, *145*, *146*
money (use of), 72, 74, 135
mysteries, the, 34, 35
  of the rosary, 25, *26*

N

natural disasters, 91
nature miracles, 142, 143
*nave, 18, *21*
New Testament, 23, 24, *26*, 34, *40*, 42, 44, *45*, *46*, 49, 50, 60, 64, *67*, 84, 100, 119, 122, *123*, 136
Non Conformist worship, 19, 22, 23, *26*
nuclear war, 45, 105-106, *107*, **167**
  see also disarmament

O

offerings *see* gifts
oil, 33, 57, 59, *62*, 70
  of catechumens, 57, 59, *62*
  of chrism, 58, 59, 68, 70, *71*, 78
  see also chrism
*Old Testament, 23, 24, 36, 44, *45*, *46*, 49, *50*, 58, 69, 84, 128, 129, 140, 142
opposition *see* conflict
organ transplants, 52, 53, *54*
Orthodox Church, 9, 14, *15*, 16, 17, 19, 21, *21*, *22*, 23, 25, *28*, 29, 30, *32*, 35, 36
  see also Eastern Orthodox Church
'orthodox' Christian, 41, 42, 43, *43*
'Our Father', 39, *40*, 58, 63
  see also Lord's Prayer
outcasts, 51, 94, 102-104, *107*, 124, 147, 148

P

pacifism, 106, *107*
Palm Sunday, 12
parables, *26*, 39, *40*, 42, 71, *76*, 88, *89*, 94, *97*, 117, 124, *127*, 136, 137, *139*, 140-142, *145*, 149, **156**, **157**
parenthood, 60, 64, 66, *67*
parents, 61, **163**, **168**
parish, 18, 69, 74, *76*, 81-82, *82*, 92, *93*, **162**, **163**
passion of Jesus, 12, 152-153
Passover, 12, 14, 36, 83, *86*, 126, 152, *154*, **157**
Paul, 8, 24, 30, 31, 36, *36*, 38, 42, *43*, 50, *50*, 57, 63, 65, 66, 71, *76*, 87, 100, 106, *107*, 122, **158**
peace, 49, *50*, 68, 80, 88, 89, *107*, **159**, **161**, **167**
*penance, 11, 69

*penance (Sacrament), 94-97, *97*, 106, *107*
  ceremony/rite, 95, 96, *97*
  meaning (forgiveness/
    reconciliation), 94-97
Pentecost, 11, 14, 15, 16, 21, 24, 37, 44, 68, 70, *70, 71*
pentecostal, 23, *26*, 30, 35
*persecution, 127, *127*, 135, 136, 149, 150, *150*, 154, **156**, *162*
personal prayer, 24
  see also prayer
Peter, 16, 38, 39, 68, *70*, 74, 76, 77, 80, 120, 122, *127*, 128, 131, 134, 135, 138, 151, 152, *154*, **159**
*Pharisees, 65, 74, 94, 119, 140, 145, 146, *150*
Philemon, 100-101, *106*, **158**
pilgrimage, 110, 111, 113
places of worship *see* church buildings, synagogue, temple
Pope John Paul II, 60, 66, 68, *71*, 106, *107*
  see also documents of the Church
population, 60, 61, 90-93, *93*, **161**, *164*
poverty/poor, 52, 88, 90-93, *93*, **158**, *162*
prayer, 11, *15*, 18, 20, *26*, 27, *28*, 39, 76, 95, 126, 134, 144, **160**
  liturgical, 23, 24, 78, **160**
  personal, 24
  petition, 39
  praise, 25, 39
  silent, 24, 26
  vocal, 24, 25, 26, *28*
*preaching, 20, 22
prejudice, racial (South Africa, U.S.A.), 6, 101-104, *107*
  see also discrimination
Presbyterian Church, 22, 35
priest, 23, 35, 57, 58, 60, 63, *67*, 69, **159**
  see also Holy Orders
promises, 30
  see also vows
*prophet/prophecy, 9, 10, 12, 23, *26*, 41, 58, 69, 70, 124, 131, 132, 140
prostitutes, 74, 103-104, *107*
*pulpit, 18, 19, *21, 26*, 35
punishment *see* crime

Q

Quakers, 26, *28*, 30, 31, *33*
  see also Society of Friends

R

race discrimination, 101-104, *107*
  see also prejudice
*reconciliation, 69, 82, 94-97, *97*, 98, 104, 106, *106*, *107*
  see also penance
reform, 98-101, *106*
  see also crime
religious congregations, 51, 52, 74, 75, 76, *77*, 78, **162**
  apostolic, 76, **162**
  contemplative, 76, **162**
Religious Society of Friends *see* Quakers *and* Society of Friends

*resurrection, 11, 14, 25, 31, 37, *40*, 41-43, *43*, 58, 59, *70, 71*, *97*, 112, 122, 127, 151-154, *154, 155*, **165**
revenge, 49, 98-100, 104, *106*
rings, 63
  bishop's ring, 79, 80
*rites *see* Anointing of the Sick, baptism, confirmation, Eucharist, Holy Orders, marriage, penance
Roman Catholic worship, 9, 12, 14, 21, *22*, 23, 24, 35
Romans, 16, 68, 104, *107*, 117-119, *119, 123*, 128, 131, 134, 136, 141
rood screen, 18, *21, 22*
rosary, 25, *26*
royal doors, 17

S

*Sabbath, 47, 121, 124, *127*, 129, 145, 146, 147, *150*, 152
*Sacraments, 8, 12, 23, 34, 57, 68, 72, 82, **159**, **160**
  see also Anointing of the Sick, baptism, confirmation, Eucharist, Holy Orders, marriage, penance
*sacrifice, 35, 85, *86, 154*, **160**
*Sadducees, 118, *120*, 146, 148
Samaritans, 70, 103, *107*, **157**
*sanctuary, 17, 18, 21
  sanctuary lamp, 21, *22*
*Sanhedrin, 68, *70*, 118, *119*, 132, *139*, 148
Satan (Devil), 39, 57, 88, 124, 130, 140, 142, 149, 150, *150*
*Saviour, 10, 20, 23, 34, 57, 128, *131*
*scribes, 119, *119*, 128, 146, 148, **157**
*Scripture, 16, 29, 31, 32, 57, 84, *93*, 95
  authority, character, inspiration, interpretation, 44-45, *45, 46*
  in worship, 22-26, *26*
  private reading/meditation, 19, 25
  sermon (homily), 23, 27, 63, 80
Sermon on the Mount, 49, 64, *67*, 100, 105
sick people/sickness, 108-113
sign/symbolism, 57, 58
*sign of peace, 23, 70, 80, *81*, 84, 85
silent prayer, 24, 26
  see also prayer
*sin, 57, 68, 94-97, *97*, 146, 148
  mortal, 94, *97*
  original, 57, *62*, 94, *97*
  personal, 94, *97*
  venial, 94, *97*
Society of Friends, 14, *15*, 16, 20, 21, *21*, 23, 27, 51
  see also Quakers
stained-glass windows, 21, *22*
stations of the cross, 21, *21*, 25
statues, 21, 25
stewardship, 71, 72, *76*, 135
suffering, **166**
  Christ's, 151-154, *154, 155*
  vicarious, 152
Sunday, 15, *15*, 24, 51, **160**
symbolism, 32, 57, 59
  see also sign/symbolism
*synagogue, 16, 142
Synoptic Gospels, 122

T

*tabernacle, 21
talents, 72, 74, *76*, **156**
tax-collectors, 74, 77, 103, 118, 124, *135*, 147, 148
teaching of the Pope(s) *see* documents of the Church
*temple, 16, 65, 71, 124, 149, *154*
*temptation, 59, 124
Ten Commandments, 21, 38, 47, 48, *50*, 64
test-tube babies, 53, *54*, **168**
  see also in vitro fertilisation
Third World *see* developing nations/ Third World
*Torah, 146
transfiguration (of Jesus), 11, 125, 129, **157**
*Trinity, 8, 29, 59

U

United Reformed Church, 22, 35

V

*vestments, 23, *26*, 32, 78-80
*Viaticum, 108-110, *110*, **165**
Virgin birth, 41, *43*
vocation, 70, 71, 72, *76*, 77, **161**, **162**, **163**
vows/promises
  baptismal, 57-58, *62*
  marriage, 63, 64, *67*
  priestly (Holy Orders), 77-80
  religious (poverty, chastity and obedience), 76, *77*, **160**, **162**

W

war, 98, 104-106, *107*, **161**
water, 28-30, 32, 57, 94, 108
weapons of war, 51, 105, *107*, **167**
  see also war
white garment (baptism), 30, 58, 59, *62*
wine, 24, 80, *86*, **157**
witness, 31, 42, 44, 68, 70, *71, 123*
worship, 8, 16, 18, 20, *21*, 22, 34, 35, 36, *45*, 47, **160**
  Anglican, 23, 24
  Charismatic, 23-24
  early Christian Church, 16
  House Church Movement, 24, *26*
  Non Conformist/Free, 19, 23, *26*, 35
  Orthodox, 9, 23, 28
  private, 24, 26, *28*
  public, 22, 26
  Quaker, 23, 26
  Roman Catholic, 9, 27, 83-86

Z

Zacchaeus, 103
*Zealot, 118, 132